The Amber Room

By the same authors
The Stone of Heaven

THE AMBER ROOM

The Fate of the World's Greatest Lost Treasure

Catherine Scott-Clark

&

Adrian Levy

VIKING
CANADA

VIKING CANADA

Penguin Group (Canada), a division of Pearson Penguin Canada Inc.,
10 Alcorn Avenue, Toronto, Ontario M4V 3B2

Penguin Group (U.K.), 80 Strand, London WC2R 0RL, England
Penguin Group (U.S.), 375 Hudson Street, New York, New York 10014, U.S.A.
Penguin Group (Australia) Inc., 250 Camberwell Road, Camberwell, Victoria 3124, Aus
Penguin Group (Ireland), 25 St. Stephen's Green, Dublin 2, Ireland
Penguin Books India (P) Ltd, 11, Community Centre, Panchsheel Park,
New Delhi – 110 017, India
Penguin Group (NZ), cnr Airborne and Rosedale Roads, Albany, Auckland 1310, New Ze
Penguin Books (South Africa) (Pty) Ltd, 24 Sturdee Avenue, Rosebank 2196, South Af

Penguin Group, Registered Offices: 80 Strand, London WC2R 0RL, England

Published in Viking Canada 2004.
Simultaneously published in Great Britain in 2004 by Atlantic Books, an imprint of
Grove Atlantic Ltd, Ormond House, 26–27 Boswell Street, London WC1N 3JZ, and in
United States by Walker Publishing Company, Inc., 104 Fifth Avenue, New York, NY 10

1 2 3 4 5 6 7 8 9 10 (FR)

Manufactured in Canada.

NATIONAL LIBRARY OF CANADA CATALOGUING IN PUBLICATION

Scott-Clark, Cathy, 1965–
The Amber Room : the fate of the world's greatest lost treasure / Cathy Scott-Clark a
Adrian Levy.

ISBN 0-670-04432-6

1. Amber art objects—Russia (Federation)—Pushkin. 2. Art treasures in war—Russi
(Federation)—Pushkin. 3. World War, 1939–1945—Art and the war.
I. Levy, Adrian, 1965– II. Title. III. Title: Amber Room.

N9165.R9S38 2004   736'.6   C2003-905202-8

British Library Cataloguing in Publication data available
American Library of Congress Cataloging in Publication data available

Visit the Penguin Group (Canada) website at **www.penguin.ca**

In memory of Muriel Claudia Worsdell
and
Gerald Anthony Scott-Clark

'There are different truths... foolish truths and wise truth, and your truth is foolish. There is also justice...'

Irina Antonova, director of the Pushkin Museum, Moscow[1]

'Some of the splendour of the world
Has melted away through war and time;
He who protects and conserves
Has won the most beautiful fortune.'

J. W. Goethe, 1826

Contents

List of Maps and Illustrations   xi

Acknowledgements   xv

Note on Transliteration   xviii

Dramatis Personae   xix

Maps   xxv

Introduction   3

The Amber Room   9

Notes   359

Bibliography   372

Index   377

List of Maps and Illustrations

MAPS

Page
xxv   Königsberg Castle, pre-April 1945
xxvi   Kaliningrad, c.2004
xxvii   East Prussia, c.1945
xxviii   Germany, c.2004
xxix   St Petersburg and environs, c.2004
xxx   USSR, post-1947

ILLUSTRATIONS

10   The original design for the Amber Room, 1701
11   The Catherine Palace *(Vera Lemus, Aurora Publishers,
     St Petersburg, Russian Federation)*
13   Alexander Kedrinsky with colleagues from Leningrad's palaces
     after winning the Lenin Prize in 1986 *(Vica Plauda archive,
     St Petersburg, Russian Federation)*
18   Anatoly Kuchumov with Anna Mikhailovna, his wife, and others
     shortly before the Second World War *(Vica Plauda archive)*
21   Curators pack up Leningrad's palaces after the Nazi invasion of
     the Soviet Union in 1941
34   Tsar Peter I *(State Hermitage Museum, St Petersburg, Russian
     Federation)*
44   The amber workshop at the Catherine Palace
46   Vladimir Telemakov *(Catherine Scott-Clark)*

60 Vica Plauda, granddaughter of Anatoly Kuchumov, holding the only surviving colour plate of the original Amber Room *(Catherine Scott-Clark)*

61 The Amber Room

62 Soviet troops re-entering the Catherine Palace, 1944

65 The ruined Catherine Palace after Nazi occupation

72 Olaus Magnus's sixteenth-century map of the Samland Peninsula

73 Seventeenth-century amber fishermen

74 Pre-war photograph of Königsberg Castle *(Königsberg City Museum, Duisburg, Germany)*

76 Professor Alexander Brusov of the State Historical Museum, Moscow, and his diary *(Avenir Ovsianov archive, Kaliningrad, Russian Federation)*

77 Soviet tanks on the streets of Königsberg during the final attack, April 1945 *(Günter Wermusch archive, Berlin, Germany)*

78 The surrender of General Otto Lasch, 10 April 1945 *(Kaliningrad City Museum, Kaliningrad, Russian Federation)*

80 Amateur painting of the post-war remains of Königsberg Castle *(Avenir Ovsianov archive)*

81 Alfred Rohde *(Avenir Ovsianov archive)*

91 Anatoly Kuchumov and colleagues from the Leningrad palaces during the 1950s *(Albina Vasiliava archive, Pavlovsk, St Petersburg, Russian Federation)*

97 The St Petersburg Literature Archive reading room *(Catherine Scott-Clark)*

101 Prince Alex Dohna-Schlobitten *(MPR Productions, Munich, Germany)*

107 Entrance to the Knight's Hall of Königsberg Castle *(Königsberg City Museum)*

112 Blutgericht, the Nazi restaurant located in the former torture chambers of Königsberg Castle *(Königsberg City Museum)*

119 Caricature of Anatoly Kuchumov at his desk researching the fate of missing Leningrad palace treasures *(Tsentralny Gosurdarstvenny Archiv Literatury i Iskusstva, St Petersburg, Russian Federation – TGALI)*

120 Caricature of Anatoly Kuchumov with a wheelbarrow of books *(TGALI)*

123 Anatoly Kuchumov and colleagues at Pavlovsk Palace *(Albina Vasiliava archive)*

127 Victorious Soviet troops pose in front of the Berlin Reichstag, 1945 *(Kaliningrad City Museum)*

146 Gerhard Strauss *(Avenir Ovsianov archive)*

159 Doodle of Anatoly Kuchumov searching for the Amber Room with a magnifying glass, 1949 *(TGALI)*

160 Doodle sent to Anatoly Kuchumov, depicting clues as to the post-war location of the Amber Room, 1949 *(TGALI)*

161 Friedrich Henkensiefken *(MPR Productions)*

165 Intelligence files of the Stasi, the East German secret police, bundled up ready for shredding, January 1990 *(Die Bundesbeauftragte für die Unterlagen des Staatssicherheitsdientes der ehemaligen Deutschen Demokratischen Republik, Berlin, Germany – BStU)*

176 Surrender of Königsberg, April 1945 *(Günter Wermusch archive)*

184 *Bernsteinzimmer Report*, by Paul Enke, 1986 *(British Library, London)*

187 Paul Enke, c.1960 *(BStU)*

190 The Stasi files *(BStU)*

193 Dr Ernst-Otto Count zu Solms Laubach *(Avenir Ovsianov archive)*

205 Günter Wermusch *(Günter Wermusch archive)*

218 News footage of the trial of Erich Koch in Warsaw, 1959 *(MPR Productions)*

247 Art works stolen by the Nazis, hidden in German mines and found by American troops in April 1945 *(Kali und Salz GmbH, Erlebnis Bergwerk Merkers, Thuringin, Germany)*

256 George Stein *(Avenir Ovsianov archive)*

260 Viktor Chebrikov, KGB chairman, with Erich Mielke, East Germany's Stasi chief, at Stasi headquarters, East Berlin, 1987 *(BStU)*

272 Baron Eduard von Falz-Fein reporting at the 1936 Munich Olympics *(Falz-Fein archive, Liechtenstein)*

274 Julian Semyonov *(Falz-Fein archive, Liechtenstein)*

275 Marion Dönhoff *(Avenir Ovsianov archive)*

284 Police photograph of the body of George Stein, 20 August 1987 *(MPR Productions)*

294 Pre-war Königsberg *(Königsberg City Museum)*

295 The 'Monster' *(Catherine Scott-Clark)*

305 The amber coastline of the Samland Peninsula *(Catherine Scott-Clark)*

306 Avenir Ovsianov, digging for the Amber Room in Kaliningrad Province, 1970s *(Avenir Ovsianov archive)*

308 Kaliningrad Geological Archaeological Expedition team photograph *(Avenir Ovsianov archive)*

317 Anatoly Kuchumov reading in the mauve boudoir of Empress Alexandra, Alexander Palace, Pushkin, 1940 *(Vica Plauda archive)*

346 Dr Ivan Sautov, director of the Catherine Palace, signing the deal with German energy provider Ruhrgas AG executives to sponsor the reconstruction of the Amber Room. From left to right: Dr Ivan Sautov; Vladimir Yegorov, former Minister for Cultural Affairs of the Russian Federation; Mr Friedrich Spaeth, former Chairman of the Ruhrgas AG Executive Board and Dr H. C. Achim Middelschulte, Member of the Ruhrgas AG Executive Board.

351 Damaged Monighetti staircase, Catherine Palace, 1945

353 Insect in amber

357 Last surviving pieces of the Amber Room *(Günter Wermusch archive)*

Acknowledgements

In the face of recalcitrant institutions, long journeys, sub-zero temperatures and many other excuses, a dedicated group of Russian curators, Red Army veterans, academics, friends and family kept us sane and helped us complete this book.

Galya and Kolya, Vova and Tanya in St Petersburg made a great contribution to our Russian work. They will not agree, or even like everything we have written, but despite this we hope we can still eat pickled mushrooms together. Vladimir Telemakov was endlessly generous with his writings, which have yet to find a publisher, and has a remarkable memory and passion for Russian culture. A friend in the Hermitage found us somewhere to stay and we apologize for being terrified by her apartment.

A close circle of curators in St Petersburg and Tsarskoye Selo, including Valeria Bilanina, Albina Vasiliava and Albina Alya, spent hours recounting anecdotes as well as searching out journals, books and addresses. Nadezda Voronova shared her family photos with us and told stories about her father, M. G. Voronov, and his close colleague Anatoly Kuchumov. Vica Plauda had wonderful memories of growing up with Kuchumov, her grandfather. Alexander Kedrinsky kept us rapt for several days, and although he will find it hard to agree with our conclusions, he may recognize the truth in them. Alex Guzanov tried hard to help us at Pavlovsk.

Valera Katsuba explained the subtext to our ongoing correspondence with the St Petersburg authorities, while Yura danced and baked fish. Catherine Phillips, a great Russian scholar, was always at the end of a phone with suggestions (and could sing all the male roles in *Eugene Onegin*). Dr Ivan Sautov, director of the Catherine Palace, prevented us using his archive but his refusal led to our finding a wealth of new material elsewhere. Stuart M. Gibson was endlessly optimistic and lent us his name on several occasions.

Avenir Ovsianov in Kaliningrad has spent three decades looking for lost treasure and has found many things, although not the Amber Room. He shared many of his files and memories with us. We have not met, but Konstantin Akinsha and Gregory Koslov are informative on the history of the trophy brigades, having opened up the subject. Susanne Massie, likewise, was a pioneer, as one of the first American writers to work inside the Soviet Union. She produced a poignant account of the life of the Leningrad palaces.

In Germany, Professor Wolfgang Eichwede invited us for coffee that became a dinner and eventually ended in breakfast. A great diplomat with a profound love for his field, Eichwede was a sound guide to Russian–German negotiations. Günter Wermusch was always good company and even though we will never agree with each other it will always be a pleasure to listen to his well-argued theories. A friend in the German Foreign Office probably shouldn't be named but was an adviser and sporadic translator. Gerhard Ehlert works harder than anyone we know and has an encyclopaedic knowledge of the Stasi.

Rainer Schubert tells his story with passion and provided us with a vivid insight into prison life in the GDR. Friends on the *Frankfurter Allgemeine Zeitung* provided background on the Stasi and party archives. Klaus Goldmann explained the backdrop to the 'Trojan Gold' débâcle. Maurice Philip Remy in Munich was great company and has broken much new ground on many projects (including the Amber Room) that remain sensitive areas for most Germans. George Laue in Munich has written some interesting catalogues about amber. Helmut Seling in Munich was the first German to be allowed into the Kremlin's secret stores after the war. Tete Böttger tried very hard to offend but his heart was just not in it. Robert Stein agreed to meet us and then wished he hadn't, but we wish him luck. Baron Eduard von Falz-Fein was wonderful company and exactly what he appears to be, which is a rarity in any age. Stephan Strauss was extremely generous in agreeing to meet, although we may never agree about the role played by his father, Gerhard Strauss.

In Britain we owe thanks to Freddy and Kitty Liebreich. Freddy translated hundreds of pages of Stasi-talk and then translated hundreds more and came out of it no madder than when he began. Kitty tracked down maps and donated them to our research. Pamela Scott-Clark steered us through the history of amber. Dorothy Levy was always prepared to listen. In particular we owe thanks to our publisher, Toby Mundy at Atlantic Books, who believed in the project from the start. His skilful, blunt and energetic readings of all of the drafts of our manuscript have shaped it beyond recognition. Clara Farmer at Atlantic has also helped greatly. In the US, George Gibson, publisher at Walker & Company, has been a calming influence on the project and provided a depth of ideas that has added greatly to the finished manuscript.

Catherine Scott-Clark and Adrian Levy,
Chiang Mai, Thailand,
January 2004

Note on Transliteration

Russian names are spelled in this book according to the standard Library of Congess system of transliteration, but common English spellings of well-known Russian names and placenames (for example, Tolstoy, Tsarskoye Selo) have been retained. To aid pronunciation, some Russian names (Grigorii and Vasilii, for example) have been changed (to Gregory and Vasily).

Dramatis Personae

Larissa Bardovskaya Head curator at the Catherine Palace in the St Petersburg suburb of Tsarskoye Selo, Bardovskaya was responsible for writing the official account of the mystery of the Amber Room for a summary catalogue published by the Russian Ministry of Culture in 1999.

Professor Alexander Brusov Professor of archaeology at the State Historical Museum in Moscow and brother of Valery, a famous Soviet modernist writer. Brusov led the first search for the Amber Room in May 1945 and reported that it had been destroyed.

Empress Catherine II of Russia German-born princess who seized control of the Russian throne in 1762. Catherine the Great restyled the Catherine Palace and vastly augmented the Amber Room. Visitors would describe it as the 'Eighth Wonder of the World'.

Professor Wolfgang Eichwede Director of the Research Centre for Eastern Europe at Bremen University. Wolfgang Eichwede mediates between Germany and Russia over the return of war artefacts stolen during the Second World War.

Empress Elizabeth Daughter of Peter I. Elizabeth became Empress of Russia in 1741 and within two years began supervising the construction of her father's Amber Room. In 1755 it was moved from St Petersburg to the Catherine Palace.

Paul Enke Stasi agent who used the code-name of Paul Köhler. Enke was a researcher at the GDR's State Archives Administration in Potsdam and began the Stasi's inquiry into the fate of the Amber Room. In 1986 he published *Bernsteinzimmer Report*, the most popular and influential book on the search.

Baron Eduard von Falz-Fein White Russian exile living in Liechtenstein. Von Falz-Fein bankrolled the search for the Amber Room in West Germany and returned looted art to Russia and the Ukraine, from where his family originated. Von Falz-Fein's 'Amber Room club' included Julian Semyonov, George Stein and Georges Simenon, the creator of Inspector Maigret, among its members.

Frederick I Crowned 'King in Prussia' in Königsberg in 1701. Frederick realized the Hohenzollerns' aspirations of transforming Prussia into a monarchy and funded the creation of the Amber Room.

Frederick William I The Soldier King. Frederick William I was the son of Frederick I and ascended the throne in 1713. Uninterested in the Amber Room, which he considered too costly, he gave it to Tsar Peter I as part of a diplomatic treaty in 1716.

Uwe Geissler Stasi informer working inside the 'Kripo', the East German criminal police. Geissler was used by the Stasi to cross-examine potential eyewitnesses during the GDR's Amber Room inquiry. He investigated the top-secret source 'Rudi Ringel'.

Otto Grotewohl President of East Germany from 1949 to 1964. Grotewohl cemented ties with the Soviet Union at a time of great unrest in the Eastern bloc. He received from the Soviet Union millions of German cultural treasures looted by the Red Army during the Second World War.

Alexander Kedrinsky One of the Soviet Union's most famous architects and restorers, Kedrinsky led the project to rebuild the Amber Room in the Catherine Palace, which was unveiled on 31 May 2003.

Erich Koch The Reich's Commissar of the Ukraine and Gauleiter of East Prussia. Koch evacuated his private collection of looted art to Weimar in 1945. Later (while being held in prison in Poland) he hinted at having played a part in saving and concealing the Amber Room.

Anatoly Kuchumov One of the Soviet Union's most famous curators. Kuchumov headed the investigation in 1946 that established that the Amber Room had survived the war, having been concealed in an unknown hiding place by the Nazis. His 1989 book *The Amber Room* would become the second most famous publication on the subject.

Erich Mielke Minister for State Security. The head of the Stasi from 1957 to 1990, Mielke became obsessed with finding the Amber Room. He pumped millions in hard currency into 'Operation Puschkin', a special task force that excavated in the GDR throughout the 1980s.

Martin Mutschmann Gauleiter of Saxony, to where the Amber Room was apparently evacuated in the last months of the war. Mutschmann vanished in May 1945. It was claimed that he was abducted by the Red Army and taken back to the Soviet Union.

Our Friend the Professor Pseudonym of a Soviet academic who still lives and works in St Petersburg, without whose contacts we would never have found the Kuchumov archive or met many of the curator's contemporaries.

Avenir Ovsianov Former Red Army colonel who worked for the secret Soviet Kaliningrad Geological-Archaeological Expedition (KGA), which searched for the Amber Room during the 1970s. After the disintegration of the Soviet Union so many treasure hunters applied for permission to dig in Kaliningrad that the province formed the Kaliningrad Centre for Coordinating the Search for Cultural Relics. Ovsianov became its director.

Tsar Peter I Having become mesmerized by the Baltic amber trade while touring incognito in 1696, Peter the Great of Russia waited another twenty years before receiving the Amber Room as a gift. His craftsmen were unable to assemble it in St Petersburg.

'Rudi Ringel' The code-name for a top-secret Stasi and KGB informer, 'Rudi Ringel' claimed that his father was an SS Sturmbannführer and evacuated the Amber Room from Königsberg Castle to a location known only by the call-sign BSCH, on the advice of Gauleiter Erich Koch.

Alfred Rohde Writer, curator, amber specialist and director of the Königsberg Castle Museum. Rohde took charge of the Amber Room in the winter of 1941 and was responsible for it until it vanished in April 1945. Rohde vanished too, some months later, along with his wife.

Alfred Rosenberg Hitler's ideologue and the Minister for the Occupied Eastern Territories, whose organization, the Einsatzstab Reichleiter Rosenberg, was involved in the transport of the Amber Room to Königsberg. It was also accused of evacuating the room out of the city in 1945.

Professor Dr Ivan Sautov A major figure in the St Petersburg cultural establishment and director of the Catherine Palace. Sautov oversaw the rebuilding of the Amber Room and presided over its opening on 31 May 2003.

Andreas Schlüter Sculptor to the Prussian court. Schlüter came up with the idea of a room panelled with amber in 1701. He lost his job before the project could be completed in Berlin.

Julian Semyonov Soviet writer whose creation was a spy named Maxim Stirlitz, the Eastern bloc's 'James Bond', who could speak almost every European language 'with the exception of Irish and Albanian'. Semyonov spent two decades searching for the Amber Room and denying that he had any connections with the KGB.

Hans Seufert Oberst in the Stasi, Seufert was a career agent who supervised Erich Mielke's Amber Room investigation, 'Operation Puschkin'. Seufert was also agent Paul Enke's senior officer.

George Stein Strawberry farmer from the village of Stelle outside Hamburg and Germany's most famous amateur treasure hunter. Of East Prussian descent, he spent a quarter of century hunting for the Amber Room, only to die bloodily, having apparently uncovered evidence that it had been secretly shipped to America.

Jelena Storozhenko Head of the secret Soviet investigation into the fate of the Amber Room in 1970s and 1980s. Storozhenko led a team that worked under the cover of the Kaliningrad Geological-Archaeological Expedition (KGA), sometimes codenamed 'the Choral Society'. Storozhenko retired in 1984, disaffected after her operation was shut down.

Professor Dr Gerhard Strauss Influential art historian and professor at Humboldt University in East Berlin. Strauss was closely connected to the Soviet and East German state investigations into the Amber Room.

Vladimir Telemakov Journalist for a car workers' daily in Leningrad, Telemakov spent decades researching a biography of Anatoly Kuchumov that has yet to find a publisher.

Stanislav Tronchinsky A Pole by birth, Tronchinsky worked as a senior cultural bureaucrat in Leningrad and also held a high-ranking position within the Leningrad Communist Party. He assisted Anatoly Kuchumov in his hunt for the Amber Room during the critical mission of 1946.

Paul Wandel GDR Minister for Education during the 1950s. Wandel was the person to whom Professor Dr Gerhard Strauss reported and was the inspiration behind the early searches in East Germany for the Amber Room.

Günter Wermusch Editor at the former East German publishing house, Die Wirtshaft. Wermusch worked on *Bernsteinzimmer Report*, Paul Enke's influential book on the Amber Room.

Gottfried Wolfram Master craftsman to the Danish court. Wolfram, an ivory cutter by trade, travelled to Berlin in 1701 to work with Andreas Schlüter on the original Amber Room, only to see the project collapse twelve years later.

Field Marshal Georgy Zhukov Leader of the Red Army offensive against the Third Reich, as well as a key player in the battle for Berlin, Zhukov's subsequent military and political career in the Soviet Union was ended in 1946 by allegations of looting during the Second World War.

Maps

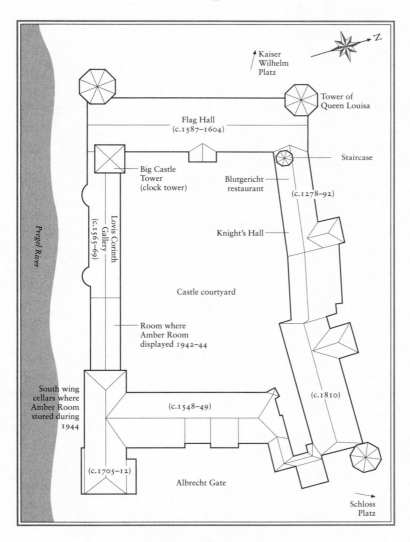

Kaiser
Wilhelm
Platz

Ｚ

Tower of
Queen Louisa

Flag Hall
(c.1587–1604)

Staircase

Big Castle
Tower
(clock tower)

Blutgericht
restaurant

(c.1278–92)

Lovis Corinth
Gallery
(c.1565–69)

Knight's Hall

Pregel River

Castle courtyard

Room where
Amber Room
displayed 1942–44

South wing
cellars where
Amber Room
stored during
1944

(c.1810)

(c.1548–49)

(c.1705–12)

Albrecht Gate

Schloss
Platz

1. Königsberg Castle, pre-April 1945

2. Kaliningrad, c.2004 (Historic names are shown in brackets.)

Alfred Rohde's house

Alyabeva
(Bickstrasse)

Moskva Hotel

Prospekt Mira

Place Pobedy

Site of Hofbunker

Leninsky Prospekt
(Steindamm Strasse)

Barnulskaya
(Lange Reihe)

Kaliningrad Hotel

Frunze Ulitza
(Frunze Strasse)

Monster (site of
Königsberg Castle)

Moskovsky Prospekt

Kaliningrad Dom
(Königsberg Cathedral)

Church of the
Holy Family

Kaliningrad
railway station

Pregolya River
(Pregel River)

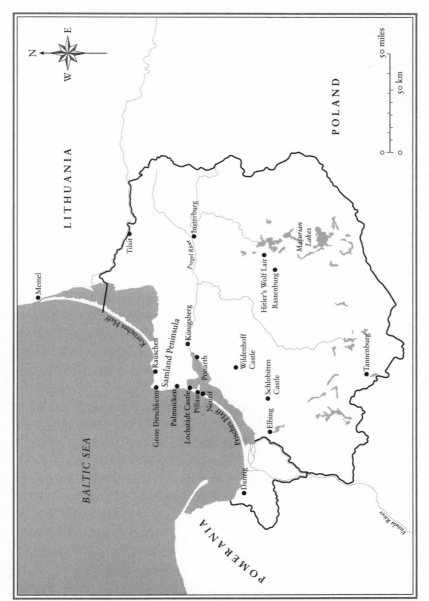

3. East Prussia, c.1945

N

W   E

S

SWEDEN

DENMARK

BALTIC SEA

NORTH SEA

POLAND

NETHERLANDS

•Hamburg
Harburg• •Stelle

•Bremen

Berlin
Lake Krossinsee•

Frankfurt
an der
Oder•
Ziegenhals

•Brocken Mountain

Volpriehausen
Göttingen•
•Duisburg   Kassel

Recklinghausen •

•Bonn   Langenstein•

Wechselburg
Castle ■

Kriebstein
Castle ■

Görlitz•

Weimar •
•Merkers

Gera
•

Dresden
•

Crimmitschau•
Elsterberg•
Freiberg•

•Chemitz
Schlema
•Deutschneudorf
•Tellerhäuser
Erzgebirge
Nature Park

•Wiesbaden

CZECH
REPUBLIC

Colmberg
Castle

B A V A R I A

Tittingwald• •Altdorf

FRANCE

•Munich
•Starnberg

•Linz

AUSTRIA

•Berchtesgaden

SWITZERLAND

Vaduz• —LIECHTENSTEIN

- - - - Divided Germany
1947–1990

0   100 miles

0   150 km

4. Germany, c. 2004

xxviii

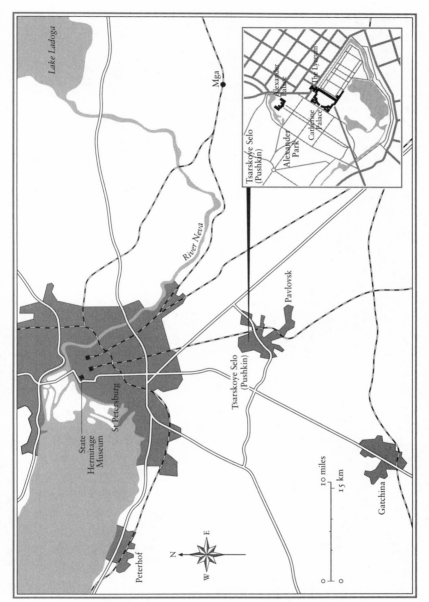

5. St Petersburg and environs, c. 2004

Lake Ladoga

Mga

River Neva

State
Hermitage
Museum

St Petersburg

Peterhof

Tsarskoye Selo
(Pushkin)

Pavlovsk

Gatchina

Tsarskoye Selo
(Pushkin)

Alexander
Park

Alexander
Palace

Catherine
Palace

The Lyceum

N
W E

10 miles

15 km

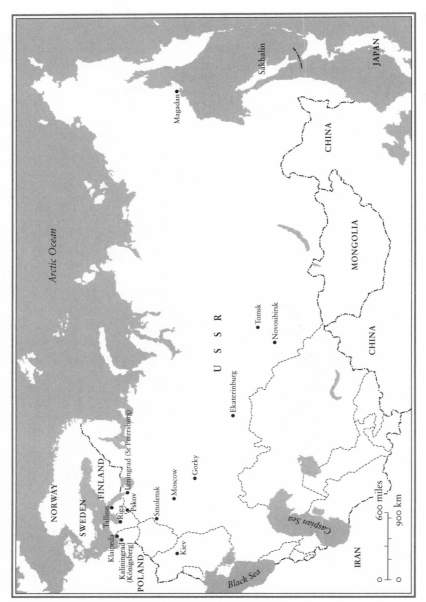

6. USSR, post-1947

THE AMBER ROOM

Introduction

An urgent order arrived just after midday on 22 June 1941: pack up Leningrad. The Nazis had invaded the Soviet Union at 4 that morning without a declaration of war. So rapid was the advance that the Kremlin calculated Leningrad's southern gateway of Moskovsky Prospekt would be overrun within weeks.

But 22 June was a radiant Sunday, the first in what had been a lousy year. Weekend revellers strolled along the banks of the River Neva, popping bottles of sweet Soviet champagne, or headed out to the suburban estates of the former tsars, their hampers filled with herrings and pickled mushrooms. The scale of the crisis only filtered through the city by 6 p.m. Grinding across the Soviet Union was the greatest invasion force in history: 4 million German soldiers, 207 Wehrmacht divisions, 3,300 tanks.

Evacuate Leningrad's treasures. The order came from LenGorIsPolKom (the city's executive committee). Everyone was listening now. Collections from the city's palaces and museums had to be saved. But there were 2.5 million exhibits in the State Hermitage, and hundreds of thousands more in the Alexander, Catherine and Pavlovsk Palaces as well as the collections housed at Peterhof, Oranienbaum and Gatchina.

A curator at the Catherine Palace in the town of Pushkin scribbled in his diary: '22 June. Flown through the halls this evening, packing what we can.'

But there was too much work: '24 June. Comrades having nosebleeds from leaning over the packing crates. Run out of boxes and paper... Had to use the tsarinas' dress trunks and their clothes to wrap up our treasures.'[1]

And what should they do with the city's most unique treasure, an arte-fact that was often said to encompass old Russia's imperial might? At the centre of a chain of linked halls on the first floor of the Catherine Palace, where salon opened into salon, stood a gorgeous chamber made of amber, a substance that, at the time of its construction, was twelve times more valuable than gold.

The idea of panelling a room entirely in amber had first been mooted at the Prussian court in 1701. The resulting radical and complex construc-tion came to symbolize the Age of Reason in which it was conceived. Tons of resin, the Gold of the North, had been fished in nuggets from the Baltic Sea, then heated, shaped and coloured before being slotted together on huge backing boards like a gigantic jigsaw puzzle. When, sixty years later, the panels of the Amber Room were gifted to Russia, they were heralded by visitors to the court in St Petersburg as the 'Eighth Wonder of the World'. 'We have now reached one of the most remarkable rarities – I want to tell you about the Amber Room,' wrote a French novelist. 'Only in *The Thousand and One Nights* and in magic fairy tales, where the architecture of palaces is trusted to magicians, spirits and genies, can one read about rooms made of diamonds, rubies, jacinth and other jewels.'[2]

Even after the Revolution, when the estates of the tsars were trans-formed into Soviet museums, the Amber Room remained Leningrad's most popular exhibit.[3] But by the summer of 1941, the installation of central heating had made the amber brittle and the Catherine Palace staff feared dismantling it. When, eight days after Germany invaded, the first Soviet train loaded with exhibits steamed out of Leningrad and east towards Siberia, the Amber Room was not on board.

The curators left behind had no more time to think about it. They were enlisted to bolster the town's defences. One wrote in her diary: 'We carry out the work of guards, office workers, cleaners. All walls are bare.' Apart from the walls of the Amber Room.

By the end of August, the Nazis had taken Mga, a railway terminal 10 miles south of Leningrad, isolating two million citizens who would not see the outside world for almost 900 days. It was now too late to evacuate anything else. By 1 September a Nazi perimeter bristling with munitions had fenced the city in. The British monitored the advance: '9 September. XVI Panzer Korps is moving to Leningrad.'

On 13 September the town of Pushkin came under fire. 'Koluft Panzer Group Four now in Detskoye Selo [Pushkin].' The following day, the attack came from above. 'Fliegerkorps have landed. Attack on Pushkin has been carried out. All bombs have landed in the target area.'

Inside the Catherine Palace, a handful of curators continued to work, attempting to safeguard what they could, scattering sand on the floors to protect the precious inlaid wood, packing all but the most cumbersome pieces of furniture into storerooms. But there was still one thing that no one had properly secured.

Couriers carried reports from Pushkin back to the city authorities in Leningrad. The last came on 17 September at 5 a.m.: 'The park and north of the town are battling hard. Everyone is moving to the west. We have even taken the typewriters. We will leave nothing for them.'

Apart from the Amber Room, which was hidden in the dark beneath another, plainer room constructed out of muslin and cotton. Rather than evacuate it, Catherine Palace staff had decided to conceal the delicate treasure in situ. The irreplaceable amber walls had been covered over with layers of cloth and padding. If the Nazis managed to force their way into the Catherine Palace, it was hoped they would be deceived into thinking that here was just another ordinary, empty room.

Within hours the palace was overrun. One German officer described how almost immediately crude signs were nailed to the gilded doors, listing them 'reserved for the 1st Company etc., etc. ...'⁴ Everywhere there were 'sleeping [German] soldiers with their muddy boots resting on the precious settees and chairs'. The Nazi advance had been exhaustingly rapid. Then a cheer went up and the German officer raced to see what his men had discovered. On the first floor, in a room in the middle of a long corridor, 'two privates in curiosity toiled in tearing protective... covers off [the walls]. They revealed wonderfully shining amber carvings, the frames of a mosaic picture.'

When Soviet curators returned to the Catherine Palace in March 1944 they entered through the buckled iron gates and across a courtyard strewn with barbed wire and Nazi graves. Up to the first-floor suite of rooms they climbed – not by the marble stairs, as they had been blown to smithereens – and discovered that where they had concealed the 'Eighth Wonder of the World' there was now just a void. The Amber Room had vanished. All the Nazis had left behind were bare boards and a tangled mystery.

In the Autumn of 2001 we pieced together this much of the story about the Amber Room using a handful of published sources and the declassified Enigma files at the Public Records Office in London, in which are recorded some of the 2,000 signals intercepted every day by the Ultra project that eavesdropped on German communications throughout the Second World War.[5]

Our curiosity about the fate of the Amber Room, then a subject of which we knew very little, had been roused by a stream of press releases and news stories coming out of Russia and Germany. In 1999, a German company had stepped in to help the Russians construct a replica of the original Amber Room with a gift of 3.5 million dollars. Now, one and a half years later, the project was almost complete and the stage was set for a grand unveiling.

The St Petersburg and Moscow authorities gushed about their new Amber Room, describing it as a memorial to everything the Soviet Union had lost in the Second World War. Publicity from the German sponsors extolled the rebuilding project as a symbol of the new Europe, without a Wall or Iron Curtain. The Kremlin announced it would invite forty heads of state and government to the opening, which was set to coincide with the three-hundredth anniversary of the founding of St Petersburg on 31 May 2003. The event was to be televised live from a specially constructed press centre that could house 1,000 journalists. The budget for the celebrations would run into billions of roubles. So much was being invested in the new Amber Room and yet no one seemed able to resolve the fate of the original masterpiece. It was now said to be worth more than 250 million dollars, a figure that made it the most valuable missing work of art in the world.

There are, we discovered, many different types of treasure hunters. Key 'Amber Room' into an Internet search engine or any online newspaper library and see over 800,000 entries pop up.

A group of salvage experts have for years been scouring the catacombs that run beneath the German city of Weimar in the belief that the Amber Room was secretly transferred to the Baltic city of Königsberg and then on to Weimar by Nazi agents acting for the Gauleiter of East Prussia.

Divers regularly explore the rusting wreck of the *Wilhelm Gustloff*, a German liner torpedoed on 31 January 1945 as it sailed from the Baltic port of Gotenhafen, north-west of Danzig. The liner was evacuating 10,582 wounded Germans away from Königsberg and the advancing Soviet front. It was also said to be carrying the Amber Room.

Mining experts regularly congregate in western Saxony and Thuringia where the countryside is honeycombed with deep ore and potash pits in the belief that as the Nazis had used mines and caves to hide important art works, the Amber Room too had been secreted in the subterranean tunnels.

These different theories and their backers, a league of treasure hunters from Europe, the United States and Russia, have spawned thousands of potential leads and a dizzying world of conspiracy. As we write this, there are more than a dozen German digs under way, each underpinned by a different theory.

However, in Russia there is an information black hole. Almost every official directly connected to the original Amber Room is dead or missing. Political and economic conditions have led to their files, diaries and memorabilia being broken up, stolen, concealed and classified. Even after glasnost and perestroika, the most important Russian archives that might contain material on the official searches for the Amber Room are arcane. The museum authorities in Moscow and St Petersburg are awkward and often inhospitable (especially to those who come without offers of international funding or research exchanges).

We had no previous experience of working in Russia or the former Eastern bloc, but had for more than a decade earned a reputation for chasing difficult stories, researching out in the field and inside archives in America, Britain, China and India, for British newspapers and broadcasters. Russia seemed like the best place to start. It was vast, obstreperous and secretive. It was also therefore likely to be the place that had retained the most secrets, even if they were difficult to extract.

In December 2001 we flew to St Petersburg and made slow progress through official channels. However, friends from the former Leningrad University, experts at living creatively, suggested another, more lateral strategy. They helped us piece together a network of subordinate characters, Red Army veterans, old comrades, serving and retired museum curators. One knew another. An introduction led to a dinner invitation. Slowly – so slowly at times that we felt as if we were going nowhere at all – we reached back in time and unearthed the stories of those directly involved in the Amber Room mystery.

In dachas and apartments, on park benches and in faceless offices, memories came alive, loosened by vodka, sweet black tea and white beer. For every official file, diary or briefing paper said by archives and libraries to be missing or inaccessible, we found draft or duplicate documents stashed away in living rooms and in hallways. For every government album that had been emptied or was lost, we discovered framed photos above mantelpieces and in bedroom drawers.

Six decades of secret and often frantic searching for the Amber Room came alive, as did the extraordinary efforts of those who struggled to suppress the truth about its fate. Our first faltering weeks in Russia grew into a two-year investigation and finally, having travelled thousands of miles from St Petersburg to Moscow, London to Washington, and from Holland, through Germany to Liechtenstein and Austria, following a paper trail that took us into the parallel worlds of the KGB and the East German Stasi, we arrived in the beat-up Russian enclave of Kaliningrad and at the heart of an extraordinary cover-up.

It was here, in a dying city on the Baltic, as the winter began to thaw, that the final pieces of the Amber Room mystery came together and we were forced to confront the truth about a story that would challenge the way we perceive the Soviet Union and its place in the Cold War.

I

'I am a complicated man,' he says through teeth that gleam like May Day medals. A little finger prods at the bridgework, poking the Soviet dental engineering back into shape. 'I committed fifty years to the Great Task – the reason why you are here. Correct?'

The old man's rolling Russian Rs clatter like falling pencils, reminding us that we have not yet explained why we are here, where we should not be, in the staff quarters of a palace museum on the outskirts of St Petersburg. We have barely recovered from getting in: squeezing between the guarded great gates crowned by double-headed eagles, tapping in a key code at an inconspicuous door, talking our way past a *babushka* huddled against the December freeze in five coats who, in her fur-lined hood, swayed like a cobra. Once inside we clanked up four flights of cast-iron stairs, past gargoyles with broken noses – casualties of war that have waited more than sixty years for restoration – until we found the old man sitting in silence in his vast studio, sporting a fine, red jersey. On the wall behind him hangs an intricate blueprint, a curious bird's-eye view, labelled: 'Imperial Prussian Study'.

Straight away he begins, a series of disconnected thoughts springing from thin, dry lips: 'I could have retired, like some I could name. But a man like me, whose work is of national importance, can never really retire. Then I had my second heart attack.' He accentuates the words as if reading from a public copy of the *Leningradskaya Pravda*, which the state once pasted to the notice-boards beside Ulitsa Nekrasova, where, we have been told, he used to sip bitter coffee in a Georgian café called Tblisi.

The old man ruffles a small hand over his white hair. 'I am a patriot.

The original design for the Amber Room, 1701

And yet here I am considering talking to *you*. Pah.' He grinds a filter-tipped cigarette into a viscous beaker of coffee and glowers out of the window at the blizzard that tears across the parkland of the tsars. His baggy face is a map of broken capillaries.

The Catherine Palace estate. Here, Peter the Great, who battled Sweden in 1702 to capture the region, built a simple manor that he presented to his fiancée, Catherine, to mark their engagement in 1708. Fifteen miles further north, his new model European capital of St Petersburg was also rising out of the mosquito-ridden delta of the River Neva. Today every statue in the frozen garden, planted more than 220 years ago, wears a jacket of wood and wire as protection against the gales that roar down from the Gulf of Finland.

Empress Elizabeth, Peter's daughter, inherited the manor in 1752, ordering her Italian architect, Bartolomeo Rastrelli, to transform it into a Baroque imperial summer residence. A 'wide, light-blue ribbon, a palace with snow-white columns', rose above the birch, maple and cherries.[1]

The exterior of the Catherine Palace was gilded with 220 pounds of gold and its interior was a jewelled chain of linked halls, salon opening into salon, white, then crimson, green and then amber, to create the golden enfilades.

Soon other palaces sprang up around it and the suburb became known as Tsarskoye Selo, the Tsar's Village. In the 1770s, the new Empress, Catherine the Great, ordered her Scottish architect, Charles Cameron, to remodel the Catherine Palace in a Classical style. It was here that she entertained her legion of lovers, the last being twenty-five-year-old Count Platon Zubov, whose name still graces the ground floor of the southern wing.

The adjacent hall, which we can see through the old comrade's window, became the Imperial Lyceum, a school that would in 1811 enrol the twelve-year-old Alexander Pushkin, who later immortalized the town: 'Whatever partings destiny may bring, whatever fortunes fate may have in hand, we're still the same; the world an alien thing, and Tsarskoye Selo our Fatherland.'[2]

The Catherine Palace

From the rooms of the Alexander Palace, behind us, Tsar Nicholas II unsuccessfully petitioned 'Cousin Bertie' in England for help before being taken to Ekaterinburg where his bloodline ended in a dank cellar. Below us, in the Great Courtyard, the Cossacks of Alexander Kerensky surrendered to the Russian people in October 1917, bringing down the Russian Provisional Government and handing power to Lenin and the Bolsheviks. At the first opportunity, the great-coated heroes of the Revolution flocked in to jockey for a peek at the decadent world of the aristocrats.

And here too, in 1952, arrived the old comrade before us, Alexander Alexandrevich Kedrinsky: one of the Soviet Union's most fêted architects; fellow of the hallowed Russian Academy of Arts; winner of the Lenin Prize; his life's work commended by LenGorSoviet (the former city council); his achievements recognized by general secretaries, premiers and presidents – Brezhnev, Gorbachev, Chernomyrdin, Yeltsin and Putin.

But difficult as it has been to reach Kedrinsky (and there have been many meetings in London and St Petersburg since we began researching the Amber Room story in September 2001 and as many letters, faxes and phone calls to émigrés and functionaries, distant voices lost in a storm of static), we have an even more delicate task ahead of us: telling Kedrinsky that it is not him we have come all this way to see.

We are searching for another elderly Russian curator who once cared for his country's most loved treasure: Anatoly Kuchumov, the Amber Room's last guardian and one of Comrade Kedrinsky's oldest colleagues. The men had worked together for more than forty years. But Kuchumov's telephone is disconnected and there is no one who remembers him at the state retirement home on the outskirts of Tsarskoye Selo.

Kedrinsky is distracted. 'There is a new order at the court, you know,' he says, rising to shut the door. 'Bardovskaya will cut off my head if I utter one word to you.' Bardovskaya? The name means nothing to us but we do not challenge him. Elderly cadre like Kedrinsky are sticklers for formality and instead we endure a long silence. It is stifling in his cavernous studio. The centralized heating system has yet to experience perestroika. Kedrinsky sharpens his pencil the old-fashioned way – with long assured strokes of a knife. Caviar tins of paint-wash that resemble various shades of snow-melt litter his desk, as do his holy triptych:

Alexander Kedrinsky (far right) with colleagues from Leningrad's palaces after winning the Lenin Prize in 1986

a disposable lighter, an ashtray and a black and gold packet of Peter I, the city's newest cigarette brand.

'Blow Bardovskaya,' he suddenly announces. 'We shall proceed. I will tell you about the Great Task when you have learned something of me. My father. He was a real Russian hero – killed in the first war. My mother – she died too, shortly after I was born, in the year of the October Revolution. An extraordinary aunt raised me.'

Comrade Kedrinsky enjoys the value everyone places on his knowledge. The sights he must have seen as the party's restorer, one of only a handful of people allowed into every locked store. And there is no interrupting. No chance to ask about Anatoly Kuchumov, the last guardian of the Amber Room.

'My aunt had studied at the Sorbonne and spoke French. Met Toulouse-Lautrec and Modigliani. Arriving back in our city in 1919, she began teaching at the ballet school – just down the road. A strange time.'

We have already noticed how Russians talk about terror. It crops up obliquely; most times indistinctly and often inaudibly and in the form of omission – what was permitted rather than what was forbidden. Here in St Petersburg, a living museum of the eighteenth and nineteenth centuries, whose architecture was barely affected by the most momentous and bloodiest events of the twentieth century, long-suffering citizens are happy to dream that they too were untouched by it all.

It is 1919. The height of the Red Terror. A city reduced from 2.3 million to 720,000 by disease, poverty, panic and the Cheka. 'He who seeks to protect poor people will harden his heart against pity and will become cruel' was the motto of the All Russian Extraordinary Commission to Combat Counter Revolution and Sabotage (Cheka), formed in December 1917 in a small office minutes away from the city's Winter Palace. Peter the Great's metropolis of canals, town houses and ornamental gardens, conceived as part Amsterdam, part London, part Paris and part Venice, soon appeared damned. A character in Alexei Tolstoy's *The Road to Calvary* claimed to see the Devil himself riding in a horse-drawn *droshky* to the city's Vasilevsky Island. 'Ranks, honours, pensions, officers' epaulettes, the thirtieth letter of the alphabet, God, private property, and the right to live as one wished all were being cancelled,' Tolstoy would write.[3]

And what of Anatoly Kuchumov? Was Kuchumov also raised during the Red Terror?

'Kuchumov was a liar. Took the glory for things he didn't do,' Kedrinsky spits, jabbing his pencil into the blotter on his desk.

We are shocked. This is not what we expected to hear from a close colleague who had supposedly worked in Kuchumov's pocket for so many decades.

Kedrinsky rails: 'Kuchumov spent his childhood trailing through the mud banks of the Volga in bark shoes. At thirteen I was painting portraits of Lenin. And by the time I was seventeen I was filled with a passion for my country. I worked hard and won a place at the Leningrad Institute of Engineering. I could continue to paint and learn to be an architect, acquire the skills I would need for the Great Task.' His words chug like old locomotives, each one capped in small puffs of smoke drawn from cigarettes that he strokes fondly before putting to the flame. 'I studied under marvellous professors, Eberling and Zedenberg. I loved their classes. But we Russians do not always get to keep what we love.'

And Kuchumov? We are insistent. What of his education?

'Pah. Kuchumov. He had no formal education. His good taste went only as far as the fat cherubs and roses he ordered to be painted on to palace ceilings when they were restored. And yet the staff had to bow and scrape before him. Kuchumov became the tsar of the museum stores.'

We try another tack. What happened in the summer of 1941, we ask, when the Amber Room vanished from this palace?

'I was not in Leningrad. I was in the southern Urals. Building mills and military factories,' the old comrade says, looking out of the window at the *troikas* skimming children over the whitened lawns.

We are beginning to wonder if we have made a mistake in coming to see this man.

But Kedrinsky presses on: 'I am writing a book about the Great Task. The manuscript is top secret.' These words are whispered. 'How we rebuilt the Motherland, restored our bombed-out palaces. Bardovskaya says I cannot die until I complete it. And the work must be ready for publication in May 2003.'

Bardovskaya. That name again. But before we can ask about her Comrade Kedrinsky produces from his schoolboy desk drawer a sheaf of Soviet-era paper, thin leaves that curl like ferns with the first touch of a warm hand.

'All of my research,' he says. Some pages are typed and others are filled with meticulous and tiny handwritten Cyrillic letters. Outside, the snow is falling in great folds, the windows creaking as ice crystals blind them. Kedrinsky reads: '"22 June, 1941. Summer was coming into its own. The fresh green foliage of the old parks, gardens and squares perfumed the air. From early morning orchestras were playing, bold and happy songs, full of energy and joy. Through the streets streamed a variegated crowd."'

But Kedrinsky said he wasn't in Leningrad in June 1941. Whose recollections are these, we ask?

He pauses and looks up over the thick black frames of his glasses. 'Your friend Anatoly Kuchumov's. His memories. He was here in that summer of 1941.' Where did Kedrinsky get Kuchumov's diary from, we ask?

'Pah. No matter,' he snaps. 'I must have access to everything for my book about the Great Task.' Kedrinsky pulls out dozens of papers: official Soviet reports, his own recollections and extracts from his colleagues' personal papers, material embossed with the stamp of the Catherine Palace archive. The pages in his hand are part memoir and part reference material.

Kedrinsky goes back to Kuchumov's diary entry for 22 June 1941:

'In one flow the holiday crowd moved towards the palaces. There, old men rested on the lawn while young people danced to the music of the *bayan*. Others played volleyball and, in a constant stream, crowds flocked into the museum to see the work of those artists of genius – Rastrelli, Cameron. One group after another flowing as if on a conveyor belt through the golden enfilades.'

How passionate Kuchumov seemed about his Russia. His words don't sound like those of an uneducated man. He seems a very different character from the one presented by the dogmatic old comrade sitting before us.

Kedrinsky continues:

'Everything was as it had always been, then Klava, the supervisor, rushed into my study with the breathless news that Comrade Molotov [Vyacheslav Molotov, Stalin's Commissar of Foreign Affairs] was to go on air with an emergency announcement. I ran through the rooms to the palace colonnade, where there was a loudspeaker.

'A large crowd was already gathering, listening to Molotov's gruff voice, full of emotion, uttering simple, terrible words: "Men and women, citizens of the Soviet Union, the Soviet government and its head, Comrade Stalin, have instructed me to make the following announcement. At 4 a.m., without any declaration of war and without any claims being made on the Soviet Union, German troops attacked our country..."'

Zhitomir, Kaunas, Sevastopol and even Kiev, Mother of Rus, had been bombed in flagrant contravention of the German–Soviet non-aggression pact signed by Molotov and Hitler's Foreign Minister Joachim Ribbentrop on 23 August 1939. Now it fell to Molotov to rouse the Soviet people: '"The government calls upon you, men and women, citizens of the Soviet Union, to rally even more closely around the glorious Bolshevik Party, around the Soviet government and our leader, Comrade Stalin. Our cause is just. The enemy will be crushed. Victory will be ours."'

In his diary, Kuchumov recalled how he stood motionless: '"War. New trials. New disasters. The whole happy new life of summer vanished and in its place there was only trouble and the premonition of terrible grief."'

Kedrinsky straightens the research papers on his desk and turns to us: 'Kuchumov didn't have long to ponder the war, as within hours he had been ordered before Comrade Vladimir Ivanovich Ladukhin, the Director of the Catherine and Pavlovsk palaces, a party man. Instructions had come from Moscow. Everything of value in the city was to be evacuated: heavy machinery, factory equipment and the treasure of the tsars.'

It was a daunting task. The State Hermitage had millions of exhibits and there were thousands more in the palaces ringing Leningrad: Catherine, Alexander, Pavlovsk, Peterhof, Oranienbaum and Gatchina.

'There was not much time,' Kedrinsky says. 'Comrade Ladukhin assured Kuchumov that there was a plan and that he'd be all right if he stuck to it by the letter.' He sighs. 'Such a mistake. Kuchumov was just twenty-nine. The son of a carpenter, brought up in a log *izba*.'

Only nine years before, Kuchumov had been a peasant without qualifications or money. Somehow he had won a post as junior inventory clerk at the Leningrad palaces and, in less than a decade, risen to being chief curator of the Alexander Palace. He had been in the job for only two years when Ladukhin singled him out, instructing him to coordinate evacuating all the palaces of Tsarskoye Selo.

Why was such an important order from Moscow entrusted to a young and inexperienced curator, we ask?

Kedrinsky frowns. He hands us a photograph of a group of four people standing outside the Catherine Palace. 'Kuchumov, taken just before the war,' he says, pointing to the man on the right.

The young curator fits snugly into his double-breasted jacket, the broad white lapels of a weekend shirt spread carefully over it, hands clasped behind his back. A pair of circular rimmed glasses adorns his mousy, feminine features and an unruly forelock falls forward. A fountain pen is

Anatoly Kuchumov (right) with Anna Mikhailovna, his wife,
and others shortly before the Second World War

clipped in his breast pocket, signalling his recently acquired status as an intellectual. In the midst of the group is a woman. Who is she?

'The blue-eyed Anna Mikhailovna,' Kedrinsky says, wrinkling up his nose. He tells us that Anatoly Kuchumov and Anna Mikhailovna met at Leningrad Art Institute, where he attended night classes. She followed him to the Tsarskoye Selo to become a curator there, before they married in 1935.

'May I read on?' Kedrinsky asks sarcastically. 'According to Kuchumov's diary, on 22 June 1941 Comrade Ladukhin handed him an envelope.' Across the front was typed: 'Acts and instructions, only to be opened if war is proclaimed'. The sealed envelope had been kept in a safe by the city's security chief and the evacuation plan it contained was similar to one devised over a century before. In 1812 Russian curators had packed up and shipped out thousands of exhibits from the museums of St Petersburg and Moscow to remote storage depots in the east as Napoleon headed for the Russian border with specially trained 'trophy brigades', whose job it was to hunt down suitable art works for Paris.

Kedrinsky says 'But according to Kuchumov's diary, the list had been drawn up in 1936 by two curators who had included only 2,076 treasures out of a possible 110,000 items from the Alexander Palace, the Catherine Palace and Pavlovsk. If Kuchumov were to follow these orders, then only 259 pieces would be saved from the Catherine Palace and only seven from his own museum. According to the papers before him, he was not to bother with the French furniture created by the famed Jacob brothers, the extraordinary clock collection, the tsar's famous arsenal of weapons. There was no mention of works by Fedot Shubin, the Russian sculptor, no examples of prized Chinese lacquerware, no paintings by Serov, Roerich or Markovsky, some of Russia's greatest artists. Incredibly, there was also no Amber Room. Instead, included were a plaster death mask of Voltaire, undated, unsigned paintings and an export-quality copy of an eighteenth-century Japanese dish.[4]

'No Amber Room! Kuchumov made some discreet inquiries and was relieved to learn that the 1936 lists had been judged to be inadequate as far back as 1939. New lists had been drawn up. But where were they? Kuchumov discovered that they had been lost by the Leningrad security chief himself. Who would dare challenge him?' Kuchumov would have to improvise. He would seek help from the senior staff, familiar with the collections. 'But by June 1941, many of the steadying hands, those with the old expertise, had vanished,' Kedrinsky says.

The assassination of Sergei Kirov, head of the Leningrad Communist Party, in December 1934 had been used by Stalin as an excuse to purge the Leninist old guard. Show trials, mass executions, the exile of millions, the peeling back of layers of the party, followed. And down swooped the Black Crows, agents acting for Nikolai Yezhov, Russia's new General Commissar of State Security, a limping, diminutive figure who had become the head of the NKVD, the successor to the Cheka, and created a whole new genre of violence that would come to be known as *Yezhovshchina*. The people of Leningrad called him Karlik, the Dwarf. Paranoia leached into every tenement as heavy boots clumped up limestone stairwells in pursuit of careless words; neighbours were betrayed over the washing line, sisters and brothers collided over a rash phrase. Sometimes a failure to confess, even if it were a lie, would still bring Karlik down on your own head. After the secret police executed her husband, Anna Akhmatova, the city's favourite poet, wrote:

> In the west the earthly sun is still shining,
> And the roofs of the cities gleam in its rays,
> But here the white one already chalks crosses on the houses,
> And summons the crows, and the crows come flying.[5]

Many of those who worked in Leningrad's cultural institutions were descended from the nobility (as they were the only ones who had had access to further education and travel) and they also came under scrutiny. The Black Crows flew through Leningrad's museums, whisking away so many curators that the NKVD holding centre spilled out into the corridors. 'It was very, very full and people were sleeping on the mattresses on the floor. I couldn't guess what I had been arrested for,' wrote curator Boris Piotrovksy, a future director of the Hermitage. 'I had to occupy a place under someone's bed.'[6] Piotrovsky was released but twelve others were shot: Orientalists (possible double agents and/or Armenian nationalists), coin collectors (a Germanic passion), armament historians (obviously capable of rallying a mob) and anyone who had ever published abroad (disloyal/spy/saboteur).[7]

It was in the wake of Karlik's purges that relatively inexperienced curators like Kuchumov, young men from the working and peasant classes, rose quickly. But who from the old school was left to assist the country boy in June 1941?

Kedrinsky rustles in his desk. 'My manuscript,' he declares, slapping down a pile of papers. He reaches for a cigarette and pushes his fishbowl glasses back up the greasy bridge of his nose. '"All of the palace workers had been dismissed on 22 June apart from the most trusted, and that evening, after the crowds had departed, Kuchumov went with his team to the reserve halls of the Catherine Palace,"' Kedrinsky reads aloud. '"As he had been instructed, Kuchumov ripped the seals from the doors, placed there by the Commissariat of Internal Affairs. Inside he found piles of boxes and wadding, waterproof canvas and sawdust, with which to begin to pack the palace treasures."'

However, none of the boxes fitted the exhibits they were supposed to house and too few of them had been set aside. Just like the lists drawn up in 1936, this task had also been poorly carried out.

Kedrinsky sets aside his manuscript and shows us a party report written in 1941. 'It is necessary to make hundreds of new boxes,' an unnamed official stated. 'There is insufficient wadding. No packing materials. And the storeroom chosen for the sealed crates is flooded and too narrow.' And time spent remaking boxes and worrying over packing material would lead to rash decisions later.[8]

Kedrinsky begins to read another extract from Kuchumov's diary:

'June 22. Flown through the halls this evening, packing what we can.

'June 23. After we packed what was on the 1936 list I asked the director if we could pack more. "Do what you can," Comrade Ladukhin told me. And so we have done what we can. We never stop. We do not stop even at dawn. Few electric lights are needed; it is light all night. We will carry on working.

'June 24. Not stopped for forty-eight hours. Comrades having nosebleeds from leaning over the packing crates. Run out of boxes and paper. Cutting grass and using the fresh hay. Had to use the tsarinas' dress trunks and their clothes to wrap up our treasures.'

Curators pack up Leningrad's palaces after the Nazi invasion of the Soviet Union in 1941

Kedrinsky hands us a summary report submitted by Kuchumov to the NKVD:

'Vice-director (science), the directors of the palaces, and three museum workers, including a wallpaper hanger and two carpenters, have supervised the first stage of the evacuation. Miniatures, Gobelins, Sèvres, Meissen, gold and silver, paintings and books, ivory. Passports have been made for every crate – inventories written up by palace scholars. To date more than 900 items are now in fifty-two boxes, each one sealed with black canvas.'

All were secretly taken to the Armoury, where each box was logged in by a member of the People's Commissar of Internal Acts. The entrance was sealed and a sentry posted.[9]

Kedrinsky lights another cigarette, lingering over the smoke. 'Listen to this, from Kuchumov's diary: "What should we do with Amber Room? What can we do? I sent for Comrade V. A. Alspector, the specialist from the palace restoration department, and gave him instructions to prepare the Amber Room for evacuation."' Kedrinsky savours the moment before reading on. '"Amber panels are to be tightly fastened with cigarette papers on a special glue solution."'

Since the eighteenth century the amber panels had been attached on to wooden backing boards and now would have to be pasted over with cigarette rolling papers to prevent the brittle resin from splintering when Kuchumov attempted to prise the amber free from the boards.

Kedrinsky hesitates and then continues: '"A trial moving of one of the panels has resulted in disaster. The amber facing has come off the mount and shattered completely. We cannot move the Amber Room. We dare not move it. What are we to do?"'

The old comrade rises from his desk, rifling through pages: 'References, references, archival references, all recorded by Anatoly Mikhailovich Kuchumov. That's all that's left – nothing more, nothing less – in this report.'

The Prussian sculptor Andreas Schlüter waited almost a lifetime to achieve greatness.[10] He underwent years of training with some of the most distinguished master craftsmen of his time. Guild records show that he was apprenticed in Warsaw and in Danzig (now Gdansk) to amber and ivory cutters. But it was not until 1694, when he was over fifty years old, that Schlüter received a summons from the Hohenzollerns in Berlin to work at the court of Prussian Elector Frederick III.[11]

Schlüter's first creations were accomplished, formal pieces: a bronze of the Elector himself and a statue of the Elector's late father, Frederick William, sitting astride his horse. Frederick William had overhauled Prussia's financial systems, uniting fractious ducal states as part of his campaign to transform Prussia into a fully fledged kingdom. His son was now attempting to finish the job and to be recognized by European powers as a monarch in his own right.

Then in 1695 Andreas Schlüter had some luck. Arnold Nering, the Elector's Superintendent of Building, died unexpectedly and the sculptor was asked to participate in Frederick III's plans to transform Berlin into a city of parks and palaces more suited to a king. Schlüter began sculpting the exterior of the Zeughaus (Arsenal) and the Royal Palace.

The Elector's second wife, Sophie Charlotte (the great-granddaughter of James I of England), admired Schlüter's designs. Sophie Charlotte's marriage, arranged when she was sixteen, was largely a political affair and she withdrew from the bombastic Prussian court, investing her passion in dance and literature. Chamber music filled her time. 'It is a loyal friend,' she wrote to Agostino Steffani, director of the Hanover Opera. 'It does not let you down or deceive you; it is not a traitor and it is never cruel. No, it gives you all the charms and delights of heaven, whereas friends are indifferent or deceitful and loved ones ungrateful.'[12]

Sophie Charlotte wanted Berlin to ring with music and its drawing rooms to be nourished by intelligent conversation. Her palaces were to be intimate, divided into small but elaborate salons decorated with muted bronze and burnished gold. It was Charlottenburg, a *maison de plaisance* and the Prussian equivalent of Tsarskoye Selo, that was to be the expression of these ideas. In 1696 Sophie Charlotte asked Schlüter to begin working on the interior designs of the building.

However, in 1699 Johan Friedrich d'Eosander, a brilliant Swedish architect and Sophie Charlotte's favourite, returned to Berlin from study leave and took over the Charlottenburg project. Schlüter was so rankled at being usurped by a man twenty-five years his junior that he abandoned Charlottenburg and reverted to the Royal Palace renovations. He was determined to create something eye-catching, lavish and innovative – rooms embellished with luxurious and novel materials: rare minerals, wood and fabrics. However, the idea for the Royal Palace's most radical feature, the one that he hoped would outshine the work of Sophie Charlotte's favourite, would come to him only by accident.

Searching the cellar stores of the Royal Palace for raw materials, Schlüter found dozens of chests packed with nuggets of golden resin that he recognized from his days in Poland. It was East Prussian amber, scooped from the Baltic Sea, a substance whose trade was controlled by the Hohenzollerns. More than 40 million years ago this region had been part of Fennoscandia, a vast forest that stretched from the Norwegian coast to the Caspian Sea. For centuries this humid, coniferous jungle, teeming with reptile and insect life, exuded hundreds of millions of droplets of resin on to the heavy clay floor, trapping countless frozen moments: a fly touching down on to a branch, the brush of a lizard's skin against it. Then the landmasses separated, ice sheets froze and thawed, flooding the Baltic, creating seas and inland lagoons, fossilizing and scattering the Gold of the North, throwing it towards the spits of land that would later be home to the cities of Danzig, Königsberg and Memel.[13]

Because of the primitive methods used to collect amber – it was fished from the Baltic Sea by men wielding giant nets – it was exorbitantly expensive and used almost exclusively to create small decorative or devotional objects like altar sets, cabinets and rosaries. However, in this cellar lay more amber than Schlüter had ever seen before.

Schlüter would have appreciated that Baltic amber had a particular resonance for Prussian aristocrats. In 1681 the Great Elector Frederick William had used amber to forge diplomatic ties with Russia, sending Fedor III in Moscow a throne made from the resin that was proclaimed by the tsar to be 'the greatest curiosity in the world'. When reports reached Prussia the following year that Fedor was sick, Frederick William sent more amber to nine-year-old Grand Duke Peter, who spies told him was to be the tsar's successor. An amber mirror was dispatched, accompanied by a deal: access to strategic, unfrozen Baltic ports in exchange for Russia's support for Prussia's claim to a crown.[14]

In the cellar, Andreas Schlüter must have conceived his idea. There was enough amber here to panel an entire chamber. His plan crystallized on 18 January 1701, when Frederick was at last crowned 'King in Prussia' at Königsberg Castle, with Queen Sophie Charlotte at his side, resplendent in amber jewellery. The monarch had consciously chosen the historic capital of his forefathers on the Baltic coast and crown jewels fished from the Baltic Sea. Schlüter immediately sent to Copenhagen for a carver.

Gottfried Wolfram, master craftsman to the Danish court, was an expert in fashioning ornate miniatures from ivory and was captivated by Schlüter's audacious idea. The workshops in Copenhagen were capable of producing only thirty amber pieces a year and all of them were small icons or jewellery.[15] To manufacture an entire chamber would require hundreds of thousands of slivers that would, somehow, have to be laced together like an enormous jigsaw puzzle. New thinking was required. Gottfried Wolfram arrived in Berlin in April 1701 with a reference from King Frederick IV of Denmark.[16] He would need to work quickly. Eosander's influence was growing. Sophie Charlotte wrote to her mother about the young architect on 3 May 1702, describing him as 'the oracle as regards all... building affairs'.[17]

Wolfram painstakingly fashioned palm-sized leaves of amber, gently heating them to a temperature of between 140°C and 200°C, using a new technique developed by Christian Porschin of the Königsberg Guild, who was experimenting with manufacturing amber sunglasses.[18] Any hotter and the amber would catch light and burn. The moulded pieces, dipped into heated water infused with honey, linseed and cognac, to give a subtle tincture to the resin, were set to harden on cooling racks before being polished and slotted into place on a paper scheme. Wolfram joined the pieces with gum refined from the acacia tree, the finished panels resembling stained-glass windows. Backed by feather-thin gold or silver leaves and wooden boards, these amber walls (comprising a dozen large panels twelve feet high, ten panels just over three feet high and twenty-four sections of amber skirting board) would come alive in candlelight.[19]

Construction went well, but soon the inspiration behind it fell sick.

Sophie Charlotte contracted pneumonia during a journey to Hanover for the carnival of January 1705. 'Don't grieve for me, for I am about to satisfy my curiosity about things that even Leibniz was never able to explain – space, the infinite, being and nothingness – and for my husband, the King, I am about to provide a funeral-spectacle that will give him a new opportunity to display his pomposity and splendour!' she wrote, before succumbing to her condition on 1 February, aged thirty-seven.[20]

In 1707 Schlüter's career also suddenly expired when another piece of ambitious engineering, a 325-foot tower he had designed for the Berlin Mint, collapsed. An investigation concluded that he had mistakenly built the tower on a sandbank. The sixty-three-year-old was exiled from court. He made his way to Russia, where he would assist in the building of the new St Petersburg – on a marsh.[21] In Berlin, court favourite Eosander took over the amber chamber project and dismissed master carver Gottfried Wolfram, accusing him of overcharging and lingering unnecessarily. In his place Ernst Schacht and Gottfried Turau, carvers from Danzig (the latter a master trained at the ancient Danzig Guild), were hired.

When Wolfram demanded compensation and refused to hand over the amber pieces, Eosander broke into his workshop and seized the partially completed frames, panels and lozenges. Wolfram hired a lawyer and sued Eosander, who in turn had him jailed.

When Wolfram was finally released he was exiled. His last and most passionate appeal to King Frederick I coincided with the death of the monarch on 25 February 1713. Frederick William I, who succeeded his father, had no time for the budget-draining frivolities of the salon or the prohibitively expensive amber chamber. The Soldier King was more interested in creating a military super-state than a folly that came attached to an irritating legal battle. Eosander was sacked, as were amber masters Schacht and Turau, who had been unable to solve Wolfram's cryptic amber puzzle that still lay in pieces, consigned to the cellars of the Zeughaus.[22]

Anatoly Kuchumov, the Soviet guardian of the Amber Room, had worked hard to compile this piece of German history. His notes, shown to us by Kedrinsky, reveal that five scholars assisted him through 1940 and 1941 (continuing their work even during the period of the Leningrad palace evacuations): an academic from the Union of Scientific Research and Restoration, one from the Hermitage, two from the Central State Historical Archive, including the head of the reading hall, and a Soviet student stationed abroad who scoured Germany for material to send home.[23]

Reading these notes, compiled in 1942, it is clear that Kuchumov was attempting to understand the mechanics used by Wolfram in constructing his amber panels. Kuchumov's references identified a cluster of files that recorded how, in 1716, Tsar Peter I set off for France via Germany, where he held an unscheduled meeting with Frederick William I, during which they discussed the Amber Room. Tsar Peter's court diary stated: 'In Habelberg their majesties saw each other and were together from 13 to 17 November, where they assured each other of their friendship and had some discussions for the use of both majesties.'[24] Etiquette dictated an exchange of gifts and yet both monarchs were unprepared. Thrifty King Frederick William's first consideration was cost, a fact confirmed by a Russian spy working in his court:

The King has assigned 6,000 talers for the meeting. But the financial ministry has been told that they should use this money so that the King can satisfy the expenditure of travelling from Wesel to Memel [today Klaipeda in Lithuania]. He ordered that the Tsar should be especially well looked after in Berlin but stated that he would not give a pfennig more for this occasion. 'You must tell all the world around I have paid 30–40,000 talers for meeting Peter the Great,' he added.[25]

King Frederick William decided to present the tsar with two of his father's lavish commissions that were of no interest to him. One was a once-famous yacht *Liburnika,* and the Russian court diary showed that the tsar was delighted with it, unaware that it was in such a parlous state that his crew would nearly drown when sailing it from Hamburg. The *Liburnika* eventually limped into Copenhagen, where it was repaired, only to be refitted for a second time when it at last arrived in St Petersburg in 1718. (According to the court records, it was renamed the *Corona* and did not leave the Neva embankment until it was towed to the naval junkyard in 1741.[26])

The second money-saving idea was the Amber Room. King Frederick William had been told of Tsar Peter's love for amber. In 1696, one year after Peter I had come to the Russian throne, the twenty-four-year-old had embarked on a secret tour of Europe. Assuming the alias of 'Sergeant Petr Mikhailov', he had travelled the Swedish Baltic, Poland and Prussia. In Königsberg, in East Prussia, 'Sergeant Petr Mikhailov' had been mesmerized by amber, assailed by the city's quacks, who touted it as a cure for everything from rheumatism, lung disease and toothache, to throat infections and the evil eye. 'Sergeant Petr Mikhailov' had even bought a copy of P. J. Hartmann's *Succini Prussici*, the authoritative amber treatise of the day.

Anatoly Kuchumov also rooted out an article written in 1877 by the head of the Moscow Archive of Foreign Affairs that confirmed how the unfinished amber chamber was dispatched to Peter the Great in 1716. A team of amber masters were hired by King Frederick William I to pack Wolfram's puzzle into eighteen crates that were each covered with flannel.[27] They were then wrapped in straw and waxed waterproof cotton before being loaded on to eight carts that were to be maintained by an engineer and guarded by a watchman. The Russians appointed Count Alexander Golovkin, a close friend of the tsar, to oversee the operation.

The amber cargo set off for St Petersburg via Königsberg, the capital of East Prussia. Such was the poor condition of the road that the carts had to be rebuilt. Leather was stitched around the crates as rain had destroyed the waxed cotton. The amber caravan's next destination was Memel. It arrived six weeks later, the convoy having travelled at a snail's pace to ensure that no further damage was caused by potholes. When the gift eventually reached St Petersburg the entire operation would have cost the miserly Prussian king only 205 talers.

When Kuchumov studied a file called 'Letters of the Russian Tsars', which was compiled in 1861 and lodged in the Hermitage library, he found several from Tsar Peter I to his wife. 'Dear Catherine, friend of my heart, hello to you,' Peter wrote from Habelberg on 17 November 1716. 'Concerning my visit: I want to tell you that it was useful. We will leave from here today and with God's help we will see you soon.' There was a postscript: 'The King gave me a rather big present in Potsdam, a yacht which is well decorated and the Amber Room, which I have dreamed of for a long time.'[28]

The tsar had nothing to give in return so he presented the Prussian kitchen with thirty-six ducats and gave a sable to the King's commandant. Later, a letter sent to the Prussian King from Tallinn, the capital of Estonia, revealed that Peter eventually thought of an appropriate gift:

The man who will give you the document, valet Tolstoy, will have the honour to present Your Majesty [with] fifty-five giants, that is how many I could find in my land up till now. I also want to give Your Majesty a barge built in St Petersburg and a lathe. Without doubt Your Majesty will be glad to have these small presents. PS We also send Your Majesty a goblet made by ourselves.'[29]

Kuchumov found the Soldier King's reply, sent in October 1718. Thanking his 'kindest brother and friend', Frederick William I wrote: 'I want to say that I have got the giants and also a goblet made by your own hands and also the barge built in St P. and the lathe which Your Majesty gave me as a present. It was a wonderful gift to me.'[30]

It took a considerable time to locate and dispatch to Prussia enough 'giant' Russian soldiers to adequately reward the Prussians for the gift of the Amber Room. In June 1720 Count Golovkin, now the Russian ambassador at the Prussian court, wrote to his tsar: 'Captain Chernishov came here with ten giant soldiers and passed on your orders, after which these soldiers were given as a present to his Majesty of Prussia.'[31] Then, in 1724, yet more giants were sent, twenty-four of them, including one named in the records as Captain Bandemir.

The crates containing the panels of the Amber Room were delivered to Peter's Summer Palace on the Neva in mid-1717 and received there by Governor General Alexander Menshikov. From the historical references sought by Kuchumov it is clear that he was pursuing a particular line of thought: whether Peter's court achieved what the Prussians could not. Kuchumov was attempting to discover how the Amber Room fitted together, information he was desperate to acquire in the summer of 1941 so that he could dismantle it before the Wehrmacht arrived.

Kuchumov would have been disappointed when he read what Governor General Alexander Menshikov wrote in his diary on 2 July 1717: 'Had a dinner for two hours and after dinner stayed in the rooms for an hour to look through the amber boxes that had arrived from Prussia.'[32] However, what the governor found appalled him. He records in his diary that pieces were broken. Many were missing. Others crumbled in his hands. Three days later he wrote to Peter, then in Paris, and put a brave face on the disaster.

I have looked through this Amber Room which was sent for Your Majesty by the King of Prussia and placed it in the same crates in the big hall where the guests gathered and almost all the panels were in good order. Some small pieces fell out but some of them could be repaired with glue and even if some of them could not be, you could insert new pieces. I can honestly say it's the most magnificent thing I have ever seen.[33]

Did any assembly instructions accompany the room? Kuchumov searched in the Central State Document Archive and found a section called the 'Cabinet of Peter the Great' and within it 'The inventory of the Amber Room presented by His Majesty of Prussia to His Majesty of Russia'. But the document, dated Berlin, 13 January 1717, contained no advice on how to construct the Amber Room.[34]

Peter had intended the Amber Room to become his *Kunstkammer*, a walk-in cabinet of curiosities, an idea he had borrowed from Versailles. But there was no one in Russia who was capable of reassembling Wolfram's puzzle and Peter the Great's dream was stored in pieces at his Summer Palace until his death in 1725.[35]

Kedrinsky wipes a winter sweat from his forehead. 'By 24 June 1941 everyone was glued to the radio. Scouring the *Leningradskaya Pravda*. Reading and rereading *Izvestiya*. Even the smallest piece of information was better than nothing. But there was no comfort for poor old Leningrad.' As the Russians liked to say, there was no 'truth' in the News and no 'news' in the Truth.[36]

But then came some direction from the city authorities. Quoting Trotsky's instructions during the Civil War, citizens were ordered to begin transforming Leningrad into 'an enigma, a threat or a mortal danger'.

Kedrinsky recalls: 'Posters appealed for help to save the Motherland

and work details were issued. Everyone fell in, we all began digging and building. Out in the countryside, even as the fascists neared, women and men built tank traps and trenches with their bare hands. For fifteen hours at a time. Barrage balloons blocked out the sun.'

Netting obscured monuments and statues. Catherine the Great's bronze horseman beside the River Neva became a pyramid of sandbags. Mountaineers scaled the golden pinnacle of the Peter Paul Cathedral on the opposite bank to throw camouflage over it. 'Instead of defending my diploma, I defended the city,' Kedrinsky says darkly. He was ordered to the far end of Moskovsky Prospekt with a transport of 'steel hedgehogs' that the Red Army hoped would slow the Nazi tank advance. 'On every roof we built anti-aircraft emplacements.'

And beyond, towards the palaces of Tsarskoye Selo and Pavlovsk, was a strangled strip of deserted dachas and allotments overlooking the city. They had been abandoned by everyone apart from Kuchumov and his hand-picked team, who were still packing the treasures of the tsars. They would be the first to feel the full force of the Nazi invasion whenever it came.

But what of the Amber Room, we ask?

Kedrinsky looks irritated to have been snapped back from his past. But he cannot leave the question unanswered. He is, after all, the oracle of the Catherine Palace. And so he slyly slides papers out from under his blotter. 'You must understand that this is material entrusted to me for my book, my history of the Great Task. These are the last words written by Kuchumov before we fought for our lives.'

He begins to read from Kuchumov's diary: '"An order came from LenGorIsPolKom. About the Amber Room. Instructions are to execute measures to conceal this unique treasure in its place rather than risk damage."'

Kuchumov's recommendation to abandon the evacuation of the Amber Room had been sanctioned. He was to hide it where it was, constructing another room on top of it. '"Wadding was delivered from the sewing factory along with sheets of gauze."' The amber panels were carefully covered in muslin cloth and then a layer of *vatzim* [cotton padding]. The entire room was then redecorated with hessian strips. Its inlaid parquet floor made from rare, coloured woods was strewn with sand. Water was placed inside every vase too large to be evacuated so that they might absorb a blast. The windows were criss-crossed with tape and then boarded up from the inside. The wall-mounted bronze candelabras were removed and placed in boxes, as were four Florentine stone mosaics that depicted the senses and were hooked on to the amber panels. Twelve chairs, three card tables, two chests of drawers, a spittoon and an icon were also left behind.

Kedrinsky looks up from the pages: 'Kuchumov could do no more and anyhow new orders came for him.' He continues reading from the diary.

Comrade Ladukhin told Kuchumov that he was no longer needed at the palaces. The young curator's thoughts must have turned immediately to the front, where tens of thousands of under-prepared young soldiers were marching almost unarmed towards the long guns of General Wilhelm von Leeb's highly trained Army Group North. But Anna Mikhailovna, Kuchumov's wife, was also ordered to pack her bags. Kuchumov records what happened next in his diary: '"Anatoly Mikhailovich, I am afraid that you are to leave Leningrad," Comrade Ladukhin told me. "You will accompany Leningrad's children, the first shipment of evacuees. You and your wife are to take the treasures with you to their hiding place."'

Kedrinsky pauses: 'They left that evening – 30 June 1941.'

According to his diary, Kuchumov made one last, frantic round of the palace, rushing through the empty halls and rooms, snipping and cutting strips of fabric as he went from the curtains and seat covers, from tablecloths and bedlinen – swatches that nestled in his jacket pocket, preserving in his mind the decorative scheme of the palace to which he was determined to return. And among the things he carried with him were twenty-eight fragments and shards that had dropped off the walls of a priceless, intriguing, infuriating Amber Room that now had the appearance of another, stuffed and packed, wallpapered and pasted.

Kedrinsky reads on:

'Commissar Ivanov was waiting for me at the station. We shook hands. I then stepped inside the goods carriage and bound the door shut with wire for our safety, lying down on the boxes, awaiting our departure.

'The strong shunt of the locomotive woke me. It was now dawn. 5 a.m. The sunlight dazzled. The morning was fine. I took my leave of my city and from the train it looked like an enormous green island in the middle of a plain. Golden domes of the palaces shining above it. When will we ever come home and what will be our future and what of those we leave behind?'

Locked into seventeen train carriages, 402 crates were bound for the Soviet interior alongside Anatoly Kuchumov and Anna Mikhailovna.

'And I remained behind,' Kedrinsky says. 'I climbed up on to a rooftop with my sniper's rifle. I was not allowed to flee Leningrad. Sitting in a steel bucket, I gripped the rim. Waiting. Waiting. Comrade Molotov ordered that the city improvise our defence of the Motherland and we followed his instructions. To. The. Letter. Filling bottles with petrol and a dry rag. Fire-bomb the Hitlerites. Waiting to bury them in our Soviet soil. And then, when my duty was served out on the rooftops, I was called to the front.

'Inside a bunker I went. Full to the brim with fear. Can you imagine, as the slaughter began, what the orders from Moscow were for me? "Paint," the generals said. I was ordered to be Artist to the Red Army. Comrade Stalin wanted posters for field hospitals and canteens of General Suvorov, the victor at Kinburn in 1787, leader of men across the Alps, to boost the morale of the men at the front. He also wanted paintings of Alexander Nevsky, our canonized Prince of Novgorod, who had halted the first great German invasion, 700 years ago. I painted Russian heroes and made a little history for our exhausted boys on the battle lines.'

The slamming of a door brings the old man out of his trance. Walking towards us is a wiry figure in a felt jacket whose mouth twitches suspiciously beneath a rusty ginger beard. He mutters into the old comrade's ear. Kedrinsky immediately stands up, swaps the woolly slippers he is wearing for outdoor shoes and throws on a great coat. 'My son says I have told you more than enough and I will get into trouble with Bardovskaya.'

What of the Great Task? We have come so far and surely we can go a little further, we say. What of Kuchumov? At least take us to Anatoly Kuchumov, the guardian of the Amber Room.

'That, my friends, is beyond even *my* considerable powers,' Kedrinsky says, as his son holds open the door. 'Kuchumov is dead.'

Kedrinsky rattles his desk drawer to check that it is locked. The man who rebuilt Leningrad stubs out a Peter I and shuffles off with his suspicious son. We follow a few paces behind, stepping out into the squall that has thrown a great billowing dustsheet over a frozen Tsarskoye Selo, obscuring all of our exits.

Tsar Peter I

2

We have been in Russia for six weeks but our bell never rings. We live like rats in an Empire-style mansion block at the eastern end of St Petersburg's Nevsky Prospekt. The building's cast-iron front door is fastened with a combination lock: 279. Its tumblers grind like teeth and the door opens on to a gloomy stairwell. The hall light bulbs have been stolen but we can feel with our feet a sticky patch on the granite porch slab. A struck match reveals spots of blood carelessly left by the man on the fourth floor, a shipyard foreman who lost his job earlier this year and now comes out only at night to club stray animals on the landing.

Every day we climb three darkened flights of limestone stairs, reaching a steel shutter, which is the first door to our apartment. Behind it is another padded, wooden inner door. The gap between the two is just large enough for someone to be immured. There is nothing physically restraining us but we feel trapped in our flat around the corner from where the drunks fighting outside Hotel Oktobrsakaya are so blinded by vodka they can hardly see the old sign above them: Leningrad Hero City.

Occasionally the telephone rings. The socket is at the far end of the hall and we sprint to it, only for the caller to hang up. Outside in the city the libraries are closed. It is the end of January 2002 and the temperatures of minus 35°C have ruptured the pipes. No one seems to know what happened to Anatoly Kuchumov's private papers or (if there are any) the files on the Amber Room. The state, central, history, party and literature archives deny possessing anything connected to either and anyhow will not let us into the building until our applications have been cleared in an opaque process that has no real beginning and possibly no end. The city's chief archivists are said to be at their dachas beside Lake Ladoga, to the east, where housekeepers cheerfully tell us, 'No one's home.' And the director of the Catherine Palace has been trying to find a slot for us in his appointment diary for more than a month. So we sit and wait, trying to suppress the feeling that we are trapped like herrings in a Russian barrel, going over our notes from Kedrinsky, deciding on a strategy to break the deadlock, reading and rereading the history of Leningrad, hoping that we will not wake up on one of these cold mornings to find ourselves accused of a crime we did not commit.

There are at least nine Sovetskayas in an urban grid and we are renting in the seventh. Private ambulances touting for business in the new frantic free-for-all lurk on our street corner. Dozens of downpipes from the guttering high above randomly disgorge tubes of ice, the frozen projectiles hurtling towards the legs of unsuspecting pedestrians with such velocity that they can shatter bones. The road is buckled after decades of freeze and thaw and quickly becomes bogged down in a slick of brown snow, the detritus left by incontinent pit bull terriers dressed by their owners in canine combat jackets. And every afternoon on Sovetskaya 7, even when the cold becomes acidic, small boys scrub the salt off the new Mercedes parked along the kerb, polishing cars bought with murky wealth until their raw faces shine in the bodywork.

St Petersburg's residents have a favourite saying: 'Everything is forbidden but all things are possible.' It is an epigram loved by the flat-headed goons who waggle their guns outside the Golden Dolls erotic cabaret. And by the women with all-year-round Black Sea suntans who gorge on the new Japanese buffet at the exorbitant Tinkoff restaurant (a chopstick held in each hand with which to impale the sushi). For the people of Alexei Tolstoy's damned city, the motto describes a Russian confidence trick, the illusion of a transfer of power where one terrifying élite bows out to reformers who prove to be equally vindictive and greedy, people who will do anything for you only if you can name their price.

We call a friend of a friend, a retired professor from what was Leningrad University. She is said to be something of an expert at identifying potential sources. The archive of a patriot, particularly someone of Anatoly Kuchumov's standing, and a mystery of the calibre of the Amber Room are commodities of immeasurable value. A Soviet hero or legend doesn't die as much as evanesce – partly classified and mostly stolen. Therefore, even before Kuchumov was in the ground, many of those he considered his peers had, no doubt, begun salting away his papers, mementoes of his life and work, in the hope that at some time they could be cashed in.

Information is hard currency in post-Soviet Russia, a trend bolstered by Russian academics who are able for the first time to comb through the past and Western academics who pay handsomely for exclusive access to history that they crate up and export.

The professor suggests we meet at Kolobok (The Ginger-Bread Man), a canteen near Sovetskaya 7, where every lunchtime staff pinned into red pinafores serve up thousands of uniform platters of mutton *khatlyeta* and *shuba*, small cubes of salty fish dressed in a coat of beetroot and dill.

Is there such a thing as a Russian *Who's Who*, we ask the professor as she munches and we calculate how to reach Kuchumov's contemporaries? 'Very funny,' she says. 'Whose business was it to know who's who? We learned to suppress our curiosity.'

How should we proceed, we ask?

'Do nothing,' she says. This weekend our friend will visit her dacha outside St Petersburg, populated by artists and museum curators. She will poke around. See what turns up.

Do nothing. We walk back to our apartment that straddles the new and old worlds. One half (kitchen and bathroom) has been renovated with pearlescent wallpaper, heated floors and mirror tiles, while the other (bedroom, dining room and living room) is gnarled boards and greasy plaster. A long-forgotten dog leash hangs by the door. A tuneless upright piano with its Empire candelabras stands in the living room. Photographs of another family: children, a picnic, a tryst beside a lake. A cabinet of crystal – belonging to whom? – tinkles as the icy wind in the courtyard plucks at the windows. These are the remnants of people we don't know and yet they live among us, former residents of Sovetskaya 7, spectres that we often sense but never meet, like everything else in our Russian life: Anatoly Kuchumov and his most important charge, the missing Amber Room.

The phone rings and we rush to it. We have placed it halfway down the hall, stretched to the very end of its cable. This time we manage to whip off the handset. The caller hangs up.

Lying fitfully in someone else's bed, we wonder if it was the director's office at the Catherine Palace. We will check with them in the morning.

First light on a winter's day, worn and dreary like hospital laundry. Our fax machine creaks into life: 'Appointment confirmed with Dr Ivan Petrovich Sautov, Director, Catherine Palace. 10 a. m. 2 February 2002.' Tomorrow.

We are delighted and nervous. There are so many stories about Dr Sautov's flamboyance in this city that it is just conceivable he started some of them himself. One of his former colleagues, forced out of the Catherine Palace, likes to call him the Tsar. It is said that on his fiftieth birthday he lined the long road to Tsarskoye Selo with pageboys bearing cups of vodka. His colleagues may have been flabbergasted but surely they would also have been awed, which we presume would have been the effect that Sautov wanted to achieve.[1]

Attached to our invitation to meet the Director are his credentials: Ivan Petrovich, fifty-five, born into a military family in Tallinn, Estonia, graduate of the prestigious Leningrad Institute of Engineering, where Alexander Kedrinsky's studies were brought to an abrupt halt. For thirteen years Sautov served as head of the State Inspection of Landmark Preservation. In 1987 he was promoted after being unanimously proposed to the post of director of Catherine Palace, at the Tsarskoye Selo. The word 'unanimously' is underlined. He took up his position while Kuchumov was still a senior consultant there, which means that he should know what happened to the great curator's personal papers.

It is an impressive CV: Winner of a gold National Achievement medal in 1984; awarded the Order of Friendship by President Yeltsin in 1997; presented with the Russian State Federation Award and the Order of St Daniel. 'Dr Sautov's innovative work and everyday heroism is [sic] devoted to the eternal purpose of preserving Russia's culture for future generations,' the CV concludes. What do we have to offer the Tsar?[2]

We are not good at doing nothing. We need to think and to plan and after all to celebrate away from the gloom of Sovetskaya 7, out in the satin light of the wintering Gulf of Finland. We take the Nevsko–Vasileostrovskaya Metro, the green line, and thirty minutes later emerge at Primorskaya, where apartments pile on top of one another. Navy veterans in ragged blue-and-white-striped sweaters dive into the gutters as if they are swallows at dusk trapping flies. Couples roll in and out of each other's arms, waltzing in Primorskaya's frozen fug of alcohol. Beyond, we can finally smell the wide-open Baltic blasted by gulf winds that are as sharp as cut glass.

As the last daylight slips away, an umbilicus of lights reaches around the sandy coast inside hundreds of plastic marquees and faux-wood *izbas*. Outside, the shallows begin to freeze. Some girls beckon us over. 'Come on, drink, our friend is pregnant.' Plastic cups are pressed into our hands at this improvised baby shower, all of us toasting in Baltika beer the good fortune that has brought strangers together to get drunk by the sea. We are pulled into an *izba* where a boy plays the squeezebox and we all sing along to songs that we have never heard before. 'Dance, André, dance,' the darker-haired girl cries, spinning faster and faster.

The beer is replaced with Russki Standard vodka so we can seriously celebrate the conception of a child whose parents we have yet to meet. One measure of vodka, the Russians believe, is medicinal. The second is sweet but slightly vulgar, passing the time before the decisive third shot, the no-going-back slug that unlocks lust and buries sobriety in a deep trench. And soon enough we can taste nothing but the air that we are gulping and all we can see is the cabin door opening and all we can smell is the Baltic and all we can feel is the gritty Russian sand.

The Catherine Palace is muffled by snow as our *marshrutki* pulls up. We jump down from the shared minibus-taxi and into the soft, white powder, away from our brooding fellow passengers, who have been staring at our drawn faces as if we are the dead. The metro trip to the *marshrutki* stop at the end of Moskovsky Prospekt was equally appalling, pickled in a gaseous train carriage of early-morning boozers, the whole journey spent

crushed against an advertisement for Molotov Cocktails ('a revolution-
ary new bottled drink') while four pickpockets from Mongolia clumsily
fumbled at our bags.

We cannot face Dr Sautov yet and so at the public entrance to the
Catherine Palace, we pay our roubles, slip *tapochkis* – cobalt-blue plas-
tic-bag slippers – over our snow-damp shoes and follow the crowds up
the Monighetti staircase, past Brodzsky's marble Sleeping Cupid and
through the gilded doors, salon opening on to salon until we reach
what resembles a half-finished stage set, one side alight with candelabras, gilded cherubs and a mosaic of amber lozenges and the other, bare
plyboard, stepladders and plastic sheeting. Packs of tour groups file
through, gasping – French, German and Russian: '*La chambre d'ambre*',
'*Bernsteinzimmer*' and '*Yantarny komnata*'. Dr Sautov's craftsmen are
constructing a replica of the Amber Room and even though it is difficult
to see Andreas Schlüter's vision in this building site yet, it enthrals in any
language.

We feel better and head for the staff department. Outside Dr Sautov's
office a group of naval officers is bidding him farewell with bear hugs
and cheek kisses, the brims of their hats rising like sails. Ushered into
the Director's office, we stand to attention before an expanse of polished
wood. Dr Sautov can see that we can see the line of photographs of him
taken with Presidents Putin and Clinton and Queen Elizabeth II.

The Director wears a glossy Italian suit. His fountain pen, with which
he now tap-tap-taps on his desk, has an amber clasp. Behind his huge
face, with its well-tended salt-and-pepper moustache, is a drawing, the
same plan for an imperial Prussian study that we saw in Kedrinsky's office
and that we now know is Andreas Schlüter's eighteenth-century blueprint
for the original amber chamber. A smiling woman in her sixties sits at the
other end of the office with a pansticked face framed by a 'Zsa Zsa' of
platinum hair.

'Welcome to the Catherine Palace,' Dr Sautov intones. 'May I introduce
Larissa Bardovskaya, our head curator?'

Bardovskaya. The woman whom Kedrinsky mentioned. Someone he
evidently feared. How much do Bardovskaya and the Director know
about our unauthorized meeting with Kedrinsky? The Director tap-tap-

taps with his amber-clasped pen on the desk again, calling the room to order.

We launch our introductory speech – a rickety vessel that takes on a little water: no one is better placed to help us learn about Anatoly Kuchumov and the Amber Room than Dr Sautov, the book we intend to write will be a wonderful platform for his museum. Sautov interrupts with a speech of his own. 'Understanding amber is the key to everything,' he says. Tap-tap-tap with that pen on his pate. His fuggish study is beginning to send us to sleep. 'The prehistoric residue carries a small static charge and that is why in Russia we use amber for therapies. Every year I go to Svetlogorsk and take off all my clothes to roll in Baltic amber.'

We stifle an urge to laugh at the thought of his fleshy body rolling around in granulated amber and distract ourselves by thinking of dour Svetlogorsk. During Soviet times party officials built palatial dachas here, a seaside town on the Samland Peninsula, at the source of the Gold of the North. They would arrive by the shores of the Baltic in fleets of blacked-out Zil sedans to imbibe tea while their mistresses rubbed them down with amber resin.

Dr Sautov nods at Bardovskaya and then says to her, 'What is it that they want from me?' We notice for the first time his huge hands, like baseball mitts, clasped upon his desk. 'What experience do they have? What is their specialism?' He turns to us. 'Have you ever worked with museum staff before? Do you understand the nature of archives?'

All of these are apposite questions although the tone of the meeting is noticeably chilly. We perform a brief résumé. Reasonable people. Can take instruction. Will cooperate.

Tap-tappity-tap with the amber-clasped pen. 'I don't think we understand each other,' Dr Sautov says, sipping his tea.

Poached in vodka on the Gulf of Finland, parched in this humid study, we too would love a glass of tea, but we press on with our dry lips cracking, explaining about this book.

The Director bangs his fists on the table in irritation and Bardovskaya intervenes: 'What information do you require?'

Has the vodka made us foolish? We don't know what we want until we know what he has.

Bardovskaya leans towards us: 'What does the Catherine Palace get?'

Sautov booms, 'Ours is not a charitable enterprise. Why should you make money from what we know? Precious knowledge. Expensive knowledge. There will have to be a contract.'

Bardovskaya has been doodling a clutch of 2s on her notepad and now interrupts: 'The second day of the second month in the second year of a new millennium is a very unlucky day for making deals.'

The Director ignores her. 'A binding legal document. I am used to dealing with things in a professional manner.'

Bardovskaya draws closer. 'Everyone has to sign a contract. Steven Spielberg signed and paid half a million to hire the mirrored ballroom. True. Elton John threw a party and he signed for 250,000 dollars. It doesn't have to be money.' She smiles. 'A film crew from Hollywood provided the staff department with air conditioning units. One publisher donated 1,000 free copies of its book. The whole world deals with us. Anyone with information comes here, to Dr Sautov, and so we know better than anyone the cost of trying to find the Amber Room,' Bardovskaya says, pulling a buff envelope out of her handbag.

She flourishes pages on which are collages of black-bordered memorial cards, photographs, identity cards, all of them with RIP scrawled across. And on one page are grainy photographs of crime scenes, houses recently ripped apart by gas explosions, car crashes, a body lying under fallen beech leaves.

Are these incidents related to the search for the Amber Room, we ask?

'It is confidential material,' she snaps, putting the papers back into her handbag. 'It was posted to us from Berlin after we held an exhibition there: *Mythos Bernsteinzimmer*, and is not for publication.'

Director Sautov leans over his desk and whispers, 'I will get forty heads of state here, in May 2003.' He flexes his huge hands and we nod even though we have no idea what he is talking about. 'And I will lead them into my newly restored Amber Room. Have you seen it? It's your last chance.' He stands up to walk an idea around the humid office. 'I intend to cover up the half-built reconstruction until it is ready. Yes, cover it up in, let us say, in a couple of days' time.' Bardovskaya nods vigorously.

'And then in May 2003, on the three-hundredth anniversary of the founding of our great city, I will throw back the curtains and show the world the miracle we have re-created. Can you see it?' We are afraid we can, and it doesn't bode well for our book. 'We have a master architect who has studied the old ways, a veteran who has learned how the original chamber was pieced together. But of course you know that as you have talked to Alexander Kedrinsky already.' So they know about our meeting.

Sautov continues: 'Alexander Kedrinsky is writing a special catalogue about our tragic loss and the Great Task. How we have put the pieces back together again. And obviously you are writing just another book and it should not, cannot, compete with ours.' The Director is now standing at his desk and someone has opened the office door from the outside.

But just as we fear that Sautov has decided against helping us, the Director changes his tone. 'Fax me today with what you want and Bardovskaya will calculate what *what you want* is worth.'

But we still do not know what your archive possesses, we say.

Bardovskaya grins. 'Make a deal,' she squawks. 'We'll work out a contract. Everybody has to pay. Isn't that so? Only nothing comes from nothing. An old English proverb, I believe.'

The Director has his 'farewell' smile fixed in place. 'Fax me,' he says. 'A member of staff will have to be appointed to supervise your work.' And the closing door muffles these last words as all the while we have been seamlessly manoeuvred backwards into the antechamber.

A whistle-stop tour has been arranged for us of the Director's amber workshop and we are pointed at an unmarked iron door, only ten paces through the snow from his office. Inside is a furnace of activity, with fifty-two workmen, former miners, stonecutters and welders, feverishly drilling, sanding and buffing, filling the air with a sweet-tasting powder. '*Dobry.*' A podgy hand wiped on an overall is proffered. Boris Igdalov, head of the amber workshop, introduces himself and from the tone of his voice it is evident that we are not the first foreigners to be handed on to him.

Wearily Igdalov begins his routine. 'Reconstructing the Amber Room is a lifetime's work.' He mops his brow with a rag. 'Almost twenty years and it's still not finished.' He guides us through the workshop. 'We boil

The amber workshop at the Catherine Palace

the amber in different oils.' Pots bubble and flasks steam. 'The amber can be subtly infused with herbs, grasses and even cherry stones. But,' he says, pulling us into another room, 'all of them are trade secrets.'

He stops beside a man slotting slivers of amber into a tray, who looks up and laughs when he sees that yet more guests have been foisted on to his patient boss. 'I was a military shipyard foreman before glasnost,' the craftsman chimes, having been coached on foreigners' expectations. 'From party man to artisan.'

Boris Igdalov marches on and we enter the raw amber store, which is filled with muddy-looking pebbles and barley-sugar hunks. 'All of it comes from Kaliningrad.' The reconstruction will absorb six tons of Baltic amber. 'Most of it was confiscated from foreign traders. We can't afford to buy it. In 1997 Viktor Chernomyrdin [then Russia's Prime Minister] gave us several tons and more recently the customs authority in Kaliningrad gave us more, taken from a Japanese businessman.' Igdalov marches to his office and continues the lecture on the move. 'Still not enough.'

We are now in a draughty hallway.

'In 1999 we ground to a halt and if it had not been for a German company, Ruhrgas AG, who agreed to sponsor us, then our new Amber Room would never be finished,' he says, once again offering us his hand after wiping it on his overalls. We have arrived back at the heavy iron door and are once again out in the snow.

Although barely perceptible, there is a small chink opening at the Catherine Palace. That evening, we fax a comprehensive list detailing the research we are eager to begin. We have hazarded a guess at what might be in the Catherine Palace archive.

Later, Our Friend the Professor calls, but she is strangely quiet as we regale her with stories of how we charmed Dr Sautov into considering our requests.

'I too am happy,' she says finally, in a clipped voice. Her weekend at the dacha has flushed out one of Kuchumov's contemporaries who knew him intimately but did not achieve his greatness. We have to come now, she says. He is an old man.

Ozerki – the penultimate stop on the Moskovsko–Petrogradskaya line, on the wafer-thin edge of the city. By the time we emerge from the metro, darkness has once again rolled over St Petersburg. There is fresh snow on the ground and it bathes the suburb in a cool blue light. We soon find the apartment, a concrete block from the 1970s containing small hutches that tenants have humanized with varnished spruce front doors. Up eight flights, we press a bell that tolls 'The Volga Boatmen'. The door opens just enough for a pair of glacial eyes to peep out. A face then creases into a broad smile. 'Welcome, welcome. Please.' He points inside to a large reed mat upon which stand his grey felt snow boots and several pairs of slippers. 'I am Vladimir Telemakov.' A petrol-blue tie, a navy V-neck, beneath a crumpled nylon suit jacket. He has dressed for the occasion. We wish we had too.

There is sweet tea and black bread. A large folder sits on his desk. There are herrings and pickled mushrooms. He picked them in the summer from the pine forests beside Lake Ladoga. He places his hands around the pastel-green file. There is small thimble of sweet Georgian wine that he has been saving for many, many months. 'You know, I am a journalist too,' he says, strumming the elastic that binds his papers together. We tell him that we know absolutely nothing.

Telemakov is lean. Everything about him is spare. His clothing and his

Vladimir Telemakov

sentences. His complexion suggests moderation. He tells us he graduated in journalism from the élite Leningrad University as a star student at the age of twenty-two. The state sent their prodigy to Sakhalin Island. Where's that, we ask? 'I too had no idea.' He pulls out a map and draws his finger as far to the east as it can go across a great pink atlas of the Soviet Union until we are almost in Sapporo, Japan. Sakhalin was the wild new frontier, a former tsarist penal colony where Anton Chekhov came to research a book on the life of a convict, a distant land between the Tatar Strait and the Sea of Okhotsk that took ten days to reach by ship, bus and plane. 'For three years I reported in Sakhalin City. Not much news.' It was, though, an evocative location for those who wished to affirm the sheer breadth of their Motherland.

'And then finally I got a telegram.' Telemakov was recalled to Leningrad. He hoped for a national bureau posting, maybe *Pravda* or *Izvestiya*. 'I was posted to a workers' newspaper published by a factory that made car parts. There I stayed for thirty-three years. It could have been worse. As the Poles are fond of saying, when I sank to the very bottom, someone knocked from below.'

Telemakov worked diligently, but on Sundays he satisfied his real passion by catching a train from Vitebsk Station to the palaces of Pavlovsk and Pushkin, as Tsarskoye Selo was renamed in 1937. 'One day I caught sight of a man in the carriage. Slightly stout. Round glasses. His jacket frayed. A fountain pen in his breast pocket. He was reading and so I introduced myself. Told him I wanted to write about art. Everyone knew Anatoly Kuchumov. I was afraid that such an important man would not talk to me. But I told him I wanted better things than the car plant and he said I could join him on his journeys . If I could find the time. We would talk about art and the Great Patriotic War.'

Each Sunday, the journalist for the car workers' daily stole a few hours, hopping on the train to Pushkin at dawn, talking to Kuchumov about the Leningrad palaces. 'And cautiously, Kuchumov began to open up. Eventually, after many months, he talked to me about *important* things. He was flattered by my interest in him, I think. He started to relax and even lent me documents to study. Some were official reports. Others were letters sent to him during the war. Over eight years he acted as a referee, recommending me to others, museum workers, and I made notes from their diaries and their correspondence too. I made copies of everything. I was meticulous. Kuchumov knew what I was doing. He rather liked the idea of having a biographer... And of course I could be trusted. I was one of them.'

One of them? Before we can ask what he means, Telemakov reaches into the green file before him and produces a thick bundle of paper. 'I wanted to publish this as a book, a tribute to Anatoly Mikhailovich. But for three decades I have been unable to.' He opens the folder hesitantly. 'Some of it is in English,' he says. 'The kind of English spoken by spies. The only people who could speak your language were the KGB. Its office at the car factory was curious about my endeavours concerning one of the city's most famous curators. So I took the manuscript to them.' He pushes the papers back into the file.

Can we see it?

Telemakov rises shakily from his seat and begins to pack up. 'It's my work. I want to publish it.' He sees the look of disappointment on our faces. 'But then again you are fellow journalists. Maybe. Can you help me? If you can, I will help you. Take these papers. Go. But come round again when you have got to the end. Please come. And help me.'

We take Telemakov's pages and head for Sovetskaya 7. Doing as the Russians do, we shunt everyone out the way in the scrum that greets the opening metro door, and dash for a space on the turquoise plastic benches. Up the escalator at Ploshchad Vosstania, plucking the elastic binding. Down Grechesky Prospekt and towards the Baltic hot bread shop in the right-angled speed-skating posture that all citizens assume to avoid being upended on the iced pavement.

At last we are at our pine breakfast table, reading. The manuscript begins with a dedication to Telemakov written by Professor Boris Piotrovsky, the director of St Petersburg's State Hermitage museum and today the most powerful cultural figure in Russia. 'I am sure that anyone taking this manuscript in their hands will read from the beginning to the end with great interest... [Telemakov] uses archives, literature and Kuchumov's own words and truthful diary records to tell a brilliant story about the self-sacrifice of our museum workers who risked their lives to save our treasures.'[3]

We turn a page and before us is an extract from the great curator's diary that picks up where Alexander Kedrinsky left off: 30 June 1941 – Anatoly Kuchumov is on the treasure train from Leningrad.

We have come to a halt. Hours of waiting in the snow. Exposed to attack from above and each side. But nothing can be done until the Red Army has cleared the track.

I ran along the track and saw two women in another carriage washing each other's faces with snow. Then I saw a big bronze bust of Marie Antoinette. The haughty face of this Queen seemed out of place here. I glanced inside the carriage and there were dozens of paintings, none of them were even covered, thrown on to the benches. I was furious at the lack of care.

But Kuchumov learned that the women were curators who had fled from Smolensk, where they had been given even less time than he had to evacuate their city's museums. He wrote: 'They told me that the bombing of Smolensk was devastating. The fascists just descended. Some were disguised as Soviet militiamen and Red Army soldiers. The trucks carrying these museum treasures had departed the ruins of the Smolensk as the Nazis poured into the streets. What is happening back in Leningrad?'

Kuchumov was fearful not only for his own comrades but also for the Amber Room that he had left behind. 'I thought of the Catherine Palace and those things I failed to pack and then I imagined vividly the tragedy of many Soviet towns, falling victim to the Nazis,' he wrote.

It still seemed surreal to Kuchumov as he had not yet seen any evidence of war. Passing through the heart of the Motherland, the curator watched Vladimir-on-the-Klyazma slip by, founded by the Grand Prince of Kiev, twice sacked by the Mongols although its citizens, famously, were never crushed. According to Kuchumov's diary, its golden domes were untouched: 'It smelled like something native. Something very Russian. Eight hundred years of our great history rushed involuntarily into my head.'

Then, on 5 July 1941, Kuchumov's train pulled up in the forested plains of the Volga basin, 550 miles south-east of St Petersburg, and there it was ordered to wait. Over three weeks later, Kuchumov at last gleaned some news from back home when a letter arrived by courier: '1 August, from Elena Nikolaievna Beliaeva, curator and party organizer, Leningrad, to Comrade Kuchumov.' Telemakov had copied this letter to the great curator. Airdrops and couriered mail would continue to reach pockets of Russia throughout the war and Kuchumov was the kind of man who threw nothing away. Beliaeva wrote: 'Everyone is now on trench duty. No families are left in the park. We are leaving *treats* behind for the fascists. Everybody is trying to be of good cheer.'

Within two weeks of writing this, the people of Leningrad would have dug 16,000 miles of trenches and 340 anti-tank ditches.

24 August, from Elena Nikolaievna Beliaeva, curator and party organizer, Leningrad, to Comrade Kuchumov. We are still evacuating Pushkin town [Tsarskoye Selo] and the palaces. Thousands of objects have now been saved. Now all walls are bare in the palaces. Yesterday in the Alexander Palace, I removed the last picture – *The Kazaki of Nicholas I* by Kruger [*sic*], which is rolled up. The situation is very hard for us. We carry out the work of guards, office workers, cleaners but nothing works.

Three days after this letter was written a night-time curfew was imposed as Leningrad became saturated by paranoia. Men with unkempt beards

or unusual clothes were shot on sight or thrown into jail. Plots by saboteurs were randomly unearthed and spies were found everywhere. Fear
strengthened the grip of the NKVD. And as Leningrad braced itself,
Kuchumov's train was finally allowed to move on, edging another 100
miles east to Gorky. The curator found a radio and tuned into the news.

On 1 September, Hitler issued orders that Leningrad and its palaces be
pounded. German bombers and artillery manoeuvred into place. Seven
days later, parts of the city were engulfed in flames as the Luftwaffe levelled the Badaev food warehouse with napalm and phosphorus, incin-
erating all supplies in an inferno that burnt for three days, fuelled by
reservoirs of fat and sugar. Huge grey plumes rose high above the Gulf
of Finland, filling every nose in Leningrad with the smell of toffee apples,
while heads and hearts faced up to imminent starvation. No rail, air or
road links. The last reserves gone. A Nazi perimeter bristling with munitions fenced in Leningrad.

In the Enigma files in London, scattered among the 2,000 signals intercepted every day by the Bletchley Park decoding station, where the British
eavesdropped on German communications, are fragments of intelligence
describing the encircling of Kuchumov's city: '9 September. Most Secret.
XVI Panzer Korps, tank division, is moving to Leningrad...'[4]

The following day the Germans began to move on Pushkin and its
palaces:

10 September, 03.28 hours, railway line to Krasnoye Selo (K.S.) has been cut.
On road between K.S. and Detskoye Selo [an old name for Pushkin] are fifteen
[Soviet] horse-drawn vehicles.

04.56 hours: motorized column moving on Detskoye Selo. Enemy column is
motorized and horse-drawn, all in about 150 vehicles.[5]

The Nazi communiqués make no mention of the load being carried by
the Soviets but what the Germans had spotted was the ongoing evacuation of treasures from Leningrad's suburban palaces.

On 13 September the attack began. 'Most Secret: Koluft Panzer Group
Four now in Detskoye Selo, reports Hauptmann Falk.' The following
day, the Nazis came from above. 'Fliegerkorps have landed. Attack on
Pushkin has been carried out. All bombs have landed in the target area.'

Inside the Catherine Palace a handful of curators who had chosen to remain continued to evacuate treasures. One of them, Comrade Sophia Popova, reported: '16 September, 20.00 hours, the situation has become treacherous.' Popova's bulletins from the front line would be combined into a longer report submitted to the Leningrad authorities in November 1941. Four decades later journalist Vladimir Telemakov would find it.[6]

Popova wrote:

Enemy is coming closer to Pushkin from the Strelna side [south-west of St Petersburg] and has begun shooting with machine guns at the cottage in the direction of the garage where Nicholas II kept his cars. It is almost impossible to move right now. Park and town are under hard artillery fire and bombing every night. We are surely going deaf. But what is deafness compared to death!

Still the museum workers crept out, throwing camouflage netting around the palaces. Late on the night of 16 September, Comrade Popova wrote: 'Firemen and military have set up posts.' Families were evacuated to shelters. 'We are told to keep in touch with commanders from regular units for when it will be time to abandon the palaces.' A German regiment broke through and moved towards the Alexander Palace, only a block away from the Catherine Palace's golden enfilades. 'We are watching the fascists. The Red Army is on Anrov Street,' Comrade Popova wrote.

A directive arrived from the chairman of IsPolKom, (the executive committee of the Leningrad Soviet): 'Comrade Pavlov [Dmitry Pavlov, Leningrad's Chief of Food Supply] has ordered work to stop in all factories ready for the evacuation of our palaces. All documents must be burned.'

On 17 September a fire-fight illuminated a grey dawn over Pushkin. '5 a.m.: the park and north of the town are battling hard. Everyone is moving to the west,' Comrade Popova wrote. Staff tried to hide in Oranienbaum, the former estate of Alexander Menshikov. 'We have even taken the type-writers. We will leave nothing for them.' Pushkin was overrun.

Stuck in his freezing cellar in Gorky, Kuchumov could only wonder at the fate of his friends and of the palaces.[7] He would not have known that on a hill overlooking Leningrad, General Wilhelm von Leeb, the commander of Army Group North, was dug in and advised Hitler on 21

September that this position in the suburb of Pushkin was to be the forward station for the final assault on the city. There was to be no infantry invasion, just remote obliteration. Relaying instructions from the Führer on 21 September, the chief of naval staff described Kuchumov's city as one of 'no further interest after Soviet Russia is destroyed'.[8]

All the while Leningrad radio played rousing messages. From her bomb shelter, the poet Anna Akhmatova recited inspirational verses, exhorting the women trapped alongside her to be brave.[9]

The war also edged towards the Volga basin. The chairman of Gorky IsPolKom ordered Kuchumov and the palace collections deeper into the Russian interior, towards the place that the Tatars call their Sleeping Land. The treasure train steamed from the west into the east, leaving Europe for Siberia and the frozen tundra of Tomsk. Four weeks later it arrived at the confluence of the Tom and Ob rivers. But it would still go 190 miles further into the blinding whiteness of the snow-fields. Leningrad to Gorky, Gorky to Tomsk, Tomsk to no one knew where, five months on the tracks, 1,600km traversed, until Kuchumov arrived in Novosibirsk, a 'town covered in hoar frost, minus 55°C on the thermometer', at the end of November 1941.[10] To the east lay the ferocious republic of Sakha, the old Cossack outpost of Yakutsk. And still further east were all that was left of the 10–40 million disappeared, who had been exiled by Stalin to the gulags of Magadan and Komsomolsk, the City of Youth.

In Novosibirsk the treasure train was finally unloaded, its precious cargo checked and aired. The theatre was chosen as a temporary store. Kuchumov wrote in his diary on 20 December 1941: 'This brightly lit town, with its white puffs of smoke, its wooden houses and churches, was delighted to receive us. We lay on tapestries in our makeshift quarters and clutched our bread ration cards.'

Back in Leningrad, Food Supply Chief Pavlov estimated that 6,000 people a day were dying from starvation. Those who were still alive were freezing to death, shredding their books and furniture for kindling. 'We've never been as remote from one another as now,' wrote the Soviet chemist Elena Kochina of her husband in her siege memoirs. 'There is no way we can help one another. We realize now that a person must be able to struggle alone with life and death.'[11]

Citizens crept out through the German lines at Pushkin, hunger over-coming their fear, to forage for root vegetables in abandoned allotments and dachas. Pavlov's team experimented with melting lipstick, smearing its fat on the hard bread ration. Leather machine belts were stewed to extract gelatine. The Badaev food factory crater was still being crawled over by a team of scientists, engaging desperately in alchemical experi-ments to transform the ruins into something edible.

In Novosibirsk, there was food but little else. 'We sit in the cellars watching our priceless charges. Sometimes we even hold small exhibi-tions. But there is nothing that can lift our mood, the frustration of not knowing what is happening to the things we were forced to leave behind,' Kuchumov wrote.

The Amber Room weighed heavily on his mind as he shivered in Maxim Gorky's 'land of chains and ice', surrounded by evacuated treasures from the Leningrad.[12] Time stood still and, in order to fill the hours of not knowing what had happened to the Amber Room, Kuchumov began to write a book about its history.

On 29 January 1743 Empress Elizabeth, who had ascended to the Russian throne one year before, issued a decree: 'Take this Amber Room to dec-orate the chambers under your command and you can use the Italian Martelli ...'[13]

We found a copy of this decree in the Hermitage library, following footnotes made by Kuchumov while stranded in Siberia. The journalist Telemakov transcribed all of them for us.

What Kuchumov had discovered was that one of Elizabeth's first acts as Empress was to take the Amber Room from its store in Peter the Great's Summer Palace and move it to her new Winter Palace on the River Neva. Her father had died without ever seeing it assembled and she was deter-mined to complete the task. Her favourite sculptor, Alexander Martelli, was placed in charge.

Using Kuchumov's microscopic footnotes we located Martelli's con-tract (signed by the sculptor), dated 11 February 1743: 'You promise to fix the [Amber] Room, sort all the pieces you have and find out what is missing and for them make replacement parts and erect the Room.'

Martelli would be paid 600 roubles to do what Peter the Great's crafts-men could not.[14]

All Empress Elizabeth had to decide was where her Amber Room should go. Initially, she ordered that it be installed in a small room in the new Winter Palace, only to change her mind and have it moved to a large hall. But there wasn't enough Prussian amber. Martelli decided to fill in the gaps between the amber panels (that had come from Berlin) with fifty-two gilt-edged mirrored pillars. The Russian court made a set but they were the wrong size; orders were sent to Britain but they were never honoured. Only on 16 September 1745 was the enlarged Amber Room completed, using mirrors that came from France.

But Elizabeth was still unhappy and ordered the Amber Room be moved three more times, into ever-larger rooms, forcing Martelli to fill more gaps with mirrors and foil-backed glass. In 1745 the new King of Prussia, Frederick the Great, heard about the travails of the Amber Room and decided to combine diplomacy with a gift. Three ornate mirror frames, also made from amber, had been designed as centrepieces for the walls of the Amber Room, but Empress Elizabeth needed four frames to complete the set. Frederick II ordered his craftsmen in Königsberg to manufacture this fourth frame for 2,000 talers.[15] It was sent to St Petersburg along with a poem, *The Allegory of the Victories and Heroic Deeds of the Empress*.

But after the four amber mirror frames had been hung, the Empress ordered that the Amber Room be moved again, to outside her bedroom. She then decided that such an innovative and luxurious curio should be used to impress foreign embassies. The roving Amber Room was taken down and reassembled again as a reception hall for ambassadors.[16]

No one was surprised when it began to fall to pieces. Kuchumov found this report dated 1746: 'Because of the changes in temperature sections [of the Amber Room] have been damaged. One post is warped. It has been repaired by Master Enger. Also rather a lot of pieces of [amber] have detached themselves from the walls and have gone missing.'[17] Rather than restore it, in July 1755 the Empress ordered V. Fermor, head of the Chancellery of the Imperial Study, to remove the Amber Room from the Winter Palace altogether and transport it, each panel and frame taken by hand, to the Catherine Palace in Tsarskoye Selo.

Here it was to be reconstructed in an even larger chamber. Bartolomeo Rastrelli, an Italian architect, was ordered to supervise the project and Martelli was once again hired to install the room. But there was no money for more amber. Instead, fake panels, glass backed with golden foil, and gilded mirrors were employed. At the centre of the golden enfilades the Amber Room was erected, between the Portrait Hall and Picture Hall, where it would be maintained by Friedrich Roggenbuch, an amber specialist brought from Prussia.

The Amber Room would not remain in its patchwork state for much longer. When Catherine, an *ingénue* from Germany, was crowned Empress of All Russia on 22 September 1762 (dressed in what Lord Buckingham described as 4,000 ermine pelts embroidered with thousands of precious stones, her crown smelted from a pound of gold and twenty pounds of silver), she decided that the palaces of the Tsarskoye Selo would be overhauled.[18]

Catherine II commissioned John Bush, her British horticulturist, to lay out new gardens with busts of Cicero, Demosthenes and Junius Brutus. Beyond them was erected *La Pyramide Egyptienne*, a necropolis for the royal greyhounds, and *L'Arc Triomphal de Prince Orloff*, a tribute to one of her many lovers, Gregory Orlov (who had helped bring her to power by overthrowing her husband, Tsar Peter III). 'There is going to be terrible upheaval in the domestic arrangements at Tsarskoye Selo,' Catherine II warned in a letter of 13 April 1778. 'The Empress will have ten rooms and will ransack all the books in her library for designs for their decoration and her imagination will have free reign.'[19]

Born in Stettin, a German town close to the Baltic coast (now Szczecin in north-western Poland), Catherine II must have appreciated the value of amber. We know from the court order books that one of the ten rooms she selected for renovation was the Amber Room. Over the next four years, the Empress ordered an enormous amount – more than 900 pounds – of prohibitively expensive amber that had to be shipped from the Samland Peninsula in East Prussia. She hired four carvers from the Königsberg Guild to carry out the work, replacing all of the fake sections that bulked out Elizabeth's room with real amber. Catherine II also commissioned Giuseppe Dzokki, an Italian craftsman, to create four Florentine stone mosaics depicting the senses to hang in the room. 'Sight', 'Taste', 'Hearing' and 'Touch and Smell' were all to be stimulated in a chamber that, when lit by candles, exuded a languorous glow, the colour of autumn and a sunset over Stettin.[20]

Almost a century later, the crowning glory of the Catherine Palace had become legendary throughout Europe. 'We have now reached one of the most remarkable rarities – I want to tell you about the Amber Room,' the poet Théophile Gautier wrote in his *Voyage en Russie* in 1866.

Only in *The Thousand and One Nights* and in magic fairy tales, where the architecture of palaces is trusted to magicians, spirits and genies, one can read about rooms made of diamonds, rubies, jacinth and other jewels ... Here the expression 'the Amber Room' is not just a poetic hyperbole but exact reality, and it is not, as you could believe, a small boudoir or study. On the contrary, the room is rather large, with... walls wholly adorned with amber mosaic from top to bottom, including a frieze. The eye, which has not adapted to seeing this material applied in such scale, is amazed and is blinded by the wealth and warmth of tints, representing all colours of the spectrum of yellow – from smoky topaz up to a light lemon. The gold of carvings seems dim and false in this neighbourhood, especially when the sun falls on the walls and runs through transparent veins as those sliding on them.[21]

Working on his book about the Amber Room can have done little to alleviate the isolation that Kuchumov must have felt, entombed in Novosibirsk. Occasional copies of *Pravda* still reached Siberia, brought by couriers, but his sense of foreboding would have only mounted as he scoured the Soviet newspapers for news. Among Kuchumov's documents transcribed by Telemakov was a newspaper article, saved by the great curator during his Siberian days.

On 17 November 1942 *Pravda* carried a front-page confession from a Nazi officer, Norman Förster, who had been captured in Mosdok, in the northern Caucasus. Förster, an Obersturmbannführer (lieutenant-colonel) in the Waffen SS, had told his NKVD interrogators an intriguing story, one that in less than two years would be cited at the International Military Tribunal in Nuremberg. Förster had bumped into an old schoolfriend while in Berlin in August 1941, a 'Dr Focke', who was a fellow graduate of Berlin's Friedrich Wilhelm University, and was currently working for Ribbentrop, Hitler's Reichsaussenminister (Foreign Minister) as a press officer. Focke offered to get Förster assigned to a new and prestigious job with the 4th Company of a secretive Special Task Battalion.

The Sonderkommando Ribbentrop, as it was known, was headquartered at 6 Herman Göring Strasse in Berlin and staffed by 800 members of the SS. In August 1941 three of its four companies were placed on active service on the Eastern front, attached to troops who were converging on the Soviet Union. According to *Pravda*, Dr Förster's company was to follow Army Group South, led by Field Marshal von Runstedt. Förster told his Soviet interrogators, 'Prior to leaving, we were instructed that when we arrived on enemy territory in Russia we were to comb thoroughly all scientific establishments, institutions and libraries and all the palaces; search all the archives and to lay our hands on every cultural treasure, sending everything to Germany.'

Förster's troop set out across the Ukraine, but he learned that the 2nd Company of the Sonderkommando Ribbentrop, attached to Army Group North, had headed straight for the palaces of Pushkin. 'There they captured and removed property from the Catherine Palace museum. Chinese silks and carved décor were taken from the walls. The parquet floor was even removed,' *Pravda* reported Dr Förster as stating.[22] It looked as if the 2nd Company of the Sonderkommando Ribbentrop might have also removed the Amber Room.

Telemakov's manuscript peters out at this point and at the bottom he has scrawled, 'Please call me.' But his phone is out of order. An operator says that it has been this way for a year or more. We will have to return to Ozerki. It is too late to make the journey tonight. The phone is ringing. We dash down the hallway and snatch up the handset. For once we are on time. But someone is trying to send us a fax.

Slowly the message unfurls.

Thank you so much for your interest in the Catherine Palace. It was good to meet the other day. All the materials we have are the result of our staff's work that has taken years and years to pick up, crumbs of information, and we intend to publish this material in a book currently being written by our curators, headed by Alexander Kedrinsky, whom you met some days ago. I find it beyond our physical powers to answer your questions or meet the scheme suggested by you. I find it just the same as to write another book. With respect...'[23]

What can we do? It took us five months to secure a meeting with Director Sautov and three weeks for him to reject us. Maybe we should have done nothing after all. We recall that some of the Catherine Palace archive was uploaded in Russian on to the Internet. We log on to the official Catherine Palace website (www.Tzar.ru) and a message pops up where once there were essays and articles. 'Under Construction. Thank you for your interest. Please return later.' The next morning the local television news carries a report that the replica Amber Room being constructed in the Catherine Palace has now been closed to visitors and will not reopen until May 2003. Months after beginning our investigation into the fate of the Amber Room, we have still not seen any original documents. Now we face another 15 months of official obfuscation, until the reconstructed room is unveiled.

We are back out in the cold. We remind ourselves of the city's favourite saying and catch a *marshrutki* to Pushkin. We will find Alexander Kedrinsky and explain the situation to him. He was more helpful than Sautov. We punch the code into the inconspicuous side door, guarded by the hissing *babushka*. At least no one has thought to change it. 'Kedrinsky,' we say, brushing past her and up the flights of cast-iron stairs. But the door to the old architect's studio is locked, even though he has told us that he works every day.

We hear a noise from above and gingerly climb the last flight. A tiny door is ajar and we push it open. We are in the first of three low-ceilinged rooms. Every inch of every wall is plastered with black-and-white photographs of the Catherine Palace, some of which show goose-stepping Nazis parading across the Great Courtyard. A young woman emerges, ashen-faced, huddled in sweaters, her neck wrapped in scarves and, around the acrylic swathes, an enormous red cardigan. 'Yes?' she asks abruptly. 'And you are?' We say nothing. She reaches for the phone. She is dialling for the guards. Two of her colleagues, whose socks spill over their calf-length plastic boots, pop their heads up over the partition, pointing and gawping. Foreigners are in the private archive of the Catherine Palace.

Like phosphorus dropped in water, the more we speak the more our English words transform the room into a hubbub of spinning and whirling, gesticulating arms and raised voices. We throw in Alexander Kedrinsky's name. We are friends from London, researching the lives of Catherine Palace curators. The women relax. The handset is replaced. Tidying away the wisps of hair that fly around her button-round face, the woman in the red cardigan asks: 'Who? Anyone in particular?'

Kuchumov, we say. Anatoly Mikhailovich.

She smiles, introducing herself as Vica Plauda, head of the Photographic Section. 'I am his granddaughter,' she says. 'I am his only living relative.' Kuchumov's wife had died before him, his brother after him. His children had recently passed away. Finding Kuchumov's granddaughter, here in the Catherine Palace, is a stroke of luck that could happen only somewhere like Russia, where families follow each other through the same institutions. 'I grew up with my grandfather's stories on the rebuilding of these palaces, and here I am working in them and here you are looking for him.'

We tell her about our meeting with Kedrinsky and our falling out with Director Sautov. She nods, her eyes lifted to the heavens. We tell her that although Kuchumov's friends and colleagues have obtained extracts from his diaries and correspondence, the bulk of her grandfather's papers are proving impossible to locate.

'I too have virtually nothing to remind me of him,' Vica Plauda says. 'When he died, in 1993, there were boxes and boxes of material. But I live in a communal apartment, one room only. I loaned the papers to the library at Pavlovsk Palace. He was the director there for years. I haven't seen them since.' We make a note of a name and number in the library at Pavlovsk. 'I kept only a couple of things, including a painting. It hangs here,' she says, pointing to an oil of roses in a vase, a gift to Kuchumov from Anatoly Treskin, one of the most prolific palace restorers: a bouquet from the artist to his patron.

Vica Plauda is silent, thinking. And then, 'Maybe these will interest you.' She produces some papers. In the soft light of the snow-covered window we can now see her likeness to Kuchumov. 'They are copies of letters to and from my grandfather. I had never seen them until I was sent them from New York last year. I have no idea how they got there. Or who has the top copies.'

Is there anything else? Vica Plauda leaves the room. She returns with a tattered folder and slides out a postcard-sized glass plate that she holds with care between thumb and index finger up to the window. The light transforms the dark rectangle into a golden glowing portal. Here is the heart of the Catherine Palace, lit with 565 candles, their flames glancing off prehistoric air bubbles and fish scales trapped in the viscous resin, illuminating the faces of carved cherubs that balance on cornices and flocks of amber parrots and eagles that fly across antique friezes. In our hands is the only surviving colour record of the 'Eighth Wonder of the World', a photographic colour positive of the original Amber Room, made in 1917 by a Russian officer who fled with it to Paris. Vica says, 'The Catherine Palace had bought it back from his relatives two decades ago and now it must be priceless.' We photograph it.

Vica Plauda, granddaughter of Anatoly Kuchumov, holding the only surviving colour plate of the original Amber Room

The Amber Room

The telephone in the next room rings. Vica comes back shaking her head. 'It's for you,' she says. Dr Sautov's assistant is on the line. He has enjoyed watching our covert operation, dressed in black coats and hats, stalking like ravens across the snow-whitened courtyard, the assistant says sternly. And Director Sautov has charted our progress into the staff quarters. Security has been called. We are advised to wait.

We run. Down the back staircase with the documents Vica has given us, out of the palace and to the bus stop where we throw ourselves to the head of the queue, pushing our way into seats.

That evening, behind our locked doors, we pore over the paperwork.

On 24 January 1944 the museum workers in Novosibirsk, enduring one of the harshest winters in living memory, gathered around the radio to listen to an announcement. The Red Army had launched a counter-attack on the German forces besieging Leningrad and was now approaching Pushkin and Pavlovsk. Three days later, 872 days after the siege began, Leningrad was liberated. It was, according to the recollections of siege survivors, as if an enormous boulder had been lifted from the grass, everything beneath it flattened, sour smelling and anaemic.

'We could not sleep for two days, listening and waiting for every scrap of news,' Kuchumov wrote in one of the letters given to us by his granddaughter.[24] He found a 'cherished bottle of wine' and produced some goblets that had belonged to the tsars. 'People drank for the success of the Red Army. They were inspired and agitated, hopeful too. From this day on the packing begins. Everyone has the same objective – to return the treasures.'

In February 1944 Kuchumov boarded a train in Novosibirsk, summoned back home by a telegram from the Leningrad IsPolKom, 'travelling in a lettered train carriage, on a seat as if I was a foreign diplomat'. It was March before he arrived in 'our favourite beautiful Leningrad that still looks the same, but advanced in age, as a man after a wasting disease'. But before he had time to dwell on the terrible scenes of death and destruction that greeted him, the authorities promoted him to Chief of the Department of Museums and Memorials and head of Leningrad's Central

Soviet troops re-entering the Catherine Palace, 1944

Stores. Kuchumov was placed in charge of returning all evacuated treasures to their original palace locations.

He immediately asked for permission to visit the Catherine Palace. 'The situation in the suburbs, I hear, is much worse, but I have not seen it for myself yet. The permit to the suburbs is in the process of validation and I will get it in two or three days. I hear that quite a few items have been found in the fields around Gatchina, pieces of furniture from Nicholas I,' Kuchumov wrote.

On 27 April 1944 the permit arrived and, accompanied by photographer Mikhail Velichko, Kuchumov 'took a tram to the outpost of the Four Hands, near the Middle Turnpike, and waited till a passing car bound for Pushkin came'. It was 'impossible to recognize the land, the traces of bitter battles are to be seen everywhere... pillboxes, obstacles, shell-holes, barbed wire and signs for mines are all about. Bodies in the road,' he wrote.

Kuchumov recorded practically every footstep and sent these accounts to his colleagues in Novosibirsk – letters that Vica Plauda now cherishes. 'I will describe every unit as I see it with my own eyes,' Kuchumov wrote. The parkland was 'ten stems without branches', a 'fountain's cup lies on the pitted ground, high burdocks and goosefeet grow on the places of former houses'. Along the way where once there were villages were only 'empty boxes, burnt from inside. Nuovo Suzi gone. Rekholovo demolished.'

Kuchumov glimpsed Pushkin in the distance across 'ditches, trenches, numerous rows of barbed wire, minefields'. There were mountains of abandoned helmets, great pyramids of German gas masks. 'A hurricane has swept over the park.' Along the roadside was a 'garbage heap of palatial doors, frames and even pieces of furniture'. He recognized a broken chair from the Silver Dining Room. What had happened to the Amber Room, the thing he had decided to disguise rather than evacuate?

Kuchumov and Velichko reached the Lyceum. 'Rejoice! The Pushkin statue is undamaged! My dream has come true: I am in Pushkin, I am home.' Then Kuchumov noticed 'five thick ropes hanging from the branches of the old birch before the church'. Here was the gallows used by the Gestapo: 'dreadful pictures were to be seen here... Oh, if only the walls could talk'. Despite his 'pain and fear', the curator made his way to the blue-and-gold-painted gates of the Catherine Palace, determined to complete the task he had set out to accomplish. 'I enter the Great Courtyard through the bright opened gates. I feel pain and fear while looking at the destroyed palace, empty and burnt. The sky is to be seen through the windows. The mighty statues of athletes are broken. Charred beams, broken things lie around.'

Strewn across the Great Courtyard was 'garbage, iron beds, broken furniture, scrap, dung, boxes from mines and shells and unbelievable variety of dirty clothes, a queasy, filthy stench'. Stepping gingerly through the mess, Kuchumov neared his goal, the first-floor rooms of the Catherine Palace, the golden enfilades. And he felt sick with every step.

He climbed up, although not by the Monighetti marble staircase, as that had been destroyed, but by the administration staircase used by staff. 'I enter the administration quarters and there is no single wooden partition left, everything is broken off, the rooms are empty. On some of the doors we can still see the pre-war doorplates, People's Commissar and Director's Assistant. It seems that the palace is still living like before the war.' But the roof had collapsed and shell-holes pitted the walls. 'A carbonized *plafond* [ceiling painting] is hanging... like a black mourning banner.'

Kuchumov moved slowly through each chamber, absorbing the scale of destruction. 'Everything from the doors is hacked off with axes. The sculptures are without heads. The bas-reliefs are hardly damaged but the parquet and fireplaces are smashed and broken.' And then, 'climbing over heaps of burnt beams, bricks and iron', Kuchumov held his breath.

The Oval Anteroom was as far as he could get. 'The whole room was covered with soot from when the suite of rooms had burned. This is the last room left in the whole suite. Next we see a terrible site of fire. Naked brick walls covered with soot. Neither floors nor ceilings have survived. Nothing but a huge collapse through all three floors.' Nothing stood where once had been the thing that he had painstakingly concealed with gauze and wadding from the Pushkin sewing factory. The Amber Room had been destroyed.

'Every step kills me,' Kuchumov wrote. 'These beasts made stables of the palace-museum, of our pride. But even the animals couldn't have soiled the rooms worse than the beasts with two legs have done. We have to begin again.'

The ruined Catherine Palace after Nazi occupation

3

At a small apartment in Ozerki, we press the doorbell that tolls 'The Volga Boatmen'. We have come to return Vladimir Telemakov's manuscript and we need his help again. He was not expecting visitors, Telemakov says. But still he wears his smart jacket and trousers. 'Welcome. Welcome. Please come in.' He glances at our bag and smiles at his green document file poking out. 'Did my manuscript help? The diary extracts and letters. All those intricate details. It was difficult for me to gather. The material is extremely rare.'

It is fantastic, we say, a work of great dedication. But we are confused. If Kuchumov found evidence in 1944 that the Amber Room had burned when the Catherine Palace was partially destroyed (whether by German troops in retreat or the Soviet blitzkrieg), why are people still searching for it today?

Telemakov walks off and returns with a blue file. From it he pulls a notebook. 'I was invited to Kuchumov's old apartment in Pavlovsk only once and when I went there I saw he had volumes of newspaper cuttings stretching back to the Great Patriotic War. They, like everything else, vanished after he died. But I copied down one or two articles.'

Telemakov begins to read:

'*Pravda*. 15 May 1945. Our Special Correspondent writes: Could we imagine that Königsberg has fallen, the fortress of central eastern Prussia, the city that the Hitlerites named the springboard to the East? We could not imagine – because the Germans not only lost in Königsberg a strategically important nerve centre but also the "crucible" of Nazism from where the citizens of the dark world rose. London radio has also confirmed our great Soviet success, saying that Königsberg is the epicentre of Prussia and it was its capital even when Berlin was a swamp.'¹

Telemakov looks up. 'Be patient,' he says. 'There is a second article from *Pravda* on the same day. "Colonel D. D. Ivanyenko, Third Belorussian Front. 12 May 1945. By telegraph."' It had taken three days for the report to get into print.

'In the ruins of Königsberg Castle, where the museum of Prussia was located, we have found nearly thirty armchairs from the Tsarskoye Selo palaces of Pushkin town. On them are labels written by Tsarskoye Selo officials and over the top are stuck labels written in German Gothic script. We have continued our searches and discovered [picture] frames from the Kiev Museum, a selection of catalogues and books, and a Gift Book consisting of an inventory of purchases and presents received by Hitlerite curators in Königsberg.

'The two hundredth item in this Nazi Gift Book, recorded on page 141, as received on 5 December 1941, is the Amber Room from Tsarskoye Selo, to which the whole page is devoted. In this inventory are listed 140 items [from the room]... and it is written that these items were *gifted* to the Königsberg museum by the German authorities.'

Telemakov fixes us in his gaze. 'The Amber Room had survived, you see? While Anatoly Mikhailovich was stuck in Siberia, worrying about its safety in the Catherine Palace, the Nazis dismantled the room and transported it to Königsberg. The Amber Room arrived in East Prussia less than three months after the siege of Leningrad began. Even when Anatoly Mikhailovich told me this story, thirty-five years later, there were tears in his eyes.'

On 16 May 1945 Anatoly Kuchumov sent three telegrams: one to LenGorIsPolKom, another to Nikolai Belokhov, the director of the Government Directorate of the Preservation of Monuments, and a third to Igor Grabar in Moscow. Grabar was director of the Committee on Architecture of the Council of People's Commissars of the USSR, a Titan of the Soviet art world, winner of the Stalin Prize, a man who had the General Secretary's ear.

'Kuchumov was the obvious person to bring the Amber Room home. He wrote requesting funds and a travel permit. He packed a small bag and said goodbye to Anna Mikhailovna,' Telemakov says. 'A telegram from Moscow arrived. Yes, Comrade Kuchumov was correct, Moscow was running a rescue operation to bring home the Amber Room. And yes, Moscow needed an expert. But someone was already on the way. Professor A. I. Brusov, from Moscow.'

Telemakov shrugs. 'Brusov! Anatoly Mikhailovich was shocked by the decision. Was he being punished? He wondered if the party blamed him for failing to take down the Amber Room while the Nazis seemingly managed it.' Telemakov sighs. 'I can't tell you more other than I heard that Brusov gave an interview to the Soviet press. Go and find it. I hope my little bits and pieces help you.' And, as the spruce front door closes, 'Please don't forget me. Your promise to help. Do come back.'

The National Library of Russia, set back from a statue of Catherine the Great dominating her circle of advisers and lovers (Suvorov, Orlov, Potemkin), is a sprawling citadel of books. One of the largest libraries in the world, it houses more than 32 million volumes. In Soviet times, the books' spines were turned away from the reader, its catalogue room planted in a maze of corridors, patrolled by the KGB.

The Soviet reader could not be trusted with potentially contagious thoughts, such as Andrei Sakharov's calculations of what would happen if Khrushchev had gone ahead and test-blasted in the Soviet atmosphere a 100-megaton hydrogen bomb. Such ideas had to be quarantined. All library research was chaperoned, readers standing in line waiting for the patrician 'inquiry apparatchiki', who flicked up and down unseen stacks like beads of an abacus, sorting and sifting. And even though the system had prominent critics, among them Maxim Gorky, who boldly advised Stalin, 'the one-sidedness of our treatment of reality – created by us – exerts an extremely unhealthy influence on our young people', still it prevailed.[2]

Nowadays anyone can roam the corridors, but in New Russia the profit-driven state barely pays library staff and, flat broke, they are elusive. We eventually find a woman sitting at a rucked baize desk littered with dribbling glue pots and official stamps. To her left is a mechanical crank-driven calendar, embossed 'Leningrad'. Grudgingly, she admits to having been a member of the old 'inquiry apparatchiki'. Now she is responsible for issuing temporary readers' tickets and she sends us down into the basement.

One, two, three corridors along, an old red rug and portraits of Lenin, new busts of Catherine, Peter and Paul, hundreds of people scurrying in different directions, gaunt men with Gogol hair, old women wrapped in girlish polka dots pinging down corridors steeped in naphthalene. Up to a fourth-floor office in a lift, along and down to the third by the stairs, until, after three hours in the building, we find ourselves breathless in a windowless hexagonal basement room filled by silent figures absorbed in their research, hunched against great tiers of drawers that line this catalogue room.

K is for Königsberg: 'see Kaliningrad'. Between articles on 'Modern Dance for Balls' and 'How to Make Better Work in Cultural Area with People from the North' there is a reference to a Telegraph Agency of the Soviet Union (TASS) story: 'Successful return of Professor Alexander Brusov and Tatyana Beliaeva from Königsberg, 13 July 1945.'

Brusov. However, a librarian informs us that the article has gone missing. We return to the catalogue room, waiting for the Bs to become free.

B is for Beliaeva and Brusov – nothing listed. But in a decrepit almanac of Soviet museums, we find: 'Brusov, Alexander Ivanovich, Professor of Archaeology, State Historical Museum, Moscow'. And a telephone number.

The man Moscow sent to Königsberg in search of the Amber Room held a prestigious post in an institution at the heart of the Soviet Union, housed in a red-brick Gothic-style building at the western end of Red Square. We call the State Historical Museum from the library payphone. 'Brusov. Brusov? *Nyet*,' the switchboard operators says, hanging up.

We try Our Friend the Professor. Can she extract some information from the tight-lipped Moscow museum world? She'll see what can be done. 'Everything is forbidden but all things are possible,' the professor choruses. 'Wait by the phone.'

Twenty minutes later, she calls. 'Alexander Brusov is dead. In 1965,' she says. Nothing is ever straightforward in our Russian lives. 'But I gather there are some papers of his. Classified. In the Leninka. The Lenin Library in Moscow. I might be able to get you copies.' The chances of us getting classified files opened are slim. Copies are fine, we say. 'I have a colleague in the Leninka and she will try and send the papers to you in the National Library of Russia,' the professor says. 'Please be patient. Do nothing.'

We wait, on tenterhooks, like Kuchumov. However, while Anatoly Mikhailovich waited for the return of his Amber Room, he began some new research into Königsberg. And while we wait for news from the Leninka, we go in search of a book from which, according to Kuchumov's diary, he took notes in May 1945. 'Study P. J. Hartmann,' the curator wrote, as Brusov set off for the Baltic, taking the place Kuchumov believed should have been his. We are not good at doing nothing.

Succini Prussici, physica et civilis historia was published in Frankfurt in 1677 by Philipp Jacob Hartmann, a 'professore medicine extraordinario'. The book's patrons spared no expense in binding the text in caramel-coloured calf hide, in commissioning engravings for the frontispiece and bookends. It was an exposition on the origins of amber and Hartmann concluded that it was 'undoubtedly petrified vegetable juice'. His book became a bestseller, one that generated such interest in the year it was published that the celebrated British physicist Dr Robert Hooke, who would discover the laws of elasticity and energy conservation, led a series of discourses on Hartmann's theories at the Royal Society in London.[3]

The debate about amber's genesis was still raging at the time Tsar Peter I became entranced by the Gold of the North and bought a copy of Philipp Hartmann's book when he travelled to Königsberg in 1696. The book's appendix reproduced the earliest eyewitness account of the amber trade in East Prussia, written by Simonis Grunovii, a Dominican monk who arrived in 1519 in an area that was then known as the Samland Peninsula.

Grunovii wrote that he wished to buy a perfect nugget of amber to give his Pope, from whom he hoped to buy salvation. Leo X, the Church's most extravagant patron of the arts, had recently begun one of the most ambitious civil engineering projects in Christendom, the construction of St Peter's Basilica in Rome. It was being financed in a unique way, by the sale of original sin – treasures and cash given in exchange for Papal Indulgences.

To reach Samland, Grunovii would have followed one of three ancient Amber Routes that had linked the Classical world and northern Europe since before the time of Herodotus. Ancient thinkers held in great fear those who lived beyond the 'tired world' that stopped abruptly at the line of the Alps.[4] In the north was *ultima Thule*, the furthest region of the world. Until the early sixteenth century many people still believed the stories of Adam of Bremen, an eleventh-century chronicler who claimed, in his *Descriptions of the Islands of the North,* that here lived a race of Amazonians who gave birth to male children with the heads of dogs.

Recent archaeological studies have revealed that the three Amber Routes were twenty-foot-wide log roads constructed on beds of branches, fastened together with pegs and topped off with sand and sod. Grunovii would almost certainly have followed the eastern Amber Route. This would have involved boarding a ship in the Gulf of Venice and crossing the Adriatic bound for Trieste, where he would have ridden with traders' caravans heading over the Alps for the Danube. Continuing to the River Oder, Grunovii would have gone north, eventually reaching the eastern Baltic.[5]

Olaus Magnus, Archbishop of Uppsala, was among the first to illustrate Grunovii's destination in a hide-bound *Encyclopaedia of Natural Products* published in Rome in 1555. Across one page was a crude map of Samland, a clearly recognizable peninsula reaching out into the Baltic. Along the coastline were dotted ominous-looking watchtowers and beside one was the figure of a man dressed in cap and pantaloons, whose foot rested on a shovel, his finger pointing to a barrel at his feet from which exploded a fountain of light. Beside him was printed the word *succinu* (*succinum,* the Latin for 'juice', also meant sap, and then later amber). The Samland Peninsula was the source of the Gold of the North.[6]

Simonis Grunovii described what he saw: 'When there is a northerly gale all the peasants in the vicinity must come to the beach and run with nets into the sea to fish for the floating amber... but many will drown.[7] When the sea roiled and the wind rose in November and December, amber resin was shaken loose from the seabed and could be scooped into nets. The men who fished for it wore leather 'cuirasses with deep pockets' and became 'frozen in icy waters and have to be thawed before they can be taken to their huts or put out again to work and for this reason big fires are kept upon the shore'. Men were roped together to battle the treacherous undertow and carried twenty-foot poles up which they clambered when the highest waves crashed down.

Grunovii wrote that these amber 'fishermen' were slaves, bonded by the Teutonic Knights, a German religious army that seized control of the region and grew rich by monopolizing the amber. 'The High Master of Prussia profits greatly... because he is paid approximately eighty marks for a ton.' It was a monopoly enforced by terror. An edict published by one of the order's judges 'prohibited the free collection of amber by

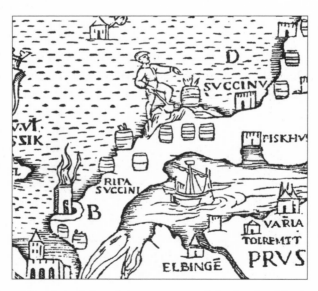

Olaus Magnus's sixteenth-century map of the Samland Peninsula, showing the amber fishing grounds and burning barrels beside which fishermen thawed out after wading through the freezing Baltic Sea

*Frontispiece
depicting amber
fishermen from
P. J. Hartmann's
book, published
in 1677*

hanging from the nearest tree... his henchmen applying instant justice, these servants having the right to kill anyone committing the deed
without interrogation'. And riding to the coast, through Elbing, Pillau,
Fischhausen and Gross Dirschkeim, the Dominican monk glimpsed car-
casses swinging from the gallows.

Grunovii was directed to the main city on the Samland Peninsula, from
where the Teutonic Knights, who had taken control of the peninsula in
1254, administrated the amber trade. The Knights had purged the land
of non-believers and, to commemorate the battle, built in 1255 an enormous castle on the banks of the River Pregel 'whose roots and cellars
were thrust as far below the surface of the earth as its pinnacles scaled the
heavens'.[8] It would become known as Königsberg Castle and its Knights'
Hall, crowned with a tower, rose above a flagged limestone dungeon lit by
burning torches where prisoners were suspended from iron trapezes. This

Pre-war photograph of Königsberg Castle

was the castle where, 691 years later, Colonel Ivanyenko, of the Third Belorussian front, would find a Nazi Gift Book containing a reference to the arrival of the Amber Room.

The Dominican Grunovii paid the Knight's Grand Master Albrecht, ten *vierdings* – equivalent to a small bag of gold pieces – for a 'gleaming amber – a half finger's length'. It took a team of men from the nearby Danzig Guild, working in shifts, six weeks to 'carve from it an image of John the Baptist as a child'. (In 1707 the same guild would send carvers to Berlin to assist architect Eosander in trying to assemble the original amber chamber.)

Grunovii rode home with the icon in his saddlebag, arriving at the Vatican only to find Rome preoccupied with Martin Luther, who attacked, among other things, the practice of Papal Indulgences. Grunovii sought out 'Cardinal John N', the Pope's private secretary, and showed him the amber carving. 'It was surely worth more than 2,000 florins [over fifteen pounds of gold] to Rome,' the Cardinal said, but he had bad news for Grunovii: Leo X was now gravely ill. In December 1521 the Pope died, along with the Dominican's bid for salvation.

The Protestant Reformation rapidly reached across the Baltic and in 1525 the Teutonic Knights' Grand Master Albrecht also converted to

Lutheranism, detaching the religious order from Rome. This transformed the region into a ducal state, which it would remain until Frederick I was crowned 'King in Prussia' in Königsberg Castle on 18 January 1701 (a celebration that spurred Andreas Schlüter to begin building the original amber chamber).

We can see that P. J. Hartmann's book would have taught Kuchumov how the Amber Room captured the Nazis' ethos. Its transportation to Königsberg was far from coincidental and its preservation in the ancient Teutonic castle would have been of paramount importance to German curators.

On the fifth morning in the National Library of Russia a packet from Moscow arrives for us. We are directed to the Bolshoi Reading Hall, where a waddling librarian escorts us to one of hundreds of identical worn wooden desks. We eagerly pull apart the bundle from the Leninka. Inside are photocopied pages and a small photograph of a melancholic figure with ice-white hair and jet-black eyebrows whose dark eye-sockets recede like metro tunnels. His serge suit is crumpled. His tie looks to be strangling him. His features are more Semitic than Slavic. The caption says that this is Professor Alexander Ivanovich Brusov and the picture was taken around the time of his mission to Königsberg. We wonder why he looks so tired of life.

We leaf through the photocopies. They are extracts from Brusov's desk diary, seven days to a double page.[9] We had not been sure what we would be sent from Moscow but this is better than we could have hoped for.

The desk diary began on 25 May 1945. It reveals that only a fortnight after the German surrender, while Europe was still in chaos, SovNarKom (the Council of People's Commissars), the highest authority in the Soviet Union, ordered Professor Alexander Brusov to find and bring back the Amber Room. It must have been of tremendous significance for the Soviet leadership for it to have acted so quickly.

Brusov was to be assisted by Ivan Pozharsky from the Moscow Theatre Library. The expedition leader was Comrade Tatyana Beliaeva of the Lenin Library. According to Leninka records, Comrade Beliaeva was

Professor Alexander Brusov of the State Historical Museum, Moscow, and his diary

chief of the 'inquiry apparatchiki'. All three were to leave for Königsberg the next day, 26 May.

It would take Beliaeva, Brusov and Pozharsky five days to complete the 1,000-mile journey, squeezed into a military van that looped around the chaos of surrender. Brusov wrote: 'Insterburg, spent the night. Gerdawyen, stayed in a hotel. And Villan...' The professor could not remember what they did in Villan.

'Königsberg: city in ruins,' Brusov wrote on their arrival on 31 May. 'Conditions very hard, no cooperation from anyone – the army or the people.' The place was still on fire, the stench of decomposing flesh hanging in the air. The Red Army had reduced the medieval city to a pile of rubble fogged by acrid smoke. Surviving citizens wandered past jeering Soviet soldiers. Covered in soot and ash with shredded clothes, the Germans were unable to comprehend the savagery of the assault or the suddenness with which defeat had overcome them.

But despite the top-level orders they were acting upon, Brusov's team was forced to wait by the Soviet Military Administration, which warned them the area was still not secure. It was barely two months since a Soviet artillery bombardment had smashed Königsberg's last defences.

On 2 April 1945 Red Army officers had recalled seeing the buildings 'crumble into piles of stone', leaving thousands buried alive.[10] On 6 April, the Soviet's 11th Guards Army and 43rd Army had fought their way into the city, flame-throwers scorching the buildings, rousting residents hiding in cellars, while citizens hung sheets from their windows, desperately signalling surrender. Hundreds attempted a futile breakout on 8 April, only to be spotted by Red Army artillery units that cut them to pieces.

One survivor, General Otto Lasch, the Nazi Kommandant of Königsberg, would write a book about the last days of the city. In it he described how the castle briefly became a safe haven for German citizens until the Red Army attacked its main gates in the late afternoon of 9 April, forcing its surrender at 9 p.m. As lines of communication between the castle and his bunker on the city's Parade Platz had been severed, Lasch would not learn of the capitulation until 1 a.m. Early on 10 April, General Lasch and his fellow officers emerged on to the broken streets carrying bedrolls and knapsacks.

Within three days Hitler had sentenced Lasch to death, accusing him of cowardice. Königsberg had meant a great deal to Hitler. More than

Soviet tanks on the streets of Königsberg during the final attack, April 1945

*The surrender
of General Otto
Lasch (centre),
10 April 1945*

50,000 German soldiers had died in three months of intensive fighting and 92,000 prisoners were taken by the Soviets in the campaign for East Prussia. Hitler warned all commanders on the Eastern Front that 'he who gives orders to retreat... is to be shot on the spot'.[11] However, by 30 April, Hitler was dead and on 8 May Marshal Zhukov, mastermind of the Soviet assault on Berlin, received the German Chief of Staff's unconditional surrender in the officers' mess of a military engineering college in Berlin-Karlshorst.

And so it was unsurprising that the Red Army still needed time to secure Königsberg, and while they did Brusov readied his search team, recruiting two translators, Lieutenant Sardovsky and Captain E. A. Chernishov, of the Third Belorussian Front. In his diary Brusov wrote that Chernishov was '[aged] thirty, sympathetic, not a silly man. Studied at the department of foreign languages in Moscow. Musically talented. It is so pleasant and easy to work with him.'

Brusov also looked for the officer whom *Pravda* claimed had located the Königsberg Castle Gift Book, Colonel D. D. Ivanyenko. He was still in town but was being chaperoned by Major Krolic, a political commissar, and was not available for debriefing. The Gift Book 'appeared to have vanished', Brusov noted, perplexed.

Brusov tried to interview some of the remaining German citizens. 'No one wants to cooperate with us,' he complained to his diary, having learned that Germans had come forward with information about looted art works to the Soviet Military Administration and that this intelligence was not being passed to him. One man who claimed to have found a Nazi stash, including large crates of amber, had been sent away, only to be found the next day hanged from a tree, his hands tied behind his back. Brusov discovered that two more German informers had died in the same manner, hog-tied and hanged, after promising to reveal the location of German treasure. It was difficult for Brusov to fathom what was going on.

The German civilian population was being squeezed through a security sieve, although now there were only 193,000 people left in a city that was once populated by 2.2 million.[12] The city was encircled by nine NKVD regiments sent by Stalin's security chief Lavrenty Beria, who had succeeded Karlik, after the Dwarf had himself become a victim of the purges in 1938. Beria's men were bolstered by 400 operatives from the NKVD's special department (christened SMERSH in 1943, a name chosen by Stalin that was an acronym for 'Kill All Spies'). SMERSH acted as the Soviets' counter-intelligence service, snuffling around Königsberg for collaborators, fascists, double agents and traitors.

On 2 June, Professor Brusov and Tatyana Beliaeva were permitted to begin searching the ruins, assisted by German recruits. They headed straight for Königsberg Castle, whose barrelling watchtowers and arrow-slits still dominated the city. According to Brusov: 'It is in complete ruins. Only a few rooms remain untouched – in the north wing. On the top floor we are collecting things, using it as a storeroom.' Large sections of the roof had collapsed on all four wings of the gigantic cloisters that rose above the River Pregel. The sixteenth-century southern wing was smashed to pieces. The west wing, constructed at a similar time, was also largely destroyed. Only the north-western corner, the oldest part of the castle, dating to the thirteenth century, incorporating a ceremonial Knights' Hall, remained relatively unscathed.

Beneath this hall was a complex of deep cellars, lit by chandeliers suspended from iron trapezes. The dank walls were lined with giant kegs of

Amateur painting of the post-war remains of Königsberg Castle

wine and beer and the flagstone floors were covered in planks upon which stood refectory tables and banquettes. Here the Nazis had eaten off red-rimmed china plates embossed with the Prussian eagle and the name of the restaurant, Blutgericht, the Blood Court.

It is hard to imagine the scale of the operation and the conditions under which the Soviet team toiled. The castle site was enormous and perilously fragile, with sixty-foot-high walls threatening to topple and fallen castellations so widely scattered that a rope was required to clamber over them. And then there was the dust, choking, all-pervasive, leaching into every crevice and pore, making work inside the ruin intolerable. Brusov and his comrades were starved of resources. He had nothing more advanced with which to excavate than a pair of shovels. There was no paraffin, he had been told by the military. And therefore there was little light by day or night. There was also no sign of the Amber Room.

After a few days conducting random surveys, the professor came across an old German man. He was wandering through the castle rubble, a shambling figure who, with his penny-round spectacles, bore an uncanny likeness to Himmler, Brusov noted.

Somehow this man had bypassed the security cordon Brusov had him arrested and under interrogation the old man admitted to having worked for the Königsberg Castle Museum. He had come back only to see if the Soviets needed help clearing it. He identified himself as Alfred Rohde. Brusov thought little about him. Rohde cooperated but seemed distracted, repeatedly denying knowledge of Soviet treasures. In his former life he was possibly a figure of consequence, but now every time he pointed to the destruction around him his eyes welled up. Alfred Rohde had been severely traumatized, Brusov reasoned.

Alfred Rohde

It was only when the professor began to interrogate others who had worked in the castle and to study Rohde's demeanour that his view changed. 'Rohde looks like a very old man with a shaking right hand. His clothes are very shabby,' the professor wrote. 'But he is actually very experienced. An art critic. He has several scientific works published.' It is not clear how Brusov pieced the truth together but he eventually discovered that Dr Alfred Rohde was director of the Nazis' Königsberg Castle Museum.

When Brusov confronted him, Rohde barely reacted. 'Perhaps he is an alcoholic. Doesn't look like a man I can trust. I think he knows more than he tells us and when he talks he often lies,' the professor scribbled in his diary. 'When you look at him when he's not looking at you, his hand stops shaking. He always tells us that the best collections were evacuated but when we ask where to he says he doesn't know.' Professor Brusov had heard rumours of art works being stored at a castle in a nearby Prussian town and put them to Rohde. 'I suggested that they [the Germans] had sent things to Rautenburg and Rohde exclaimed: "Oh, have you found them?"' The old man was broken, infuriating and also probably concealing something.

As they laboriously cleared masonry from the Albrecht Gate, Brusov became suspicious. 'Digging started for the Amber Room before I arrived,' the professor confided to his diary. 'They started in the south wing of the castle. I noticed the small hall was already excavated.' He was further concerned to discover that the Nazi Gift Book identifying the arrival of the Amber Room had been found by Colonel Ivanyenko on 25 April, almost three weeks before the news reached Moscow. During this significant interval unofficial investigations to find the Amber Room could have been conducted. But by whom?

No time to think. They dug on. Since there was little left of the south wing, the Brusov team began knocking their way through the Queen Louisa Tower to reach the blocked-off north wing and the Knights' Hall. Pre-war photographs show a large vaulted chamber with a sweeping ribbed roof beneath which the Teutonic Knights conducted their ceremonies, watched over by the sombre portraits of their forefathers.

On the morning of 5 June, Brusov broke through into the Knights' Hall and, stumbling over blocks of stone and wooden beams, he and his team found there had been an inferno. The carved thirteenth-century columns were charred, the ancient banners incinerated, the glass was blown and distorted, the flagstone floor cracked by falling masonry. They crawled through the ash on their hands and knees. In one corner Brusov found some chair springs and old German iron locks. In another, recognizable Russian mouldings and frames. That night Brusov returned to his quarters and wrote: 'Found bronze hangings from the Tsarskoye Selo doors... Cornice pieces that could have been in the Amber Room... Iron strips with bolts with the help of which parts of the Amber Room were boxed into crates... We should give up looking for the Amber Room.'

It was a devastating conclusion. Three days into his mission and Brusov had gathered evidence that strongly suggested that the Amber Room had been stored in the Knights' Hall, where it had been destroyed by a devastating fire. Yet we already know that the search for the Amber Room would continue until the present day. This could not possibly be the end of the story.

No one dared return to Moscow or the powerful SovNarKom empty-handed. No one – least of all Stalin – was in the mood for bad news. These were euphoric times with Soviet radio broadcasting on 5 June the sound of celebrations in Red Square as Stalin awarded the Order of Victory to Montgomery and Eisenhower.[13]

Brusov returned to the ruins of the castle, surely determined to find more evidence before reporting his terrible finding that the Amber Room had been incinerated. He would have to try to find something else to mitigate the bad news, something of high value with which to sweeten his dismal conclusions. He recruited dozens more German volunteers to sort through the rubble in return for food.

The professor's diligence began to pay off almost immediately, with caches of art extracted from air pockets in the rubble. 'We have dug continuously,' he wrote, 'and we have eventually found success: 1,000 items, Italian paintings, porcelain and many silver items.' But still no sign of the Amber Room. The search was widened to incorporate other areas of the city.

On 10 June, eight days after their dig began, Brusov and his team forced their way into a municipal building on the corner of Lange Reihe and Steindamm Strasse, the city's former high street. Here was evidence of a hasty evacuation. Tens of thousands of loose pieces of amber lay on the floor. Others had been packed into boxes. Besides them an inventory in German suggested that scores more crates also containing amber had already left Königsberg 'in the care of Karl Andree'.

After an initial flush of excitement, Brusov learned from one of his German workers that Karl Andree was director of the Institute of Palaeontology and Geology at Königsberg's Albertus-University. Brusov concluded he had found the remnants of an amber collection once famed throughout Europe, consisting of more than 120,000 pieces, the most valuable being 'a life-size reptile carved from the resin'.[14] Although Brusov had stumbled over something of immense value, this collection was not connected to the Amber Room.

That evening the professor composed a communiqué to Moscow that was witnessed by Captain Chernishov and copied to the Soviet commandant in Königsberg.

We have examined a building on the edge of Lange Reihe 4 where there was a collection of items from the amber and geological museum. It seems that the Germans started packing but something disturbed them. Most of the items are labelled. It is probably a good idea to pack all of these items and transport them to somewhere safer, a protected building. It really is one of the best collections and perhaps could be sent to Moscow. Geological collection, beautifully systematized and very wide.

Brusov was clearly thinking of his museum in Red Square and calculated that packing would take 'eight or ten days with the help of ten workers'.

Brusov ventured further afield in search of anything connected to the Amber Room. He investigated claims of a Nazi stash at Wildenhoff Castle (today Zikova in Poland), the ancestral home of Countess von Schwerin, an East Prussian aristocrat. Dr Rohde claimed it was pointless. When the Soviet team arrived, Wildenhoff was in a dismal state. Eyewitnesses claimed to have seen a retreating SS unit set fire to it. But not everything had been destroyed. 'In three chambers were heaps of remarkable documents, handwritten papers and legal articles from the sixteenth century, all in order with numbers. Because of our small car we could take only a few of these documents and will have to come back with bigger car on 16th,' Brusov wrote. But no Amber Room.

The night before he was due to return to Wildenhoff, Brusov could not sleep. He was in his sixties and suffered from insomnia. Before dawn he went for a walk in the ruins of Königsberg Castle where he noticed smoke rising from behind a broken wall. Clambering over the rubble to investigate, Brusov found Alfred Rohde, the German curator, crouched over a smouldering bundle. As he had cooperated with the Soviets, Rohde had been given special privileges. He was not locked up at night as other German prisoners were, although he had been ordered to observe a dawn to dusk curfew. 'Today I found some documents,' Brusov wrote, revealing that he had rescued from Rohde's fire thirty charred letters. Rohde claimed he was burning rubbish, but Brusov dismissed the excuse as 'plainly absurd'. Brusov would have to translate the papers that Rohde was so keen to destroy. But Captain Chernishov warned that he had little time as he was also attached to the NKVD, which was still processing German citizens.

Brusov returned to the castle site now even more wary of Alfred Rohde, although the Soviet mission was determined to make progress. '21 June – all day we were searching and we found Italian and Flemish paintings,' Brusov wrote, noting that among the canvases were works by Andrea del Verrocchio and Brueghel the Younger.

And then, with only a few days before the Brusov/Beliaeva mission was due to return to Moscow, Chernishov appeared with a rough translation of a selection of the documents partly burned by Rohde. According to Brusov's diary, one of them was a draft letter to Berlin written on 2 September 1944, confirming that the Amber Room had been packed into crates, having narrowly escaped an Allied air raid on the night of 27–28 August 1944. Rohde's office in the castle had been flattened and he noted that he was now working from his home in Bickstrasse. Among the other charred fragments were travel permits issued to Rohde, including one for a five-day trip to oversee the evacuation of Countess Keyserlingk's 'furniture, weapons, marble sculpture and 100 paintings' from Rautenburg to Königsberg Castle. There was also correspondence between Rohde and other East Prussian aristocrats, among them Prince Alex Dohna-Schlobitten of Elbing and Countess von Schwerin. There was a passing reference to Soviet pictures from Kiev. Another missive mentioned paintings taken from Soviet museums in Minsk.

Chernishov was puzzled by one document in particular. In it Rohde wrote to Berlin that he had lost the key to an underground palace storage facility called the Hofbunker. Rohde had never mentioned a Hofbunker before. Brusov immediately summoned the German curator. Had the remains he had found in the ruins of the Knights' Hall been placed there as a decoy? Was the Amber Room in fact concealed in this secret Hofbunker?

Rohde was nonchalant. 'He said the Hofbunker was on Steindamm Strasse and that he would lead us there. He said he had now found the key,' Brusov wrote in his diary. The professor and Rohde walked there in the last week of June, accompanied by a young Red Army lieutenant, Ilya Tsirlin, who had been asked to come along as a witness. Near to the corner of the crossing with Rosen Strasse, they found a cellar, four storeys deep, on the left side of the street and a long staircase that led down 'until we found ourselves in a very well-equipped bomb shelter'. This was no ordinary air-raid bunker. Brusov wrote: 'Here were rooms for sleeping and things thrown over the floor. There were paintings and sculptures. We chose two or three of the better things and then left.' Although there was nothing to indicate that the Amber Room had ever been stored here, Brusov still could not give up hope that it was hidden elsewhere.

As Rohde had lied about this Hofbunker, Brusov decided to interrogate him formally. He forced the German curator to sign a confession: 'Destiny of Museum Treasures for Which I was Responsible'. We have it before us.

The German curator's story changed. Rohde admitted that Alfred Rosenberg, Hitler's ideologue and the head of the Einsatzstab Reichleiter Rosenberg (ERR), an art-looting organization, had used Königsberg as a store for plundered art works. In autumn 1941 Rohde had been sent works stolen from the Minsk Museum, 'eighteenth-century paintings from the historical dept, items from the heritage of the tsar's department, including furniture'. All of them 'became the target of Anglo-American aviation attacks in August 1944 and were destroyed' in the eastern wing of Königsberg Castle. In the summer of 1943 Rohde received 'the properties of the museum of Kharkiv, Western and Russian paintings as well as icons'. These had been sent to Wildenhoff, only to be transferred back to Königsberg in January 1945, when the Red Army loomed. Treasures from Kiev arrived in December 1943, 'packed in ninety-eight boxes and sent to Wildenhoff Castle. There were about 800 icons – the most significant collection of icons in the world.' All had now vanished.

But what about the Amber Room? Rohde finally addressed the central issue. 'Yes,' he admitted, he had personally 'received the Amber Room from the Tsarskoye Selo' in November 1941, 'which I placed in Königsberg Castle in a suitable hall'. So the Gift Book (now missing) had been a true and accurate record of all things received at the castle. But, Rohde added, 'four weeks before the Allied air attack' the room had been 'transferred to a safer place to make sure it would not be damaged'. Some time later, Rohde ordered the room be returned to the castle and he 'packed it in boxes and placed it in the north wing of the castle and there [the crates] were preserved until 5 April 1945', along with pieces of furniture belonging to Countess Keyserlingk. The Red Army had by then encircled the city. All plans to evacuate the Amber Room were abandoned, frustrated by time, Soviet bombers and troop movements.

Although Brusov did not reveal it to Rohde, this statement tallied almost exactly with what he had discovered in the Knights' Hall: chair springs and iron locks of German design (the Keyserlingk collection); bronze Russian door hinges and cornice pieces (the Amber Room). The fact that Brusov had also found iron strips of the kind the Germans used to strengthen wooden crates bolstered Rohde's story.

The Soviet team had run out of luck and time. Thankfully, it had not only discovered the depressing truth about the Amber Room but also recovered more than sixty crates of treasures. On the journey back to Moscow, Alexander Brusov prepared his report for SovNarKom.

When TASS called, Brusov must have thought everything was well. The state news agency could not possibly have known about his secret mission, unless SovNarKom had informed them of it. So Brusov gave an erudite interview about his discoveries in Königsberg in the belief that this was what was expected. The Amber Room had been stolen by the Nazis and transferred to Königsberg, where it had been put on display in the castle. It had been taken down and packed into crates shortly before the British bombing raids of 1944 that had levelled much of the city. Dr Alfred Rohde, the director of the Königsberg Castle Museum, had confessed that these crates were in Königsberg Castle until 5 April 1945. An eyewitness had corroborated this story, telling how, the day before, Rohde received a severe reprimand from Erich Koch, the Gauleiter of East Prussia, for having failed to evacuate the Amber Room. Soviet troops smashed the fascist defences two days later, making it impossible for the boxes containing the Amber Room to be moved without being spotted. So they remained in the north wing of the castle and there, in the hours after the German surrender, between 9 and 11 April, they had been destroyed in a terrible fire that gutted the Knights' Hall.

Great discoveries had been made by Soviet investigators in Königsberg, including thousands of Soviet treasures looted by the Nazis, but sadly Brusov had also discovered the hinges and mouldings from the Amber Room. No one knew who was responsible for its destruction. The Nazis, savage and barbaric, under siege? The victorious Red Army, which broke their will and fired the Knights' Hall? This was a war in which both sides had fought bestially, doggedly and unremittingly for a city that appeared as if it was at the heart of the Third Reich, the professor told the man from TASS.

Brusov's TASS interview, published on 13 July 1945, was picked up by the British Ministry of Economic Warfare's Broadcast Unit at Heddon House, who translated it on 27 July:

Confidential. Soviet scientists are carrying out excavations at Königsberg Castle, in order to return the cultural treasures concealed there looted from USSR. In an interview with TASS, A. I. Brusov said that under rubble just over three feet deep they found an inventory of amber from Tsarskoye Selo... The amber panels themselves have not yet been discovered, although treasures from Kiev, Minsk and Kharkiv have been revealed ...[15]

But the Allies would overhear nothing more on the subject. Soviet newspapers didn't follow it up. Tatyana Beliaeva made no public comments on her mission's finding. Within days Brusov had withdrawn into the cloisters of Moscow's museum world, only ever making one more public comment about his mission to Königsberg – but that would not be for another fourteen years. In the meantime his report was overturned and his diary was impounded by the NKVD and exiled to the Leninka. After all, there was no safer place for state secrets than a Soviet public library.

4

We slip-slide through the melting snow along the darkening Dvortsovaya Embankment that runs beside St Petersburg's River Neva. 'Our twentieth century was so ugly,' Our Friend the Professor from Leningrad University had repeatedly complained, as we forced her to revisit the Soviet Union so that we could investigate the Amber Room mystery. 'We had to live through the Stalin times and we now choose to forget them. Instead we study Russia's nineteenth century, an epoch of innovation and elegance, the time of our Grand Duke Vladimir. You must see this side of our history too. I promise it won't be a waste of your time.'

She has been helping us for many weeks and so we are here for her tonight, outside No. 26, a Florentine-style palazzo built by Grand Duke Vladimir for 1 million roubles. He constructed it in 1865 on a site facing the Peter Paul Cathedral that was originally owned by the rear-admiral of Peter the Great's rowing fleet. The professor presents us with a book she has written about this palace. Later we will meet her publisher, she says.

Grand Duke Vladimir, third son of Tsar Alexander II, was Commander of the City Guard and President of the Academy of Arts, the professor says, as she climbs the Italian marble staircase writhing with mermaids and cherubs, its handrail upholstered in purple velvet. 'Our great operatic bass Shaliapin and even Rachmaninov came here to dine,' she says, pulling open the door into a hall of oak panelling painted with Russian fairy tales. Leading us through the state rooms towards the boudoir of Grand Duchess Maria Pavlovna, she throws back another door to reveal a Moorish antechamber with an inlaid cupola.

The professor guides us along a corridor. 'The Grand Duke's exiled son proclaimed himself Russian Emperor Cyril I in August 1924, having convinced himself that the stories of the execution of the Romanovs in Ekaterinburg were true,' she says. 'This vacated palace was handed over to Soviet researchers and thinkers on the request of Maxim Gorky, becoming our House of Scientists.'

There is no time to linger. We are here to attend a meeting of the Club of Scholars of the Russian Academy of Science in honour of a curator from Pavlovsk Palace who died last year. Although we dare not say this to the professor, we hope it won't take too long. 'The people you will meet tonight live, like me, for Russian history. Come,' she says, opening a plain door to what must have been the staff quarters.

Men and women, young and old, in pressed suits with frayed cuffs, their skin translucent, are crammed beside a grand piano that is not needed tonight but fits nowhere else. The room is filled with locksmiths, clocksmiths, painters and hangers, sculptors and carvers, gilders and seamstresses, specialists in Meissen, miniatures and Sèvres, all of them earning no more than twenty dollars a month at Pavlovsk or the Catherine Palace, where they work as curators.

The gathering is called to order and a sturdy woman stands and begins to speak. 'Albina Vasiliava,' the professor whispers. 'Bolshoi Albina we call her. Porcelain curator at Pavlovsk. Great friend of Anatoly Kuchumov.'

Albina delivers a tribute to her recently deceased colleague, who worked for forty-six years in the sculpture department of Pavlovsk. The audience listens reverently to the story of how this curator in 1941 saved palace statues from the Nazis by burying them so deeply that, though the Germans dug, they never discovered them. And then, when the park was liberated in 1944, the curator came back and disinterred every one of them, even though the land was mined, recording the salvage operation in photographs.

'Some sculptures were broken in more than seven places,' Bolshoi Albina says gravely. Heads nod. 'We don't have a projector or a photocopy machine. So I'll pass these things around while I talk.' A ribbon of documents wraps itself around the room, members of the audience lingering over every item. 'We have only these few things, thanks to the curator's daughter,' Bolshoi Albina says as a photograph comes towards

*Anatoly Kuchumov (left) and colleagues from
the Leningrad palaces during the 1950s*

us of a picnic in Pavlovsk park, men in black berets puffing on cigarettes. All of them are enjoying a joke, including the man to the left. We recognize him. Anatoly Mikhailovich Kuchumov. We in the West are so accustomed to photographs of Soviet citizens in fur hats and great coats that it is disconcerting to see these comrades in such relaxed poses. We have caught a glimpse of the private world inhabited by museum curators like Kuchumov and Brusov.

As the lecture comes to an end, the room breaks up into smaller memory floes. A waistcoated clock repairer glides past. 'Can I tell you something?' he asks. 'Do you know why we all cling on, even though we are barely paid and rarely respected? Do you know why we never left? Because of those who came before us. Every night I walk through the halls of Pavlovsk, winding up the clocks in the dark, and I feel the souls of my predecessors watching me.'

We go from group to group, listening, introducing ourselves, meeting as many people as we can, explaining about our search for the Amber Room and how we were trying to find out why the story did not end in Königsberg in 1945 with Professor Alexander Brusov's findings.

Heads shake. Eyebrows are raised. And then a dark-eyed woman shyly introduces herself. Nadezda Voronova. She tells us that her father worked with Kuchumov for decades, helping to research his book on the history of the Amber Room. 'You know very little,' she says. 'I hope you don't mind me being so direct.' Voronova stares at her feet. 'The search didn't end in 1945. Anatoly Mikhailovich went to Königsberg in 1946 to reopen the investigation into the Amber Room. My father told me.'

But Professor Brusov's report had been emphatic: the Amber Room burned in the Knights' Hall between 9 and 11 April 1945, we say. Voronova shrinks back: 'Sorry, I can't help you more. My father is dead. My mother is very old. Alone in our apartment in Tsarskoye Selo. I must leave. It's a long way. On the metro and then the bus.' She looks anxiously around the room and draws closer. 'Try the Pavlovsk library. Kuchumov's papers must be there. He was director of Pavlovsk for many years. Kuchumov knew the truth about the Amber Room.'

Vica Plauda, Kuchumov's granddaughter, had given us the same advice and we had forgotten to follow it up as we had become gripped by Brusov's mission to Königsberg.

The next morning we head for Vitebsk Station and catch a train bound for the Catherine Palace's neighbour on the River Slavyanka, twenty miles south of the city, travelling the route taken by Vladimir Telemakov as he snatched interviews with Anatoly Kuchumov. It is early April and the rain has stopped so the train is crowded with families heading for their dachas.

A thin line of country men and women bustle down the aisle with handfuls of chewing gum and sticking plasters for sale. A raucous band follows, serenading passengers. A ragged veteran of Chechnya rolls along, with an outstretched hand and a missing foot. Every woman slips him roubles. The man sitting next to us tries furiously to get our attention. He motions towards a large glass bottle poking from his khaki pack. He mimes drinking the aquavit with an empty hand, pinging the bottle with his fingernail. 'Going for some fun in the countryside, eh? Don't you know? You only take a whore on the electric train! A lady goes by taxi.'

Half an hour later we are walking across the parkland, passing bronze figures cast after Bonaparte's return from Egypt with pharaonic trophies that started a craze for all things related to the Nile. Pavlovsk. A gift from Catherine the Great to Paul, her strange and ugly son, a boy with a bee-stung nose who managed to reduce Russia from imperial super-power to a vacillating state at war with France, in conflict with Britain, ignored by Austria and embarked upon a perilous expedition into the savage khanates of central Asia on the back of a foolish plan to mount a surprise attack on India. Paul would be assassinated in 1801 by courtiers wielding cushions. But visitors get no sense of this looking at the majestic Classical halls with their reserved beauty and elegant proportions.[1]

We explain the purpose of our visit to the urbane palace director and he summons a sullen librarian, his frame long and thin, hanging beneath a hand-knitted yellow jumper. 'There is not much,' the librarian blurts out, loitering in the doorway but refusing to make eye contact. He produces four books from behind his back and tosses them on to the desk. 'There is nothing else here belonging to Kuchumov. That will interest you,' he says, turning his back and vanishing. Forty-five years employed at the Leningrad palaces, a multitude of postings and offices, a leading role played in the cultural life of the Soviet Union's second city and four second-hand books to his name?

We leave, depressed, and a diminutive curator calls us over and leads us up the back stairs to her office, bursting with furniture that has just returned from an overseas exhibition. 'You are my guests, please.' She points shyly to two chairs labelled 'Tsar Paul I'. We sit and flick through Kuchumov's four books while she scrabbles around on her haunches, searching for the smallest fissure in the patina of a walnut writing desk. 'Put them away,' the curator advises. She stands and we at last recognize her from the meeting at the House of Scientists. She introduces herself as Malinki Albina (Small Albina, not to be confused with Bolshoi, her larger namesake, who also works here).

'There's nothing in those books. I've read them.' She scrapes back her silken grey hair to reveal eyes brimming with stories. 'You know the librarian is writing a book – on Kuchumov. I bet he didn't tell you. But of course it will never see the light of day. No money for books in Russia.'

We think of Telemakov. To return his generosity, we have passed his manuscript on to Our Friend the Professor's publisher, but even he doesn't hold out much hope that he can raise the cash to get it into print.

'And because the librarian knows in his heart that his book is a pipe dream,' Malinki Albina continues, 'he will ensure that you don't get his information. He is young, he can wait.' As we gather our coats, Malinki Albina catches us by surprise, embracing us warmly. 'We are old. Not so beautiful as we were.' She stubs out a cigarette in an onyx Romanov ashtray. 'But we will help you to find Kuchumov's Amber Room files.'

We make our way back into the city. The carbon-thin air smells of bonfires even though we can see none. The source is probably the hiccuping incinerators on the Neva, where the wide waters of the river are pearlescent in the moonlight. A tall ship driven into a low bridge by a sozzled captain has spilt 875,000 gallons of fuel. The entrance to every metro is choked with citizens rushing to get out of the chill. A quick shot of Russki Standard and an ice cream (even in the coldest winter) and then away. The takeaway bottle shops, glazed in armoured Plexiglass, are mobbed by commuters and list under the weight of their security precautions. We are back in Sovetskaya 7.

Midnight. The phone rings halfway down the hall. We sprint to reach it. A clicking and whirring. Then a voice. 'Try the Central State Archive of Literature and Arts.' It is Malinki Albina. 'Make for the Bolshoi Dom. I hear they might have Kuchumov's papers, though I can't get you in.'

The landmark that locates the literature archive today is the nearby Bolshoi Dom, a huge white edifice whose stone walls are not its own. The masonry originates from a cathedral dedicated to sailors who died in the Russo-Japanese war of 1905. The story goes that Stalin had the cathedral demolished and gave the bronze plaque with the names of the drowned to a local butcher as a chopping block. The stone was wheeled in barrows to the builders of the Bolshoi Dom, the new KGB headquarters for Leningrad to where, citizens used to joke, people came from all over to see the view of the Siberian gulags from its windowless basement.

The looming Bolshoi Dom is today the headquarters of St Petersburg's

FSB (the successor to the KGB). But even after we find it, the literature archive is still difficult to locate. Concealed in an alleyway that runs off the broad Ulitsa Shpalernaia, its double front doors are obscured by a burnt-out Lada and the poorly laid tarmac path is sticky, trapping would-be researchers like flies. Although we have applied for a meeting with the director, we are a long way off from seeing any files. An assistant has refused to confirm whether any of Anatoly Kuchumov's papers are actually here. Even if they are, access to them might be restricted. We have been told that archivists require ten years to catalogue every new bequest before its contents can be made available to selected researchers. The director herself may be at her dacha and if so a deputy who has no executive powers will take her place.

Many former Soviet institutions are caught between their desire to profit from the future while being wary of revealing their past. We have been in Russia for several frustrating months now and we need this meeting to work. So we have taken a precaution, bringing with us a letter of recommendation that we have been advised to use if we encounter any obfuscation. We present ourselves to a frothy blonde guard who spurts up from her desk like a bottle of warm Soviet champagne. She leads us up a broad staircase lined with heavily barred windows. In the stairwell, an ancient document lift rises, its file-filled car attached to a steel cable with a reef knot. The steps are bowed, worn down by legions of clerks employed to keep researchers out and their applications in limbo. We are following a vapour trail of raw alcohol that emanates from somewhere up above us, wafting past photographs of a city caught singing, writing and dreaming (despite the regular firestorms): dancer Natalia Makarova thrown bouquets for her performance in *Giselle*, author Daniil Granin lauded after publishing his recollections of the siege of Leningrad; painter Alexander Vokraniv in his studio.

We are shown into an office. On the desk are half a dozen calendars and as many diaries. Another three calendars hang from the walls. Two clocks, three watches and a bedside alarm. A small, elderly woman with sculpted hair enters. Her nails, cardigan and blouse are all ribbons and rose pink, her tiny feet bunched into imposing heels. '*Dobroye Utro,*' she demurs, slipping into her high-backed captain's chair, spinning it around in a ghostly hush. 'Alexandra Vasilevna Istomina, director of the Central State Archive of Literature and Art. Can I be of assistance?'

We plunge into Anatoly Mikhailovich Kuchumov. The director shakes her head, we slip our letter of reference across her desk. Alexandra Vasilevna's painted nail follows every word. It is from Our Friend the Professor's publisher, head of an important St Petersburg house. His company subsidizes the printing of Russian archive catalogues and he strongly recommends that we be allowed entry. A passionate man who had bowed deeply in his long coat when we had met, the publisher recalled Anatoly Kuchumov fondly and is also keen to know if the great curator's private files have survived.

The archive director smiles broadly. She produces three cups of black tea and a box. Out of it tumbles glittering foil wrappers embossed with a Soviet pantheon: red stars, saluting heroes, fairy-tale cottages in the Karelian woods, fiery rockets scorching the firmament, chocolates produced by a company founded by Nadezda Krupskaya, the wife of Lenin.

Alexandra Vasilevna sucks noisily on a Soyuz 10, making it soft and malleable. 'I joined the Leningrad archives in 1950,' she says. 'I have had no other job. I know it is not fashionable to talk about the Stalin times, but I will be honest with you. That time was good. We travelled everywhere in our USSR and we paid very little for everything.'

She spins her chair round to watch the rain falling through a porthole-like window. 'We still have to get used to letting people in. To this *openness*, as you would call it. You are the first *Angliyski* I have ever met. Do you know that the only time I talked with an American was last year? At a social function at his embassy. I watched and I listened. He told me we were soulful, long-suffering, our leaders corrupt.' She tuts and shakes her head. 'They come here like children, quoting Orwell: "Four legs good. Two legs bad."' The director is asking for our understanding before advising us of the archive fees. But is there anything worth buying?

Alexandra Vasilevna begins to calculate, her pink nails tapping on a row of numbers she scribbles on a pad. 'All files will have to hurdle a vetting procedure'. Well, at least there are files. 'Their contents are to be assessed by a censor who will decide what is and is not pertinent. You

The St Petersburg Literature Archive reading room

may come in for one day next week,' the director rules cheerily. In Russia it is never today. And even though she has given us a day pass into the reading room, we are not sure what we have been granted access to.

The following Wednesday the frothy guard barely fizzes as we enter. She knows we know the way. The reading room on the second floor is disappointing, in its ordinariness, with formica-topped tables and red kitchenette chairs. Unloved cheese plants clutter the windowsill. Infused with tobacco smoke, with gloss mocha walls, the room feels like we are in a railway waiting hall. The only other notable feature is Vitalia Petrovna, the buck-toothed superintendent, who is sporting a pair of mohair leg-warmers.

But on our desk is a file wrapped in ribbon. The file contains a batch of Kuchumov's private papers. Our names are the only ones written in the readers' record that has been stuck inside the folder so recently that the spittle to moisten the glue is still damp. Not even Kedrinsky has seen these documents. We are consigned to a far corner with the virgin file. Our Friend the Professor has agreed to translate for us and we begin to read.

A form printed on sugar paper:

Order 88, 1 March 1946, Kuchumov, Anatoly Mikhailovich, former curator of

Amber Room and Chief of Central Stores, Leningrad, is sent on *komandirovat* from 3 March to Moscow, for several questions in connection with searching for museum treasures. Expenses to be paid by GA [General Administration], State Historical Museum.

The form is stamped: Staff Department, Catherine Palace. At the bottom someone has written, 'Kuchumov is to say he is on vacation.'[2]

Komandirovat is 'to be sent on a business trip' and in Soviet times it was a regular feature of working life, but citizens sent on these routine exchanges were never normally instructed to assume a cover story, telling friends and colleagues they were on holiday. This first document seems to confirm what Voronova told us. Anatoly Kuchumov had embarked on a clandestine state-sanctioned mission in 1946.

A letter is attached to the *komandirovat* form, written by the Soviet Ministry of Culture to the Leningrad authorities: '1 March 1946, ref 04-18, to LenGorIsPolKom. Kuchumov, Anatoly Mikhailovich, *komandirovat* to Moscow on orders of SovNarKom. *Komandirovat* also for Tronchinsky, Stanislav Valerianovich. Mission status: Secret.'[3]

The document confirmed that SovNarKom, one of the highest authorities in the Russian Federation, ordered Kuchumov's mission. He was to be accompanied by Stanislav Tronchinsky, who, according to museum workers at the House of Scientists, was a senior cultural bureaucrat stationed in Leningrad. They had met during the evacuation of the palaces in the summer of 1941 and corresponded throughout the war: Kuchumov in Novosibirsk and Tronchinsky in Leninsk-Kuznetsky, in the foothills of the Alatay Mountains.

The next documents are notes, an impromptu diary written in purple ink on graph paper, in a delicate hand that we recognize as Kuchumov's. We have seen his writing before in letters shown to us by his granddaughter.

Kedrinsky has read diary extracts to us. Telemakov has transcribed sections too. But this is the first time we have seen an original part of Kuchumov's diary.

Arriving in Moscow, Kuchumov wrote, he called at the State Historical Museum, looking for Alexander Brusov, the man who had led the previous year's unsuccessful search for the Amber Room. The museum told

Kuchumov that the professor was working from home. When Kuchumov and Tronchinsky eventually found him, they revealed that this was not a courtesy call. They had been ordered to Königsberg to reinvestigate the fate of the Amber Room. They wanted to debrief the professor about his findings. There is no explanation here of why Moscow was at this time questioning the professor's conclusions. But by going to the expense of sending a second mission in search of the Amber Room, the Soviet authorities demonstrated the significance they attached to it.

From Brusov's interview with Kuchumov it is clear that he was nervous. Had Kuchumov and Tronchinsky read his report from July 1945, he asked them? Yes, they had, but was there anything else he would like to add for the record? Brusov thought. He did have something new that might assist them. The professor produced a translation of the correspondence that he had rescued from the bonfire set by Königsberg Castle Museum director Alfred Rohde. The work had been done by V. F. Rumiantseva, an expert in German paintings at Moscow's State Tretiakov Gallery, who had spent nine months reconstructing the charred documents.

Brusov confided in Tronchinsky. There was one event from his 1945 trip that now unsettled him. Kuchumov made notes:

It was the Hofbunker. In September 1944 Rohde reported in a letter to Berlin that he couldn't get into the Hofbunker because he had lost the key. But when we went with Rohde to find this bunker, he said he had a key. But there was no door to unlock. As soon as we got in we were excited and forgot all about Rohde. Suddenly, I realized he was not with us and he only reappeared when we all left. Where had Rohde been? We didn't search the whole bunker on that trip. Were we taken to the right bunker? Were there more rooms in this bunker that we were not shown? That is my regret.

In Brusov's diary we had read a confident account of how he had thoroughly searched this Hofbunker and found nothing connected with the Amber Room, and yet this account was shot through with self-doubt. Brusov must have felt threatened by having his conclusions queried. Kuchumov and Tronchinsky did not commit their impressions to paper. Instead, they thanked the professor. They had to rush if they were to catch the train to Königsberg.[4]

March 1946 was an ominous month for a journey from east to west. On 5 March, Winston Churchill warned an audience in Fulton, Missouri, that 'from Stettin in the Baltic to Trieste in the Adriatic, an iron curtain has descended across the Continent', while Stalin in Moscow responded by blaming the West for a war in which the USSR had lost more souls than anyone else. The General Secretary also warned that the 'Imperialist Camp' was planning to do it all over again.

Kuchumov and Tronchinsky spent the journey to Königsberg poring over the newly translated Rohde letters, several of which concerned the security of treasures for which Rohde was personally responsible.[5] Brusov's latest statement implied that Rohde might have lied to his Soviet captors. The letters that he had tried to destroy might provide an explanation.

The earliest was written by Rohde on 2 September 1944, the day after a second wave of British air raids on Königsberg, and was addressed to Dr Gerhard Zimmerman at the Kaiser Friedrich Museum in Berlin. 'In spite of the destruction of Königsberg Castle with explosives and incendiary devices... the art collection up to now did not lose any important items,' Rohde wrote. 'Those items which we are keeping from your collections survived in the cellars without any damage.' Next he mentioned the Hofbunker, to which 'we have lost the keys to its iron door and so cannot get inside'. Brusov's story.

Kuchumov underlined in red crayon this paragraph and the next, in which Rohde asked for an urgent message to be relayed to his superior, Dr Ernst Gall, Director of Administration for State Palaces and Gardens in Berlin. 'To Herr Dr Director: there is no damage to the Amber Room at all apart from to the *sockel-platten*.' While the twenty-two large and medium-sized amber panels, the most important parts of the room, had survived the air raid intact, this letter confirmed that six of the twenty-four sections of *sockel-platten* or skirting board had been destroyed. The larger amber panels had obviously been kept separately, perhaps in the so-called Hofbunker, Kuchumov reasoned in his notes.

The second category of correspondence was letters that Rohde had dashed off immediately after the Allied air raids. Believing that the city was now a target, he tried to find new storage facilities in the East

Prussian countryside. He must have sat with a map of provincial castles, Kuchumov speculated in his notes, calculating which ones were furthest from the front as well as the most bomb-resistant.

Rohde's first letter, written on 6 September 1944, was to Prince Alex Dohna-Schlobitten. Prince Alex's castle (Schlobitten is today Slobity, in Poland) was a Teutonic fortress fifty miles south-west of Königsberg and at the time seemed far from advancing Red Army units. Rohde would have known that the prince was not only 'anti-Bolshevik' but a patriot and a veteran of Stalingrad, where he had served with the German 60th Mechanized Infantry Division. Rohde wrote, 'Art treasures and also the Amber Room should be moved to a less dangerous place, so I am asking you to give two to three rooms of your castle.' This letter confirmed that Rohde was looking to evacuate the Amber Room. Kuchumov underlined the passage in red and put a question mark against one word, 'moved'.

*Prince Alex
Dohna-Schlobitten*

Rohde sent a second letter on 6 September 1944 to Countess von Schwerin, advising her that he had already dispatched a shipment of art works to Wildenhoff, her country house twenty-five miles south-west of Königsberg. Kuchumov made a note. He needed to clarify what this shipment consisted of. There seemed to be a lot more possible hiding places emerging from the Rohde letters than Brusov had investigated in 1945.

With the front advancing by the day and Königsberg under threat of further raids, Rohde needed assistance quickly. But Prince Alex replied on 11 September: 'The cellar rooms are very wet so they can't be used for placing art treasures. One room that is more or less dry is not very big. I can give you this space but I am afraid that it will not do for the Amber Room.' The panels were unwieldy and required a sizeable hall to store them in. They had not gone to Schlobitten Castle.

Countess von Schwerin's reply was not in the bundle that Brusov gave to Kuchumov, but from a second letter Rohde wrote to her on 17 October 1944 he noted that the unnamed art shipment arrived safely at Wildenhoff and that the German curator planned to inspect it in the last week of October. Maybe the Amber Room had gone there.

But due to the fragmentary nature of the letters saved by Brusov from the fire, Kuchumov and Tronchinsky found Rohde's movements difficult to follow. What did this partial document, sent to 'Very Respectable Herr Lau' on 21 October, mean? 'I would be deeply grateful if you could give me notice if something changes in our plan and if the packed boxes have to be moved again. I have to tell my superiors. At the moment I don't know if I can go any further than Insterburg.' Kuchumov underlined the section in red. There was no address for Herr Lau and no other reference to him in the bundle. Kuchumov drew a circle around Insterburg, noting that it was fifty miles east of Königsberg. He also knew that by January 1945, three months after Rohde had written to Herr Lau, the town fell to the Red Army. If the Amber Room had been evacuated there, then the Red Army would surely have found it.

The Soviet team analysed travel permits made out in Rohde's name, from which they fished dates, times and places. On 18 October, the day after his second letter to Countess von Schwerin, Rohde received permission to travel to her castle, Wildenhoff. On 2 November he was issued with a permit to embark on a five-day trip to the home of Countess Sabina Keyserlingk in Rautenburg, fifty-five miles north-east of Königsberg, near Tilsit (today Sovetsk in Kaliningrad Province). The outcome of this journey was confirmed in a letter to her, written by Rohde on 10 November, three days after he returned, in which he advised the Countess that he had brought from her abandoned manor to Königsberg 'two cars' of art works. Rohde's mission to find a new hiding place for the Amber Room, Kuchumov noted, was complicated by the need to evacuate art works from country estates belonging to aristocrats who had already fled East Prussia.

Gauleiter Erich Koch, the highest authority in East Prussia, signed the next permit, issued on 8 November 1944. He gave Rohde a mandate 'to take any measures in guarding, moving and evacuating any pieces of art from Prussia'. Clearly the German curator was at the centre of the Nazi art establishment in East Prussia and treasures were being shipped in every direction.

Rohde must have barely had time to catch his breath. On 15 November he wrote to the Ministry of Culture in Berlin about plans to evacuate Soviet art works from one East Prussian safe house to another. On 26 November he received orders to travel to Castle Binanen to transfer another art collection back to Königsberg. But it was the permit issued on 1 December 1944 that caught Kuchumov's attention, authority to travel to Saxony, several hundred miles to the south-east, in the heart of the Reich. In the bundle was a report of this mission: 'My trip from 3 to 10 December 1944 in Saxony'. Rohde had visited two castles, Wechselburg and Kriebstein, both west of Dresden, and concluded that they were secure and watertight hiding places, the perfect locations in which to secure 'irreplaceable treasure'.

A picture was emerging. Here in Rohde's letters was clear evidence that art stored in East Prussia was evacuated further west by the Nazis before the Soviet advance. It was possible that Brusov had been too quick to conclude that the Amber Room had been destroyed in Königsberg. The last letter in the bundle gave Kuchumov further hope. It was from Rohde to the Ministry of Culture in Berlin and was dated 12 January 1945: 'I have been packing the Amber Room into containers and they are being sealed. The moment is ready for these panels to be evacuated to Saxony and more correctly they can be sent to Wechselburg in Rochlitz.'⁶ The letter appeared to conflict with Rohde's statement to Brusov that the Amber Room had remained in Königsberg Castle until 5 April 1945. Kuchumov concluded that Rohde had lied.

Kuchumov and Tronchinsky began compiling a thirty-three-point list of questions for Alfred Rohde, comparing his statements to Brusov with his letters. Tronchinsky would begin the interrogation light-heartedly with information that was only really of interest to fellow academics: the arrival of the room at Königsberg Castle and its display there. He would create the impression that he was an amiable party man marking time. Kuchumov calculated that if Tronchinsky could make himself small in the face of Rohde's arrogance, then the German would be unable to resist bragging to his poor Soviet cousin. The plump Russian figure in spectacles, Kuchumov, would remain in the background throughout the interrogation, a silent, brooding force who would conceal the fact that he was running the operation.

On 19 March 1946 their train pulled in. General Vasilev, one of Königsberg's commanders, met Kuchumov and Tronchinsky at the station and insisted on giving them a tour. 'The only buildings that were standing were single cottages at the end of streets, villas in the middle of the rubble that were now occupied by the Central Commandant and the Narkomats [representatives of the People's Commissariat],' Kuchumov wrote. 'One could only walk down certain streets at certain times, depending on the roster of demolition. There were about 25,000 German refugees that we could see living in cellars and ruined buildings in the suburbs.'[7]

Kuchumov and Tronchinsky were so on edge on the first night that, rather than resting in the city's only hotel, they walked two miles in the freezing dark to the ruins of the castle. Early the next morning they were back again, taking photographs of locations and masonry, plotting their approach like detectives at the scene of a crime.

They could not resist taking a few pictures for themselves, two men standing like mice before the forbidding hulk of the castle's blasted Albrecht Gate. Kuchumov pasted them into an album of black cartridge paper and wrote captions in chalk. This book, which has found its way into the literature archive, has been opened so infrequently that the tracing paper dividers are still pristine, as if the album had just been bought at the stationery counter of the Dom Knigi bookshop on Nevsky Prospekt. We gently turn the pages but we are not allowed to photograph it.[8]

Two beaming men in heavy tweed trench coats and worn leather shoes, their socks rolled over their trousers, Tronchinsky in a black beret, Kuchumov wearing a pork pie hat, both of them overshadowed by the mountains of rubble that they would soon have to clear. In another frame they sit by the remains of the Knights' Hall, serious, composed, Kuchumov carrying a small leather attaché case. And in a third and a fourth, both men pose awkwardly before unrecognizable heaps of bricks that rise up far above their heads. In all of the pictures the two men wear identical suits, given to them in Moscow to make them inconspicuous. Two grown men in a post-war hell-hole, walking everywhere like shelled peas, their unnaturally pressed suits and white shirts contrasting with their undertaker's ties.

Dear Katya, We are here in Königsberg for the third day. One and a half days have been taken up with bureaucracy. We found the grave of Immanuel Kant, remaining miraculously intact among absolute ruin, and visited a house where Richard Wagner had once stayed. We have now been allowed into the ruined castle. We begin to search through the rubble.[9]

Several documents in our file are informal letters like this one, written by Stanislav Tronchinsky, who, despite being on a covert mission, obviously kept no secrets from his wife. Every three days he had sent an extraordinary missive to Katya in Leningrad, a fact that Kuchumov only learned of in the 1960s when Tronchinsky's widow gave the letters to him to assist in the research of his book about the Amber Room. The ambiguity and innuendo in them suggests that Tronchinsky was aware that a censor would read them, but he was presumably senior enough within the party not to be afraid of recriminations.

Kuchumov wrote no such letters to his wife, Anna Mikhailovna. He confided only to his diary. Kuchumov is emerging as dogged and patriotic, putting to one side his personal life, while conducting the business of the state. Everything he typed went straight to the Ministry of Culture in Moscow, pages of reports, the carbon copies of which are here in these files.[10]

'First, we have made a detailed inspection of the castle cellars and tunnels that lead out of its precincts,' he wrote. We can imagine Kuchumov at his hotel dressing table, squinting in the candlelight as everyone else slumbered. Wearing his Moscow-issue black suit, his fleshy body pressing at its seams, the itchy woollen fabric taking on a sheen having wriggled with the curator over broken beams and masonry. Kuchumov stabbed at the typewriter keys, making frequent mistakes, which he hatched over with Xs.

The underground passageways were numerous and beguiling, Kuchumov noted. 'Many of them were flooded and all of them were dangerous.' Some had even been sabotaged, the water electrified or poisoned. Others were simply crumbling and filled with the smell of gangrene, the gasses of decomposition that could kill a man as easily. 'Forty Soviet specialists died,' Kuchumov wrote without comment, as if forty men killed in one incident was an unremarkable fact. Given what we know about the culture of checking, cross-checking and counter-checking in Moscow then, the incident was certainly investigated by another agency. We have no idea whether these deaths were connected in any way to the search for the Amber Room.

When Kuchumov and Tronchinsky began inspecting the ruined castle itself, they immediately made discoveries. Kuchumov wrote to Moscow: 'In different parts of the structure that was burned and destroyed we found a great number of fragments of furniture from the Catherine and Alexander palaces (including furniture from the Great Hall, the Karelian Reception Room of Alexander I, the Chinese Room and many others).' Then, in the East Wing: 'Near the main gate, we discovered big bronze locks that had once belonged to the Lyons Hall of the Catherine Palace.'

All of these pieces had been found within a few days and yet Brusov claimed in his report to have made a thorough search of the castle. But perhaps it was not entirely surprising, as Brusov was an archaeologist with no specialist knowledge about the Leningrad collections. And he had been working just weeks after the German surrender.

According to Tronchinsky's secret letters home, he and Kuchumov soon discovered more:

Dear Katya, we have found fragments of the Catherine Palace floor. Broken furniture from the Bolshoi Hall and the Chinese Drawing Room, as well as a cabinet from Alexander I. Anatoly Mikhailovich has to be careful. He was in the east wing when he fell through two floors, masonry pouring down on his head, he was only stopped from crashing into the cellars and killing himself by an old oak beam.

Kuchumov wrote to Moscow: 'While surveying the castle, in a small ground-floor room in one of the semi-ruined towers in the middle of the south wall, we also found among the rubbish more copies of Rohde's official correspondence.' One of the letters was from General George von Küchler, who in 1942 had replaced General Wilhelm von Leeb as commander of Army Group North, which was barracked in the Catherine Palace. Küchler asked his 'good friend Alfred Rohde' about the safe arrival of the Amber Room 'that had been sent to East Prussia'. This new letter proved that Rohde had some useful and influential connections.

Kuchumov and Tronchinsky systematically worked their way through the north wing. The Knights' Hall was to be the focus of their investigation. Kuchumov wrote to Moscow: 'Here, according to Rohde, was where the Amber Room was located at different times.' Here too Kuchumov and Tronchinsky quickly found items that Brusov had missed. Kuchumov wrote: 'Our detailed searches of layers of soot, garbage and debris that

Entrance to the Knight's Hall of Königsberg Castle

covered the stone floor of the Knights' Hall where the Amber Room had possibly been burned have revealed gilded pieces of wood varnish and great amounts of furniture springs and iron parts from German wardrobes.'[11] Kuchumov concluded that he had discovered more of Countess Keyserlingk's incinerated furniture collection – pieces that Rohde had told Brusov had been packed beside the Amber Room.

Hinges, cornices, iron strips. Kuchumov ventured that if the entire Amber Room had burned here then there would be far more evidence still lying in the rubble. There had to be something left of the twenty-two large and medium-sized amber wall panels, the four amber frames that contained the four Florentine stone mosaic pictures and the stone mosaics themselves, commissioned by Catherine the Great.

Then, on 22 March, Tronchinsky wrote to his wife that Kuchumov had found something significant, something that they could directly connect to the Amber Room: 'Dear Katya, We found copper frames from the stone mosaics, but only three of them. Here they were, literally under my feet.'[12]

Kuchumov made the formal report to Moscow:

Near the entrance to the [Knights] Hall, where the staircase runs, covered in three layers of ash, totally burned and discoloured, we have found the mosaic pictures. Examining the profile of the bronze frames and the small decorative tendrils of wire that surrounded the stone pieces one could confirm that they were of Italian production and therefore the ones that once decorated the Amber Room.[13]

The findings appeared to bolster Brusov's theory that the Amber Room had burned. But Kuchumov argued the reverse. Having learned about the mechanics of the Amber Room while researching his book, Kuchumov advised Moscow that he had left all four small stone mosaics in the Catherine Palace in June 1941, and only three had now turned up in the rubble of the Knights' Hall.

The stone mosaics could be detached from the amber panels and the fourth might have survived elsewhere. If this fourth stone mosaic had been packed and stored elsewhere by the Nazis, then surely the possibility existed that the amber panels and thick carved frames that had comprised the Amber Room were still concealed alongside the fourth mosaic, in another location.

Space. When it came to them, Kuchumov wrote that both men burst out laughing. Kuchumov had memorized the Amber Room's original dimensions – a dozen large panels twelve feet high, ten medium panels just over three feet high and twenty-four sections of amber skirting board. He knew that the large amber wall panels could not be broken down into smaller pieces and so, when they had been packed up by Alfred Rohde in January 1945, they would have required large, cumbersome crates. Kuchumov wrote to Moscow:

More important than the number of stone mosaics is the issue of size. If we suppose that these stone mosaics were packed together with the large amber panels being still mounted upon them, all of which burned in the inferno [in the Knights' Hall], then the cases for the panels and mosaics would have had to be vast. And yet this place, between the two doors and the windows where we have found the three stone mosaics, is cramped and tiny.

Tronchinsky and Kuchumov studied the pile of ash on the floor before them. In the searing temperatures, the stone mosaics had been perfectly preserved in a neat stack, although they were now more fragile than a spider's web. The picture on the uppermost mosaic was even discernible, until Kuchumov touched it and it imploded in a puff of ash. Kuchumov wrote to Moscow:

If the mosaics had been stacked still hooked on to the amber panels, a layer of amber panel with its wooden backing, a layer of stone mosaic, and so on and so on, when the panels burned individual amber pieces would have separated as the glue that bound them melts at low temperatures, and the board that backed the panels ignites at around the same mark. Some trace of the amber, now loose and insulated by the stone mosaics, would have remained trapped. But we found nothing.

Nothing. It was inconceivable that not a single piece of amber from more than a dozen twelve-foot-high amber wall panels, each one of which was made up of thousands of slivers of the resin, had survived. In addition, Kuchumov advised Moscow that the Amber Room was decorated with twenty-four mirrored pilasters that, according to *Pravda*, had been marked as received in the castle's Gift Book. Kuchumov wrote to Moscow: 'Above these pilasters were twenty-four bronze wall chandeliers. Inspecting the ash we did not find a single trace of bronze or mirrored pilaster.'

Three mosaics not four. A tiny space in which to store only the smallest crates. No bronze or mirror fragments to be found in the ash. Nothing sandwiched between the stone mosaics. Kuchumov's reasoning was at times hard to follow but he argued that the evidence – much of which he had decided not to burden Moscow with – pointed to the Amber Room having been packed up and stored in multiple locations, or at the very least not solely in the Knights' Hall, where Dr Rohde and Brusov had said it was. Rohde's correspondence made it clear that the Germans had separated parts of the Amber Room as early as August 1944, when six *sockel-platten*, part of the amber skirting board, had been destroyed by fire in the south wing, while all other pieces had survived.

On 25 March 1946 Tronchinsky wrote again to his wife: 'Dear Katya, We have to work very hard indeed. We walk and run each day about six miles. We have revealed something.' But he did not tell his wife exactly what they had discovered.

But three days later, when he wrote again, he was in an altogether different mood: '28 March, Dear Katya, Yesterday was a week since we arrived in this city. We have walked now about 90 miles. Results of our work are small. We did not find the main thing: the mystery of the Amber Room has not been revealed to us.' Tronchinsky had good reason to be deflated. '[Rohde], the castle director is dead. He died three months ago. We cannot find any other collaborators.'

The man at the centre of the Soviet inquiry. The well-plotted thirty-three questions. The mystery of the evacuation to Saxony. Kuchumov and Tronchinsky were to have squeezed Alfred Rohde hard. No one had seen Rohde since December 1945. Not General Vasilev. No one at the NKVD headquarters in the Moscow Hotel. None of the SMERSH operatives. It was thought to be impossible to get in or out of the city and yet Alfred

Rohde, together with Ilse, his wife, and Lotti and Wolfgang, his daughter and son, had vanished.

A German informant claimed that they had died from malnutrition. Kuchumov found this hard to believe as the Soviets had been feeding Rohde emergency rations to keep him alive. '*Werwolfs*, members of the secretive Nazi resistance, had taken or executed them to conceal the secret of the Amber Room,' an anonymous letter that found its way to Kuchumov stated.[14] He dismissed this out of hand. Tronchinsky knew that Germans who offered to collaborate had been hanged and that there were now ten such incidents under investigation. However, Kuchumov conducted his own inquiry and wrote to Moscow: 'I have learned that Alfred Rohde committed suicide. His wife is also dead. That's what people in the hospital have told me.' But Kuchumov also admitted in the same report that he had been unable to find the graves, the post-mortem reports or the death certificates. No doctors in Königsberg could recall treating Rohde or any of his family. This was a city living in terror where it was virtually impossible to keep a secret, a city that had dematerialized along with Alfred and Ilse Rohde and their children.

But Tronchinsky and Kuchumov struggled on and on 1 April Tronchinsky wrote to his wife:

Dear Katya, we once again have found tracks of the Amber Room... If the room was demolished... it was not here in Königsberg [Castle]... We have also found important furniture from the Amber Room... and are about to go on and follow the trail left by the Amber Room... We shall go to Moscow on 10 or 12 April.

Kuchumov wrote to Moscow that he and Tronchinsky had located three of Rohde's close associates. Paul Feyerabend, owner of the Blutgericht, the Blood Court historical restaurant that Kuchumov noted with distaste was 'located for 200 years in the old Teutonic Order's torture chambers beneath the Knights' Hall', had come forward claiming he was a Communist who had been forced to conceal his party card. Feyerabend claimed to have witnessed a puzzling event in July 1944. The interrogations were attached.

Blutgericht, the Nazi restaurant located in the former torture chambers of Königsberg Castle

Feyerabend. Statement 1, 2 April 1946: July 1944 – two cars entered the castle yard, heavily loaded with cases. Small cases among the larger load were then placed on the ground. But the rest, the huge cases, were left on the cars. I asked Rohde what were these gigantic cases and Rohde said to me they were the amber walls from Russia.[15]

Feyerabend described how Rohde was called to an urgent meeting with Dr Helmut Will, the Oberbürgermeister or Lord Mayor of Königsberg. Kuchumov noted: 'Find Helmut Will.'

Feyerabend said:

Following the meeting, the cars, still loaded down, left the yard and Rohde then arrived at the Blutgericht restaurant to order a case of wine from me, telling me that he would be away for several days. He came back three weeks later and I saw him again. Rohde told me that he had been to a big country estate. Some time later he told me that his mission concerned the amber hall from Russia, which had been packed on these cars.

Following Kuchumov's prompts, Tronchinsky tore into Feyerabend. There was no evidence that Rohde had made any trips out of Königsberg until the air raids of 27–28 August 1944. Rohde had told Brusov that after he had dismantled the Amber Room in July 1944, it had been stored in the cellars of the castle's south wing. What was the date of Rohde's expedition with the room? 'July 1944,' Feyerabend insisted.

The restaurant owner was asked to think hard about his statement, but he had nothing to add or take away. He could, however, recall other conversations he had had with Rohde after that date: 'Rohde told me many times that the room should and would have gone to Saxony in the end, but due to logistical problems in March [1945], it had not been moved there. Gauleiter Erich Koch had wanted it evacuated to Saxony too, but the tight military situation would not allow it.' But was Feyerabend in a position to know, Kuchumov asked? He might have poured wine for the élite but did he drink with them? How likely was it that a man of Rohde's intellect would trade secrets with a restaurateur?

The interrogation continued but the transcript before us abruptly finishes. We make a note to find the missing pages.

The next interrogation was of Ernst Schaumann, a war artist and friend of Rohde. He described Rohde as an amber expert. Rohde had written a seminal book known as *Bernstein* in 1937.[16] 'Must get a copy,' noted Kuchumov.

In April 1942 Rohde had also prepared an article illustrated with photographs for *Pantheon*, a German art digest, to celebrate the Amber Room going on display in the second-floor gallery in the south wing of Königsberg Castle.[17] 'We must get this too,' Kuchumov wrote. Schaumann came up with the name of a new witness for the Soviets to find: Jurgen Sprecht, a Königsberg restorer who had been sponsored by Rohde to study in Berlin. 'He was later assigned to work on the Amber Room,' Schaumann told Tronchinsky. 'Find Sprecht,' Kuchumov wrote.

Schaumann recalled one notable conversation he had had with Rohde: 'After my return from France in October 1944, I asked Dr Rohde about the destiny of the amber and picture collections,' Schaumann told Tronchinsky. 'He answered that by order of the authorities in Berlin they were packed and transferred to safe places at estates in

East Prussia and Saxony. Later, at the time when Königsberg was surrounded by the Red Army, Rohde repeated the claim.' Tronchinsky lost his cool. Feyerabend and Schaumann could not both be right. The Amber Room was either evacuated or not. One of them was lying. Kuchumov said nothing. He could not decide if Schaumann was credible or confused.

Finally, Otto Smakka was called. Smakka worked as a translator for the fisheries in Königsberg. He confirmed the Amber Room had been on display. 'Yes, I saw it in the summer of 1942. It had obviously suffered in transportation. Several pieces of amber were either stolen or lost. Even the printed information sheets mentioned that parts were missing in the walls. It occurred to me that they were probably stolen.' The vast and opulent room that we have in our mind's eye, candles blazing, walls glowing, as it appears in the glass plate we were shown by Kuchumov's granddaughter, was not the Amber Room that had reached Königsberg in the freezing winter of 1941. Since then, Kuchumov had established that three of the four Florentine stone mosaics had been destroyed, as had parts of the amber skirting board. Kuchumov noted that the scale of the Amber Room they were searching for was significantly different from the one installed in the Catherine Palace. But it did not affect his general conclusions that the space in the Knights' Hall, where the stone mosaics had been found, was not large enough to have accommodated the amber panels themselves.

Only one man, Alfred Rohde, knew the truth and he could no longer speak for himself. Kuchumov began to analyse the character of the German curator. He considered the letter sent by General Küchler, the commander of Army Group North. Had Rohde actually sought out the Amber Room, requesting troops stationed beside it to transport the treasure to Königsberg? Then there was Rohde's text book, *Bernstein*, published seven years before Operation Barbarossa began, and the scholarly article he wrote for *Pantheon*, apparently celebrating the arrival of the room in Königsberg. Kuchumov wrote: 'Rohde dreamed for a long time of having the Amber Room in his collection. He expressed more than once his regret that it had left Prussia, that the Prussian King had made a great mistake in giving it to Russian barbarians.' Why would such a man leave his greatest treasure to the mercy of an army besieging the city, Kuchumov reasoned?

He concluded: 'The described circumstances force us to reject the claim of Dr Rohde that was treated as the truth by Professor Brusov about the destruction of the Amber Room in the fire in the Knights' Hall of the Castle.' Kuchumov was convinced that the answers lay outside Königsberg.

He began to research the four months leading up to the fall of the city:

By mid-January the railway connections between Königsberg and the rest of Germany had been cut off. So if they had used the road rather than the sea, they could only have taken the clumsy and heavy crates as far as some location within East Prussia. Moving the Amber Room to Germany by air or sea could have been done later, until mid-March, but these were the most dangerous ways possible, taking into account the proximity of the front and the domination of our air forces.

Kuchumov compiled a wish-list of Rohde's former friends and colleagues to interrogate. Where was Oberbürgermeister Helmut Will? The NKVD reported that he had disappeared. Königsberg Schlossoberinspektor Friedrich Henkensiefken? He was said to have fled to Germany. A 'Dr Gert', known to have been close to Rohde? No one even knew his full name. Erich Koch, the Gauleiter of East Prussia? There had been no confirmed sightings of him since March 1945. Jurgen Sprecht, the restorer and amber craftsman? Sprecht did eventually turn up. He had been held in a Soviet detention camp but was discovered hanged in circumstances that were still under investigation. It was a criminal inquiry. 'Bodies, bodies,' Kuchumov wrote gloomily. 'Dead and missing.'

It would be virtually impossible for the two men to find these witnesses without outside help, since millions of Germans, soldiers and civilians, were in flight – a mass migration of half of Europe. Kuchumov wrote to Moscow for permission to place a letter in *Vo Slavu Rodini* (For the Glory of the Motherland), a journal read by Soviet soldiers in the field. 'Help Us Restore the Museums of Leningrad', the letter was entitled, and it contained Kuchumov's exhortation for 'soldiers, sergeants and officers to advise us through the editors of locations where valuables of historical and artistic significance might be found so that they can take their place again in our museum'.[18]

'We shall go to Moscow on 10 or 12 April,' Tronchinsky wrote to his wife, and he and Kuchumov caught a train to the capital. They went back to Professor Brusov, who was still working from home. They discussed the chaos of Königsberg: how there were only potatoes to eat; the depravity of the fascists. And then Kuchumov began to probe. He was confused, he said. Witnesses claimed that the Amber Room had been removed from the castle in July or August 1944, while Rohde had told Brusov that the room was concealed in the south wing. Kuchumov handed Brusov the statements by Feyerabend and Schaumann. The professor read in silence before defending himself.

Schaumann had got it wrong. When Rohde had talked about 'the amber and picture collections' being evacuated he was not referring to the Amber Room but to the Albertus-University's scientific amber collection. It was the most famous in the world. Brusov had located part of it, tens of thousands of pieces, and, judging by the communiqué he had sent to Moscow, he regarded it as the crowning achievement of his mission. 'Claims he found nearly all of the amber collection. Catalogued it. Sent everything to Moscow. Has witnesses,' Kuchumov wrote. 'Why, then, did this collection never turn up in Moscow?'

Brusov became agitated. Why was he being criticized given that he had found so much while enduring such appalling conditions? Was he being accused of theft, or lying, or treason? What had they found, the professor demanded, of Tronchinsky and Kuchumov? Nothing, they said, as they left.

This is what they wrote to SovNarKom in Moscow:

The conclusion is self-evident. The Amber Room was kept and hidden in safety in a place that was without doubt familiar to Rohde and the version he told [Brusov] about the destruction of the Amber Room in the fire in the Knights' Hall distracted the attention of the Beliaeva/Brusov commission from future searches.

The mistake of Professor Brusov was that he believed easily the words of

Rohde, taking as truth the words of this museum co-worker, forgetting that he was dealing with a Nazi fanatic. Brusov didn't know the Amber Room or details of its decoration, so he couldn't check the veracity of Rohde's words by digging in the area where the fire occurred and so he couldn't tell truth from fiction. The most direct and best way to know the location of the Amber Room has been lost to us – Dr Alfred Rohde – but we now have the opportunity to gather additional information from former workers of the Königsberg Castle Museum.[19]

Kuchumov submitted a list of names of those he wished to interrogate to SovNarKom and applied for a special permit to travel to Berlin.

5

After lunch at Kolobok restaurant, another file is waiting for us at the literature archive, an enticing box three times the size of the previous file. No one looks up as we scrape our chairs across the parquet floor, even though the reading room is bustling with men and women in white dustcoats. All of them are preoccupied, armed with small pencil erasers, which they feverishly apply to sections of files, as if rubbing out entire episodes from history.

We spring open the box and pick through the contents, but there is no response from Moscow to Kuchumov's list of German eyewitnesses to interrogate or a reaction to his taking apart of Brusov. No instructions or orders. Only greetings cards.[1]

We double-check the readers' record slip. Our names are freshly inked on it. But when we examine the file number, we see that it is not the one we have requested. The only sign of Vitalia Petrovna, the reading-room supervisor, is a lukewarm cup of tea and a trail of biscuit crumbs across her desk. So we walk down past the photographs of Makarova, Granin and Vokraniv to the director's office, where we find Alexandra Vasilevna Istomina studying the rain falling outside her window.

'We must assess what is pertinent to your research. We have decided that certain files are extraneous.' Alexandra Vasilevna smiles weakly. 'Well, of course you may resubmit your application. Errors are sometimes made. Decisions faulty. I can't vouch for all of my staff. We are dreadfully overworked.' We nod and she fumbles under the desk. A bell rings in the corridor. Vitalia Petrovna, pops her head around the door, wiping her mouth, only to be hit by a raging gust of Russian invective.

Alexandra Vasilevna spins back to us on her chair's silky castors: 'It takes two days to locate a new file normally. The archive for which I am responsible is vast. There are several million files to pick through.' She motions up to the rafters and we nod appreciatively. 'But if you pay double rate, yes, pay a double rate, you can make an emergency submission. If I recall, an emergency submission comes back in only twenty-four hours. Is that right, Vitalia Petrovna? Come back tomorrow. I will extend your readers' tickets for three hours in the morning.' Everything is forbidden but all things are possible. We have no choice but to wait another night.

The next morning, the same file of greetings cards is waiting for us on the table and the director is not expected back for several days. We might as well read what we have.

'In celebration of your eighteenth anniversary as a Leningrad Museum Worker, from your friends and collaborators': this first greetings card is illustrated with a sketch of a scene in a library; rows of desks, and sitting at one a bespectacled researcher, sandwiched between two great towers of files. It looks like the Bolshoi Reading Hall in the National Library of Russia. The next card shows the same man in a black suit, pushing a weighty wooden wheelbarrow of books, a pork-pie hat balancing on

Caricature of Anatoly Kuchumov at his desk researching the fate of missing Leningrad palace treasures

*Caricature of Anatoly Kuchumov with a wheelbarrow of books marked
'archives, extracts, documents' in which he researched the reconstruction
of missing treasures from the Leningrad palaces*

top of them, their spines embossed with the words 'Archives', 'Extracts',
'Documents'.

'Upon your 47th birthday': a card edged in red from 27 May 1959.
Here is another ink drawing of a plump man in a black suit striding
purposefully across the page, a scholar with a forelock and little round
glasses struggling with a tome under each arm inscribed *'arkivie'*. Falling
all around him, against a backdrop of the Leningrad palaces, are multi-
coloured parachutes that, on closer inspection, cradle pianos, chairs and
candelabras, the returning treasures of the tsars. Inside is written: 'To
Anatoly Mikhailovich from your grateful comrades at the Pavlovsk and
Catherine palaces.'

1962: 'On the occasion of your 50th birthday, 27 May.' A lilac card
with gold trim. Inside is a watercolour of a figure swathed in a blue toga,
riding a chariot accompanied by a phalanx of maidens in lilac robes. Small
photographs of faces have been pasted on to all of the torsos. The chari-
oteer is Anatoly Kuchumov, his sylphs curators at the Leningrad palaces,
including several faces that we recognize from the House of Scientists.

That year Kuchumov also celebrated his thirtieth anniversary as a
Leningrad Museum Worker, and greetings were more formal: 'From the

Workers of the Western European Art Department at the State Hermitage; heartfelt congratulations to you. We fully appreciate your great knowledge and Soviet patriotism, your acute taste and good eye that is so important.' Eight members of staff from the Alexander Palace also sent salutations: 'Many people died and were scattered to the winds by war. But we were all joined by former times to the Alexander Palace, where you were once director. We thank you, Anatoly Mikhailovich.'

The pile is several inches deep and it takes us all morning to pick through to the bottom of the box. One card catches our attention. It is from Kaliningrad, the Soviet name for Königsberg, given to the city in October 1947 following the death of Mikhail Kalinin, chairman of the Presidium of the Supreme Soviet. Sent on 27 October 1975, the card is decorated with a bouquet of blue irises and contains the dedication: 'Dear Anatoly Mikhailovich, from our hearts congratulations on your honourable notation. We wish you health, creativity and success and we invite you as our guest, members of the Expedition, Chairman Storozhenko.' An expedition in Königsberg. It may have been connected to the Amber Room. We note the name of the chairman, Storozhenko.

There follows a dedication written by Valeria Bilanina, the vice-director of Pavlovsk Palace, on 27 November 1977:

> Why, my brother, are you lying in bed?
> You have left us in trouble and now this year is nearly finished.
> I can hardly carry my burden alone.
> When it is all over we will all lie in rows.
> Kuchumov, Kuchumov, Kuchumov!
> Take notice, you must have more courage and instead of medicine you
>   must have good health and return to our circle.
> Through tears, Valeria Bilanina.

The box finishes with a gift from Albina Vasiliava, porcelain expert at Pavlovsk, surely the same Bolshoi Albina who gave the lecture at the House of Scientists: a hand-painted silk pennant.

Plaudits, caricatures, tears and a pennant. None of them can help us resolve what became of Anotoly Kuchumov's Amber Room investigation.

We wonder if any of Kuchumov's adoring colleagues knew about his other life, the secret investigations into the Amber Room that we have only just begun to uncover in these papers that the literature archive has sat on for so many years. The orders from SovNarKom. The furtive *komandirovats* business trips to Moscow and Königsberg. A request to the highest Soviet authorities to be allowed to pursue suspects to Berlin. Kuchumov's growing obsession with the Amber Room.

Our Friend the Professor says that she will speak to the archive director about the Kuchumov file we had actually requested, but in the meantime we contact Bolshoi Albina and tell her we have found her silk pennant. We hope her curiosity will get the better of her shyness.

Bolshoi Albina laughs when we call and agrees to meet. Two weeks later, sitting with her at a dinner table in the new suburbs, warmed by crimson Georgian wine, she is unstoppable, in the way that elastic unravels from a split golf ball.

'We all adored Anatoly Mikhailovich. And I remember painting the pennant for his birthday. How embarrassing it ended up in an archive,' she says, tucking a stray wisp of hair back into her bun. She is blushing. 'He fired us all with his enthusiasm. He said we should never give up the search for Russian things stolen from us by the fascists.' She takes another sip of wine. 'I had heard so much about him even before I started work. I thought that he would be tall and handsome, but actually he was quite small, with a thick neck, like a bullfrog. Quite clumsy.'

Bolshoi Albina pulls some photographs out of the pocket of her tweed skirt. 'Anatoly Mikhailovich was a man of simple origins. He didn't act like a director. He had only one suit and all of us used to dust him down when the high officials came.' In the first picture two young women are dressed up in imperial gowns, one of them sitting crossed-legged, her stilettos peeking out from beneath a long lace petticoat. 'That's me,' she says. 'Wearing the dress of Maria Fedorovna, the wife of Alexander III. In another picture a male curator sits on a throne wearing the gold crown of Paul I, laughing colleagues crowded around him, including a familiar figure, Kuchumov. Albina explains: '*Capusnik*, we called it. It means chopping cabbage for winter. But it came to mean a staff party. Letting your hair down. Relieving the tension.'

*Anatoly Kuchumov (left) and colleagues at Pavlovsk Palace;
the crown was once worn by Tsar Paul I*

We try to steer the conversation back to the private Kuchumov. Did he talk about the Amber Room?

'Not publicly. He would go off on *komandirovat*, certainly. He said he was going to conferences. About restoration work. Or he would tell us he was on holiday and leave us in chaos for a couple of weeks.'

All of the *komandirovat* forms we have seen so far suggest that when Kuchumov said he was on holiday or a work trip he was actually on Amber Room business.

Albina shrugs. 'When he returned all he wanted to know was what we had been doing. He had important friends with high ranks as party leaders. We were lowly. It was a difficult time. Perhaps the most difficult. He brought us together. You have no idea, I think, about what we had all gone through during the war.'

Albina smooths the creases in her skirt. 'On 2 October 1941 German soldiers running a slave caravan abducted me from my village near Smolensk. I was only five. We were stripped naked, disinfected and loaded into vans.' Her cheeks burn. 'We were bundled into Poland,' she says, fixing her memory on a harrowing journey to an unknown place. 'All the time the convoy was bombed by Soviet planes. Children are so simple. We used to try and hide in the craters as we thought that a bomb could not land in the same place twice. A German farmer bought us.

'When we were liberated the Red Army came to escort us back. Our brave soldiers. We walked or sat on carts pulled by heavy horses. The road was wide and deep with mud. We went through a big German city. I think it was Königsberg. We were then in Smolensk and my mother said "This is your city," although I could see no city. But even then we were elated. Eventually we arrived at the village and saw that it too had gone. Still we got down on to our hands and knees and dug in the mud, proud of the Motherland, happy as we excavated holes. Over them we threw tin and wood, pits that became our temporary homes. But then the NKVD came.'

In the post-war Soviet Union there would be no room for anyone exposed to a foreign ideology that could unsettle the programme. By the summer of 1945 Stalin had rounded up Soviet citizens who had been prisoners of war in Germany, 126,000 of them, like those in Albina's village, who were now damned as 'capitulators'.[2]

Bolshoi Albina says, 'When we thought we could be no happier, living deep inside the Soviet earth, our friends and neighbours began to disappear. "Don't say you were captured," the whisper went. "Don't ever let the NKVD know that you were a prisoner of the Germans."'

Despite the purges, at the end of the war the vast majority of Soviet citizens felt deeply patriotic, and this sense of nationhood would become a valuable tool. In 1946 Andrei Zhdanov, leader of the Leningrad Communist Party, proposed to the Central Committee of the Communist Party of the Soviet Union (CPSU) a new theme, 'no servility before the West'.[3] Emancipation meant recouping everything Soviet. Victory over the Hitlerites was now the Great Patriotic War, in which Soviet losses and the ability to endure were brought to the fore: the battle of Stalingrad, the 900 days of siege, the desecration and rebuilding of the Leningrad palaces. All that was Russian had to be found, brought back, reconstructed and celebrated. Every treasure looted had to be tracked down and returned to its rightful place, and the world was to be advised of these Soviet losses and triumphs through the new Communist Information Bureau (Cominform), established by Zhdanov in 1947.

We walk to the metro and Bolshoi Albina links arms with us as we dodge between speeding *marshrutkis*. 'It was when I began working at the palaces that I learned how to be proud of my country. Anatoly Mikhailovich, with his ceaseless searching for looted treasure, made sure of that.'

Our Friend the Professor calls. The literature archive has found the missing Anatoly Kuchumov file we requested several weeks ago and we have been given permission to come and read it, as a special favour from the director. When we open it the next morning we find a report entitled 'Document Defending the Character of Mikryukov'. The document is stamped 31 October 1945 and was compiled by the colleagues of Ivan Mikryukov, director of Pavlovsk, who had been arrested on suspicion of being 'anti-political'.[4]

It states, in his defence, that he led the packing of treasures at Pavlovsk Palace in the late summer of 1941, after the first shipments had left with Kuchumov for Novosibirsk. Like Kuchumov, Mikryukov had 'improvised wadding and containers, salvaging curtains and linen to bulk out cases that were sewn together from old sheets and carpets, saving 42,000 treasures valued at an estimated 1.5 billion roubles'. How could Mikryukov be anything other than a patriot? Many risked their liberty to sign this document, but on the reverse is stamped the verdict: attempted to 'pack too early', a defeatist. The sentence: '*komandirovat* to Kazakhstan'. The official wording suggests a business trip to the Central Asian state, but Mikryukov never returned.

Surprisingly, Kuchumov's name was not attached to this petition to save Mikryukov and yet he preserved the document for many decades. Within six months of the defence document being submitted to the Leningrad authorities, Kuchumov was on his way to Königsberg, searching for the Amber Room. It seems certain, then, that on that long train journey to Königsberg, Kuchumov would have been preoccupied with not only the letters that Alfred Rohde had tried to burn (given to him by Professor Brusov) but also the fate of his close colleague from Pavlovsk, whose actions had been condemned as unpatriotic.

The second document in the file is a telegram dated October 1947. It is yet another *komandirovat*, a supposed business trip, this one to Moscow. Once again Kuchumov was to tell his colleagues that he was on holiday. In Moscow, he reported to the Committee for Cultural Institutions, a body that came under Zhdanov's empire and received instructions from Committee Chairman Comrade T. M. Zuyeva.[5]

The next document is an account of the meeting, written by Kuchumov in purple ink on graph paper. Chairman Zuyeva introduced Kuchumov to Comrade Georgy Antipin of the State Historical Museum, who was attached to a 'special unit of the Military Department', and Comrade David Marchukov, representative of the Committee for Cultural Institutions. Kuchumov noted that Antipin was an intense, brooding man. All three were issued with special passports and permits to travel and were then driven to the Sheremetyevo military airstrip, where they boarded a DC3 bound for Kaliningrad.[6] It seemed that Kuchumov was being sent back to reinvestigate the Amber Room again.

The whole region was under the tightest security and at Kaliningrad airport the border guards inspected the three men's papers and luggage. According to Kuchumov's notes, he was held up for hours by security staff. He had packed 500 photographs of the pre-war palaces of Leningrad in his suitcase and was accused of being a spy. It was Marchukov who eventually persuaded the guards that Kuchumov was on a classified mission. Only then did the DC3 take off again, this time heading for Tempelhof airport. The final destination of the mission was not Kaliningrad but Berlin.

Kuchumov wrote that his digs in that city were 'not far from the Gestapo headquarters' in Prince Albrecht Strasse and that he, Antipin and Marchukov 'rambled through the streets, eager to see what this capital of terror was really like, this city that gave birth to the Third Reich'. In *Pravda* Kuchumov had read how the Soviet Fifth Shock Army had been first into the city and by the morning of 25 April 1945, when US troops met with their Soviet counterparts on the River Elbe, the noose had been pulled tight, Berlin surrounded. Russians pressed on to the Brandenburg Gate, fighting house by house, using T-34 tanks and katyusha rockets, devastating firepower for such a close-quarters battle. The rows of bombed-out houses reminded Kuchumov 'of skulls with hollow eye sockets'.[7]

When the mint at the National Bank of Prussia fell in April 1945, Soviet riflemen had forced their way into its vaults to find piles of banknotes as well as remarkable antiquities from Assyria and Persia that had once been displayed in the city's Pergamon Museum. By 27 April 1945 the Soviet Eighth Guard Army had reached the Zoological Gardens, in the western suburbs, where they pounded the Zoo Flakturm, an enormous concrete anti-aircraft tower with thick steel shutters, inside which more than 3,000 civilians cowered alongside paintings and collections (including a priceless golden hoard excavated from Anatolia that was said to have once been worn by Helen of Troy).[8]

Allied air raids during the first three months of 1945 had levelled much of Berlin's historic Prussian centre and in 1947 Kuchumov was anxious to see what remained of Museum Insel, the small island on the River Spree, in which had been housed priceless treasures excavated by German archaeologists from Turkey in the 1860s and 1870s. Here should have been the legendary altar of Zeus from Pergamum with its delicately

Victorious Soviet troops pose in front of the Berlin Reichstag, 1945

carved frieze. But Kuchumov could find nothing. A British soldier who was there at the same time wrote of a 'shambles of crumbling rubble, with the great monuments from Mshatta and Miletus peering like ghosts over ruins, more sudden than those they had seen before in their two- or three-thousand-year history'.[9]

Outside the Reichstag, where German troops had made a last stand on 30 April 1945, Kuchumov scooped up some charred masonry from the ground and could not help but smile: 'who could resist a small souvenir of the evil of fascism from this city broken into smithereens?'

Kuchumov visited all four sectors of Berlin: American, British, French and Soviet. In the British-controlled Tiergarten, when the portly curator, still in his not-so-new black suit, witnessed the sprawling side-show of whores and touts, con men and fences, most of them wearing an array of military uniforms, he was filled with a deep sense of revulsion. 'It is enough for me to smell the rottenness of the bourgeoisie that is so foreign to the heart and soul of every Russian man,' he wrote. It was an aside that was surely written for any of those charged with implementing Comrade Zhdanov's new campaign, who might (accidentally) peruse this log.

Exhausted, Kuchumov caught a lift to Berlin-Karlshorst through the khaki traffic jam of jeeps and trucks, to where the Soviet Military Administration was now based. 'It was the only place that seemed in any kind of order,' he wrote. Anyone reading Kuchumov's account would believe that he kept only Soviet company, shunning contamination by the West. The next day he moved into the Berlin-Karlshorst district and was immediately called to a meeting. This was to be the first time he saw the general.

General Leonid Ivanovich Zorin, head of the Department of Reparations and Supplies, supervised the tracking and return of Soviet art works plundered by the Nazis. He had a small team of Soviet experts working for him, one of whom Kuchumov might have known by sight, Comrade Xenia Agarfornova, a curator from the Hermitage in Leningrad.

General Zorin gave Kuchumov his orders. His report from Königsberg had been received warmly. The evidence – that the Amber Room had survived the fall of Königsberg and might be concealed elsewhere – was compelling. The Committee of Arts of the Council of Ministers of the USSR had been deluged with replies to Kuchumov's appeal for help published in *Vo Slavu Rodini*. So he was to continue with his Amber Room investigation as a matter of urgency, but as well as chasing down witnesses he was to scour a vast warehouse of looted Soviet art works that had been assembled by the Americans at the end of the war. Kuchumov warned the general that his *komandirovat* was for only one month since he was needed at the Central Stores in Leningrad, which was still receiving a constant flow of treasures. The general replied that a month was probably enough to trace the Amber Room.

'Taken down to the banks of the Spree by the general,' wrote Kuchumov. 'In the east harbour was a long, grey building of sombre stone, at least a third of a mile of it.' The gigantic riverside property was the warehouse known as the Derutra building. The Deutsch–Russische Transport-Aktiengesellschaft (German–Russian Storage and Transport Association) had been formed in the 1920s. The general, Kuchumov and Comrade Antipin unlocked the huge steel doors. 'Believe me, we could not trust our own thoughts,' Kuchumov wrote.

Here the notes have been annotated at a later date. Kuchumov has copied down Comrade Antipin's first impressions of the warehouse:

Enormous heaps of pictures in frames and rolled canvases. Can you imagine it? Icons, wood and marble sculpture, manuscripts and books, ceramics, tapestries and carpets, glass, porcelain, drawing and ancient arms, hundreds and hundreds of thousands of exhibits from museums in Kiev, Minsk, Pskov, Novgorod, Kirch, Pavlovsk and Pushkin. Dizzying all of it. Dizzying.[10]

The building was filled with dismembered Soviet collections that had been stolen by the Nazis and hidden all over the Third Reich. Kuchumov was told that the majority of these works had been found by US troops and transferred to Berlin from US Army collection points in Munich and Wiesbaden, where they had been gathering over the past twenty-four months. But there was a problem. Many of the treasures had been stolen from the Soviet Union by roving units of Alfred Rosenberg's ERR, the

Third Reich's art theft squad, whose knowledge of 'culture of the Russian and Soviet empires' was negligible. Original Soviet inventories had been destroyed and replaced with German index cards that were inaccurate. The Americans had relied on these indexes to determine the provenance of the stolen art. Kuchumov wrote: 'The crates had also been opened. Many of the pieces inside were missing.' The task of matching individual items to their original institutions was enormous. But not as large as opening every single box to check for traces of the Amber Room. Kuchumov would need staff, he told General Zorin. He would need transport. A lorry and a jeep were on call. He would need time.

He hired 100 German workers from the labour exchange. Every box was opened and resealed with a Soviet official present as a witness. Kuchumov was so eager to work quickly and comprehensively that he roped in all able-bodied people, even his German housekeeper 'Paul', who was sent off to search an annexe at Derutra.

And 'Paul' almost immediately came running back with news. Inside the annexe building, a former grain warehouse, he had found wooden-backed sheets poking out from beneath a tarpaulin. Having been told by Kuchumov that the panels of the Amber Room were backed with wooden boards, he was sure he had found it.

Kuchumov wrote: 'We scrabbled around with our hands. But what we found was a parquet floor, inlaid with Australian mother-of-pearl and rare hard woods, rose and amarantus, that had once been in the Lyons Hall in the Catherine Palace.' It might not have been the treasure he was after, but it taught Kuchumov a lesson. The Lyons Hall had been dismantled by the Nazis, who had then scattered pieces of it across Europe, a plaster mould abandoned in a field outside Pushkin, the bronze locks and a door in Königsberg, and here in Berlin the floor itself. Kuchumov noted in his diary that the fate of the Lyons Hall demonstrated a Nazi methodology that might also apply to the Amber Room – stolen, packed and then spread about.

The Germans working in the Derutra warehouse went through tens of thousands of crates in the flickering paraffin lamplight, kneeling over artefacts long into the night. Kuchumov wrote: 'They brought with them food and thermoses, so there was no need to take breaks. They worked diligently and professionally. They are pedantic and tireless. Our relations were cordial.'

For all the detailed description of his work at the Derutra warehouse, Kuchumov did not comment on the fact he never had time to leave Berlin, to travel to the castles of Saxony to where Alfred Rohde had planned to evacuate the Amber Room.

What is palpable is Kuchumov's exhaustion. His writing began to deteriorate. The entries became breathless. The general forced him to take a few days off. Kuchumov heard a platform performance of Wagner's *Götterdämmerung* (the apocalyptic *Twilight of the Gods*) but he thought it sounded like the torching of Leningrad. Only when he found a Russian-run cinema screening Eisenstein's *Battleship Potemkin* did he feel revitalized.

November came and his time was up. Kuchumov was dispatched to Leningrad alongside 2,500 crates packed into eleven railway carriages. Six more carriages left for Kiev and another four to Minsk. He wrote: 'A special flat-backed carriage was also used in the procession leading back to Russia and on it the huge bronze statues of Hercules and Flora, sawn from their podiums near the Cameron Gallery at the Catherine Palace.' They had been found in a smelting yard in Dresden, barely recognizable, having been dragged all the way from Russia by German tanks. 'They can be mended. Of that there is no doubt.'[11]

As he left the fallen capital, Kuchumov wrote: 'Here was the lifeblood flowing back to our cities.' But he must also have been conscious of what he was leaving behind, the unexplored lines of inquiry that had sped out of Königsberg in the spring of 1945. He had not found a single trace of the Amber Room.

The Soviet Union that Kuchumov returned to would soon become a quagmire. On 31 August 1948 Stalin's protégé Zhdanov dropped dead, starting a ferocious three-way fight between Georgy Malenkov, Deputy Prime Minister, Lavrenty Beria, Minister for Internal Affairs, and Viktor Abakumov, the Minister for State Security and former head of SMERSH. The instability also consumed the cultural establishment.

Sergei Eisenstein's rushes for *Ivan the Terrible Part II* (the Tsar was

Stalin's role model) were denounced and his new work was suppressed. Shostakovich was banned from teaching at the Leningrad and Moscow conservatories. Prokofiev, who had willingly abandoned a life in America for Mother Russia, now hid in his dacha, destroying anything that he owned from those foreign times. Polina Molotov, the Jewish wife of Stalin's foreign minister, was accused of being a Zionist plotter who intended to establish 'California on the Crimea'. Her husband left her on Stalin's orders and the following year she was renamed Object No. 12 and exiled to Kustanai *oblast* in northern Kazakhstan.[12]

The slightest hint of disloyalty could end one's career. In 1946 Leningrad writers Mikhail Zoshchenko and Anna Akhmatova were both expelled from the Writer's Union. Zoshchenko's manuscripts and letters were later thrown into a rubbish skip by workmen clearing his apartment.[13]

Those things that were deemed quintessentially Russian were fêted and, although he had struggled to find time to search for the Amber Room in Berlin, Kuchumov could not afford to give up on it now. The final paper in the file before us reveals how the curator exploited his contacts in the Red Army to revive the search for the treasure. It is a letter from someone called Simeon Pavlovich Kazakhov, who wrote to the curator:

Before my visit to Zorin, they had heard nothing from you. But they listened to me very well and the affair has now begun. Tomorrow I will go to the general commander with a report and inevitably they will send the doctor to Kaliningrad along with someone else to investigate this place, because either he really did forget or he is pretending he cannot remember.

The future destiny of the Amber Room will proceed in ways that I just don't know. We will wait for the resolutions of the Lord God, but not the one in the heavens, the one who lives on earth. I am certain there will be good results to this affair. I long to return to my native Motherland. That is my only wish. I shake your hand, yours in solidarity, Comrade Kazakhov.

The small blue envelope is postmarked '19 October 1949, Poland, Post Dept No. 40223' and the stationery is that which the Red Army issued to its soldiers in the field. There is a stamp from the military censor that confirms this letter came from an army camp. And there is a postscript. 'Don't write letters to me here. Send them to Leningrad.'[14]

It is clear that Kuchumov was engaged in an ongoing correspondence with Soldier Kazakhov concerning the Amber Room, but frustratingly there are no other references to him in the literature archive index. We have no idea who 'the doctor' was or what 'place' in Kaliningrad they were referring to. Whatever the 'the doctor' claimed to know was obviously connected with the Amber Room and was of such significance that special arrangements were being made to send him to the Baltic city. Our translator notes that in 1949 the phrase 'Lord God on earth' could only have been a reference to the Soviet secret services or Stalin himself. The Kremlin was closely connected with the whole enterprise.

We make a copy of the letter.

Alexandra Vasilevna, the literature archive director, has advised us that she intends to carry out an important audit of the Anatoly Kuchumov papers so they will not be made available to readers again for at least six months. We cannot afford to sit around in St Petersburg doing nothing. We have to find another route. We need to trace Kuchumov's contemporaries from 1949 or at least someone he confided in. But the women and men whom he employed as junior curators, like Bolshoi Albina, were not let into his private world. We need to find someone who was of equal or superior standing. We recall the fond cards sent to him and particularly one containing the question, 'Why, my brother, are you lying in bed?' written by Valeria Bilanina, vice-director of Pavlovsk Palace and Kuchumov's deputy. We call Our Friend the Professor and leave a message.

Later that night, she rings back: 'Valeria Bilanina is alive! But she is a recluse.' Nothing in our Russian life is straightforward. 'And she is unwell, about to go into hospital for surgery. She has never allowed anyone into her apartment, but perhaps you can sip tea together in Tsarskoye Selo.'

Curiosity gets the better of Valeria Bilanina. She agrees to meet at a bus stop on a small lane running through Tsarskoye Selo. When we arrive on a crowded *marshrutki,* the sun is shining but she does not show. We call and someone picks up straight away, as if they were sitting beside the phone. 'It is far too hot to be practising *détente* in the open air.' It is Bilanina. 'You had better come to the apartment.'

We climb to the second floor of a post-war red-brick block. 'Come in. Very slowly,' Valeria Bilanina rattles, pushing and pulling us along her small hallway. 'Do. Not. Destroy. Deface. Crumple. Scrumple. Anything. Sit. Stand. I don't care.'

The first thing that strikes us about her apartment is that it is so cluttered no one else can sit or stand. Towers of boxes fill every space. We ask her if she knew Kuchumov back in 1949?

'Of course not,' Valeria Bilanina snorts, flinging open a door and diving into a kitchen, from where drifts the smell of browning butter. On the wall is her graduation portrait from fifty years before, and in it she is slim, studious and beautiful. Either side of the photograph are propped drawings of Landseer lions.

Ten minutes later, Valeria Bilanina reappears to brush the living-room table clean. A bust of Catherine the Great sits on the mantelpiece, along with a collection of broken teapots. Glass flowers are propped into jars surrounded by a forest of ribbon and satin roses, every piece of gift-wrap that she has ever received. The apartment block in which she lives was built for the workers of Pushkin to commemorate the centenary of Lenin's birth and Valeria Bilanina arrived in 1970. Before then, she had shared a room in the Catherine Palace's Central Store. 'I am still waiting for the memorial plaque to go up,' she says only half jokingly. Now, having retired from Pavlovsk, Valeria Bilanina is busy curating her own lengthy life in this small flat. 'My *arkhiv*. Every one of these' – she sweeps a hand over the cardboard metropolis – 'has a different theme. This, for example.' She hauls out a bundle of yellowed cards. 'These are the evacuation indexes from 1812 and there are twelve books of them.' We wonder why these things are not in a museum. 'And this painting.' We look up at the wall. 'This was a gift from Anatoly Kuchumov. It is by Ivan Bilibin. He found it under a hedgerow and gave it to me. "Keep it," he said. "To remind you."' Obviously not everything that was recovered after the war went to the Central Stores. 'And this watercolour of Empress Anna Ivanovna was another gift from Kuchumov.'

Valeria Bilanina produces plates of hard-boiled eggs, hanks of fleshy sausage and a pot of steaming *kasha*, kernels of steeped buckwheat. Even as she eats she talks. How can she help us if she didn't know

Kuchumov back in 1949, we ask? Valeria Bilanina seems stunned. Beads of sweat glisten on her darkening face like bubbles breaking on the surface of a steaming bowl of borscht. Her great frame shivers and twitches and we wonder whether to fetch her some water. 'I got my job the day I left Leningrad University in 1952. But I knew Kuchumov better than anyone. When I first met him he was still wearing the suit given to him by the commission in Moscow in 1946. He was so embarrassed when he realized that he and Tronchinsky were issued identical clothes: tie, shoes, shirt.'

So Bilanina doesn't know what Kuchumov was doing in 1949, we ask again? She shoots out of her seat and begins tearing through boxes. Finally, she retrieves four letters from a pile. 'Kuchumov received many letters and cards from this man, a German. He was connected to what happened in 1949.' She looks triumphant. 'There are things we were not meant to know and Kuchumov knew how to keep a secret, but as he became older he was careless.'

She thrusts into our hands four envelopes that are now pockmarked with grease spots. 'How can you *Angliyski* understand? Even Kuchumov did not understand everything. I should know, I wrote his obituary.' She is quivering again. 'You see the kind of woman you're dealing with now? And all this trouble the day before I go under the knife.'

Four empty envelopes. We lay them on the pine table at our apartment in Sovetskaya 7. They bear the postmark of the former German Democratic Republic (GDR) and are addressed to 'Pawlowsk, Leningrad Schloss Museum, A. Kugumow'. They are all dated after 1949 and we wonder if Valeria Bilanina misunderstood our questions. One is from 3 January 1951, another from 1 January 1970, the third from 4 January 1973 and the last from 25 December 1976. Quite possibly they contained seasonal greetings. Each one bears the stamp of the Soviet censor.

But we notice that the envelope dated 4 January 1973 is slightly plumper than the others. We hold it up to the light. An opaque, oblong shadow runs across the envelope like a tumour on an X-ray. We slice the lining of the envelope open with a razor blade and a piece of tracing paper falls out. We open up the fragile square. It is a letter written in German with an extremely light hand in pencil, so that no discernible indentations could be felt if the envelope was patted down.

The writing is formal and outmoded. The author of this letter had so much to say that, having filled the paper his words then run vertically up one side of the page:

Dear Mr Kugumow, a long time has passed, in my opinion almost twenty-four years, since we worked together on the mystery of the Amber Room. I congratulate you from the bottom of my heart for the New Year and I wish you all the best and great successes in this year's work. You will probably not remember me after so long. On 3 October 1970 I visited Leningrad with a tour party. I wanted to very much meet you again but I couldn't remember your surname correctly and nobody could help me when I asked about the great art historian who searched for the Amber Room.

The writer was forgetful and possibly old. He also had a confession:

Very often I blame myself that I did not insist in Kaliningrad on systematic searching. This feeling was especially alive when I saw a Soviet movie last year about the Amber Room when my name was mentioned and again recently when Mr Seydervitz, the former general director of the Dresden Gallery, wrote about the destiny of the Amber Room. Not everything he wrote is quite right, but he shows well how cruelly and without responsibility the Nazis behaved towards your great monuments of art.

Then there was a request: 'I would very much like to come to Leningrad again. Could you give me in Pavlovsk somewhere to stay, since without it I am not allowed to go to the Soviet Union?' He envisaged an exchange of favours. 'Maybe you would like to visit our Republic too? I invite you as my guest and you can stay at my home. The wife of my son is a student of Slavonic studies and she can translate for us.'

Since it remained concealed until we sliced it free from the envelope's lining, Kuchumov never read this secret letter. We can only presume that what the great curator took out of the envelope and what the Soviet censor also saw was an innocuous New Year's greetings card. The tracing paper square with its mention of the Amber Room and a secret trip to Kaliningrad was presumably concealed to keep the subject matter private.

And yet from what we have learned so far it is clear that every detail of the operation to find the Amber Room was planned, funded and supervised by Moscow. Perhaps the paranoid German writer was trying to conceal his thoughts from prying eyes at home.

Finally, it is signed: 'Comradely Greetings, Yours, Dr G. Strauss, 111 Berlin, Heinrich-Mann-Platz 4, GDR'.[15]

We go back to our notes. We compare this letter to the one sent in October 1949 to Kuchumov by Soldier Kazakhov. 'Tomorrow I will go to the general commander with a report and inevitably they will send the doctor to Kaliningrad... because either he really did forget or he is pretending he cannot remember,' Kazakhov advised Kuchumov.

Before us is a letter from a forgetful doctor who is writing in 1973 and referring to a trip to Kaliningrad made by him twenty-four years earlier. There is only one way to establish if Dr G. Strauss is the same doctor Kazakhov referred to. We cannot get back into Kuchumov's private papers for another five months. But we can go to Berlin and check out Dr G. Strauss. When the Stasi, the East German secret police, was disbanded in March 1990 it left behind comprehensive files on one in every three German citizens. An East German who corresponded with a Soviet official about the search for the Amber Room must have come to the attention of the authorities in East Berlin. We call the Federal Authority for the Records of the State Security Service of the former German Democratic Republic (GDR), the bureaucratic structure that is responsible for sifting and disseminating what was left behind by the Stasi. Yes, they say that there is material concerning Dr G. Strauss and the Amber Room. But, they add, it may take several months to process our application.

Once again our research is put on hold.

6

Berlin is clear and white. Even though it is two days after Christmas 2002 the city is still festively optimistic. But beneath the iced pavements we are rolling back in time. The U2 subway revives feelings from an age when West Berliners boarded city-bound trains at the comfortable shopping and residential quarters of Zoologischer Garten and Sophie-Charlotte-Platz while their compatriots in East Berlin stepped on at tense Pankow or at functional Schönhauser Allee. But the shoppers and workers never saw each other, riding instead within their separate political systems. When the westbound and eastbound trains were forced to converge at Potsdamer Platz, each would wiggle around and retreat back along the darkened tracks. Now, thirteen years after *die Wende* (or 'the turning point', as Germans describe the process of reunification), it is still something of a novelty to travel the entire length of the U2 and see incredulous faces crease up with surprise as a brightly lit carriage rattles past their train window, in the opposite direction.

Six months after leaving Russia we are still waiting to hear if our application to see the Stasi files has been approved, and in frustration we have come to Pankow to search for Dr G. Strauss ourselves.

Outside the station, the easternmost stop on the U2, fierce winds from the Baltic slice between the cement towers, whipping woollen scarves from red-raw necks and thieving hats. We cross the street, looking for the address recorded in Gothic capitals: '111 Berlin, Heinrich-Mann-Platz 4'. We make our way down the slippery path.

The supermarkets are prefabricated, the houses muddled with concrete and pebble dash. In the 1960s and 1970s, the red brick and carved masonry of Pankow were replaced by a bloc utilitarianism that was deemed more suitable to the hard-wearing society that was being raised there. Today its residents are not so durable and beneath the ripped steel awnings are greasy drunks and fumbling dealers, elderly junkies and wrinkled skinheads, all of them more than likely former servicemen who now have no one to serve.

It has not always been so deadbeat. Pankow was once a gentile retreat for prosperous nineteenth-century Berliners and in the 1940s it became the favoured suburb of Walter Ulbricht and his clique. Within a year of the collapse of the Third Reich, in February 1946, Ulbricht, the leader of the German Communist Party (KPD), signed a pact with Stalin that tethered the East German state to the USSR. Three years on, Ulbricht, 'a scoundrel capable of killing his father and his mother' (according to Lavrenty Beria, the NKVD chief), founded the German Democratic Republic, which was to be governed by his new Socialist Unity Party (SED), and one of its first acts was to commandeer Pankow's nineteenth-century mansions as homes for its Politbüro.[1] Niederschönhausen Castle, where Queen Christine, the wife of Frederick the Great, was reputed to have died of boredom and the Nazis stored 'degenerative art', was also seized and transformed into a state guesthouse, later used by Fidel Castro and Mikhail Gorbachev.

By 1950, when the Stasi was formed, the sedate suburb of Pankow was completely encircled by its agents. Only the most trusted were permitted to enter, let alone live within the security perimeter of what was now a water-tight enclave. Dr G. Strauss was one of them.

In St Petersburg, the Kuchumov papers are still officially closed. But Our Friend the Professor has used her connections to help us once again and has secured a few documents from a correspondence file of Kuchumov's, stored in the literature archive, concerning contacts in East Berlin.

She has sent us a batch of notes she has taken and written a covering letter. She recalls we were looking for a source known as 'the Doctor'. She is excited, she writes, having come across an intelligence briefing and interrogation report of a former German internee who, in 1949, claimed to know the location of the Amber Room. His name was Dr G. Strauss and his file bears the stamp of the Soviet Ministry of State Security, Comrade Viktor Abakumov's MGB (the former Soviet intelligence and counter-intelligence agency that was a forerunner to the KGB).[2]

Abakumov, Beria's pupil, had become the Soviet's spymaster and chief of the new MGB in 1946, inheriting the old NKVD's extensive network of interrogation and holding centres that had been set up at the end of the war to imprison Nazis, collaborators and anyone else whom the system deemed objectionable. Abakumov's agents stalked the Baltic and Eastern Europe, seeking out opposition and arresting saboteurs and dissidents. Abakumov also fostered the growth of like-minded security organizations within the Soviet's new partner nations, including the Stasi.[3]

We see that the MGB file Our Friend the Professor has sent to us was prepared for Anatoly Kuchumov and it is dated October 1949, a briefing prepared for his meeting with Dr G. Strauss in Kaliningrad that December. Attached to it is a *komandirovat* for Kuchumov to travel to Kaliningrad. It stated that General Zorin, in Berlin, had finalized the arrangements for transporting Dr G. Strauss. We are now certain that Soldier Kazakhov's source, 'the Doctor' and this former German internee are one and the same.

In the MGB briefing, Strauss was described as 'an art historian' with long-established links to East Prussia. He was born there in 1908 in Mohrungen (today Morag in Poland), a market town founded by the Teutonic Knights, not far from Prince Alex's castle at Schlobitten. Dr G. Strauss studied art history at Königsberg University and on graduation was recruited by East Prussia's Provincial Memorials Office. In 1939, he was appointed as an assistant to the city's director of art collections. This makes it likely that he was a contemporary of Alfred Rohde, Königsberg Castle Museum's director.

There is more. In 1934 Strauss became a brown-shirted street fighter, joining the Sturmabteilung and three years later, while many others chose not to, he joined the Nazi Party. His service record shows that during the war he was a Wehrmacht officer, stationed in East Prussia, and for the last two years of the war he was assigned to protecting the state and its treasures from Allied air raids, a job of great importance considering the value the Third Reich placed on the haul of artefacts stashed in the region. It was a posting that also revealed a degree of political favour, as Strauss could have been ordered to the front, where so many Germans perished.

The file shows that these classified briefing papers originate from a Major Kunyn at MGB headquarters in Berlin-Lichtenberg and state that immediately after the war Strauss was interned by the Soviets at Bornholm Camp in Rossenthin, south-east of Berlin, in the verdant Brandenburg Spreewald. The vast majority of detained Germans spent years waiting to get out and another decade coming to terms with the collapse of their splintered nation. Strauss, however, was released after only four months at Bornholm and was then allotted a villa at Pankow. This is the villa in Heinrich-Mann-Platz that we are heading towards.

Many Germans secured their freedom by declaring allegiance to the Communist Party. The MGB briefing paper stated that Strauss told his Soviet interrogators that he had been a Communist since 1932. He claimed only to have joined the Brown Shirts and the NSDAP on the orders of the Communist Party that instructed him to go to any lengths to conceal his real political affiliations.[4] What should we believe? We do not know.

We enter Pankow's Gothic-style Rathaus, with its gargoyles and faded yellow Bayreuth sandstone, practically the only thing that evokes the kind of Germany to which this suburb once belonged. 'Heinrich-Mann-Platz 4,' the counter clerk says, running a finger down the electoral role. 'Professor Dr Gerhard Strauss, this is the person now living at Heinrich-Mann-Platz 4. Here is a telephone number. I'll call it right away.' The old man is still alive. We have not contemplated this eventuality. We have hoped at best for relatives or a forwarding address, perhaps a quick glimpse of the house in which he lived. No, we say, no thanks, and walk back on to the street.

We try to settle ourselves. We want to be as natural as we can when we knock on the door. Around us through the snow we can see the outlines of large, foreboding chalets, each in its own mute private grounds, the low-slung roofs insulated by thick ice. We stand before No. 4. The gate is locked, although through a downstairs window we can see the lights of a Christmas tree. We gently rub the frosted brass plate: 'STRAUSS'.

What shall we say? Something low-key and neutral. We are researching a Russian curator's life and have discovered that he had a pen pal in East Germany. We press the buzzer.

A face appears at an upstairs window. Possibly a man. 'Dr Strauss?' we call. '*Sprechen sie Englisch, bitte?*' The front door rattles. Chains are unwound. A bolt is drawn back and it opens to an archer's slit. 'Dr Strauss?' we ask.

A dark-haired man dressed in black jeans and a sweater makes his way cautiously to the gate, slipping along the frosted path, inspecting us with eyes like iced water. We shout an explanation in German so broken that we can only be English. This man is about fifty. He cannot possibly have met Anatoly Kuchumov in Kaliningrad in 1949. And yet he is opening the gate and we are following him back to the house.

Inside, there is not a mark on the new stripped-pine floors except for the large black prints left by our slush-filled boots. On the whitewashed walls are moody oils and organ pipes, pieces that give the space a chaste air. The man motions us to sit beside the tree whose hand-carved ornaments are *völkisch*. We try and clarify who he is and what we are doing in his living room. But he will not hear it. Not just yet. We must wait. A woman's voice floats through from the hall, '*Kaffee?*' she calls. After ten silent minutes, listening to the percolator bubble on the hob, *amaretti* biscuits placed on a tray, the woman has joined the man in their living room. They serve us even though none of us know who the other is.

'*Zo?*' the woman says, as we drain our cups.

'So,' we say. 'Do you know Dr G. Strauss?'

'*Ja*, of course,' the man answers in broken English, loosening the neck of his jumper, gasping a little, as if the air is now rarer. 'Gerhard Strauss was my *Vater*. *Warum?*'

'Oh, Stephan,' the woman interrupts. 'How funny you sound.' She turns to us. 'I teach English and Russian at the university. I will translate. Darling, your languages are really terrible.'

We hand over one of Valeria Bilanina's envelopes.

'Stephan, look. How strange!' the woman exclaims, her eyes scanning the handwriting. 'I remember *Vati* writing some of these.' She turns to us. 'Stephan and I were just married, in 1972, and Gerhard, my father-in-law, asked me to translate some letters into Russian. He was trying to find a curator in Leningrad, right? The one who was looking for the *Bernsteinzimmer*? You found these in Russia? *Vati* was so disappointed, you know. I don't know if he ever received replies.'

Kuchumov, we say, is unfortunately dead. And Dr Gerhard Strauss?

Stephan has had time to gather his thoughts and now his arms are wrapped tightly around his ribcage and his legs are crossed. Suddenly all of his anxieties tumble out: 'What do you know about my father's work? Who are you? Why do you want to know about him? Why are you here?'

The woman lays her hand on his lap. 'Stephan, let the people talk.'

He relaxes a little. 'It is difficult to speak of these things,' he says. 'You may know facts now that even I, we –' he squeezes his wife's hand – 'do not know about my father. There were things he had to do in the war to survive. We have come through difficult times.' He glances at his wife for reassurance. 'I'm not sure what you will do with any information I will give you. And anyhow I was a child, you must realize.' He pauses. 'But I do recall my father travelling to Kaliningrad sometime after the war.' He fixes his gaze on the Christmas tree. 'Russians came to the house. They were not wearing uniforms. At the time I was disappointed. Now I think they must have been KGB. There were whispered discussions. Papers were passed around the room. This room. But why should I tell you about these things?' He is losing his cool again, frowning deeply. 'You are strangers in my house.'

It is a beautiful house, we say, slowing everything down. And it is true that only a cup of coffee back we walked through that front door.

'They gave my father this place after the Nazis were cleared out. My father was a *Genosse*, you understand?'

Yes, we say. He was a comrade.

'He told us many stories about his secret KPD activities before the war. How he had to go underground. He had to join the Nazi Party but he hated them.' He pauses and sends his wife upstairs. She returns with a large photograph in a white wooden frame. It shows an elderly man wearing a black beret, a proud man in a park on a winter's day. You can see his breath forming as it hits the cold air.

'Gerhard passed away in 1984,' she says. 'He would have been delighted to have more visitors from Russia!'

So the doctor is dead.

'It was snowing the day he left in 1949, like today.' Stephan rocks the photo of his father gently on his knees. 'My mother was so worried. She said he would never come back. You have to understand, we were a little afraid of the Russians.' Stephan smiles at us. 'Perhaps the word is unsure. Unfamiliar.' He tries to encapsulate the feelings of the time. 'Well, the Red Army had taken away so many people. After six weeks my mother was frantic. She picked up courage and went to Karlshorst. Don't worry, they said. The weather was bad on the Baltic Coast. Father's plane was delayed. She was told to go home and wait.

'My father came home in the middle of January. He wouldn't talk much about what had happened. He mentioned that he had tried to find his parents' house in Mohrungen but had been prevented. And that he had helped in the search for the Amber Room. He felt it was his personal responsibility to find it and return it to Leningrad. Later, he became obsessed. It was a constant topic of conversation at the dinner table. On the phone. It was not good. It made him ill. Odd people kept calling. Russians, Poles, even West Germans. One called George Stein invited himself over for dinner, yes, George Stein. Have you heard of him?' Stephan sees us writing down the name and dries up again.

Why does he think his father was of such interest to the Soviets, we ask?

'During the last two years of the war my father was assigned to the air-raid protection forces in Königsberg. I suppose he must have been responsible for the safety of the Amber Room, that's why the Russians were so interested in him. His boss was called Andrei. No, not Andrei but ...'

His wife interrupts: 'Alfred, darling, Alfred Rohde.'

The director of Königsberg Castle Museum.

Stephan studies us with his iced water eyes and volunteers that he has an attic full of material belonging to his father, diaries and semi-official documents. He is a polite man who wants to be helpful. Can we see them, we ask?

He sees the excitement in our eyes and pauses. 'I have looked at them before. But not properly. I should study his papers first. Maybe if you come back. In a few weeks.' For as suddenly as he has blurted out about his father's private archive he wishes that he hadn't. He appears panicked. We can see his train of thought. Brown Shirt, card-carrying Nazi or loyal *Genosse* acting on the Communist Party's orders? And even if only a *Genosse*, what had Gerhard Strauss done for the regime? After so much time only the papers remain and Dr Gerhard Strauss's real motivations might be blurred.

We sense that Stephan is grappling with the conundrum faced by everyone reunited after a conflict. How should a family deal with the multiple histories that coexist in one life: by exposing them all or by concealing the unpalatable ones? Should one carry on oblivious, loving the person one ate with and slept with or strolled to the park with? Post-war Europe was a kaleidoscope of multi-coloured truths.

'I have my own life to live. Our own lives to live. One cannot live one's father's life although I love my father. Can I drop you somewhere?' Stephan asks, standing up. He has to leave for a meeting in town. He is a landscape architect employed by the municipal authorities to help rebuild Berlin. He leads us out to his Volvo and we sit in silence as the engine warms.

The Volvo settles and Stephan drives through wisps of freezing fog into a darkening Berlin, past Daniel Liebeskind's Jewish Museum with its Holocaust Tower. And we notice out of the corner of an eye an Arab boy on a mountain bike frantically pedalling to reach the queue for the museum before it disappears behind the armed security perimeter. Then, as he nears, he pulls a gun from his tracksuit. He has a pistol in his hand and before we can shout out he has pulled the trigger, again and again, waving the firearm wildly. But no one seems to see, apart from us trapped in the traffic behind fogged windows, boxed in on the other side of the street. However, no one is falling, crying or bleeding. The weapon must be a replica, although his hatred is real enough. We may have been the only people this day to have seen his drive-by fantasy.

Stephan pulls over at Alexanderplatz and leans across to open the passenger door. 'There are things I don't want to read and I hope you will not write them. Do you understand?' If we do come back, there will be documents in the attic that Stephan Strauss will not want us to print.

We cannot promise to censor our research to leave his father's reputation intact. With Alfred Rohde dead, finding Dr Gerhard Strauss, one of his assistants, must have been a critical moment for Anatoly Kuchumov. And it is for us too.

We'll call, we say, before diving into the hushed darkness of the west-bound U2, while Stephan Strauss drives off to his meeting in the east. Even though our paths have crossed, we have not really met at all. We have been prevented from understanding each other, our true characters and emotions blacked out, obscured (on our part) by self-interest and on his by a fear of history.

We have felt a clammy-handed excitement as the mystery of the Amber Room unravels but so far all of it has been from a distance – the story told through reports, diaries, letters and memories. Today the Amber Room has lifted off the page and into the lives of those around us, casting doubt and fear.

Two weeks later, we return to our Berlin hotel to find another couriered package from St Petersburg waiting for us. We rip open the envelope and a photo of Gerhard Strauss falls out. This Strauss is a young man, elegant and relaxed in a white shirt, his head of thick dark hair slicked back in a confident, cosmopolitan manner. While there are many similarities

Gerhard Strauss

between the younger and older Gerhard Strauss, the older man did not have this younger man's confident stare.

Our Friend the Professor writes that the literature archive has completed its audit of the Anatoly Kuchumov files and that she has obtained a reader's ticket on our behalf and found more material concerning our East German doctor.

Dr Gerhard Strauss. What did he know? Leningrad curator Anatoly Kuchumov was certain that Alfred Rohde, the Königsberg Castle Museum director, lied in 1945 and the Amber Room had not burned in the Knights' Hall. But with Rohde dead, Soldier Kazakhov had found another source whom he called 'the Doctor', a man who claimed to have important information about the location of the Amber Room. We now know that 'the Doctor' was Dr Gerhard Strauss and that in December 1949 he was sent to Kaliningrad to meet Anatoly Kuchumov.

In our latest Russian package is an MGB briefing paper dated 8 August 1949 that explains how the Kaliningrad mission came about. It begins with a letter from Dr Gerhard Strauss in which he reveals a different version of events than that remembered by his son. Gerhard Strauss wrote that he invited Soviet agents to his home in Heinrich-Mann-Platz (a decision that he had obviously not shared with his wife, who believed he was being arrested, according to Stephan Strauss's recollections). Gerhard Strauss was ready to assist the new Soviet administration, offering 'information on your missing Amber Room'.[5]

The letter was addressed to Major Kunyn, a liaison officer for the MGB in the Department of Soviet Military Officials, Berlin-Lichtenberg. Strauss must have been sure of himself and of what he had to barter to have dared contact an organization feared by the majority of Germans. 'I figured out from my chief of department, Mr Volkmann, that you are searching for the Amber Room,' he wrote breezily. 'Since the war ended I have met many people who came from Königsberg and they know only about the death of Dr Rohde and the destruction of the castle. But I know more.'

Strauss was exact and unburdened by guilt or modesty. His letter revealed that this was not the first time he had made contact and he expressed frustration that the Soviets had not reacted to three previous attempts to volunteer his services concerning the Amber Room.

One was made during his 'unfortunate' internment in May 1945, where 'I told everything'. His second statement was given in 1946 to a 'Major Poltavsev, Dept of Information, SV/V Germany'. Strauss approached the Russians a third time, in 1947, when he was questioned by Comrade Xenia Agarfornova, from the State Hermitage, the curator whom Kuchumov had met in Berlin in 1947 while cataloguing the looted Soviet art works stored in the Derutra warehouse.

'I told everything to the art historian from Leningrad, Mrs Agarfornova,' Strauss complained to Major Kunyn. 'Since nobody followed it up and I had no possibility to get in touch with you by phone, I decided to write.'

There must have been a serious breakdown in communication between the Soviet authorities in Berlin, Moscow and Leningrad concerned with the recovery of looted art works. While SovNarKom had ordered a mission to recover the Amber Room just weeks after the German capitulation, it had taken Dr Gerhard Strauss four years and four attempts to get anyone's attention.

Maybe Comrade Agarfornova had not taken Strauss seriously enough to inform her Leningrad comrade Anatoly Kuchumov of his statement in 1947. Maybe Comrade Agarfornova had not known Kuchumov was looking for clues about the Amber Room in the Derutra warehouse. We will never know, but it was only through Strauss's determination to be heard that he and Kuchumov ever met.

In the file sent to us from Our Friend the Professor in St Petersburg, Strauss reassured Major Kunyn that he was never a Nazi. Neither was Alfred Rohde. The real fascist was the Gauleiter of East Prussia, Erich Koch, a man Strauss described as 'a military criminal'. Strauss wrote about the Amber Room: 'It would really be a big loss if this piece of art were to become a victim of the Nazi war. No question, I am ready to help in this matter.' Major Kunyn marked this passage with three exclamation marks.

Strauss contradicted Alfred Rohde's testimony by saying that the Amber Room had survived the fall of Königsberg. 'But it cannot be in the Soviet Zone [of Germany] since despite my requests it wasn't moved in time,' he wrote. Major Kunyn marked the passage with a question mark. What was Strauss's exact role in wartime Königsberg? He seemed to be suggesting here that he was directly responsible for the safe-keeping of the Amber Room.

Strauss's letter continued: 'No amber objects have appeared on the Berlin art market but in March 1945 I did overhear that the evacuation of the Amber Room was assigned to one place, east of Görlitz [an area that was part of Saxony until 1949, when it became part of Poland].' Again Major Kunyn drew three bold exclamation marks. Strauss signed off 'Chief of Applied Arts Museums, Monuments and Education, GDR, Berlin'. He had been rehabilitated into the new East German regime remarkably quickly and had risen to an influential post. But drawing attention to himself in this way was a risky endeavour.

The next document is a poor carbon copy of a long interview conducted on 12 December 1949. As we slowly trace the sentences we realize that this is the transcript of Gerhard Strauss's interrogation. The man asking the questions was Anatoly Kuchumov.[6]

The two men talked at the Hotel Moscow in Kaliningrad. Pre-war photographs show it to have been a historic red-brick building. As one of the few Königsberg-era edifices still standing in April 1945, the NKVD had commandeered it as their headquarters before the MGB occupied it. In order for Strauss to have reached Hotel Moscow, he would have been driven past the ruins of the castle, past the statues of Bismarck and Prince Albrecht with missing limbs and their heads shot off, and along what he knew as Steindamm Strasse. It had been renamed Leninsky Prospekt and led into Prospekt Mira, where the Hotel Moscow stood. We wonder if seeing the levelled city of his youth shocked Dr Gerhard Strauss.

There is no scene setting in the file but we can imagine the likely circumstances, Kuchumov wrapped in his heavy tweed overcoat, wearing his pork-pie hat and black suit. No doubt the battered leather attaché case lay open by his ankles. Kuchumov's granddaughter still has it, although his former colleague Valeria Bilanina has probably obtained its contents. Opposite him, cool and confident, 'the doctor': Gerhard Strauss, his dark hair slicked so that not even one strand would become unruly.

At the outset these two men should have had much in common: a love of art history, a background in conservation, an overwhelming desire, albeit for different reasons, to find the Amber Room. But while they were now on the same side, recent events had created a gulf between the haughty Prussian and the shabby Russian.

Session One: '12 December 1949. What I know about the Amber Room. (translated by Captain Shukin)'.

Translated. Kuchumov had no language apart from Russian. We know from Strauss's daughter-in-law that the doctor could only speak German. And so all the nuances, the tucks and nips of language that help friendships settle, were lost as they sat down in the (no doubt freezing) Hotel Moscow during a Kaliningrad winter for a formal discussion, encumbered by an intermediary, the translator Captain Shukin.

Kuchumov began by asking about Alfred Rohde. What could Strauss say about the castle curator? Strauss was fluent on his former chief: Rohde had been born in Hamburg and served as an officer during the First World War, during which he had been gassed. Kuchumov noted that this might have accounted for the Parkinson's-like shakes observed by Professor Brusov in 1945. After demobilization in 1918, Rohde moved to Munich where he studied art history at Marburg University, then continued his education in Paris, before eventually taking up appointments in museums in Hamburg, Breslau (today Wroclaw in Poland) and lastly Königsberg.

Next question: what were Rohde's politics? Kuchumov suspected him of being a Nazi but Strauss informed him that Rohde was never a member of a political party. The only organization Rohde ever joined was the Union of Artists, for whom he arranged annual exhibitions of contemporary works.

Did Rohde know the Nazi élite? This was one of those probing questions, a proving ground, that Kuchumov also used with Brusov. After all, Kuchumov had read the castle curator's personal correspondence and already knew that Rohde was acquainted with Gauleiter Erich Koch and General von Küchler, head of Army Group North. Strauss performed well. He confirmed that Rohde had been acquainted with Erich Koch since 1928, the year that the curator arrived to become director of the city's art collections and Koch became Gauleiter of East Prussia. When Koch was later elected to the East Prussian Reichstag and took responsibility for the culture of the region, he and Rohde were brought into more regular contact. 'But they were never friends,' Strauss added. 'Rohde was a very modest and reserved person, respected by all of his colleagues. Politically, he certainly belonged to the middle and I even thought the left. Most people he associated with were of that persuasion. His closest friends were Hans Hopp and my teacher R. Worringer.' Kuchumov noted the names Hopp and Worringer. They mean nothing to us.

But Kuchumov pressed Strauss. Rohde must have been a Nazi sympathizer to have done so well. 'I remember how much he disliked the Nazis,' Strauss countered. 'Rohde told me so when he showed me pictures from Kiev. But professionally he was nice to them. The fact he didn't leave Königsberg only demonstrates that Rohde recognized his professional responsibility to his exhibits.' Strauss wrapped up the topic symmetrically. 'Alfred Rohde was not scared of the Soviet Union either. He had no bad intentions. That's all I can tell you about him.' Kuchumov has placed a small exclamation mark in the margin.

Kuchumov asked Strauss about the Amber Room. Strauss said: 'In 1941 I, together with Dr Rohde, was anxious that the Amber Room was going to be destroyed. Rohde contacted an old friend, General von Küchler, and asked him to save the room by sending it to Königsberg.' Kuchumov drew an asterisk here – thinking, no doubt, of the letter from General von Küchler, addressed to 'my good friend' Alfred Rohde, that he had found in the ruins of the castle in 1946. Strauss seemed to be telling the truth.

Strauss continued:

When the room arrived in 1942 or 1943, it was installed in the museum in the south wing of the castle, in a room with only one window, facing the river on the third floor. The panels were in a very good condition. It was installed with care, the broken pieces glued back together and the mosaics were put in place. The walls were sixteen feet high and it seemed as if they shone with yellow-brown light beaming from them. On a cloudy day it created a rather grotesque impression.

Kuchumov has marked another small asterisk here. He had learned from his interrogation with Otto Smakka, translator for the local fisheries, that the Amber Room was already badly damaged when it reached

Königsberg. Strauss's dates for the room's arrival also conflicted with Smakka's evidence and with the Gift Book found by the Soviets in 1945. But Kuchumov gave Strauss the benefit of the doubt.

Strauss was pressed to expand his comments and responded with a caveat. He had never seen the room before, 'so I couldn't tell if all the parts had been delivered to Königsberg'. He supposed that 'it was complete' since Dr Rohde didn't say anything about losses. 'Dr Rohde believed that the Amber Room might ultimately return to [Pushkin]. Despite the fact that its beauty was overwhelming, I was quite depressed and worried that I was an accomplice to that robbery.' Another small asterisk. Perhaps Kuchumov was becoming irritated by Strauss's clumsy attempts at ingratiation.

What could Strauss tell Kuchumov of the evacuation plan? Strauss claimed that he had attempted to get the Amber Room out of Königsberg in the spring of 1944. 'It was then that I warned Rohde for the first time that it was dangerous to keep it on the third floor of the castle as it could be destroyed. There was an obvious danger of aerial bombing.' But, according to Strauss, Rohde was reluctant. 'Only after several warnings from me did he agree to board up the window to prevent shrapnel from getting in. But even so we only boarded up the bottom third of the castle window.'

Strauss said that his persistence led to the room eventually being dismantled, packed into crates and moved to the south-wing cellars, only days before the first Allied air raids – 27–28 August 1944. Yet another asterisk. Kuchumov wrote a name beside it: 'Castle restaurateur Paul Feyerabend'. He had told Kuchumov that Rohde had temporarily evacuated the crates to an undisclosed location outside the city in July 1944, before the air raids.

Was Strauss sure about his dates? 'Yes,' he replied. He knew this was the case because, although he had missed the bombing raids, he had returned to Königsberg on 1 September 1944 and gone straight to the castle. 'It was entirely burned but the outside walls were still standing. I met Dr Rohde by chance in the castle yard outside the entrance to the south-wing cellar. He was surrounded by boxes, big and small, and told me the room had been stored in the cellars during the raids and wasn't damaged.' If it had not been for Strauss's insistence, then the Amber Room would not have been moved and would have taken a direct hit.

And then? Kuchumov was plotting times, dates and places. What happened next? Strauss thought for a moment. In December 1944 Rohde began to travel, Strauss said. Another mark in the margin. From Rohde's reconstructed correspondence, saved from the fire by Brusov, Kuchumov knew that it was in November 1944 that Alfred Rohde began looking in earnest for hiding places outside the city.

Strauss corrected himself. Yes, now he remembered. It was November 1944. Rohde had made a few local trips to find hiding places for the castle treasures in that month. But in the end these stores in castles and manors were not safe enough. Strauss had heard it said that Rohde had written in a letter that he intended to evacuate the Amber Room to Wechselburg Castle in Saxony. So did Rohde carry out the plan? 'About the moving of the room from Königsberg, I don't know,' Strauss replied.

Kuchumov asked about the Knights' Hall, where Brusov concluded that the Amber Room had burned. Was it used as a temporary store for the Amber Room? Strauss replied: 'Maybe [Rohde] told me that he wanted to put the boxes in the Knights' Hall, I'm not sure.' Strauss was becoming defensive but Kuchumov would not let up and asked about the last time that he saw Rohde. 'Some time between 11 and 15 January [1945]. But I cannot recall if the Amber Room was even discussed,' was Strauss's vague response.

Suddenly the pace and direction of the interrogation transcript changed. The cool-headed doctor asked to return to Berlin. He claimed that he needed to winkle out more witnesses. Not Nazis, but Germans, like him, silent, concealed opponents of Hitler who had weathered the final weeks of the war. 'Ernst Schaumann, for example, lives in Berlin. His address I can figure out and somebody can check it,' Strauss suggested to Kuchumov. 'Maybe it's possible to ask the general [Lasch] who capitulated and was taken as a POW? Maybe Lasch knows something about the Amber Room,' he said.

Strauss had only just arrived and, from the correspondence and files that surrounded the preparation for this trip, it had been arranged at significant political and financial cost. It was unlikely that the Soviets would let him go so quickly. We contrast Strauss's imprecise responses with his letter to Major Kunyn: 'But I know more.'

Strauss had one last thought: 'If it was lost, I suppose that such a room could be re-created with the help of photographs?' It was an unhelpful suggestion that could not have been made at a worse time.

Session Two: '12 December 1949. What I know about Soviet pieces of art taken to Germany (translated by Captain Shukin)'.

Take the pressure off the witness. Let him relax. Talk him through areas that he feels more comfortable about. Seduce him. Knead his ego. Make yourself small. Kuchumov seemed to be calming Strauss as the next session began. What had Strauss witnessed during his wartime office as an air-raid warden with access to bunkers and storerooms? Strauss replied: 'Dr Rohde showed me things he had been given by Gauleiter Koch for safekeeping: things from Minsk, Kiev and Rostock. They came in 1942, or was it 1943? It was forbidden to talk about or show these items.'

What items? More precision please? Strauss replied: 'Pictures: eighteenth and nineteenth century. Also Chinese porcelain and vases manufactured in St Petersburg. Icons too.' Names? Descriptions? Strauss couldn't recall: 'Everything was in a good condition but they were not great works. We supposed at that time that only a small section of [Soviet] treasures was in German hands, that the most famous things had been hidden by the Russians.'

Where were these small number of Soviet items kept? 'Everything was located in the first floor of the round tower in the north-west corner of [Königsberg] castle; the entrance was through the Knights' Hall.' Anything more? 'Well, there were church bells from Latvia. In 1942, or was it 1943? And not long before the end of the war, famous silver treasures from Riga and Danzig.'

Fearing incrimination, Strauss added: 'I got this information from Dr Rohde and members of his staff. This is all I know. I didn't work at the museum. I was only interested from a political and scientific point of view.' His answers were beginning to take on a defensive tone again.

Kuchumov placed yet another asterisk against this last statement.

We know from his notes that the great curator had read some of the Nuremberg depositions concerning looted art, including that of Hermann Voss, director of the Dresden Gallery, who, according to his American inquisitors, relied constantly on 'failure of memory to explain discrepancies in his testimony, a tactic that did not improve the atmosphere of the interrogation ...' Voss's captors had concluded: 'He takes the profoundly German attitude that art history is pure science, and that one can pursue it without exterior moral responsibility.'

Session Three: '12 December 1949. Where could the Amber Room be located? (translated by Captain Shukin)'.

Kuchumov returned to the events of January 1945. Strauss began: 'According to Rohde's letter of 12 January, the Amber Room was still in the city.' Asterisk. These letters were found by Brusov and passed on to Kuchumov, who knew that Strauss could not possibly have seen them. At best, he had heard about them from gossiping German museum curators.

If this information was third-hand, then what else in Strauss's statements was begged and borrowed? Strauss struggled to defend himself: 'Before 15 January [the Amber Room] could have been delivered by rail to Germany, after that it would have only been possible by sea or plane.' Asterisk. Wrong. Kuchumov had researched train movements out of Königsberg. He knew that the last one left for the German heartland on 22 January 1945.

Did Strauss believe that the Amber Room remained in the castle until the fall of Königsberg? Strauss was even more evasive: 'Dr Rohde was a lover of amber. There is no doubt that he would have tried to save the Amber Room. But I didn't see him again. I heard only gossip about hiding places at Görlitz. But there were many hiding places in East Prussia too, you know.'

Gossip. Maybe. Perhaps. If Strauss was so misinformed, why had he tried four times to gain the attention of the Soviet authorities? No answer. Then Strauss volunteered: 'There was a bunker.'

Kuchumov was very interested in bunkers – he recalled Brusov's mention of the Hofbunker. Rohde had talked about this hiding place in a letter to his superiors in Berlin, but showed it to Brusov in 1945 only after this letter was pulled by Brusov from the fire. In 1946 Brusov had told Kuchumov that he feared he had not thoroughly searched the Hofbunker after being distracted by Rohde and a story about lost keys. Was the Amber Room concealed in the Hofbunker? Strauss replied: 'Pictures from Königsberg Museum were supposed to be stored there. That is all I know.'

Where was the bunker? Kuchumov wanted an address. Strauss blurted out: 'I think, maybe on Lange Reihe or on a street in Nasser Garden. Precisely where I don't remember.'

We recall a phrase from Soldier Kazakhov's letter in which he wrote to Kuchumov about Strauss: 'they will send the doctor to Kaliningrad along with someone else to investigate this place, because either he really did forget or he is pretending he cannot remember.' It seems possible that Kazakhov was referring to the Hofbunker and Strauss's inconsistency.

On the defensive, Strauss now launched into a list of other potential hiding places in East Prussia. 'The nineteenth-century city bastions are many: Wrangel Tor, Rosegarten Tor, Friedlander Tor. All were used. There was also a room in the main railway station. And the safe of the Reichsbank near the castle.' The fortress at Pillau, had they tried there? 'But I suppose that was unlikely since it was full of wounded soldiers. Lochstädt Castle... what about that castle?'

But what about the Hofbunker, Kuchumov persisted? The other sites that Strauss mentioned had been searched already by the Soviets in 1946 and they had found nothing in them.[7]

Kuchumov challenged him. Was Strauss concealing facts about the Nazi evacuation plan? Strauss defended himself:

I buried treasure. I helped to bury books from Königsberg Library and the state archive on the lower underground floor of Lochstädt Castle. Sixty-five feet down. We wrote a message on a big piece of cotton with the help of a captured Russian soldier, 'Russian cultural treasures, open only in the presence of a curator.' Treasures were hidden at Schlobitten Castle too. Nowadays it's in Poland. There we placed furniture and paintings. People from Königsberg Museum moved them. Possibly they took some things from the museum too.

Strauss began to trail off, perhaps realizing that he was in danger of incriminating himself again. 'I wasn't there. I got this information from Helmut Hels from Hamburg... no, maybe Mrs Clomp from the Monuments Commission.' More names. More contradictions.

Strauss asked for a break, but Kuchumov returned to the Hofbunker. Strauss threw back yet more suggestions, names and locations: 'Schlobitten Castle, the home of Prince Alex zu Dohna-Schlobitten. Talk to him. He knows. Professor Voringer from Halle, he told me that things from the university and the most treasured items from Königsberg Library were moved to Langheim Palace, near Warstenburg. You should talk to him.' More names for Kuchumov's witness list. 'There was talk too of moving icons from Königsberg churches to Tilsit [Sovetsk, Kaliningrad Province] and of moving other items to Tsiten [Kaliningrad Province] and also an estate on an island at the Samland Peninsula, the name of which I don't remember.'

Think now. Don't stop. You can rest soon. You must know the name. Strauss dried up: 'No,' he said finally. 'I don't know any more. Not about art from the USSR. I can't remember anything else.'

Here was a man confident enough to contact the MGB, an organization feared by most Germans, and volunteer his services in the search for the Amber Room. He promised precision and details, even a solution, and yet, having been issued a special permit to travel and having been escorted to the closed military province of Kaliningrad, Strauss delivered nothing of substance. While placing himself at the centre of key events, claiming that the Amber Room had survived the air raids of 1944 only after he insisted on its being dismantled, Strauss failed to reveal anything concrete about Rohde's plans for the Amber Room and he claimed to know nothing about its final resting place.

What Kuchumov had to decide was whether Strauss really did not know or was playing a dangerous game. In an appendix to the official typed interrogation transcript that was compiled some time later, Kuchumov wrote:

In 1949, according to the decisions of the local party and the Soviet administration, a big and authoritative commission was organized ... A hundred soldiers and firemen, mobile generators and other equipment was provided. Giving evidence, Dr Strauss affirmed only those facts that were already known from the evidence of others and Rohde's correspondence. He didn't describe the exact location of the Amber Room in spite of our belief and hope that he must have known more about it.

There was more. Once the Soviets had decided to dig in Kaliningrad, Strauss had hindered the operation. The great curator concluded: 'Strauss tried, as Rohde also did by different means, to deflect the attention of our commission from heaps of bricks at the southern side of the castle, making recommendations to search in the north wing, discouraging the digging until the time that plans for the castle could be found.'[8]

Strauss stood accused of grave charges: wasting the time and resources of the Soviet government.

There is one last document in our packet from St Petersburg and it serves only to increase our uncertainty about Strauss's motives. We have before us a folded sheet of paper that carries obscure doodles, as well as maps, dates and names.

On one side, there is a message: 'To my best comrade from Leningrad. It's better to search in Henkanziskan! 7–19. XII.49'.[9]

The Cyrillic is poor. It's somebody's second language. But the dates are intriguing: 7–19 December 1949, the period during which Kuchumov interrogated Strauss in Kaliningrad. Only General Zorin, Soldier Kazakhov and the MGB were supposed to know about this classified mission.

The sheet is dominated by a large drawing of a man with little round glasses, wearing a pork-pie hat, a miniature shovel sticking out of the hatband like a feather. His nose has been coloured in blue, and beside this freezing figure is a thermometer measuring minus 10°C. Unlike the hand that painted Kuchumov's birthday cards, this artist is no professional, but there is no doubt about who is being caricatured.

The cartoon Kuchumov is carrying a magnifying glass inside which the word HENKANZISKAN appears again, in large wobbly letters. Although incorrectly spelt, this can only be a reference to Friedrich Henkensiefken, Schlossoberinspektor of Königsberg Castle, one of the

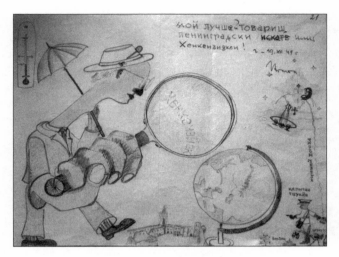

*Doodle of Anatoly Kuchumov searching for the
Amber Room with a magnifying glass, 1949*

people near the top of Kuchumov's list of missing German officials. We wonder who is taunting the curator about this man and why.

Beside the cartoon Kuchumov's feet is a small sketch of the Knights' Hall in the north wing of Königsberg Castle. And to the right is a globe, featuring a magnified detail of the Samland Peninsula and again the name 'Henkanziskan'. On the far right of the page is a strange kind of hieroglyphic: a cartoon depicting a bearded man floating in the clouds with a telephone to his ear. At the other end of the line (presumably down on earth) a Red Army soldier listens, standing amidst drawings of the Brandenburg Gate, a Christmas tree, a bottle labelled *pivo* (beer), a gun and a chicken, above which is written the name STRAUSS.

A Red Army officer stationed in Berlin (possibly Soldier Kazakhov) talks to God (maybe the MGB or Stalin) at Christmas time about a dangerous situation in which a chicken called Strauss is involved.

The reverse of the paper sheet is given over to a hand-drawn map of the Baltic coast, a railway line stretching between Leningrad and northern Germany, along which a steaming train chugs out of 'Detskoye Selo'

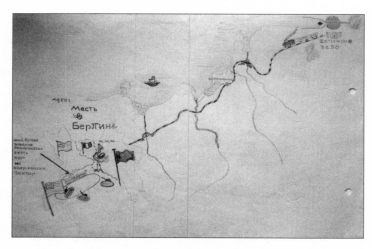

*Doodle sent to Anatoly Kuchumov, depicting clues as to
the post-war location of the Amber Room, 1949*

(Pushkin) towards Kaliningrad and then on to a Berlin that is divided into
sectors, each one highlighted by the occupier's national flag.

The chicken called Strauss is depicted again, standing in the American
sector. 'Cluck, cluck' is written over his open beak. Across the top of the
page, again in faulty Russian, is written a word that could say 'place'
or, if the letters are better formed, could also read 'revenge'. If this is the
theme, then the caption makes some sense: 'It is better for my best comrade of Leningrad to go around Berlin through the American sector.' This
is where the answer to the mystery lies, according to the cartoonist.

Someone was warning Kuchumov to beware the chicken called Strauss,
who was willing to barter the life of others in order to keep hold of a
priceless secret.

Someone else believed that Strauss was lying, despite having volunteered to assist the Soviets. And to understand why Strauss would embark
on such a high-risk venture, we need another source, an objective one
who will not attempt to filter our understanding, one who might also
lead us to Friedrich Henkensiefken, Schlossoberinspektor of Königsberg
Castle. It cannot be Stephan Strauss, the doctor's protective son.

We are torn. The material that Our Friend the Professor has obtained from the literature archive in St Petersburg is sensational and we are desperate to see what else they have. However, an official from the Stasi archives has also contacted us to say our application has been approved. We will stay in Berlin for another two weeks while Our Friend the Professor works in the literature archive in Russia on our behalf.

*Friedrich
Henkensiefken*

7

The Federal Authority for the Records of the State Security Service of the former GDR is a mouthful that most people shorten to the Ministry of Truth.

We enter its headquarters through plate-glass doors at 10.30 a.m. Female guards glower behind Perspex screens: applications for passes are to be filled out in triplicate, no cameras, no tape recorders, no ball pens. At 10.50 a.m. we are escorted to the office of the senior functionary who has been assigned to our inquiry.

From the ninth-floor windows, you can see the view clearly: right across the congested five-lane highway of Otto-Braun-Strasse and into pigeon-grey Alexanderplatz, the former hub of East Berlin. Here, on 4 November 1989 half a million demonstrators gathered to whistle at spy-chief Markus Wolf, who had been called to placate the daily public protests at the intrusions of the Stasi.[1]

The box-like office into which we are ushered has bare walls and is empty save for a large white plastic desk and four white plastic garden chairs. Sitting in one is a woman resplendent in pearls like a Japanese empress, one globe in each ear, a generous string at her throat and a delicate strand around her blue-veined wrist. As she speaks, spitting words like a slingshot, she drums the desk with a silver pen. 'So you have got your passes?' A tick in the book. 'So you have your accreditation?' A tick in the book. 'You have references?' A tick in the book. And so on and so on until she has gone through every single page in the large file of paperwork we have accrued in order to gain entry. The Ministry of Truth has a reputation for being fearsomely bureaucratic, fenced in by labyrinthine legislation. We hope our introductory interview will not be protracted.

The functionary looks at her watch, her pen hovering. 'Unfortunately, you are still not ready to see any files. I must explain the protocol.' It is now 11.15 a.m. Speaking as if to unruly children, she continues: 'Your task is difficult. I am responsible for all files relating to art theft and its investigation, from the Nazi and Stasi periods, a study that requires the examination of more than 1.1 million Nazi-era documents and tens of millions more generated by the Stasi. And there is only me and nine co-workers. Complicated research applications arrive every week from all over the world. As well as yours.'

The Stasi had begun as a smaller mirror-image of Victor Abakumov's MGB, its sponsoring organization which gifted to it Soviet interrogation records from the end of the war, a starter kit on which to build its own domestic intelligence service. But under the guiding hand of Erich Mielke, who became Minister for State Security in 1957, it underwent a kind of Marxist mitosis, its founding departments of counter-espionage, sabotage, and subversion subdividing into daughter offices responsible for coercion, intrusion and betrayal: fifteen Directorates, twelve Departments, four secretariats, the Dynamo Sports Club, the Feliks Dzerzhinsky Guard Regiment (named after the chief of the Soviet Union's Cheka), a publishing wing, a law school, a medical agency, as well as four work groups, including the fabulously titled Central Workgroup for Secrecy. At its height, the Stasi employed 91,016 staff and deployed a network of 180,000 informants (one for every sixty-two civilians).[2]

The MGB file on Strauss that we had been sent from St Petersburg contained references to three interrogations of the doctor carried out in Berlin between 1945 and 1949. Copies of these statements should be here, in the Ministry of Truth.

'Then there is the four-eyes principle.' The functionary is still talking. We can see from a typed pro forma that she is nowhere near the end of her presentation. It is now 11.30 a.m. 'The principle is designed to absolutely prevent intrusion into personal data.' There is no point mentioning that intrusion into the personal enabled the creation of these files in the first place. 'So a minimum of two members of staff are in the room with a file at any time. But these files are not actually here, so to speak, only copies. The originals are where they have always been, in another building, now controlled by the Federal Authority for the Records of the State Security Service of the former GDR.' She protectively strokes a binder.

All original Stasi and Nazi-era documents remain at the defunct ministry's headquarters three miles east, in Berlin-Lichtenberg, locked inside steel cabinets specially designed to bear the weight of a nation's secrets. The Stasi inherited this site, a block-and-a-half compound on Normannenstrasse, in 1950. Our functionary in pearls shoots out statistics: 'Side by side the paper files would stretch 122,000 metres... Microfiche: 46,500 metres. 360,000 photos. Negatives: 600,000. Slides: 24,000. Videos: 3,850. Movies: 730. And 100,000 sound recordings.'

No one would really know the scale of the Stasi's enterprise until 15 January 1990, when pro-democracy campaigners of the recently formed GDR Citizen's Committee occupied the block-and-a-half and broke into the central archive. Here they found huge motorized card indexes of GDR citizens. Above were seven reinforced floors that held the files themselves and below a vast empty room lined with copper to prevent electronic interference, inside which the Stasi had been planning to install a super-computer to accelerate the crunching of surveillance intelligence.[3]

The functionary smiles. 'We are the reading supervisors. We cannot talk to those working in the central archive at the former ministry. We are prohibited from visiting the Stasi central archive – as are you. All decisions on what is released by them are final,' she declares. Those files that are approved for public consumption are sent down Karl-Marx-Allee to Otto-Braun-Strasse under guarded transport, where reading supervisors like the one before us will censor them yet again.

'Can I be frank with you?' She has so far. 'You will see only a skeleton of information as we only have a fraction of what the Stasi actually produced. What is preserved in our archive are the deactivated papers. Cold cases put back in the store. Files on live objects or those out in the field have all vanished.'

Strauss died in 1984, six years before the Stasi ceased to exist. Is this enough time for him to become a cold case? And what of Kuchumov (dead in 1993)? And Schlossoberinspektor Henkensiefken (who, the author of

*Intelligence files
of the Stasi, the
East German
secret police,
bundled up ready
for shredding,
January 1990*

the cryptic doodle insisted, was a vital source for Kuchumov)? We have no idea if he is alive or dead. It is now 11.40 a.m.

'Even that which had been filed was got at by agents in January and February 1990.' Photographs in the lobby of the Ministry of Truth show the interiors of Stasi offices and depots as they were found: documents bulging in mailbags, heading for thousands of shredders employed by agents to turn them into bails of paper straw. As the first thing that any prospective applicant to the Federal Authority sees, it marks every trip of discovery with a disconcerting air. One is further reassured as one rides to the ninth floor in the lift by a poster that tells how, in a small village outside Nuremberg, a Federal Authority team, known as the Puzzle People, is employed to stick back together more than 15,000 sacks of those files recovered in a partially shredded state, an exercise that will take more than 375 years to complete.

'Laws too,' she explains. It is now 11.50 a.m. 'Reading of files is regulated by the Stasi Records Act, 1991. According to Section 32, I must decide whether the people you are investigating are "contemporary historical personages". These files are available for study only if "no overriding protection-worthy interests of such persons are adversely affected".' Her finger traces the wording of the law. 'Therefore, I will black out all information unnecessary for your research. I will black out anything that relates to third parties. You will not receive any original documents, only photocopies. Photographs? They may be obtained only if they are already in the public domain.' We nod even though all of it is barely comprehensible. Although the Federal Authority was set up so that victims of the Stasi could read their files, it seems that the process of extracting one's own can take a lifetime.

'Unfortunately for you –' we thought she had reached the end – 'there are also new considerations.' We sigh. 'The law has recently been amended and any files we have already censored will have to be censored again.' Former West German Chancellor Helmut Kohl fought to introduce the legislation to open up the Stasi files in 1991. But now Kohl has brought about their closure. Having been found guilty of receiving 900,000 dollars in illegal funding for the Christian Democratic Union (CDU), for which he accepted a fine so that the charges would be dropped, Kohl then took an action out against the Federal Authority when it appeared that Stasi files (including transcripts of Stasi phone taps at CDU headquarters) might throw a brighter light on his activities. A court ruled in March 2002 that Kohl's privacy would be invaded if these Stasi files were accessed and as a result millions who were afforded no privacy at all in GDR times will find it far harder to find out how, who, what and why.[4] Every time a request is made for a personal file the subject of it, even if they are former Stasi agents, must give permission before it is released. 'But you are lucky. As the re-censorship process for these files has not yet begun you have a small window of opportunity.'

We have only twelve days left in Berlin before we are scheduled to return to St Petersburg. The functionary's watch reads now 12.10 p.m. 'You might find a few helpful references in here,' she says, passing an A4 ring binder over the desk.

Before us are fourth-generation photocopies that have been scored through with so much thick black marker that they are barely legible. Someone zealously wielding a hole-puncher has cut words out of pages and whoever made these most recent copies has aligned them so badly that the reader has to guess the first word of every line. Then there is the prolific stamp of the Federal Authority itself. It recurs with such frequency that more words are obliterated beneath it. The indelible marker is lazily applied. On one page a name is blacked out but then mentioned in full seven lines beneath. Two small passport photographs of individuals wear sad Zorro-like masks of black marker. The only obvious fact that we can initially derive from these papers is that all of them have been prepared or filed by a Stasi agent with the initials P. E.

However, what we have before us is something completely unexpected. Although the date has been obscured on the first document, it is not difficult to work out the year from the text. It is not an MGB interrogation of Gerhard Strauss but an official report written by him for Dr Paul Wandel, concerning Strauss's trip to Kaliningrad in December 1949. So now we get to see the Hotel Moscow interrogation from the other side of the desk.

This version is strikingly different from Kuchumov's. In it Strauss accused Kuchumov of holding him under virtual house arrest after being interrogated. He said that he was detained in Kaliningrad for several weeks while his Soviet counterpart decided on an inadvisable excavation. Strauss wrote that 'the ground is hard as rock due to the sub-zero temperatures. Several days were taken up with clearing a passageway through the [castle's] former Albrecht Gate for the required Soviet excavator to pass through. It was far too big.'

Strauss claimed that Kuchumov was so desperate to find the Amber Room, he excavated at random:

I told him it was pointless without a proper set of plans for the castle, which I could find in Berlin. He shouted at me, accused me of knowing less than him about the layout of somewhere I had worked for years. It was most exasperating. Several days were wasted digging out the rubble that covered the remnants of the south-wing cellars. I tried to tell him that he would find only collapsed chambers there, but he did not believe it until he saw them for himself.[5]

There is no mention here of the gossip, the second-hand intelligence, the desperate lists of names, the scene of Strauss stammering under the weight of Kuchumov's questions. But then Kuchumov failed to mention the short-sightedness of embarking on a major dig in the midst of a Kaliningrad winter. We have no idea who is telling the truth.

It is only when we look up a biography of Paul Wandel, the recipient of Strauss's report, that we truly appreciate its significance. An early supporter of the German Communist Party (KPD), Paul Wandel had fled to Russia in August 1931. In Moscow, he had been selected for the Lenin School (for spies), entrance to which was limited to only the most promising cadre. Wandel graduated to the Marx-Engels Institute, where he was introduced to a senior German comrade, Wilhelm Pieck. During the war, Wandel acted as Pieck's personal secretary and in his spare time broadcast anti-fascist propaganda directed at weakening the morale of the Wehrmacht. After the return of the KPD leadership to Berlin in July 1945, the German Communist leader Walter Ulbricht appointed Wandel and Pieck to his inner circle, Wandel becoming Minister for Education and Pieck the GDR's first President.[6]

By writing to Paul Wandel, Strauss was effectively reporting his thoughts on the Amber Room to President Pieck and, by extension, to Ulbricht, General Secretary of East Germany's ruling Socialist Unity Party (SED). Although it was barely a year old, the SED Politbüro must have been as concerned with the fate of Amber Room as SovNarKom. We are beginning to appreciate the political muscle pushing the ongoing search for the Amber Room. We cannot yet comprehend why.

'May I have?' The functionary is back and has her hand out. 12.30 p.m. 'We are closed for the day.'

The next morning. In one of the anodyne white rooms at the Ministry of Truth, a file awaits us. Inside are more chewed-up pages, stamped, blotted, scribbled over, but we can see that all of them are authored by Dr Gerhard Strauss. In Kaliningrad, Strauss performed so poorly that he seemed to us to have nothing to contribute to the search for the Amber Room. An incidental witness who would fade away. And yet before us, in classified documents submitted to his superiors in the GDR, Strauss appears unstoppable, generating piles of intelligence about the Amber Room. Vain, naïve, treacherous, arrogant, whoever the real Gerhard

Strauss was, he was far more central to the search for the Amber Room than we had previously thought.

The first document in this file is another report written by Strauss in 1950 for Dr Paul Wandel. Strauss provided a detailed breakdown of all that he could recall about the events of 1945. And there was a lot. He wrote that on 15 January 1945 he returned to Königsberg from a tour of castles in East Prussia, having learned of plans to evacuate art works from the city's castle. He found Dr Alfred Rohde and ten workmen surrounded by half-packed crates, duvets and pillows in the castle yard. Strauss even recalled the names of the blacksmith and joiner employed to make the crates: Herr Weiss and Herr Mann. Rohde complained that the task to evacuate treasures was being slowed down due to his additional responsibilities as a Leutnant with the Volkssturm (the Nazi home guard). Instead of spiriting priceless art works from the doomed city he was digging defences.

Strauss wrote that he advised Rohde to take urgent action, particularly regarding the Amber Room. But Rohde informed him that it was of such value to the Nazi hierarchy that he could not move it without authorization from Dr Helmut Will, the city's Oberbürgermeister. Getting permission from Dr Will was proving difficult. Strauss then left the city on other duties as an air-raid warden and returned only at the beginning of March 1945, by which time there was no sign of Rohde. The last thing Strauss heard about the Amber Room was from a junior civil servant at the Königsberg office of the Ministry of Culture, who told him that it had been evacuated to 'somewhere east of Görlitz'. So this was the source of his Görlitz story, the hook in Strauss's letter of 1949 sent to Major Kunyn in Berlin, offering his assistance to the Soviet's Amber Room search. Strauss had then written: 'in March 1945 I did overhear that the evacuation of the Amber Room was assigned to one place, east of Görlitz'.

Nothing about his coming forward in 1949 had been down to chance. Prior to travelling to Kaliningrad in that year, he had spent four years researching the fate of the Amber Room using documents from the Soviet archive of Nazi files at Potsdam, a heavily militarized area south-west of blockaded Berlin. The Soviet Military Administration had discovered caches of Nazi files all over Germany that they locked into this high-security archive. To gain access to them Strauss must have offered his services as a translator and convinced the Soviets of his Communist credentials. We cannot yet understand why a man who must have been trusted by the Soviet authorities in Berlin treated his comrade Kuchumov in Kaliningrad with contempt.

Strauss studied the Nazi plan to evacuate art from Königsberg thoroughly and, even though he would not meet Anatoly Kuchumov until December 1949, this research shows that both men were working independently on the same theory as to the fate of the Amber Room – that it was not destroyed in the Knights' Hall.

In the dossier prepared for Wandel in 1950, Strauss cited a letter dated November 1944 from Gauleiter Erich Koch to Martin Mutschmann, the Gauleiter of Saxony, in which Koch advised his counterpart that, due to the worsening military situation in East Prussia, he was sending a museum official to Dresden, in Saxony, to search for potential storage facilities.

In November 1944 Saxony was still a safe haven, with an array of disused mines, caves and medieval fortresses in which things of value could be concealed. It was also a gateway to Bavaria and Austria, where the Nazi High Command had built its eyries and Hitler had his southern headquarters, the Eagle's Nest at Berchtesgaden.

The next wartime document in Strauss's dossier for Wandel was a report from the man chosen by Koch as his emissary, Helmut Friesen, head of the Provincial Memorials Office in Königsberg. Friesen arrived in Dresden on 22 November 1944 and met Arthur Gräfe, chief of Saxony's Department of State Collections of Art, Science, Castles, Gardens and Libraries. An account of this meeting written by Arthur Gräfe revealed that the two men discussed 'the storage of irreplaceable art treasures of high monumental value' and identified one of them as 'the famous Amber Room, a present from Frederick the Great to Tsar Peter III [sic] that had been rescued after the terror air raid on Königsberg'.[7]

Strauss had proved that in November 1944 two senior figures in the cultural apparatus of the Third Reich, acting on the orders of two Nazi Gauleiters, had begun to discuss the evacuation of the Amber Room in the certain knowledge that Königsberg was no longer safe.

According to Arthur Gräfe, storage depots in Saxony were in short supply and there were just six locations that Friesen could view: castles Sachsenburg, Kriebstein, Wechselburg, Albrechtsburg, Augustusburg and Grossgrabe Manor. On 24 November, Mutschmann approved the use of these six castles as stores for East Prussian art and Friesen returned to Königsberg.

On 1 December 1944 Arthur Gräfe was advised to expect a second official from East Prussia who would oversee the transfer of treasures from that region. Strauss found a telegram from Königsberg to Gräfe naming him as Dr Alfred Rohde. Strauss's research in Germany dovetailed with the documents found by Brusov in the bonfire set by Rohde in Königsberg Castle in June 1945: a report of Rohde's trip to Saxony and his travel permits.

However, by the time Rohde arrived in Dresden on 4 December 1944, Sachsenburg Castle, west of Chemnitz, was being used as a test centre for biological weapons. Albrechtsburg, near Meissen, had been filled with the Dresden Gallery collection, including Raphael's *Sistine Madonna*. Reichsleiter Martin Bormann, Hitler's shadow, had requisitioned Augustusburg, also near Chemnitz, as a storage facility for the Reich Chancellery and it now contained personal items belonging to Hitler, including portraits of him, several grand pianos and Otto von Bismarck's furniture. Grossgrabe Manor, near Kamenz, was full of museum treasures from Dresden. This left Alfred Rohde with only two choices: the castles of Wechselburg and Kriebstein.

We know from Rohde's report on his Saxony mission, analysed by Kuchumov in 1946, that on 4 December 1944 Rohde and Gräfe drove fifty miles west of Dresden into the heart of the Zwickauer Mulde valley. Before the war this sleepy region had been popular with German tourists, who were captivated by its turreted castles and craggy forts. Now it served to remind the Nazi High Command of the indomitable nature of the Allies. Here was Camp Colditz, a maximum-security holding centre for Allied officers, from which 130 POWs had managed to escape to date, scaling the seven-foot-high walls and abseiling down the 250-foot crag.

In a later interview, Gräfe recalled that it was snowing when they arrived at Wechselburg, a Baroque castle built next to an 800-year-old basilica, twelve miles south of Colditz.[8] Monks were preparing the church for Christmas and Gräfe and Rohde were shown around by one of them. Rohde asked permission to use 'unoccupied rooms in the palace's church and [in the palace itself], the large hall on the first level, as well as about five or six other rooms'. Even though this would displace hundreds of refugee families, Gräfe ordered the district capital of Rochlitz to requisition the space 'in favour of the municipal art collections of Königsberg'.

Strauss wrote in his dossier for Paul Wandel that Rohde and Gräfe left Wechselburg as dusk fell and travelled to Kriebstein, a Gothic fortress twelve miles to the east. In December 1944 this journey would probably have taken more than an hour. Tensions were high and Rohde and Gräfe would have been overtaken by dozens of military convoys heading towards the Eastern front. Small huddles of German soldiers manned checkpoints along the road. One can imagine the scene, their car flagged down in the snow, shivering sentries waiting impatiently at the driver's window to inspect papers by torchlight.

Rohde and Gräfe arrived at Kriebstein around 8 p.m. The 600-year-old castle, perched upon an icy spur above the River Zschopau, must have been an impressive sight in the moonlight. From photographs we know that, inside, its dark vaulted corridors were hung with antlers, while long crimson banners bearing swastikas fell from the ceiling of a banqueting hall. Several rooms were already filled with museum exhibits from Dresden. However, space was still available for things of 'irreplaceable value'. In a report submitted by Gräfe to his superiors (and found by Strauss), he wrote: 'Four heated rooms in the gatehouse of Kriebstein Castle to be placed at the disposal of the municipal art collections of Königsberg. In addition Herr Rohde would be very pleased if he could obtain the banqueting hall for the storage of larger-scale goods from the Königsberg collections.'9 Larger-scale goods could also mean the Amber Room, Strauss advised Paul Wandel, adding that Rohde had chosen the location well. Beside Kriebstein Castle was a small factory that manufactured aeroplane parts. It had its own railway siding connected directly to the Reichsbahn.

Having proved the Nazis' intention to evacuate the Amber Room to one of two castles in Saxony, Strauss now attempted to confirm that the transportation happened. However, he advised Wandel that he could locate in Berlin only one letter concerning either castle. It was from a Reichsbahn official to the manager of Kriebstein Castle and was dated 19 December 1945. It mentioned that two specially chartered train carriages were on their way from the East Prussian capital. Here Strauss stumbled. The carriages could not have contained the Amber Room since the date and location contained in the Reichsbahn letter conflicted with one written by Alfred Rohde on 12 January 1945. Three weeks after the two specially chartered train carriages had left for Kriebstein, Rohde advised his superiors that the Amber Room was still being packed in Königsberg in preparation for its evacuation to Wechselburg Castle.

Strauss's research was interrupted by his journey to Kaliningrad where he seems to have withheld almost everything he had gleaned from the Soviet files from curator Kuchumov. As an East Prussian who had been based in Königsberg, maybe Strauss felt possessive, that this mystery was his to solve, and he alone hoped to win the glory and rewards. Or maybe Kuchumov's files have been cleansed.

What we do know from the Ministry of Truth files before us is that when Strauss returned from the failed Kaliningrad mission he was rewarded by his own government. A letter signed by Wandel, dated June 1950, praised Strauss for having 'on his own initiative' diligently searched the Soviet zone for missing art treasures, including the Amber Room. Strauss now received an official commission from the GDR government to head a new investigation into the fate of the Amber Room.[10] A race was on, two parallel inquiries were under way. One was headed by a senior palace curator from Leningrad and the other by a senior cultural bureaucrat from the GDR.

According to this file in the Ministry of Truth, Strauss began his new investigation by writing to every jeweller in the GDR, asking them to report any noticeable increase in the number of carved amber pieces coming on to the market since 1945. He was looking for evidence that the Amber Room had been brought to Germany and broken down.

Strauss also ordered that every one of the new republic's 921 castles be searched and that all resettlers living in them be interrogated.

Strauss received permission to personally head investigations in Saxony, a place Kuchumov had been unable to visit in 1947 as his time in Germany had been monopolized by cataloguing Soviet art works in the Derutra warehouse in Berlin.

A report written by Strauss for Wandel in June 1950 confirmed that his first stop was Kriebstein Castle, one of the two castles that Rohde had selected in December 1944. Strauss did what Kuchumov could have only dreamed of – he located an eyewitness. He found museum curator Walfried Kunz, who described how, in April 1945, Kriebstein Castle, packed with art from all over the Reich (including Königsberg), had been stormed by the Red Army. Kunz told Strauss that the Soviet commander, based at the nearest town of Waldheim, immediately commandeered the art crammed into the banqueting hall, gatehouse and other rooms. Kunz had been ordered to help open and sort through the crates. But the Amber Room was not among this haul.

That was not all. Kunz informed Strauss that a special Red Army brigade arrived at Kriebstein in July 1945 and carried out another search. They seemed to know about art and, Kunz claimed, he overheard them talking about Königsberg and missing treasures from there. But, as far as Kunz knew, the Soviets found no more. Strauss turned his attentions to Wechselburg Castle, dismissing Kriebstein as a possible location for the Amber Room.

At Wechselburg, he found an old Catholic father, Gottfried Fussy, who had been caretaker of the basilica for more than thirty years. Fussy confirmed to him that in December 1944 he had shown Dr Alfred Rohde and a museum administrator from Dresden (Arthur Gräfe) around but had heard nothing more until Gräfe returned shortly before Germany's surrender. Strauss wrote: '[Fussy] was then told [by Gräfe] that the transports from Königsberg had not got through. The railway lines were cut by the Soviet army near Elbing.' According to Father Fussy, the next visitors to Wechselburg were American soldiers in mid-April. Strauss reported to Wandel: 'They found a few crates which they took away.'

There was only one conclusion that Strauss felt able to convey to his superiors. High-level plans had been made for the evacuation of the Amber Room to Saxony that were thwarted by Allied troop movements and the interruption of transportation routes out of East Prussia. However, given the status of these plans, the high-ranking Nazi officials involved in them and the cachet attached to the Amber Room as an 'irreplaceable treasure', Strauss wrote that it was 'inconceivable' that the Amber Room would have been abandoned in the unsecured Knights' Hall, in a wrecked castle at the epicentre of a besieged city whose future was getting bleaker by the hour. It had survived the war, concealed somewhere in Königsberg.

There is only one more document in this Ministry of Truth binder, a June 1959 edition of *Freie Welt*, an illustrated magazine published by the German–Soviet Friendship Society that contains an 'exclusive' two-part series entitled 'Where is the Famous Amber Room?'

The article began: 'For the first time all citizens of the GDR will learn the true and fascinating story of the Amber Room, thanks to the generosity of our guest editor, Professor Dr Gerhard Strauss, director of the Faculty of Art History, Humboldt University, Berlin.'

We are surprised to see Strauss revealing to his fellow citizens something that had up until then been a state secret: 'a covert investigation conducted into the fate of the Soviet Union's greatest treasure'. Strauss informed readers that contrary to the earlier conclusions reached by Professor Alexander Brusov of the State Historical Museum, Moscow, the Amber Room was not destroyed in the defeat of Königsberg. It was still missing and readers were encouraged to write in to *Freie Welt* with any information that might help their Soviet comrades find this national treasure.

It is unthinkable that such a revelation would have appeared without the blessing of the Stasi and the KGB. And that raises the possibility that the recently promoted Professor Dr Gerhard Strauss was a Soviet agent of influence or a Stasi informer. The strands of Cold War intrigue are becoming increasingly difficult to disentangle.

We revert to the Russian files. In an attempt to understand the precise nature of the relationship between Anatoly Kuchumov and Professor Dr Gerhard Strauss, we have requested all material from the Leningrad curator's papers relating to the 1950s. A slim package has arrived from St Petersburg. Our Friend the Professor says she is busy and has not been able to visit the archive as frequently as she had hoped. Also, she tells us that the archive director intends to limit our research – we can only have six further days. We cannot return to Russia just yet so will have to rely on the professor.

What we have been sent is a photocopied scrapbook on which is written in large unsteady letters the words YANTARNY KOMNATA, the Amber Room.[11]

It contains pages of newspaper articles, and must have been one of those volumes seen by Vladimir Telemakov when the journalist for the car workers' daily visited Kuchumov at his Pavlovsk apartment.

We flick through wartime reports until we reach three long cuttings from *Kaliningradskaya Pravda*, a densely written Soviet broadsheet. The use of pictures is spartan as nothing must be allowed to interrupt the columns of minuscule dogma that run page after page like machine code. However, when we notice halfway through the first piece a smudged shot of war-torn Königsberg and the words '*Yantarny Komnata*' we decide to translate them.

Written by Vladimir Dmetriev, the first article, dated 6 July 1958, was headlined: 'The Search Continues for the Missing Amber Room'.[12] Dmetriev revealed to his readers that this was the start of an exclusive three-part series in which 'for the first time all citizens of the USSR will

Surrender of Königsberg, April 1945

learn the true and fascinating story of the Amber Room'. We have just read a similar phrase – in German.

Dmetriev wrote of what had, up until then, been a state secret: the covert investigation into the fate of the Soviet Union's greatest treasure, the Amber Room of the Catherine Palace. He informed his readers that contrary to the earlier conclusions of Professor Alexander Brusov of the State Historical Museum in Moscow, the Amber Room had not been destroyed in the fall of Königsberg and was still missing. Strauss would make exactly the same claims a year later in *Freie Welt*.

Reporter Dmetriev claimed that, in December 1949, he was a member of the 'top-secret mission to search for the Amber Room in Kaliningrad', an investigation ordered by ObKom (the *oblast* or provincial committee of the Communist Party of the Soviet Union) and authorized by SovNarKom in Moscow. 'I was really involved and excited. I had never done anything so interesting before. We reported every day to ObKom our measurements of the castle and during the evening analysed results, as if it was a difficult crossword.' We are certain that Dmetriev was referring to the same expedition as the one led by Kuchumov, to which Gerhard Strauss was called. It was supposed to be covert.

However, Dmetriev continued: 'This was vital work. Soldiers were assigned, sappers, engineers, officers, drainage experts with water pumps, generators to light up the rubble, tunnels and bunkers. I looked through fortresses and estates, wondering where the Amber Room could be hidden.' We are puzzled that Kuchumov made no mention of a valued team member called Vladimir Dmetriev and realize that our view of the 1949 mission has until now been restricted to the interrogation room in the Hotel Moscow, where Kuchumov faced down Gerhard Strauss.

The *Kaliningradskaya Pravda* report revealed that a crack team of specialists and Communist Party cadre were on the trail of those surviving Nazis who knew the coordinates of the Amber Room's secret location. 'Write in,' Dmetriev urged his readers. 'Write to us with all your information.' Dmetriev was particularly keen to have help in finding Helmut Will, Helmut Friesen, Gerhard Zimmerman, Ernst Gall and Friedrich Henkensiefken. Surely it was not a coincidence that these names were also on Kuchumov's list of missing Germans and that one of them,

Friedrich Henkensiefken, was the Schlossoberinspektor of Königsberg Castle referred to on the cryptic doodle sent to the great curator from Berlin.

The second article from *Kaliningradskaya Pravda* was published three days later, on 9 July 1958. In this piece, Dmetriev revealed that the first Soviet investigation into the fate of the Amber Room, in May 1945, mounted by Professor Alexander Brusov, was a débâcle. Using a series of transparent pseudonyms, Dmetriev launched a stinging attack on 'Viktor Barsov' (Alexander Brusov) and team member 'Comrade Beliaev' (Tatyana Beliaeva), accusing them of being slipshod and failing to follow even the most obvious clues. 'Barsov' was 'muddle-headed' and omitted to question the key witness in the inquiry, Dr Alfred Rohde, director of the Königsberg Castle Museum, about the Amber Room, partly because 'Barsov did not know that [the Amber Room] was taken from the Catherine Palace'.

These claims wildly conflict with Professor Brusov's own diary in which we read that his primary objective was to travel to Königsberg to bring home the Amber Room and that Rohde was his key source. Dmetriev was lying.

He then claimed that 'Barsov' came into contact with Rohde and his wife only by chance, when he hired them to help search the castle for other missing treasures, giving them the same pay and food rations as those received by Soviet helpers. 'Rohde and his wife had a wonderful, comfortable life and work,' Dmetriev wrote, 'until they disappeared.'

From 'a high-level military source' Dmetriev learned the true fate of Rohde and his wife, who did not die of sickness, malnutrition or suicide. 'Both had been poisoned,' Dmetriev revealed, 'murdered to stop them giving away the secret location of the Amber Room.' Dmetriev wrote that two death certificates found by 'Barsov', stating that Rohde and his wife had contracted dysentery, were fakes and that the doctor who allegedly signed them after carrying out post-mortems had vanished. When the Soviet authorities opened the graves to re-examine the bodies, there was nothing inside them. 'Even today, we have not found [Rohde's] real tomb,' wrote Dmetriev. Yet Brusov had written in his diary that Rohde was still alive when he left the city in July 1945.

The second Dmetriev article concluded with a confession from 'Barsov' that we read in astonishment. 'I am a historian,' he told the newspaper. 'I am naïve about the character of people. I am not able to see their mood. I cannot understand if a person is joyful or sad. This became a problem after I got orders to search for treasures with the Soviet Army.'

It is hard to reconcile this voice with the one in the diary we have read. Either 'Barsov'/Brusov must have been compelled to make this humiliating public statement for reasons that we do not yet understand or the entire article was a fabrication.

The third and final piece for *Kaliningradskaya Pravda*, published on 12 July 1958, was far shorter but equally explosive, as it touched on the issue of treason. Reporter Dmetriev wrote that military sources had revealed to him that a number of Soviet museum curators were traitors who collaborated with the Nazis: 'Our German friends and their little Soviet helpers know the secret of the Amber Room. It did not burn. It is still not found. The search continues. Dear comrades, send your notes and proposals to *Kaliningradskaya Pravda*.'

The *Freie Welt* and *Kaliningradskaya Pravda* articles contained identical idiosyncrasies and errors. They both called Rohde's daughter Ilse, claiming she left Königsberg in 1944, when her name was Lotti and she had stayed in the city until 1945. They both used the same awkwardly worded retraction made by muddle-headed 'Barsov'. Both contained the identical revelations that Alfred Rohde had been murdered and the Amber Room had survived the fall of Königsberg. It would be easy to dismiss these articles as spurious if we had not then discovered that the same story was also carried by *Soviet Russia* on 21 June 1959 and by the Soviet newspaper *Front* six days later, as well as by all the regional editions of *Pravda*.

After all the years of silence following Professor Brusov's interview with TASS on 13 July 1945, with not so much as a word said about the fate of the Amber Room, an entirely new story had tumbled out. And when all the versions of it, published in the Soviet Union and the GDR, are placed side by side, it strikes us that what we have before us is a deliberate campaign to end any lingering speculation that the Amber Room was destroyed in the Knights' Hall of Königsberg Castle in April

1945. The public focus was being drawn away from loss and towards the Nazis accused of evacuating the Amber Room from Königsberg Castle to no one knew where. With the spectre of traitors in their midst, all good comrades would have to rally together and help track down these Nazis, so that the Amber Room could be restored to the Soviet Union. There had to be a purpose behind such a campaign.

We need help, ideally from one of those responsible for the story. It first broke in *Kaliningradskaya Pravda*, but when we call no one there has heard of Vladimir Dmetriev. A contact in Moscow, who has assembled a database of journalists, says that no one by the name of Vladimir Dmetriev has ever been registered. That makes Vladimir Dmetriev more than likely a pseudonym and the thought suddenly occurs to us that Dmetriev might be Anatoly Kuchumov, the man sent to reopen the Amber Room search, a key opponent of Professor Brusov. It would have been in Kuchumov's interests to discredit his predecessor's findings. For the first time we notice that Kuchumov's name was absent from all of these articles about his 1949 Kaliningrad mission (articles that are pasted into his scrapbook).

But Kuchumov is dead. Gerhard Strauss too. *Freie Welt* closed down in 1991. We are not scheduled to go back to Russia for another ten days. However, since the Stasi controlled all publications in GDR times, we contact an information trader from former East Berlin who, we have been told, sells contacts with old apparatchiks.

Could he broker a meeting with a former editor of *Freie Welt*, we ask? 'No,' the information trader says, 'but there's someone else who might be able to help. I do have contact with a former Stasi lieutenant-colonel who worked in propaganda. Pay up and I'll get you an introduction. Maybe he knows something about it.' The information trader hangs up.

It is said that if you put the right number of coins in the box these days in Germany, former Stasi officers pop up. And yet when the Stasi lieutenant-colonel calls us, we are still surprised to be talking to him. It is a brief conversation, devoid of any niceties. The man demands a pseudonym. We settle on Herr 'Stolz'. He asks the topic of discussion. We keep it tight. We say we want to talk about his specialism – state propaganda. He asks for our address. We give him the room number at the Berlin Swissôtel.

*

Overlooking the Swissôtel's glass atrium from the eighth floor, we watch a middle-aged man in a black felt beret pacing the lobby in black zip-up boots. He observes the minimalist scene with its stained pine, marble and chrome, stopping to press the plush cream furnishings and stooping to sniff the pink lilies, all the time keeping an eye on everyone who emerges from the lifts.

Once in a while he sits down on the sofa beside the lobby bar, his black boots easing themselves into the luxurious pile, his suede gloves sliding over the smooth leather seat covers. And then off he goes again. The flowers. Rising and sitting. Stooping and sniffing. This must be 'Stolz'.

We ring down to reception and a few minutes later he is at our door, his milky blue eyes studying our faces, while a gloved hand strokes an immaculate Walter Ulbricht beard.

Only when our room door is locked does he signal that he is ready to talk. Can 'Stolz' tell us anything about Gerhard Strauss's articles in *Freie Welt*? Hunched on the bed facing the window, his back to us, 'Stolz' is monitoring the shoppers milling along Kurfürstendamm. Suddenly he looks over his shoulder. '*Freie Welt* was a textbook case,' he says. What does 'Stolz' mean by a 'textbook case'? He ignores our question but takes off his gloves and his black felt beret. We notice that his rosy cheeks and thin pink fingers have an expensive spa sheen as he launches into a lecture about the art of propaganda and disinformation.

We interrupt. Can he be more specific? Can 'Stolz' tell us about *Freie Welt*? The Amber Room? He picks up his beret and starts to pull on his gloves. 'I don't know anything about the Amber Room. Have you brought me here under false pretences?' he snaps. 'I thought I had come here to talk about me. My expertise. My career in the disinformation unit at the Stasi's foreign affairs directorate.'

We try to calm things down. Talk him back. He is almost at the door. We do need your expertise, we say. We are interested in your career. But we also need to understand the *Freie Welt* articles, what they really meant. Would he like a coffee? 'Stolz' goes quiet. We point to the room's personal chrome Gaggia machine and push a small black button marked ESPRESSO. A lush coffee oozes out. 'OK,' says 'Stolz'. The former Stasi officer is hypnotized by such sophistication and he sits back down at his perch by the window.

'You're never going to understand *Freie Welt* until you understand the nature of disinformation,' he says, savouring the espresso shot.

'Our textbooks were Lenin. Of course.'

We nod.

'And Sefton Delmar.'

Who was Sefton Delmar, we ask?

He tut-tuts. 'Sefton Delmar was the genius behind the science of disinformation. I am surprised you have never heard of him, as he was a famous journalist with your *Daily Express*.' He's deviating again, but we do not interrupt this time.

'Stolz' explains how all Stasi operatives in his directorate were ordered to study Delmar's two-volume autobiography, *Trial Sinister* and *Black Boomerang*, in which the former *Daily Express* Berlin bureau chief revealed his double life.[13] In 1940 Britain's Special Operations Executive (SOE) had employed Sefton Delmar, a fluent German speaker, to devise methods of weakening the morale of the Wehrmacht. Delmar set up a phoney German radio station, Soldatensender Calais, perfect in every way apart from the fact that it broadcast from Ashdown Forest in Sussex and its presenters were British intelligence officers.

Delmar's radio persona was a belligerent Prussian diehard, an army officer known to German listeners as Der Chef, who was deeply loyal to the Fatherland but outspoken on certain policies. 'Stolz' recounts how in one of the first broadcasts, Der Chef bitterly attacked Hitler's deputy Rudolf Hess, who, a few days previously, had made his flight to Scotland. Stolz becomes animated: 'I have studied the transcripts. Delmar was a subtle master. Der Chef stormed, "As soon as there is a crisis, Hess packs himself a white flag and flies off to throw himself and us on the mercy of that flat-footed bastard of a drunken old cigar-smoking Jew, Churchill!" 'Don't you see,' 'Stolz' says, putting down his empty cup. 'The message was plausible. What was false was the source.'

Is 'Stolz' saying that *Freie Welt* (which we know to be a genuine GDR publication) ran a phoney story about the Amber Room, one that had been generated in the Soviet Union?

'No,' 'Stolz' says. 'It wasn't the story that was false. The story was partially true, although some details may have been exaggerated. It was the source of the information that had been disguised. New evidence had been unearthed that confirmed that the Amber Room had been evacuated from Königsberg to a secret location, but there were conflicting stories about its precise location.

'A major investigation was being planned. But to be certain, the authorities needed to identify anyone out there who knew about the Amber Room, who was connected with it, and who had gone to ground after the war. They needed assistance in testing and honing their hypothesis. Thousands of GDR citizens had been convicted of being Nazi collaborators, of looting, of war crimes, and the Stasi was still hunting down people. No one would come forward voluntarily if the request was made by the state, but a respected East German academic like Strauss, a former citizen of East Prussia, a man already connected with the Amber Room story who was not afraid to say so in public, gave people the confidence to write in. And thousands of letters arrived in response to the *Freie Welt* articles.'

What did the letter-writers reveal?

'It was not my responsibility. All I know is that *Freie Welt* was dealt with at the very top, by the Committee of the Minister for State Security, Comrade General Erich Mielke, and that soon after the Stasi formed a highly secret study group to find the Amber Room. I know this because I used to be in contact with its chief, Oberst [Colonel] Seufert.'

Did Oberst Seufert ever hint at what new evidence the Stasi was working on, we ask?

'No. I told you I was not involved. I worked for a different directorate. But I do recall strict instructions about informants who came in with leads about art thefts. We were to pass them immediately to the office of Generaloberst Bruno Beater, Mielke's deputy during the 1970s. Particularly if they concerned the Amber Room. Generaloberst Beater apparently took the issue of the missing Amber Room very seriously. Sometimes we would get questions back from Beater's office. But I did not deviate from my orders. I only asked the questions I was ordered to.'

Was Strauss then working for the Stasi, we ask, or perhaps a Soviet security agency? The story he wrote had originated in the USSR after all.

'I couldn't possibly say,' says 'Stolz'. 'I never met Strauss but I knew him by reputation. The Herr Professor Doctor was well respected among the upper echelons of the SED Politbüro.'

Can 'Stolz' put us in touch with Oberst Seufert, General Beater or anyone else connected with the Stasi's Amber Room study group?

No response. From a leather folder 'Stolz' produces a slim volume with a cheap cellophane cover decorated with a drawing of the Amber Room, tinted yellow and white: *Bernsteinzimmer Report*. 'Have you seen this? The author was the GDR's foremost Amber Room expert. Amassed a lot of information.'

Paul Enke's book on the search for the Amber Room, published in 1986

'Stolz' throws the book on to the bed and turns back to look down on Kurfürstendamm. *Bernsteinzimmer Report*, published in 1986 by a man who might or might not have been a Stasi agent, is the most famous German book about the Amber Room mystery. But it is long out of print and this is the first copy we have actually seen.

Was Paul Enke part of the Stasi study group, we ask? 'Stolz' isn't listening. He's at the mirror, moulding his black felt beret back on his head. We flick through the book to see in the flyleaf a handwritten inscription: 'To my Comrade ['Stolz'], with thanks, Paul Enke.' You know the author, Paul Enke, we say? No response. Can we at least speak to Enke directly?

'Stolz' stifles a little laugh with a gloved hand, brushing the leather against his lips. 'I don't think so,' he murmurs. 'Enke's dead. Quite unexpected. A relatively young man. We were all very shocked. *Bernsteinzimmer Report* had only just been published.'

'Stolz' holds out his hand. 'Give. I need it back. Must go. Have to pick up my daughter from the airport.' And with a waft of cheap soap, he is gone although we have held the book just long enough to see the name of its editor, Günter Wermusch, and the quote that begins Paul Enke's story, something he had taken from Johann Wolfgang von Goethe: 'Some of the splendour of the world has melted away through war and time.'

8

We ring round the second-hand bookshops in Berlin that specialize in publications from the former GDR, but none of them has a copy of Paul Enke's *Bernsteinzimmer Report*. One outlet in Ackerstrasse, in former East Berlin, suggests we contact Enke's editor directly. 'Günter Wermusch. He is still alive,' he says.

But there are several G. Wermuschs in the phone book. Eventually we connect to this weary voice: 'Wermusch, *ja bitte?*'

A hacking cough interrupts our prepared speech. The man at the other end sounds consumptive or very old. He drops the receiver. Hack, hack, clunk. We call back again, mention a name and wait for his answer.

'Paul Enke? *Scheisse. Nein, nein.*' Clunk.

We try again: 'Hello?'

Silence. Then Wermusch manages a few words: '*Sprechen sie Deutsch?* I don't speak English. Not since 1992.' Clunk.

One final attempt from us: '*Guten Tag*, we have flown from London …'

Hack, hack. Then Wermusch hoarsely whispers: 'Ach. Nah. What did you say your name? OK. Who told you about me? In three days' time you come. 5 p.m. *Nur eine halbe Stunde, ja?*' Clunk.

We return to the Ministry of Truth, where we have applied for files on Paul Enke, Oberst Hans Seufert and the Stasi's Amber Room study group. They are not ready. Two days later we are contacted to say that a single personal file has been located. It will take longer to find and release any files from the study group, the Ministry of Truth functionary says, and we will not be allowed to see Seufert's file without his permission. He is still alive.

Paul Enke, KSII404/82, is waiting for us on a white plastic table in a sterile reading room. This personal file on the author of *Bernsteinzimmer Report* is a brick of paperwork. With Enke dead, Wermusch reluctant and the book out of print, getting hold of it is better news than we could possibly have hoped for and there is plenty to read. Enke's book jacket carried no biography. There was no author photograph. No explanation as to *how* he had become, as the blurb claimed, '... involved in the inquiries and investigations about the fate of the Amber Room ...' Judging by the length of what we have before us, Enke was obviously significant to the Stasi and we open his file, unsure whether we are about to read of a lowly informer and weekend Amber Room fanatic or discover between the pages a forensic investigator at the heart of a state-sponsored inquiry.

First are pages of photographs. The earliest, a black-and-white shot, is clipped to a 1950 Volkspolizei service record. Enke was a people's policeman. It shows him as a dashing young recruit, proud of his gilt epaulettes, his collars stitched with the emblem of the force. The next frame portrays Enke, about a decade later, now dressed as a purposeful bureaucrat in a tight black suit, wearing heavy-framed glasses. We wonder if he became

Paul Enke, c.1960

a plain-clothes officer. The last pictures are of Enke in his late middle age with receding hair, his face now puggish. He wears a look unique to the GDR, a garish checked sports jacket, a black shirt, a clashing light tie and a distant expression. This strip, probably taken in the early 1970s in a photo booth, recurs throughout the file.

Next is a report by Major Schmalfuss, a Stasi departmental director, who seems to know everything about Paul Enke.[1]

Born: Magdeburg, 20 January 1925. Social class: worker. 'In his parents' home, Paul Enke received a Protestant education and consequently joined a Christian youth organization in 1931,' Major Schmalfuss wrote.[2]

Left school at thirteen. Apprenticed as a lathe operator. Early political development: 'Christliche Jugend and Hitler Jugend'. The Stasi had uncovered a serious black mark against Enke that would surely impact on his adult life in the GDR, membership of the Hitler Youth. But Major Schmalfuss was satisfied that the blame lay with Enke's parents: 'Due to the inadequacy of positive political-ideological influences [at home], Comrade Enke became a member of the Hitler Jugend in 1935 and volunteered in 1942.'

Enke was seventeen when he set out to fight for the Fatherland. Schmalfuss wrote: 'Served in fasch. Wehrmacht, Funkmeßer [radar technician] Marinebrigade (1 May 1942 to 8 May 1945), lance-corporal, stationed in Gdingen, Poland; in Kiel, northern Germany; in Courland, on the Baltic coast. He has never been decorated.'

Enke served through the war in and around the Baltic's amber coast, which might provide a tenuous personal connection between him and the Amber Room. We wonder if he heard about the triumphal arrival of the Amber Room in Königsberg Castle after it was opened to the public in the spring of 1942.

The war ended for Lance-Corporal Enke on 8 May 1945 when he surrendered to the Red Army that marched him and hundreds of thousands of others to prison camp. Major Schmalfuss listed Enke's POW record: 'Soviet Camp 27/2 Moscow (May 1945 to January 1946); Soviet Camp 7711 Leningrad (January 1946 to May 1949); Zentralschule 2041, Kursant (June to December 1949).

Zentralschule 2041. By 1949 Enke must have convinced his Soviet captors that he could be rehabilitated, and while thousands of others languished in camps until 1955, he spent six months on political study leave at the Soviet Central Training School in Kursant. Here, according to Schmalfuss, Enke 'worked as a lathe operator, fitter, blacksmith and bricklayer'. We are becoming a little concerned. The Paul Enke we are reading about was not promising material for a high-velocity secret inquiry in pursuance of the Amber Room

Major Schmalfuss did have something positive to say about Enke's days at the Soviet Central Training School, Kursant: 'He had his first contacts with anti-fascists, becoming a member of the Anti-Fascist Committee in Leningrad, and was employed as Brigade and Company Propagandist after short training courses. Comrade Enke's theoretical knowledge of Marxism-Leninism is good.'[3]

Enke may not have been bright, but he clearly was cunning. He understood that he would have to change to fit in with the new world that had sprung up around him. Major Schmalfuss wrote: 'Comrade Enke arrived at the realization that the ideological view of life that he held hitherto had been incorrect. This realization and the world view he is holding nowadays are separating him from his parental home but Comrade Enke places the political necessities in the foreground.' Enke had returned from the war a different man, willing to denounce his parents – and his religion. 'Against his parents' wishes [Enke] resigned from the Protestant Church,' wrote Major Schmalfuss. His file is beginning to illustrate a man edging towards the state apparatus.

But what would Enke do with the rest of his life? 'Joins GDR Volkspolizei (25 January 1950), Magdeburg.' This must have been when the first photograph of Enke was taken, in his uniform. Oberrat Bähr, the Volkspolizei school director, wrote a glowing report on 23 October 1950: 'Comrade Enke's class-consciousness is well developed. Through his continuous self-studies he will eventually succeed in becoming a good propagandist... Nothing disadvantageous or detrimental is known about his social life.'[4]

By 1952 Enke had been promoted to the rank of Oberrat (senior councillor) and a superior wrote: 'Enke possesses a healthy ambition and makes efforts to fulfil his tasks, sacrificing his free time... Enke's fighting spirit becomes apparent during discussions about deeper problems.'⁵ We can almost feel Enke maturing, greedy for success and knowledge.

Five years later, on 1 April 1957, he was seconded to the Ministry of the Interior at Potsdam, employed to 'deal with the administration of the cadre and teacher seminaries'. He won a law diploma, grade 'Good', from the Walter Ulbricht Training Academy at Potsdam-Babelsberg. Enke's diploma certificate was embossed with the recently adopted Soviet-sponsored emblem for the state, a hammer and a compass ringed by a crescent of rye, symbolizing the GDR's new social divisions: the worker, the intelligentsia and the farmer. He had come a long way since leaving school at thirteen.

A handwritten report appended to the file noted that Enke began to use his position in Potsdam to access the wartime archives, conducting on his weekends 'private research into a hobby'. We feel a charge of excitement as we read that Enke's chosen subject was 'the fascist robbery of the Amber Room'. The note recorded that he had made 'significant finds' and located important new archive documentation.⁶

The Ministry of Truth's functionary in pearls announces that she has recently come into possession of 12,000 pages of Stasi material relating to the Amber Room. Are we interested? Of course, we say. The files have

The Stasi files

been missing since 1991 and have never been properly analysed, she tells us. Lost and found? We look incredulous. 'The papers were in the Bundesarchiv facility at Koblenz. They had been sent to the wrong archive after *die Wende*,' she explains, unflustered. 'I always thought they had been destroyed. But they were just sitting in the dark somewhere, until I got them back. Archives are very territorial places.' The functionary beams. 'You are very lucky.'

An assistant comes in and drops a bulging binder on to the white plastic table, just one of thirty volumes. 'Finish this one. Then request another.' She leaves us alone with the paper mountain. We have been warned that there are now only days left before all these files are closed so that they can be recensored under the Kohl judgment. We need to work quickly.

Straight away we find references to Enke's private research in Potsdam. But it is not clear whether he gave his material voluntarily or if the Stasi requisitioned it.

Written in a forward-slanting, purposeful hand is a report by Enke himself. It began in hyperbolic fashion with Enke describing 'the German fascist's robbery of Europe's cultural heritage' as far worse than those carried out by 'the Persians at Babylon, the Romans at Athens or the Crusaders at Constantinople'. The theft of the Amber Room was, according to Enke, 'the most painful loss of all'.[7]

Enke substantiated his claim. He set out to prove that the pillage of Europe and the theft of the Amber Room were premeditated. The Nazis had been preparing to cherry-pick Eastern Europe as far back as 1933, he reported. They had gathered information about Eastern European museum collections via a cover organization called the German Academic Exchange Service. Free excursions, conferences and training workshops were offered to museum staff from the USSR, while Germans of Baltic origin were dispatched to spy on their collections. Even while Molotov and Ribbentrop were negotiating the non-aggression pact in 1939, and Latvia, Lithuania and Estonia were being constituted as Soviet republics, this team of art spies was drawing up lists of collectables for Hitler.[8]

On 15 November 1940 team leader Dr Nils von Holst, an Eastern art expert and head of the Berlin State Museums' external affairs department, issued a secret circular to museum directors across the Reich, asking them to identify 'isolated [foreign] exhibits that for various reasons could represent an enrichment of the German cultural heritage'. By May 1941 Dr Nils von Holst was in Moscow, trying to persuade Pushkin Museum director Andrei Guber to let him view storerooms on the pretext of buying paintings. Enke wrote: 'He tried to do the same in Leningrad.' We wonder if Dr Nils von Holst met Anatoly Kuchumov and saw the Amber Room.

Dr von Holst was still writing up his Soviet findings when Operation Barbarossa was launched on 22 June 1941. Two days later he presented his report on 'the most important collections of cultural possessions in the Baltic countries' to Dr Hans Posse, then director of the Dresden Gallery and, more significantly, a key art adviser to Hitler.[9] Enke found a dispatch order dated 8 July 1941 forwarding the list of collectables on to the 18th Army headquarters, from where it was disseminated to the commanders of German units advancing on Leningrad.

On 1 September 1941 Dr von Holst was sent back to the Soviet Union, initially to Smolensk, recently captured by the Wehrmacht's Army Group Centre, with instructions to help establish the eastern headquarters for Einsatzstab Reichleiter Rosenberg, the art-looting organization headed by Hitler's ideologue Alfred Rosenberg. By 26 September, Dr von Holst was at the front, camped at the Catherine Palace with Army Group North, charged with safeguarding 'the art treasures of [the tsars' palaces at] Krasnoye Selo, Peterhof and Oranienbaum and later also Petersburg [sic]', according to a letter from the Führer's aide-de-camp, dated 26 September.[10] Although initially sceptical we are now gripped by how closely Enke was able to follow a Nazi art expert all the way into the Catherine Palace.

Next Enke reported that he had found a copy of Dr von Holst's list, attached to Hitler's order from July 1941, reserving the first pick of art works plundered from the East. But here was a set-back. The Amber Room was not on it.

Enke was undeterred. He dug on until he discovered a second list, compiled for propaganda minister Joseph Goebbels by Otto Kümmel, the seventy-year-old director of the Berlin State Museums and Dr von Holst's boss.[11] This one consisted of all German art works that had gone abroad since 1500 and were to be repatriated. Prominently placed on it was the Amber Room. If Enke's research was reliable, he had proved that the theft of the Amber Room was premeditated. And whoever had planned its theft would possibly have also worked out how to conceal it in 1945.

Enke wrote that all items on the Kümmel list were to be returned to their German towns of origin or set aside for Sonderauftrag Linz (Special Operation Linz), a Führermuseum and Aryan culture park that Albert Speer, Hitler's architect, had been asked to construct on the banks of the Danube, outside Linz, the town where the Führer had spent his childhood.

Enke found a war diary for the 18th Army and in it an entry for 29 September 1941 that, he argued, proved the dismantling of the Amber Room had been overseen by the Nazi High Command: '16.oohrs: Cavalry Captain Count Solms, from the Supreme Army Command, who has been commissioned to record the works of art in the tsarist palaces, asks for protection for the tsarist palace in Pushkin... It is now in the immediate vicinity of the front line and is endangered by the thoughtless behaviour of our troops.'[12]

Dr Ernst-Otto Count zu Solms Laubach

Enke tracked down Captain Solms's unit, the 50th Corps, and in its journal he found this entry: '14 October 1941. Krasnogwardeisk. Removal of the works of art salvaged by Cavalry Captain Dr Count Solms and Captain Dr Pönsgen in Gatchina and Pushkin, including the wall panels of the amber hall from the Pushkin Palace to Königsberg.'

From military archives held in the GDR, Enke learned that the cavalry captain's full name was Dr Ernst-Otto Count zu Solms Laubach and that he was an aristocrat from Frankfurt-am-Main and a museum curator in civilian life. One week before the Count had arrived in Pushkin, he had been in the Leningrad palace of Peterhof, supervising the looting of the Neptune Fountain, an art work that was also on the list prepared by Otto Kümmel for Goebbels. Hitler had personally requested that the Neptune Fountain be returned to Nuremberg, where it had been cast in the mid-seventeenth century.[13] If the Count had been acting in Peterhof for Hitler, then it was, Enke argued, likely that he was acting for Hitler in the Catherine Palace too.

But having established that the Nazi High Command had ordered the Amber Room theft, who had taken specific responsibility for it in Königsberg and after? Enke reported that 'General [sic] Marshal Goering, Reichsführer SS Himmler, Reichsleiters Lammers and Bormann, Rosenberg and foreign minister Ribbentrop' had all used their positions to amass large art collections and were possible contenders.[14]

However, it was Alfred Rosenberg that Enke focused on and he discovered some interesting connections.[15] Although Rosenberg was of German descent, he had been born in Tallinn, the capital of Estonia, on the Baltic coast. The son of a cobbler, he had been sent to college in Petrograd (Leningrad), where, Enke reasoned, it was likely that he would have learned of the legendary Amber Room. When Rosenberg fled Petrograd in 1917, finding common cause with 600,000 White Russian refugees who converged on Germany, he joined the Freikorps, roving counter-revolutionary units that held back the Bolshevik advance. When disbanded, these Freikorps veterans remained closely linked through the Baltic Brotherhood, an organization for ex-servicemen whose ceremonies were steeped in Norse and Teutonic myths of heroism and self-sacrifice. Many, including Rosenberg, converged on Munich, forming a pseudo-intellectual circle around Hitler and joining the secretive Thule Society, which conjured the existence of a mythical island, the source of amber, a land locked into the ice flows of the far north whose pagan inhabitants adopted a creed of strength and loyalty.

Through his tenacity and hard work, the weekends spent researching in Potsdam, Enke had identified a senior member of the Nazi High

Command who not only was responsible for looting art but also had clear links with the Baltic culture surrounding the Amber Room and the coast from where it originated.

On 18 November 1941 Alfred Rosenberg won another portfolio as head of Hitler's Reichsministerium für die besetzen Ostgebiete, the Ministry for the Occupied Eastern Territories, *The Times* of London commenting: 'Rosenberg is Hitler's Eastern expert ... Rosenberg, who hates everything Russian, will certainly conduct his office with ruthless brutality.' The only part of the USSR that was to be maintained intact was the Baltic states, Rosenberg promised, a region that he described as having been captured '700 years ago by German knights'.[16]

Enke traced the growth of ERR-Ost, Rosenberg's Eastern art-looting organization, as it spread its tentacles into every city and town. In Lithuania, ERR-Ost was operating out of the capital, Kaunus. In Latvia it was based in Riga. In Estonia it had offices at Tallinn and Tartu. It was based in the Belarus capital at Minsk and in the Ukraine, where the wealthy republic kept busy four offices at Chernihiv, Dnipropetrovsk, Kharkiv and Kherson. There were ERR-Ost operations in the Caucasus, the Crimea and in Russia proper, where units fanned out in an arc west of Moscow, 'at Pskov, Smolensk, Voroschilovgrad [*sic*] and Voronezh'. Rosenberg's staff were everywhere.

But it was all of academic interest until Enke found an ERR-Ost report about the Amber Room itself. On 28 April 1944 Dr Nerling at the ERR-Ost depot in Riga advised Rosenberg's ministry in Berlin about 'the works of art salvaged from the operational area Army Group North [in October 1941]'.[17]

Dr Nerling wrote: '[Captain Solms] sent five coaches with art treasures to Königsberg... via stations Siverskaya, Luga, Pskov and Riga... Among the treasures sent were the Amber Room and various precious paintings and furniture...'[18] If Alfred Rosenberg's ERR-Ost had supervised the removal of the Amber Room to Königsberg in 1941, had it retained responsibility for transporting it again in 1945, as Königsberg fell, Enke asked?

But our file is finished.

*

We return to Enke's personal papers. Judging by what we have just read, Enke clearly devoted all of his energies to his research, so it is surprising to read that he found time to marry (Gerda, 1950) and to have a daughter (Sonia, 1952). It is not known if he mourned the deaths of his estranged parents (Klara, 1958, and Paul, 1959).

In 1962, one year after the Berlin Wall was erected, at a time when a second reinforcing wall was being raised parallel to it, Enke faced a serious set-back that threatened to terminate his Amber Room hobby and his career. A reorganization within the Ministry of the Interior left him out of favour and his post as the deputy director of Department Administration Training was axed. On 17 September 1962, one month after GDR teenager Peter Fechter was shot, falling into the death-strip between the Berlin walls ,where he was photographed bleeding to death in full view of the GDR border guard, Enke came up with a survival plan.

The next document reveals that he was spying on his colleagues and students at the Ministry of the Interior. Stasi Oberstleutnant Hut wrote that Enke informed on his co-workers 'without hesitation' and appeared to be objective. 'In this context, it should be mentioned that good contacts had always existed between Comrade Enke and the [Ministry for State Security]...'[19] We had wondered how a lowly bureaucrat in the Ministry of the Interior was allowed unfettered access to what were obviously sensitive wartime documents. Now it is clear that he had done so by forging a relationship with the Stasi.

Oberstleutnant Hut continued: 'Towards the conclusion of [our discussions] Comrade Enke was asked whether he was prepared to cooperate with the Ministerium für Staatssicherheit [MfS] even more closely than before. He declared his agreement.' Enke was asked to submit a list of relatives who were to be investigated before he could be put on the Stasi pay roll. He signed a pledge not to reveal anything that had been discussed at the meeting. A pattern of behaviour was emerging, a man willing to sacrifice friends and family to ensure his betterment.

As security around the Berlin Wall was bolstered with minefields and trip-wires, Enke ascended through the ranks of betrayal, from casual work-a-day sneak to a dedicated informer. He was attached to Directorate XX, the Stasi department responsible for recruiting and maintaining informants: cameras mounted in tree trunks, concealed in traffic lights and car doors, microphones in matchboxes left on a bedside table. Most informers were coerced into working for the Stasi, but at a time when East German salaries were paltry, the lure of cash payment was enough to persuade some, like Paul Enke, to volunteer.

All informers were marshalled into ranks: the Inoffizieller Mitarbeiter (IM), the lowly tell-tales who lived next door; the high-ranking Hauptamtlicher Inoffizieller Mitarbeiter (HIM), senior snitches who had direct contact with the person under surveillance – your best friend or your wife; the Inoffizieller Mitarbeiter zur politisch-operativen Durchdringung und Sicherung des Verantwortungsbereich (IMS), the verbose rank of boss or a secretary responsible for reviewing the political pedigree of his co-workers. But despite all of this stratification, the Stasi handlers referred to their charges by the derogatory term *spitzel*, which translates roughly as 'nark'.

By December 1962 Enke's remaining family members had been security-cleared and Hauptmann Schliep, an officer attached to the Stasi's Department of Agitation visited him at home. [20] Schliep wrote: 'Enke placed the question on the table, what sort of income he expected to realize... He declared that he could not hope to equal his current income of 1,800 Ostmarks net. The undersigned [Hauptmann Schliep] pointed out that Comrade Enke could count on a net income of approximately 1,200 Ostmarks if he was employed by us.' Paul Enke became a Stasi IM on New Year's Day 1963. [21]

In the next document we read that on 5 October 1964 Enke joined the Stasi itself as a full-time operative, with the duty grade Oberstleutnant and the duty rank of Referatsleiter (departmental manager) in the Observation and Investigation Directorate (HA VIII, Section 8). So here was proof that several years after beginning his private research, the author of *Bernsteinzimer Report* had become a Stasi agent.

'Worker 011-747 Enke' recited the Minister for State Security's personal oath to 'protect our workers and farmers', promising 'eternal loyalty to our fatherland, the GDR', to give his life 'in defence of every enemy' and be forever 'unquestioningly obedient to the military authorities'. He pledged to protect the republic and its Ministry for State Security 'for ever and everywhere in the world'.[22] We flick back to the photograph of the purposeful bureaucrat in a tight black suit, wearing heavy-framed glasses. This was the authorized image of a man who would later become faceless.

In 1968, Enke completed his Stasi training and his Service Qualification read: 'Dr Paul Enke, Historian.' In 1970, he became an Offizier im besonderen Einsatz, a Stasi special operations officer.[23] He was given a new cover, assuming the name Dr P. Köhler, a senior researcher at the Documentation Centre for the State Archives Administration of the Ministry of the Interior, Potsdam. 'At the same time he continues his usual social activities (participation at all party and other important events connected with his service).' Enke was back in the archives in a much more senior position than before.[24]

His arc was complete: lathe worker, radar operator, informant, historian, spy. Enke's only concern now was how to make an impression in an organization so vast.

Another binder from the Amber Room study group lands on the white plastic table. It begins with a selection of wartime newspaper cuttings collated by Stasi Oberstleutnant Paul Enke a.k.a. Dr P. Köhler of the Documentation Centre for the State Archives Administration of the Ministry of the Interior, Potsdam.

On 12 April 1942 the chief editor of the Berlin *Lokal-Anzeiger* reported on the Amber Room's unveiling ceremony at Königsberg Castle. It was presided over by Captain Helmut von Wedelstädt, the deputy Gauleiter of East Prussia. There was no mention in this story of Hitler, the Gauleiter of East Prussia, Erich Koch, or Alfred Rosenberg sending their congratulations.[25]

Enke found the article in *Pantheon* magazine, an illustrated German art digest, dated October 1942.[26] It was written by Castle Museum director Alfred Rohde, but it provided no clues about who was in overall charge of the Amber Room while it was in Königsberg. It painted Rohde in a completely different light from that presented by Dr Gerhard Strauss.

Strauss had told Anatoly Kuchumov during their interrogation sessions in December 1949 that Rohde was never a Nazi and that his politics (if he had any) were centre-left. But here in *Pantheon* Rohde was describing the Amber Room as a 'Prussian cultural monument' that had been 'rescued' from the 'furthest forward fighting' around Leningrad after 'a nearly unimaginable storm of victories' by the German army. (Although, of course, Rohde may have had no choice but to frame history in this patriotic language.)

Dismissing the wreckage and plunder of the Leningrad palaces as 'unavoidable war damage', Rohde revealed that 'Captain Solms Laubach supervised several army authorities, comprising one NCO and six men of a pioneer company, [who] making a supreme effort and through sharing their common interests, succeeded within thirty-six hours in this urgent dismantling job.'

Thirty-six hours. We are shocked to learn that it took the Nazis only a day-and-a-half to unlock the complex amber puzzle that Anatoly Kuchumov had claimed was impossible to dismantle. We recall that Kuchumov had had eight days to pack up the palaces and we wonder how this article would have reflected on him when Moscow read it. Rohde concluded on a rousing note: 'In its deepest meaning of the words, the Frederick I Amber Room had thereby returned to its native land.'

Enke's most interesting cutting was from the *Königsberg Allgemeine Zeitung*, which reported how, on 8 July 1944, Bernard Rust, Reich Minister for Science, Education and Public Instruction, visited Königsberg to preside over the four hundredth anniversary of Albertus-University. During a celebratory dinner thrown at the Blutgericht restaurant (in Königsberg Castle's old torture chamber), Rust told guests that the time had come to start moving the Third Reich's treasures into the heart of the Fatherland. Enke believed that he had found the origin of the plan to evacuate the Amber Room – and it had been conceived as early as 8 July 1944.

Days later, Amtmann Mertz, one of Rust's officers from Berlin, arrived in Königsberg with orders for Alfred Rohde. He was to dismantle the Amber Room immediately and send it with other art works to a storage facility at Kassel, the medieval city on the River Fulda where the Brothers Grimm had written their fairy tales. But the Gauleiter of East Prussia intervened. According to Enke, Erich Koch argued that moving the city's treasures and in particular the Amber Room would undermine morale. Mertz returned to Berlin to seek advice.[27]

By November 1944 Erich Koch had been persuaded to let the evacuations go ahead. Here in the file we see that Enke read Gerhard Strauss's report to his minister, Paul Wandel, written in 1950. And, like Strauss, Enke highlighted the correspondence between Erich Koch and Martin Mutschmann, from November 1944. Like Strauss, Enke stated that both Gauleiters approved a plan to set aside a castle in Saxony for the Amber Room (if it could be transported out of Königsberg).

Then we reach the critical part of the file. Was Enke able to prove that the Amber Room had been moved out of Königsberg? With his access to Nazi wartime archives, he was able to reconstruct the last days and months of the battle for East Prussia in much more detail than Anatoly Kuchumov, who had attempted the same exercise in 1946.

Kuchumov had concluded that the last train out of Königsberg had been on 22 January 1945. However, Enke learned that there were two trains that day: a so-called Special Gauleiter Train, which supposedly took Erich Koch to safety, and also a D-Zug, a civilian express train. This meant there had been a second opportunity to move the Amber Room.

Reviewing orders issued by the Nazi High Command, Enke also found a record of a ship leaving Königsberg on 22 January 1945. According to an order from Hitler to Admiral Dönitz, the German navy's commander-in-chief, the *Emden*, a small cruiser that had been laid up in the Königsberg shipyard, set sail on a secret mission. Nazi footage discovered long after Enke conducted his research, shot by Goebbels's cameramen, shows how on the *Emden*'s deck two coffins lay draped with old flags from German regiments that had fought the battle of Tannenberg, east of Königsberg, where the Russian army had been crushed in one of the most decisive campaigns of August 1914. Surrounded by an honour guard, the coffins contained the bodies of former Reich President General von Hindenburg and his wife, who had been disinterred from a memorial constructed at Tannenberg. On the Führer's orders, icebreakers towed the *Emden* to Pillau, where the coffins were transferred to a passenger steamer, *Pretoria*, that set out for Stettin the same night. If bodies could be moved on 22 January 1945, Enke asked, what else might have been on board?

Pulling together orders, intercepts and old footage, Enke discovered that even after the Red Army had reached Elbing, south-west of Königsberg, cutting off all direct routes to Germany, it would still have been possible until 31 January 1945 for the Nazis to transport crates and people out of the region by heading north-west up through the Samland Peninsula before boarding a boat at Palmnicken (now Yantarny).

Enke found orders issued by Gauleiter Erich Koch for ammunition to be supplied to Königsberg using this sea route that showed it must have remained open until March 1945. Enke also deduced that between 19 February and 6 or 7 April 1945, German forces temporarily rallied, reopening roads between Königsberg and Pillau, leaving the possibility that the Amber Room could have been evacuated right up until two days before the fall of the city.[28]

Enke concluded: 'I am convinced that the Amber Room and further precious art treasures robbed in the Soviet Union by the fascists were transported to the West. If one were able to search the archives of the Wehrmacht one would find the Amber Room's destination.' There was but one small hitch for Enke, working in the GDR. The main Wehrmacht military archive was at Freiburg im Breisgau, in West Germany.[29]

'The file please.' An outstretched hand. The working day has ended. Exactly at 4 p.m.

Paul Enke must have been stuck for many months in the air-tight archives, without access to those quickening modern aids of fax and Internet. Even the telephone was a problem. He could not just pick it up and call Moscow or Leningrad when he needed to check a fact. And those responsible for generating most of the material he was reading had been hanged, hounded, jailed or had flitted to the West or South America.

But in this mêlée Enke fought to prove that the Amber Room had been evacuated to Germany, disproving the conclusions of Anatoly Kuchumov and Gerhard Strauss, who believed that it had survived the war but remained concealed somewhere in Königsberg.

Enke worked in a blizzard of foreign-sounding names, obscure locations, train timetables and shipping news. Cyrillic text was transliterated into German and back again, details eroding with every version. The

Soviet curator began life as 'Kuchumov' before becoming 'Kugumow' and then 'Kutschumow'. A Leningrad suburb was once called Tsarskoye Selo and then Detskoye Selo before becoming Pushkin. An East Prussian village now sat in Poland with a new name and resettled population who knew nothing about the past. And yet Enke stayed the course, although we do not know what he had discovered that made him so certain the Amber Room had reached Germany.

We are relieved to see that the next binder that arrives on the white plastic table is filled with far more contemporary Stasi material on the Amber Room. Most of it dates to the 1970s and we hope that it may at last give us a glimpse of the intelligence that prompted the Minister for State Security to mount a full-blown inquiry into the fate of the missing treasure.

What we notice straight away is how Enke was ordered to deploy the ministry's training manual to interrogate eyewitnesses to the Amber Room story. We flick greedily through pages of surveillance reports of 'operationally interesting persons', written up from notes probably made on the backs of envelopes, scribbled on sheets torn out of school exercise books and on U-bahn or cinema tickets.

This binder bulges with cross-references to *Operative Personenkontrolle* files (OPK), a dossier opened on any individual selected by the Stasi for further investigation. Each OPK began with a formulaic description: gender, age, height, hair colour, eye colour, distinguishing features. Then came an opening report, followed by a plan of action, requests for clandestine checks, with responses ranging from 'provisional arrest' to 'arrest' and from 'search' to 'interrogation'.

There were school and university records, curriculum vitae and statements taken from neighbours, co-workers, friends and family. There were maps of housing estates and written comments: 'Is it possible to get the keys to his apartment without telling him?' Or: 'Does this "object" have a mistress we could approach?' And: 'We are not aware of the address of Countess Schwerin in the Federal Republic of Germany. The source of the information is one of her relatives and has been passed to us by a reliable and trustworthy informant.'

From this ball of information some individuals became *Operativ*

Vorgangs or OVs, targets for a full-blown investigation. Agents used a range of technological devices that made the task of peeling back the layers of privacy easier. Again more choices: 'A' measures (telephone tapping) or 'B' measures (bugging).[30] Odour samples were requested, collected from crotches and armpits of 'hostile-negative elements'. The Stasi transferred the swatches to their 'smell conserve', to be brought out along with packs of hounds called the *schnüffeltieren* if a surveillance 'object' went AWOL.

There was also the van painted with the cheery slogan 'Fresh Fish from Rostock!' In GDR times everyone knew that inside were men and women stacked like trays of silvery mackerel, up to seven prisoners in one small vehicle that drove repeatedly around the suburban streets so everyone would know. Round up in daylight. Interrogate at night. The proliferating paranoia drove citizens to extraordinary lengths to protect themselves, secreting miniature pencils in body cavities when they feared the agents of the state were approaching, so that later they might have something with which to scribble a plea for help. The Stasi responded to by introducing the 'penis search'.[31]

Judging from the number of surveillance forms and OV files that are contained in this one binder, Enke was evidently in pursuit of a rich new seam of intelligence about the Amber Room.

Here we at last come across a small reference to the 1959 articles in *Freie Welt* (written by Gerhard Strauss, identifying for the first time that the Amber Room had survived the war). Enke wrote that much of the intelligence that he was acting upon came from readers of *Freie Welt*. 'Stolz', the former Stasi agent we had met in the Berlin Swissôtel, had been right. By disguising the source of the *Freie Welt* story (the Stasi and KGB), readers had responded in their hundreds.

However, frustratingly, almost every detail that identified these readers and what they had volunteered, has been blacked out. All our potential leads and therefore any insight into the Stasi's thinking on the Amber Room have been obliterated by the Ministry of Truth's censors.

In some files only the 'Reg-Nr', the case number for a particular 'object', remains and the Ministry of Truth will not give us access to the corresponding name index. What has not been obscured was written deploying the terminology of Erich Mielke's *Dictionary of Political-Operative Work*, a 500-page lexicon of terms and definitions that was into its third edition when the Berlin Wall fell.[32]

Take the word 'hate'. The *Oxford English Dictionary* defines it as 'A feeling of intense dislike, anger, hostility, or animosity'. The minister's favourite word, *hass*, was defined as 'one of the fundamental features of the passionate and irreconcilable struggle against the enemy', an essential attribute for any good Chekist. And although this lexicon would ultimately control the lives of everyone within the GDR, it was one of the many paradoxes of the time that it was never made available to the general public, who were left deliberately confused and at cross-purposes. As are we, reading the files now.

What we are left with in this binder is an intriguing hierarchy of code-names that we cannot decipher without help.

Günter Wermusch, the editor of Paul Enke's *Bernsteinzimmer Report*, lives in an eastern Berlin suburb where the past has been smothered with a forest of identical towers. As we walk past the sports centre, it echoes to the splash of a lone swimmer.

Before our fingers have left the buzzer a voice urges: 'You must walk up. Elevator is *kaput*.' We climb eighteen flights. A door is open. In the shadows stands a man who is younger than we had expected, wearing two days' stubble and a synthetic tracksuit. Günter Wermusch looks like a bedraggled Soviet sports coach, the kind who shouted gruff instructions to shrimpy gymnasts on television in the 1970s. 'Better come in,' he mutters, limping back through the apartment.

We smell mildewed books, boredom and emptiness. In the kitchen a solitary supper is laid out on the grey Formica: a bottle of red wine, a tin of mushrooms, a knife and fork. The hallway is stuffed with old cardboard boxes spilling papers on to the floor, files stacked precariously on top of them beside a battered photocopier. Russian paperbacks prop up homemade shelves. We notice that there are no family photographs on the walls. No finger-paintings on the fridge.

'Zo, you've flown from London, eh? I hope not just to see me. I think

Günter Wermusch

I might disappoint.' Wermusch clears his throat and fills a briar pipe from a pouch of vanilla-scented tobacco. An English dictionary sits on the arm of his chair beside several boxes of pills. 'Who gave you my name? Who have you talked to?'

We do not mention 'Stolz' or the Ministry of Truth files just yet. We stick to the *Bernsteinzimmer Report*.

'I'm a *Lektor*,' Wermusch says defensively, rippling through the pages of his dictionary. 'Yes, an editor, not quite the right word but you know what I mean? I am a historian and with *Bernsteinzimmer Report* I did what my publishing house, Die Wirtschaft, asked of me.' He limps over to the picture window that fills the far wall with a distant view of the giant TV tower on Alexanderplatz.

And Paul Enke, we ask? How did you meet him?

Wermusch has boxed himself into a corner. 'He came to me in 1984,' he says, trapped between the shelves and a chair. 'I had edited a scientific book on amber. It contained a chapter on the *Bernsteinzimmer*. Enke rang up. He said he'd been researching the mystery since the 1950s. He had a manuscript he wanted me to look at.' A kiss-curl of smoke floats over Wermusch's head.

What did he tell you about his research, we ask?

'Enke told me he had seen the Amber Room in Königsberg during the war and later became a research officer of the Volkspolizei. The Amber Room investigation was like his weekend thing. A *hobby-Historiker*, we call people like him. Why should I be suspicious?' We could think of a number of reasons but say nothing.

'At the time I presumed Enke had got interested the same way we all had. The *Freie Welt* articles in 1959 got everyone very excited. Went and bought metal detectors.' *Freie Welt* again. Gerhard Strauss's articles obviously succeeded in generating a lasting clamour.

Wermusch ponders a stain on his carpet. 'In 1959 we all thought we would find something that everyone else had overlooked. The Amber Room story did that, *ja*? So when Enke came to Die Wirtschaft in 1984, we thought it seemed like a great idea to publish his manuscript. Get people excited again.' The phone rings in the hall. Wermusch looks relieved. He limps out. '*Wer ist da? Nein. Nein. Nicht. Eine minute.*' He drops the receiver and shuffles back into the room, distracted. 'All the time, these people call. I don't know who they are.'

Are they ringing about the Amber Room, we ask? Wermusch does not answer.

'Before *die Wende* you didn't ask questions,' Wermusch says, forgetting the caller and hanging up. 'We worked on the manuscript at Paul Enke's house in Berlin-Grünau. There was always a third man present, with black hair, but he never talked. Enke once introduced him as "my friend Hans".'

You met this man on dozens of occasions and never knew who he was, we ask?

'I only found out after Enke died in December 1987.' Wermusch pauses. He stares at us. Looks at his watch. He fills his pipe and then begins again. 'The funeral. I suppose I was invited because I was Enke's *Lektor*. We were not great friends or anything. *Zo*, there were a few people to see him off. But no green policemen. You know, the Volkspolizei. No friends from the force turning up. I thought it was, er, *sonderbar*.' Wermusch rifles through the dictionary. 'Odd, *ja*? The only person I recognized was the black-haired silent man from the meetings in Enke's house. I went up to him after the service. He introduced himself as Hans Seufert.'

Seufert. The Stasi Oberst or colonel in charge of the Amber Room study group.

'I asked Seufert: "Where are Enke's Volkspolizei colleagues? Seufert laughed at me. "Comrade," he said. "We don't wear uniforms." He was laughing so much he could not get his words out. And I still didn't get it.'

We sit in silence, pondering Wermusch's claim to have worked out Enke's membership of the Stasi only after the funeral.

Can we clear up something else, we ask?

'Anything,' he splutters. 'Whatever you like.'

Were you in the Stasi too, we ask?

Wermusch jumps up, a glimpse of his old agility returning, and rustles furiously through one of his boxes. 'I was only ever paid by my publishing house,' he shouts over his shoulder. 'Look, look at the proof.' He bounds over to pass us some paperwork mutilated with the familiar stamp of the Ministry of Truth. But he sees that we linger over an abbreviation next to his name: '*Gen.*'

'*Nein. Nein. Nein.*' He pounds the arm of his chair. '*Nicht General* but *Genosse*. We were all comrades. Look here. Look at this word.' He points to *Freiwilliger*. 'Volunteer, that's what I was. Volunteer, not Stasi, not informer. Take it. I have another copy.'[33] We have no idea of what he 'volunteered' for but he has a ready supply of these non-incriminating references from his Stasi file. 'How could I be Stasi after all?' He rings his hands. 'My father was in the SS.' The warped logic of unified Germany is that someone would rather expose their family's Nazi pedigree than be revealed as Stasi. 'Maybe I was singled out to edit the book because I was good at Russian. I don't know. I had worked for Comrade Naumann as translator. I went with him to Moscow several times.' (Konrad Naumann had been the SED's party boss for East Berlin in the early 1980s and held a senior position in the Politbüro.)

Wermusch fetches three bottles of soda water and pops the lids. So what had Enke and the Stasi learned that made them certain that the Amber Room had been concealed somewhere in Germany, we ask?

'I don't know. I was not involved in the Stasi investigation,' Wermusch snaps. He stands and hobbles into the hall, reaching up to a shelf almost at ceiling height, where dozens of binders and files are stacked, their spines annotated with dates, all of them drafts of *Bernsteinzimmer Report*. 'Enke exercised total control over his material. All I have is what he showed me. There are many official papers about the search for the Amber Room and they must be in the Stasi files.' Yes, we know. That's the main reason we are here. His face takes on a sweaty sheen. 'Are you taping me?' No, we say. We need your help. To decode Enke's Stasi files. Wermusch giggles. 'You don't need me. You need someone who was on the inside.'

We read out some of the names we jotted down in the Ministry of Truth. Generaloberst Beater? 'He's dead. 1982.' Generalleutnant Neiber? 'You'll never get him to talk, not since he was sued by someone he imprisoned.' Markus Wolf, the Stasi's foreign espionage chief? 'You can't afford him. Doesn't open his front door unless the cash is on the table.' What about Oberst Hans Seufert, is he still in touch with him? 'You're a bit late. He died two days ago. His wife called me.' Our timing could not be worse.

We run through a list of codenames for Stasi informers and sources who worked on the Amber Room. 'Dead. Dead. Dead. Missing,' Wermusch recites. He is enjoying himself. 'Wait.' He stops at HIM 'Bernd' (a Hauptamtlicher Inoffizieller Mitarbeiter or senior paid Stasi informer). 'I know that one. It's the codename for a mole in the 'Kripo' [the criminal police], an Oberstleutnant. He did the strong-arm stuff for Enke. He's around. Anyhow, he appears to be your only choice.'

Will he help us, we ask?

'Depends on whether he thinks you're worth it. He told the German government where to go when they came sniffing around for information about the Amber Room after reunification.'

Is 'Bernd' reliable?

'He did time in Bautzen prison – it was said that he tried to play both sides, got caught cheating on the Stasi, allegedly selling secrets, and then found out from prison that his boss was messing around with his wife.'

So, the reason why he went to prison is unclear. We can't call him 'Bernd', we say. The Cold War is over. 'His real name is Uwe Geissler.'

Wermusch shuffles into the hall. 'I'll call him tonight. Oh,' he says, poking his head around the door, 'you might like this.' He tosses us a copy of *Bernsteinzimmer Report*.

We open it and read a few words from the introduction. 'The German fascists' robbery of Europe's cultural heritage was far worse than those carried out by the Persians at Babylon, the Romans at Athens or the Crusaders at Constantinople,' Enke wrote. And the Amber Room was 'the most painful loss of all'. We have read this passage before, in one of Enke's early reports to his Stasi masters. It made the final edit.

9

Two days later we find Günter Wermusch blinking in the stairwell of his block, dressed for a field trip in a blue bomber jacket and combat trousers. 'How are my new friends?' he asks. His mood has lifted. 'I have some things for you,' he declares, passing us some papers. 'I typed out my theories last night. Just my small hobby. Not so important. Read them later.' He hands them over with an apology. 'Writing is too painful these days. Can't seem to hold a pen.'

No one picked up the phone at Uwe Geissler's apartment near Allee der Kosmonauten in East Berlin. But Wermusch knows the location of Geissler's weekend bungalow, two hours south-east of the city, and he thinks we might find Geissler there. As we drive out, beside the River Spree, Wermusch explains that he got to know Geissler while accompanying him on trips around the GDR after Paul Enke's death, interviewing potential eyewitnesses connected to the Amber Room story. Wermusch is interested to see how Geissler has weathered, he says. We think to ourselves how curious it is that this *Lektor* accompanied a Stasi informer on official investigations. But we will broach that subject later.

After an hour we arrive at Lake Krossinsee. Nearby is a red-brick village with a stagnant duck pond, a place Wermusch, who is now visibly sweating, says has become a favoured retreat among retired Stasi officers. A side road peters out into a sandy track that feeds a cluster of identical cement chalets running down to the shore. 'Uwe Geissler lives somewhere here,' Wermusch gestures, struggling to disentangle himself from the seat belt. Ahead is a signpost announcing Ziegenhals, 'Goat's Throat Village'.

The chalet peeps over a manicured border of marigolds, tiger lilies and busy lizzies. Frogs burp contentedly beside plastic tulips. The lawn is a deep emerald green and rolled into checks and stripes. A short, pigeon-chested figure in a purple polo shirt and nylon trousers leaps up from his garden chair as we approach and rushes over to the knee-high picket fence. A neighbour has informed us that this is Geissler's spread. '*Scheisse*,' he shouts, his forehead creasing as he attempts to recall whether these are faces he would rather forget. '*Mein Gott!*' And then, as it dawns on him, he reaches out with a tanned hand. 'Wermusch? *Wilkommen. Wilkommen. Und ...?*'

Geissler leads Wermusch off, down towards the lake. We can see them gesticulating vigorously, looking back, towards us, before Wermusch places a steadying hand on his acquaintance's forearm and guides him up the path. And as we squeeze around a small plastic table we notice the family of pottery gnomes peeking out of the shrubbery. For a retired collaborator at peace in his garden, Geissler's eyes are remarkably blood-shot. He complains to Wermusch that these days he cannot sleep. He lights a cigarette and dissolves into a whooping cough, while Wermusch stares longingly at the pile of stubs ground into the ashtray.

Geissler sets some rules. Never betrayed anyone, got it? Was never a sneak, right? 'We've all been betrayed by the Ministry of Truth. I never spied. I was just trying to help. It's my natural impulse.' Wermusch stares into space. 'The Soviets were dealt such a terrible blow in the war, losing so much more than anyone else,' Geissler says. 'It was only right that we Germans help find what was stolen from them.'

Geissler's eyes track a delicate woman with prematurely grey hair who emerges from the chalet behind us. '*Liebling*, get our guests something to eat,' he barks. Geissler's *liebling* must be half his age and she silently shakes our hands with the grip of a jailer, before retreating into the chalet.

What was Geissler's role in the Amber Room study group, we ask?

'The "fraternal authorities" [KGB] were trying to locate all the old East Prussian aristocrats, those whom Alfred Rohde had corresponded with in 1944 as he struggled to find a hiding place for the Amber Room: Keyserlingk, Dohna, Schwerin. Also the high-ranking castle and museum officials: Henkensiefken, Will, Friesen, Gall, Zimmerman. Would you like a Danish butter cookie? Pass them around, *liebling*.' These names are becoming familiar to us. All are on Anatoly Kuchumov's list of missing Germans; in *Freie Welt* and *Kaliningradskaya Pravda*. We still do not know what role any of them played in the Amber Room story.

So did you find them, we ask?

Geissler isn't listening. He's talking. For a man who is supposed to have spent a lifetime keeping his mouth shut, he seems incapable of doing so. 'We were remarkably successful.' Wermusch shudders as Geissler wedges a large biscuit in his mouth.

'I tell you. The Soviets made a mistake throwing out all the eyewitnesses.' By 1949, the authorities in Kaliningrad had expelled all Germans from East Prussia, filling their homes and farms with Soviet settlers. Did Geissler ever point out the short-sightedness of the policy? 'Well, I could have done,' he splutters, 'but I was too busy. On the road. Rounding them all up again.'

Dark clouds gather overhead and the candy-striped awning above us flaps loudly. We try and steer the conversation to what we have come here to learn. What was the new intelligence about the Amber Room that the security services had obtained? '*Freie Welt*. More than 1,000 eyewitnesses came forward after the articles were published and we went checking them all out. Soldiers who'd been looting in Leningrad. Königsberg residents who'd seen the Amber Room,' he says, thunder echoing across Lake Krossinsee.

But what was the impetus for publishing the articles in the first place, we ask? *Freie Welt* was surely the second stage. We recall Herr 'Stolz's' theory but do not mention it. Rain begins to whip the chalet, water pouring down off the awning. 'There are a lot of liars out there,' Geissler shouts above the deluge. 'Sad, deluded people who wanted to be part of the mystery, wanted to be part of something special. Some of them even tried to find the Amber Room themselves. We had to stamp on that right away.' Imagine sending a letter to the editor of *The Times*, we think, and finding an MI5 agent on the doorstep.

Geissler's eyes flicker skywards. 'Looks like rain,' he says, noticing it for the first time, pushing past us into the cabin where his *liebling* kneels on the floor, picking crumbs off the carpet. He settles behind a smoked-glass coffee table, beckoning Wermusch and us inside. 'I was a specialist. Not like some of the creeps they employed. I was a criminal investigator.' He lights another cigarette. 'I'd only move in on an "object" when I was ready. Sometimes it took several attempts to break through their deception to the real story.' A nudge and a wink. 'We had to know more about them than they knew about themselves.' Geissler takes a slug of tea.

'I'd say, "If you have looted stuff, that's acceptable. Everybody nicked stuff in the war. But if you've killed people, well, that is a different matter. Not so easy to forgive."' Geissler grins. 'It was a great trick. Worked every time. So they would all eventually admit to looting, but then we would have them. Stupid pricks didn't realize we were looking for looters all along, particularly anyone connected with the Amber Room.' He bunches his hands into fists and Wermusch slips outside with a cigarette. 'There was this one guy who admitted to having stolen something quite valuable. When he realized that I was going to report him, he pleaded with me. Said he'd never told his wife and now she would find out from the Stasi. I had to call the ambulance.' Geissler is laughing and tears well in his eyes. 'The guy had a fucking heart attack.'

Geissler's *liebling* grabs her purse and marches out of the chalet, sending a beaded curtain flying. We are beginning to understand why GDR citizens would never have responded to *Freie Welt* if they even suspected that the Stasi was its source.

Is it true, we ask, that you spent time in Bautzen (a high-security Stasi prison nicknamed 'Yellow Misery' by those cast into its urine-coloured buildings)?[1] We have heard enough bravado.

Geissler reaches for a cigarette. 'It was all a misunderstanding. That's what my boss, Oberst Hans Seufert, said when he got me out in 1977. Served three years. All of it in solitary. Listen to my cough. My parents died and they would not even let me out to bury them. They accused me of selling Stasi secrets.' Did you? 'Never. A Stasi officer was giving my wife one. Wanted me out the way. I was framed. Seufert told me, "You've done your time, now shut up. If you argue you'll go back inside." It worked out all right in the end. I found a new wife, a younger one. And I was brought back into the Amber Room team.'

Geissler goes on the offensive, jabbing a finger towards us. 'I know many important things,' he shouts, motioning to an imaginary store at the back of the cabin. 'Government people came looking for me in 1993, the Ministry of the Interior and the head of the Berlin CDU. They were so impressed by what I knew about the Amber Room that they offered me money to write it all down.' His face reddens. 'Money too for my Stasi documents about the Amber Room investigation. I told them all to piss off.'

What documents, we ask? 'My papers are my pension. Took them in January 1990, when it all went to hell.' Oberst Seufert once told Günter Wermusch that his Amber Room study group generated 180,000 pages of intelligence and yet we know from the functionary at the Ministry of Truth that the files she has recently acquired run to only 12,000.[2] Someone is still sitting on the rest.

But what story do these documents tell, we ask? Geissler cannot keep it to himself: 'The Stasi had intelligence that the Gauleiter of East Prussia, Erich Koch, had successfully evacuated the Amber Room from Königsberg Castle to Germany. When *Freie Welt* came out, the intelligence was substantiated by one of the letter-writers. A man wrote that his father, an SS Sturmbannführer, had overseen the evacuation of the Amber Room on Koch's orders.'

Could this possibly be true? The existence of a plan to evacuate the Amber Room had been glimpsed by Kuchumov, confirmed by Strauss and plotted by Enke, but this is the first positive confirmation we have had that someone ordered it and that the task was accomplished. We are not yet ready to believe it. Geissler's revelation opens up a staggering range of new possibilities. We begin to wonder if we started our research at the wrong point in the wrong country, chasing the wrong line. We need to pin Geissler down. Can he show us the evidence?

He smiles, sucks in a deep lungful of smoke and then leans forward until his head is barely an inch from ours. We can see every oily pore and his chipped incisors. 'Wouldn't that be interesting? Worth something a little extra.' We have not yet discussed money. Geissler settles back into his chair. 'I'll give you a taster. For free. The letter-writer only found out his dad's secret when he discovered wartime documents hidden in a leather pouch in the family's cellar in 1949, a couple of years after his father died.

He had never spoken about these documents until he read the article in *Freie Welt.'*

What did these documents state, we ask? We must keep Geissler talking.

'There was a receipt confirming the handing over of forty-two crates and packages to the letter-writer's father and an order to take the Amber Room to a secret storage facility codenamed BSCH. Another document was a transcript of a radio message reporting the implementation of that order and it read: "Action Amber Room concluded. Storage in BSCH. Accesses blown up. Casualties through enemy action." There was also a map. But there was confusion over what location these documents identified. And there was a much more serious problem. The letter-writer was just a kid when he found them and he was so frightened by what they said – there were regular round-ups of old Nazis going on 1949 – that he burned them.'

It is a lot to believe. How did you corroborate the letter-writer's story, we ask?

'He was vetted. By the author of the *Freie Welt* articles, Professor Dr Gerhard Strauss.'

That name again.

'Dr Strauss reported back that he thought the letter-writer was telling the truth. He had little to gain by exposing his father's Nazi past. We agreed to disguise the letter-writer's identity and he became source 'Rudi Ringel'.

Where was BSCH?

Geissler brushes our question aside: 'After Strauss had finished with "Rudi Ringel" he was whisked off to Kaliningrad so the Soviets could check him out too. Comrade K. Lebedev, the chairman of the district committee on arts affairs, was in charge. All intelligence connected to "Rudi Ringel" was sent to Comrade Veniamin Krolevsky at the Kaliningrad Party Secretariat.'

You said the evidence pointed to Germany, so why take 'Rudi Ringel' to Kaliningrad and channel all of your information to the KGB, we ask?

'I told you there was some confusion over the location of BSCH because the documents were burned. The "fraternal authorities" agreed that "Rudi Ringel" was probably telling the truth but deduced that BSCH was a location in Kaliningrad. Of course we were not in a position to contradict them and while they did their work we did ours, checking out all the remaining *Freie Welt* letter-writers. Finally, "Rudi Ringel" came home to the GDR.'

What happened next, we ask?

Silence. The windows of the cabin are dripping with condensation, the rain is thundering on the corrugated roof and Geissler's wife appears at the front door, soaking wet, bearing a box of cherry pies.

'*Liebling*. Let's have a break from talking. Let's eat and drink together.' The pot is brewed. The coffee is poured and it is not until Geissler is sated that he continues. 'Enke grilled "Rudi Ringel". I did the sister and the mother. We were all over like them like a virus.' Thankfully, Geissler is unstoppable. 'We found many references in Nazi records that supported the "Ringel" family's stories.' He lights another cigarette. 'And these references revealed what we suspected all along, that the documents "Rudi Ringel" had found in the family's cellar had been misinterpreted by the KGB. BSCH could not be found in Kaliningrad because BSCH was here in Germany.'

How did the Stasi locate BSCH? What were these clues, we ask?

'That would be telling and telling equals money, but what I will tell you for free is that Enke proved that "Rudi Ringel's" father had evacuated the Amber Room out of East Prussia. The radio message – "Action Amber Room concluded. Storage in BSCH. Accesses blown up. Casualties through enemy action" – was broadcast from a location in Germany.

'Paul Enke went to Oberst Seufert but the boss was cautious. Didn't want to clash with the "fraternal authorities" who were digging in Kaliningrad. Seufert said that if we found more evidence then he would back an application for funding a dig in Germany. But –' Geissler takes a mouthful of pie – 'there was a problem. Enke identified in the GDR 700 possible locations for BSCH: salt mines, coal-mines, quarries, caves and underground bunkers. The Stasi Secretariat ordered us to whittle the list down. We went back to "Rudi Ringel" but he said he knew only what he had seen in the documents. His father had died two years after the war without ever talking about the location of BSCH. The only living person who could confirm the location of the Amber Room was the man who issued the orders, the Nazi war criminal Gauleiter Erich Koch.'

Geissler looks at his watch. 'Time's up. Nothing more for free. I'm back in the city on Monday. Call me and we'll talk cash,' he chirps. 'You'll have to. I'm the only one connected to the Amber Room study group still alive.'

Liebling struggles to hold the door and slams it shut behind us. 'Goat's Throat Village' sinks beneath the deluge.

On 28 May 1949 the *Daily Telegraph* reported the arrest of a farm labourer called Rolf Berger in the village of Haasemoor, north of Hamburg, after a tip-off from suspicious neighbours. 'In his trouser pocket was found a glass phial of cyanide of potassium, the kind issued to leading Nazis. A similar phial was used by Himmler after his arrest in 1945,' the *Daily Telegraph* revealed. Under interrogation, the labourer admitted that he was Erich Koch, the former Gauleiter of East Prussia, and that he had been living incognito for four years in the same sparsely populated north-ern-most German state where Alfred Rosenberg, the Nazi ideologue and Reich Minister for Occupied Eastern Territories, had been run to ground in May 1945.

It was a coup for the joint British-German intelligence operation code-named Old Lace, which had been tasked with chasing down missing Nazis. Erich Koch, who had been among the first to join the National Socialist movement in 1922 and bore party ticket number 90, was one of the most wanted, along with Bormann, Eichmann and Mengele. However, with no central prosecuting authority now in place, the International Military Tribunal at Nuremberg having closed, the British guarded Koch at their base in Bielefeld, while they decided what to do with him.

Stalin demanded to be allowed to prosecute Koch, since more than four million Soviet citizens had died and two million more been sent to Nazi work camps during his tenure as Reich's Commissar for the Ukraine (a position he held before becoming Gauleiter of East Prussia). While the British requested that the Soviets send a detailed legal case for extradi-tion, Koch launched his own action, submitting a plea: 'I know that as a former member of the Nazi Party... I have incurred heavy political guilt but I would ask you to believe that in all my political and human mistakes I... was servicing a good cause and the welfare of my people.'³ He wrote that he had no illusions as to 'what awaits me behind the Iron Curtain'. It was not death he feared 'but the base and inhuman treatment that this [Soviet] system applies to its opponents. It is the cold-blooded way in which a human being is made use of and then atrociously killed.' (This from the man who had ordered the corpses of Soviet prisoners in Rovno to be incinerated and the ash sold as fertilizer to German farmers.)

The British were unmoved by Koch's appeal but the former Gauleiter would not be tried in the Soviet Union. Instead of witness statements, affidavits and photographs, the Soviets submitted a terse letter claiming that Nuremberg had already established Koch's 'grievous war crimes'.⁴ Then another application for Koch arrived in West Berlin and this one was a detailed legal document accompanied by eyewitness accounts married to specific charges. It had been compiled by the Polish government. The British dispatched the former Gauleiter of East Prussia to Warsaw.

But having got him, the Poles declined to try Koch. For nine years he was held on remand at Warsaw prison, a delay that was never adequately explained, although the Poles claimed weakly that he was too sick to face trial. We contrast the Polish inactivity with Nuremberg, in which

News footage of the trial of Erich Koch in Warsaw, 1959

218

a significant proportion of the leadership of the Third Reich was tried, prosecuted, jailed or hanged in just eighteen months.

It was only in November 1958 that the Poles began the case against Koch. Televised footage shows a tearful former Gauleiter lolling in the dock with a handkerchief tied around his head like a casualty of the Great War. On 19 March 1959, after ten years in custody, and a court case of four months and seventeen days, during which 1,500 pages of evidence had been heard, the Poles finally passed the death sentence. Koch immediately launched an appeal on grounds of ill-health, further delaying his fate, an opportunity that would be pounced upon by the Soviets.

We have asked Our Friend the Professor in St Petersburg to scour the Kuchumov papers for any references to the former Gauleiter of East Prussia and with only four days left on our readers' tickets a couriered package arrives at our Berlin hotel. It contains an extraordinary series of classified Soviet documents. The first is a letter from the Catherine Palace, dated 28 March 1959, nine days after the death sentence on Koch was passed, then suspended pending an appeal. Comrade A. V. Bobidanosov wrote to the office of the General Prosecutor of the Soviet Union: 'One can add another crime to all the terrible crimes committed by Nazi troops on the territory of the occupied Soviet Union: the robbery of the Amber Room from the Catherine Palace.'

Comrade Bobidanosov reported that research to date 'clearly shows that the Amber Room has not perished in the war and could not have been taken out of Kaliningrad... One can see that high-ranking German officials were interested in the fate of the most valuable international art trophy in the world. Therefore it is possible that Erich Koch could have known about [the Amber Room's] fate.'

Comrade Bobidanosov continued:

As far as we know in the recent trial in Warsaw the Amber Room was never mentioned and therefore it is possible that this war criminal may take his mystery to the grave. Therefore the state commission for search of art treasures is urging you to address the general Polish prosecutor with the following requests: 1. Erich Koch should be interrogated about the Amber Room. 2. One should check in the trial materials to see if any witness reports shed light on transportation of the Amber Room.

The General Prosecutor of the Soviet Union replied to Comrade Bobidanosov on 3 June 1959: 'According to our request the authorities in Poland have interrogated the former Gauleiter Erich Koch. But he knows nothing of the fate of the Amber Room and he was not aware of the existence of the room and never was informed about its unique value. Also, in the materials of his trial there is no trace of the Amber Room.'[5]

It was a strange response from the Poles. We recall that in 1949 Dr Gerhard Strauss had furnished the Soviets with a dossier of evidence connecting Koch to the Amber Room: letters from him to Gauleiter Mutschmann in Dresden, asking for secure storage facilities; orders from him to Alfred Rohde to inspect castles in Saxony for places to hide 'irreplaceable treasures', including the Amber Room.

Unsurprisingly, the Soviets refused to accept the Polish response and insisted on sending their own emissary to interrogate Erich Koch. They would need a neutral figure who would not aggravate the Poles or the former Gauleiter. We search for an account of the meeting. There is no reference to it in the literature archive but in the Ministry of Truth we come across a report dated 24 June 1959.[6] In it we read that a top-secret grilling took place that month in the GDR embassy in Warsaw and, examining the list of those who attended, see that the man chosen as the Soviet's emissary was none other than Professor Dr Gerhard Strauss of Humboldt University. For us, Strauss had begun as an incidental character, a name in a grease-flecked letter discarded by a Soviet curator, but now he seems to crop up everywhere. By 1959 he must have been very highly regarded by both Moscow and the GDR Politbüro to have been chosen to front such delicate negotiations.

The minute shows that the meeting – attended by Strauss, Erich Koch, his lawyer, the GDR Deputy Ambassador Riesner and the Polish Solicitor General – got off to a terrible start. One of the prison warders had given Koch Strauss's recent articles about the Amber Room, published in *Freie Welt*. Koch immediately began to attack Strauss, saying that he was unhappy about the articles and the 'accusations raised' that he had some connection to the fate of the Amber Room. A Nazi prisoner on death row faced the emissary of the bloc, accusing him of peddling lies like a tabloid journalist. It must have been an excruciatingly embarrassing moment for Strauss, who struggled to reassure the former Gauleiter that he was in fact a serious East German academic trying to solve the mystery of the Amber Room on behalf of his government. 'It was possible to make light of it,' Strauss reported. We will never know what Strauss really told Koch about *Freie Welt*, but the former Gauleiter kept talking.

Strauss and the prisoner then discussed art concealed in bunkers. Koch's knowledge of East Prussian storage facilities, Strauss noted, tallied with his own and the former Gauleiter conceded that it was possible that the Amber Room had been hidden in a bunker or cellar. However, Koch insisted he had never given orders concerning the Amber Room, a reply that Strauss cautioned should be seen in a wider context. 'In total Koch took great care to give only such information that minimized his own responsibility and spoke in his favour.' Although the former Gauleiter claimed to have no personal knowledge of the fate of the Amber Room, he said he thought it impossible for it to have been evacuated to Germany.

Koch proposed his own radical theory. Strauss wrote: 'Koch thinks it is likely that the Amber Room was transported by the Soviet Army but when I said, "Well, in that case it would have been reinstalled in Pushkin," Koch accepted that my argument was more convincing than his.' As the ninety-minute meeting drew to a close, Koch demanded Strauss's 'word of honour' that their discussion would remain confidential. 'Nobody should find out that he was helping to find the Amber Room,' Strauss reported. 'At the moment we cannot expect more from Koch, but because he is trying to influence his appeal process, it is not impossible that shortly we shall get further statements from him.'

We had left our meeting with Uwe Geissler still unsure of how the Stasi had tied Erich Koch to the Amber Room and a hiding place in Germany. In this Stasi report Koch divulged no evidence connecting himself to the Amber Room or an evacuation plan ending in Germany. But just as we begin to think that Geissler may have been lying, the next document sent to us from St Petersburg bolsters Geissler's story. He told us that in the summer of 1959 a GDR citizen codenamed 'Rudi Ringel' had been flown to Kaliningrad and cross-examined by party functionaries. Here we read confirmation that 'Rudi Ringel' did exist and that this source was flown to Kaliningrad in the summer of 1959. The Soviet official who interrogated him there was Leningrad curator Anatoly Kuchumov.

In a typed report marked 'Ringel: Top Secret', Kuchumov summarized the witness's story. It was remarkably similar to the one Geissler told us. Kuchumov wrote:

In July 1949, two years after the death of his father, when the family was preparing to move house, ['Rudi Ringel'] was sent to clear the cellar by his mother. Under some rough moist coal he found a leather map pouch, like the ones used by soldiers during the war. It was covered in mildew. Its contents were wet through and stuck together. What could be deciphered were typewritten sheets of orders, reports, parts of a Königsberg town plan and various SS documents with passport photos of his father [SS Sturmbannführer 'Ringel'], one of which bore Himmler's signature. 'Rudi Ringel' was only thirteen but old enough to understand the significance.[7]

So the map that 'Rudi Ringel' recalled seeing was of Königsberg, not Germany. Geissler's story was still at odds with this one.

Kuchumov asked 'Rudi Ringel' to reproduce from memory the contents of the map pouch and noted that the witness reconstructed seven documents, each of which he signed as 'true copies'. Kuchumov initialled them. Comrade Wagnerman translated them. Comrade Shaposhikovna of the KGB 'certified' them.

The first reconstructed document was a letter addressed to 'Rudi Ringel's' father, dated December 1944:

To SS Sturmbannführer 'Ringel'. It is supposed that soon in Königsberg Operation Grüne will begin. It will then be necessary for you, as agreed, to assume your responsibility for the evacuation of the Amber Room. Borders B-Sch-Kniproderstrasse, Steindamm, Reihe/BU3UP, visible from streets Jakobstrasse, Gezekusplatz. After burying it, blow up the building. Then you and your officers go to place [name missing], moving there as agreed. When you have successfully completed this mission please confirm by courier. *Heil Hitler.*

Although the street names are garbled, what was almost certainly being described here was a location in Königsberg, somewhere adjacent to Steindamm Strasse.

'Rudi Ringel' recalled that the next document he read was marked 'Top Secret' and addressed to 'the Main Office of the Reich's Security Minister V.V.S. (military air forces department)': 'Order is executed. Action Amber Room is finished. Entrance according to orders has been blown up. Many victims due to enemy action. I am coming to agreed place [name missing].' 'Rudi Ringel' recalled his father, the SS Sturmbannführer, had signed the message although it was not dated.

Kuchumov sketched a map of the centre of Königsberg. At the junction of Steindamm Strasse and Lange Reihe the great curator marked Steindamm Church, a pond and a First World War monument. An area running between the church and the pond was shaded and labelled 'bunker'. If 'Rudi Ringel' could be relied on, then the evacuation of the Amber Room, codenamed Operation Grüne (Green), had gone ahead and the Soviet treasure had been taken from Königsberg Castle and concealed somewhere near Steindamm Church. We wonder how the Stasi could have reached the conclusion that the Amber Room was evacuated to Germany.[8]

Frustratingly, the five remaining documents transcribed by 'Rudi Ringel' are missing from our file. We call St Petersburg and ask the Professor to recheck the index. She soon gets back to us: 'Nothing.' We revisit the Ministry of Truth to see if the Stasi was sent a record of Kuchumov's debriefing of 'Rudi Ringel'. Again nothing.

All we have before us from the literature archive are yet more of Kuchumov's newspaper clippings and they concern Erich Koch.

As Strauss predicted in 1959, Erich Koch soon began to talk again about the Amber Room, leaking information to his guards at Mokatovska Prison. In September 1961 he also spoke to Polish journalist Vladimir Orlovsky and then in October to *Izvestiya*: 'Erich Koch knows of two bunkers where art works were hidden by Rohde and Dr Helmut Will.[9] There, among other items, are some things from his own collection. He cannot be 100 per cent sure that the Amber Room is there but he thinks it almost certainly is.'[10] Although Koch still denied any responsibility for the Amber Room, he was almost certain that it had been moved to a bunker beneath Königsberg, a story that seemed to tally with the evidence of letter-writer 'Rudi Ringel'.

Three years later the Polish authorities commuted Erich Koch's death sentence to life, publicly stating that the prisoner had been reprieved because he was suffering from a terminal illness. Shortly after, Koch was transferred to a specially built compound in the Polish countryside, from where he continued to cooperate.[11] In 1967 stories leaked out that the former Gauleiter (remarkably, still alive) had incriminated Reichsleiter Bormann, who, he said, was keen to acquire the Amber Room, which in Koch's estimation 'was worth in excess of 50 million dollars'.[12]

On 5 February 1967 TASS reported that the Soviet authorities were now certain that the Amber Room was in East Prussia after Koch finally admitted that it was he who gave the order to Alfred Rohde and Dr Helmut Will 'to take out this treasure' and conceal it in a bunker under a city church near Steindamm. Surely this was the same bunker identified by Kuchumov on a map he drew eight years earlier, having interrogated GDR letter-writer 'Rudi Ringel'. At the end of February 1967 TASS revealed that Soviet investigators were indeed heading for Königsberg – with heavy drilling equipment. There is no record here of what this dig achieved.[13]

When the articles in *Kaliningradskaya Pravda* and *Freie Welt* came out in 1958 and 1959, the public focus was drawn towards unnamed Nazis who were accused of evacuating the Amber Room from Königsberg Castle, although no location for it was revealed (or perhaps known). New information from 'Rudi Ringel', writing in response to these articles, suggested that the unnamed Nazi was Erich Koch. In 1967 Koch finally admitted that he had been involved in the Amber Room evacuation (although he insisted that it was to another site in Kaliningrad). At the same time the Stasi and the KGB seemed to be using the Koch–Ringel evidence to pull in different directions. Geissler assured us that the Stasi interpreted the story in such a way that it led them to search for the Amber Room in Germany where they believed Erich Koch had had it sent. The KGB was sticking with Kaliningrad.

*

Maybe we are missing the point. We are acutely aware of the fact that time is running out. Do we stay here in Berlin or return to St Petersburg? We take the lift to the ninth floor of the Ministry of Truth in Berlin and after half a morning searching through hundreds of censored interrogation documents we come across this draft report from 1976: 'Plan of measures for the carefully concentrated pursuit of the search for the tracks of the Amber Room on the territory of the GDR'. Here at last is a report, written in the Stasi's clumsy language, about its German operation. We hope it will explain or rebut Geissler's statement. Thankfully, because there are not many names contained in it, the censors have spared the document.[14]

Oberstleutnant Paul Enke advised his section head Oberst Hans Seufert: 'We are aware that in the Soviet Union the search is run by a government commission but based on the clues this search has been concentrated exclusively on Kaliningrad and only relatively little trouble has been taken for an intensive exposure of clues and hints pointing to hiding places in Saxony and Thuringia.' This statement suggested that by 1976, nine years after TASS reported that digging had begun in Kaliningrad, based on Erich Koch's evidence, the Soviets still had not found anything.

Enke recommended: 'Intensive, on-the-spot investigations into the large numbers of facts and clues. The veiled hint of Koch to where his private collection is located may refer to Thuringian storage depots as well as concealment locations in western Saxony.'

The report continued:

Further recommendations: it seems necessary to question Erich Koch extensively on the subject of his private collection. Such an investigation was carried out once already in 1960 [sic] by Professor Dr Gerhard Strauss, Berlin, without any result and had anyhow been restricted exclusively to Kaliningrad. Koch could nowadays be given some clues that could be of assistance to help his memory and start him thinking. (Suggested questions attached.)

This is exactly what Geissler told us. The KGB was thought to have misinterpreted the evidence provided by Koch and 'Rudi Ringel'.

Enke called for an 'investigation of the true role of SS Sturmbannführer "Ringel" in the concealment of the Amber Room'. He advised: 'The statements made by "Rudi Ringel" during questioning by a Soviet Government Commission [Anatoly Kuchumov] rest only on his child-hood memories (he was thirteen in 1949). I recommend re-questioning now.'

Why Enke felt it necessary to reanalyse the statements made by Erich Koch and 'Rudi Ringel' becomes clearer when we read a report of a research trip to Thuringia and Saxony conducted by Enke in June 1976.

He was accompanied by Gerda, his wife (a couple on holiday was a 'legend' that the Stasi used time and again). They headed first for Weimar, the birthplace of the Weimar Republic. Leaving Gerda to pace the cobbled streets down which Hitler's armour-plated Mercedes once clattered, Enke set up office in the local Stasi headquarters, a villa on Cranach-Strasse, where he spent hours poring over Nazi-era archive material.

Enke reported to Seufert: 'Everything which the Nazis had brought to Thuringia in order to continue the good life... had to be left behind. Palaces, even the dance halls of many inns, had been filled up to their ceilings with luxury goods.'[15] In the Weimar archives, Enke immediately encountered 'interesting traces' of Koch, including 'extensive stocks of files from the estate of his bloody governance of the Ukraine that had been evacuated to [nearby] Bad Sulza at the beginning of 1945'.

Many East Prussian artefacts had been evacuated to Thuringia in the spring of 1945, Enke reported, including medieval sculptures from Marienburg Castle (today Malbork in Poland) and an iron chest of the St George Brotherhood from Elbing. A few days later, Enke found an inventory from 1945 of 'museum goods delivered for storage to the State Museum of Weimar', written by its wartime director, Dr Walter Scheidig. It included valuable Gobelin tapestries, paintings and a large collection of wall-mounted silver candelabras. But what initially caught Enke's eye were paintings of insignificant monetary value: *A View of Elberfeld*, *Roaring Monarch of the Glen* and a series of third-rate family portraits.

Enke reported that Elberfeld, in the Rhineland, was the birthplace of Erich Koch and, according to papers Enke had read in Potsdam, *Roaring Monarch of the Glen* was one of many gifts received by the Gauleiter while he was in Königsberg. Enke contacted East Berlin: 'We have found the relocation site of [Koch's] robbed collection, even without Koch's assistance!' Enke added that he had once read in a GDR newspaper that Erich Koch had bragged: 'If you find my art collection then you will find the Amber Room too.' Enke believed he was closing in on something significant.

Enke went in search of Dr Scheidig, who had compiled the inventory of Koch's evacuated art works. At the remains of the State Museum of Weimar (heavily bombed in the war and still a ruin in 1976), Enke found an elderly retired art dealer who told him that Scheidig was dead. But Enke should not worry, as the dealer (name blacked out) also knew how the Weimar museum came to receive Erich Koch's collection.

The old art dealer recalled that a Nazi officer had arrived in a van on 9 February 1945, saying that he was an 'administrator for Gauleiter Koch' and was 'bringing museum treasures from Königsberg'. The officer wore the uniform of the Nationalsozialitsches Fliegerkorps (NSFK) and appeared uneasy. He was 'neither an art historian nor a museum curator' and seemed anxious to leave as soon as he had unloaded the contents of his van. The old man noted that the cargo was an assortment of 'crates, racks, suitcases and chests' that museum staff stacked unopened on the ground floor. 'Everything about the evacuation of these crates seemed to have been conducted without thought or pre-planning, leaving much to chance,' Enke wrote.[16]

After several weeks of bombing raids over Weimar, on 9 April 1945 (the day that Königsberg surrendered) Gauleiter Koch's administrator returned to remove the 'museum goods from Königsberg', cramming crates and suitcases into a small van with Swiss number plates, operating under the flag of the International Committee of the Red Cross. He came back again the next day to take another batch and said he would return on 11 April for the last. But he never returned, since the next force to arrive in Weimar was the US Third Army (on 11 April 1945) and American art experts who accompanied the troops found the unclaimed crates in the lobby of the Weimar museum. Museum director Scheidig was ordered to open them and make an inventory, noting that alongside family portraits, German etchings and prints were silver candelabras and museum exhibits that bore labels written in Russian. It was this list that Enke had discovered.

So where was this cache now, Enke asked the old art dealer? He said that he was surprised Enke didn't know. A female curator from Russia had visited Weimar in 1948, debriefed Scheidig and taken most of the contents of the crates back to the USSR. The old man thought her name was Xenia Agarfornova.

We know this name. According to Kuchumov's diary from his Berlin mission in 1947, when he worked for General Zorin, sorting stolen Soviet treasures in the Derutra warehouse, Xenia Agarfornova was part of the staff. She had come from the Leningrad Hermitage and was given a roving role to retrieve art works concealed in the German countryside. She had also interrogated Gerhard Strauss. The USSR had claimed part of Koch's collection and not thought to tell the Stasi. Why?

Enke would have to check with the Soviet authorities and sent off a letter to Leningrad. While he waited for a response he worked on mapping Koch's consignments that *had* left Weimar in the Red Cross van on 9 and 10 April 1945.

Sitting at his desk in Cranach-Strasse, with his favourite thinking food of black beer and pickled pork, Enke plotted the 1945 Allied advance on his route map of Thuringia. 'Under the conditions described, the average van speed may hardly have exceeded 30 kmh,' he wrote in his report. 'Considering the journey to the depot [Weimar museum], unloading, the return journey, controls *en-route* and resting periods, this would have allowed a maximum distance to be travelled of 150–180 kilometres from Weimar.' But in which direction had Koch's treasures been driven?

North was into the arms of the Red Army. If the van had driven west it would have run into the American troops that reached a Thuringian village called Merkers on 4 April 1945. The Americans were also advancing from the south and were at Coburg in Bavaria by 11 April, threatening the Berlin–Nuremberg A9 autobahn. Enke concluded that the only sensible route on 9 and 10 April 1945 would have been east, along the A4 autobahn to Gera and on towards Dresden. 'To simplify and shorten our description, we will call this mooted area western Saxony,' Enke wrote.

Where in western Saxony? Enke reported: 'By April 1945 all [Nazi] hope had evaporated and turned into the certainty of total defeat. At this moment the Nazis no longer searched for palaces, castles or monasteries... but for hiding places where [art] might be stored and remain undiscovered for a certain length of time.' Mines not castles. Caves not monasteries. Bunkers not safes. Enke reminded Seufert about the American discovery in May 1945 of the vast Führermuseum collection found in a salt mine beneath the Alt-Aussee mountains of Austria.

Enke sought out archives to help locate subterranean bolt-holes in western Saxony. He visited Dresden and among the papers he recovered there was a letter from Professor Fichtner, who wrote to the Reich Chancellery in December 1943: 'The best and most ideal safeguarding and rescue depots are at this moment in time decentralized accommodations in well-camouflaged areas of central Germany.' Fichtner named a limestone quarry at Lengefeld, on the northern edge of western Saxony's Erzgebirge nature park, much of which was 'laterally inside the mountain and may be considered to be absolutely safe against air raids'. At the time, the Reich Chancellery declined the offer and, as far as Enke could establish, the hiding places had remained free.[17]

Enke applied himself to the Erzgebirge region, a dense and uneven strip of pine forest hugging the mountainous border between Saxony and Czechoslovakia. Erzgebirge means 'Mountain of Ore' and the region had been heavily excavated for zinc, silver and lead since the twelfth century. Enke visited a 'mountain archive' at Freiberg, a small town on the northeastern tip of the Erzgebirge, a document centre mapping the region's disused mines. He reported to Seufert: 'It is imperative that the search must be precisely targeted because the stock of files extends to several thousands of metres of shelving, as well as around 76,000 individual mine and shaft sketch plans.'

Enke learned from local residents that on 11 May 1945 the bodies of Hitler's brother-in-law, as well as four members on the staff of the Gauleiter of Saxony, Martin Mutschmann, had been found in the Erzgebirge. He recalled the correspondence from 1944 in which Koch debated with Mutschmann about the best places to conceal the Amber Room. Mutschmann himself had been arrested in this area in May 1945, found by the Red Army in the hamlet of Tellerhäuser and allegedly taken back to the Soviet Union. Enke speculated that Mutschmann had fled to what he thought was the safest part of his state. This would be the area where the Stasi would dig for the Amber Room. All that Enke needed was the Secretariat's approval.

In an attempt to focus his inquiries, Enke began to work on identifying the Nazi officer who had transported Koch's treasures in through Weimar. Enke reported to Seufert that, using a combination of archival resources and eyewitnesses, he arrived at the name Albert Popp, an NFSK Brigadeführer in Gruppe-7 (Saxony) and, more importantly, Gauleiter Mutschmann's nephew.

Enke reported that Popp had acted for the Nazi High Command already, evacuating Angela, Hitler's half-sister, from Dresden to Berchtesgaden in March 1945. To demonstrate further the proximity of Popp to the Nazi High Command, Enke advised Seufert that, while Popp fled to the West after the war, his wife remained in the GDR and adopted the children of missing Gauleiter Martin Mutschmann.[18]

Enke tested the name Albert Popp on the old art dealer, the only surviving eyewitness to the arrival of Koch's crates at Weimar museum in February 1945. Enke reported: 'The dealer said, that if he could hear or read the name, he would probably remember it. So, we wrote down two dozen names, some of them fairly similar, with the name of Albert Popp in thirteenth place. The old man read through the names... and then he said: "Yes, the driver was called Popp."'[19]

Enke also tried out his theory on a Soviet source. Our Friend the Professor has found two letters from him to Anatoly Kuchumov in the St Petersburg archive, written while Enke was conducting his Saxony research. We never knew that the two men had ever corresponded. The first letter, dated 24 July 1976, began with 'heartfelt greetings to my battle comrade'. Enke wrote:

And now to a... problem... You told me about the last statement of Erich Koch regarding possible connections between the Amber Room and his private collection. Do you think it likely that maybe Erich Koch thought to hide them together? This idea corresponds exactly with a version of the story that I have been researching... as I told you in April in Pushkin and Pavlovsk.[20]

So Enke and Kuchumov had met, in Leningrad in April 1976, and discussed the possibility that Erich Koch had evacuated the Amber Room along with his own art collection from East Prussia. Until now we had thought that the Stasi and Soviet investigations had gone their separate ways and that Enke had never left the GDR.

Enke continued:

I have found a list of Koch's vast stolen collection and on that list is a great amount of silver candelabras. I recalled the description of the Amber Room in Pushkin and above all remembered the light emitted by the large number of candles that were reflected by the huge mirrors. According to my calculations, from photographs, there should be 132 candelabras. It is interesting to me that on this list of silver belonging to Koch is the same number of [Russian] candelabras. Maybe these are the decorations of the Amber Room.

Enke's theory (and Geissler's account of it) was beginning to make sense. He had a final question for Kuchumov:

Did you see during your searches the name of Koch's aide? Was it Popp or Poppa? I have evidence that this man was trusted and helped hide some of the treasures on Koch's list. My heartfelt thanks to you and your colleagues in Pavlovsk and Pushkin. Be sure that we from our side direct all our energy to help you reach our mutual goal, with Communist regards, P. Enke.

Enke's second letter was written on 22 October 1976: 'My respectable Anatoly Mikhailovich, first of all my wife and I personally thank you for your battle-felt regards on the occasion of our national festival of the GDR [7 October].' Enke was still keen to learn all he could about Albert Popp, the driver of the Red Cross van: 'I have a question about a man who transported the treasures of Koch in 1945 from Königsberg to central Germany and hid art pieces so successfully that some are still missing. Could you tell me anything more about this Popp, his date of birth, his real name.' Perhaps Kuchumov had not answered Enke's previous inquiry.

Enke continued, easing his way into more delicate matters:

During vacations with my wife we travelled through Thuringia and Saxony and visited useful people who gave us information. But I have a question for you. It seems that in 1948 Soviet art historian Xenia Agarfornova found part of Koch's treasure, including the silver candelabras (that I spoke of before) and delivered them back to the USSR. Is she a curator from the State Hermitage and did you establish that these candelabras were from the Amber Room? Heartfelt regards and I am sure together we are going to find the Amber Room. P. Enke.

This is the first time that we have seen any evidence that part of the Amber Room (albeit only the candelabras) might have been found in Germany by the Soviets after the war. If what Enke confided in Kuchumov in this private letter was true, it explains why the Stasi was so certain that the Amber Room was in Germany. What it doesn't explain is why the Soviets chose not to tell the Stasi about their discovery of the candelabras.

Kuchumov's replies, if he sent any, are not in the Ministry of Truth. What is here is another report dated 1976 from Enke to Oberst Seufert. In it Enke attempted to tie up all the loose ends, and addressed the issue of the evidence given by GDR citizen 'Rudi Ringel'.

His line of reasioning was as follows: Koch had hinted that his treasures were concealed together with the Amber Room; Enke had traced Koch's treasures to Weimar and then into a Red Cross van; if 'Rudi Ringel's' father, the SS Sturmbannführer, had also been involved in the secret operation to evacuate the Amber Room, that placed him together with Albert Popp in the Red Cross van heading in all probability into western Saxony and not, as the Soviets had concluded, in downtown Königsberg. It was an unconvincing and staggeringly simplistic piece of logic but the Stasi seemed to have accepted it.

To prove his theory, Enke began to prise apart 'Rudi Ringel's' family history, testing the stories told by his mother, sister and brother against available wartime records, looking for connections to Albert Popp, a Red Cross van and the western Erzgebirge. We realize, reading this document, that it must have been at this point that Enke called in Uwe Geissler to help him with the cross-examinations. According to the report, 'Frau Ringel' claimed that on 2 November 1944 she and her children had relocated from bombed Königsberg to Crimmitschau in Saxony, sixty miles west of the Erzgebirge. Her husband, the SS Sturmbannführer, stayed behind, but on 5 February 1945 he arrived in plain clothes on his family's doorstep in Crimmitschau, carrying a duffel bag, a machine gun, a pistol and some food.

According to local records, scoured by Enke and Geissler, the SS man had registered with the Crimmitschau police on 6 February 1945. His wife claimed he then disappeared for ten days and did the same in March and April 1945. In February 1946, the 'Ringel' family moved again, to Schlema (a suburb on the edge of the Erzgebirge). In nearby Greiz hospital, Enke located the death certificate for the SS Sturmbannführer, 'dated 14 October 1947 (lung disease)'. It was in the cellar of the family's Schlema house that 'Rudi Ringel' claimed to have found the map pouch in July 1949 as his family prepared to move again to Elsterberg, west of the Erzgebirge, a place that Enke discovered had been Albert Popp's hometown. Popp and the 'Ringel' family's proximity to the Erzgebirge was tantalizing for Enke (although it seems to prove little to us).[21]

We read on impatiently, as Enke reported to Seufert:

There had been many voices that claimed 'Rudi Ringel' is a swindler, a fantasist and for these reasons he does not have to be taken seriously. Initially we too had some doubts, but we wanted certainty and therefore we dealt thoroughly with 'Rudi Ringel's' past... We do not consider the radio message ["Action Amber Room concluded. Storage in BSCH. Accesses blown up. Casualties through enemy action."] to have been a mistake or a forgery, but we only query the opinion mentioned by several investigators that the message had been sent from Königsberg.[22]

Enke was so certain of his breakthrough that a few months after writing to Kuchumov he factored the Koch–Weimar–Popp–Ringel theory into a plan for a book that he gave the provisional title 'Traces of the Amber Room: A Historical Criminological Investigation'. This was the start of what would eventually become *Bernsteinzimmer Report*. Chapter 6 promised 'New Tracks That Point to Western Saxony'.[23]

We flick ahead through the file, looking for a report on the outcome of the 1976 digs in the western Erzgebirge and instead find something baffling. Two years later, Paul Enke had been taken off the Amber Room investigation altogether. Now based at home, he composed this letter to Generaloberst Bruno Beater, Deputy Minister for State Security, Erich Mielke's right-hand man, first among several deputies.

Enke wrote: '30 January 1978, 118 Berlin-Grünau, Dear Comrade Beater! I am in need of your good advice and practical assistance and I am asking for the possibility of a personal consultation. My request is for information about the BZW [Amber Room file]... With the best will in the world I cannot accept the recommendation to give up the search.'[24]

One minute he was digging in the Erzgebirge. Now he was begging for access to the Amber Room files that surely he had compiled. We read on, trying to understand what had happened to Paul Enke. What had gone wrong?

Enke continued:

The result of ten years' research is now to hand in the form of an art-historical-criminological study... in which I am furnishing proof that the Amber Room was brought on 9 February 1945 to Thuringia and was then conveyed in the beginning of April 1945 to Saxony. I am contradicting all other versions (East Prussia, Königsberg, the Baltic, Bavaria, Lower Saxony)... Dear Comrade Beater, please do find a possibility for me and ascertain how I could report directly to you... I remain, with the best regards of an old Fighter [sic], yours Paul Enke.

The situation must have been critical for Enke to go over the heads of his immediate superiors and make contact with Beater, one of the most powerful men in the GDR; with the Stasi from the start, a member of the notorious kidnapping gangs sent out by Mielke in the 1950s to bring back defectors.

Six days later, Enke wrote again:

5 February 1978, 118 Berlin-Grünau, Dear Comrade Beater! Initially please accept my most sincere wishes for the rudest of rude health and I hope that you will continue to be successful at your work! The enclosed work might perhaps be suitable to clarify somewhat the extent of the problem BZ [Amber Room]... The difference between my manuscripts and all other

publications consists to a large extent in the... constant and general use of facts and proofs indicating the exact sources and renouncing all speculative pseudo-facts.

There was a justificatory tone creeping into this letter, as if some authority had questioned Enke's research.

In case Beater still needed to be convinced of Enke's discernment and experience, there was a postscript:

Within the framework of my Service Qualification as 'historian', I presently read the newest book by David Irving (England): *Hitler and His Generals*. Eight years ago Irving had been in contact with us... and together we searched near Perleberg for items from the legacies of Nazi leaders. In the above mentioned book [Irving writes] about this matter... 'It took weeks to search a forest in East Germany with the aide of a Proton Magnetometer... but the jam jar, supposedly containing the last Goebbels diaries, [was not there] although according to the map we stood above it.'[25]

There is no suggestion that David Irving was ever in the pay of the Stasi and we do not know if Beater replied. But one month later, on 15 February 1978, Enke submitted another plan of action: he wanted permission to interrogate Koch (who was still in Poland) and to contact the Soviet authorities.[26]

On 21 August 1978 action was taken. The Stasi rejected Enke's appeals and instead called a moratorium on all investigations based on evidence given by GDR citizen 'Rudi Ringel'. The order went out: '"Rudi Ringel" to be reinterrogated'. The Stasi agent, brought in for the task, was Uwe Geissler, the man we had met at 'Goat's Throat Village'.[27] He had not mentioned this.

GEISSLER: There has never been an SS Sturmbannführer or an SS man of a similar rank with the name ['Ringel']. What is your explanation?

'RUDI RINGEL': My father was very brown [a militant Nazi]. He joined the Nazi party on 1 May 1937. Everyone knew that it was him who had burned down Königsberg's synagogue. He wore many uniforms, brown, grey and black, but he had certainly had the double silver lighting-strike runes [of the

SS] pinned to his epaulettes. The family used other names. Perhaps my father was enlisted into the SS using one of those.

GEISSLER: Why did your father keep documents after 1945 that could have sentenced him to capital punishment?

'RUDI RINGEL': My father was a Prussian wooden-head. I now think that my own behaviour can be connected to that family trait.

GEISSLER: How did you find the letters?

'RUDI RINGEL': It was while I was clearing the basement. I found a hinged pouch with the name of my father on it. It was locked and nearly rotten. But inside there were sheets that did refer to the Amber Room. On one my father was addressed as Sturmbannführer. I remember seeing the Nazi eagle and that it came from the RSHA [Reich Security Main Office]. At the time I burned the documents because I was of the opinion that it was better if they didn't exist.

GEISSLER: Under what circumstances have you been in contact with the Soviet state authorities?

'RUDI RINGEL': In the illustrated *Freie Welt* there was a request for people to come forward. I wrote to Berlin and said I could make a statement. The editors of *Freie Welt* [names blacked out] visited me. Then I flew to Moscow and Kaliningrad.

GEISSLER: The Soviet authorities state that you indicated to them that the Amber Room was stored at Ponarth [a south-western suburb of Königsberg] Church, a building that the SS blew up. There was only one church in Ponarth and it was not blown up in 1945. What do you say now?

'RUDI RINGEL': It must be a translation fault. I have never made such a statement. I only talked about a path from the castle [Königsberg] to Steindamm Church.

GEISSLER: In the statements you have made on the Amber Room to date has your imagination taken over?

'RUDI RINGEL': Today I could have made it very easy for myself and told you that everything was fantasy. But this is what I remember. I am prepared to think about it once again and if I remember anything further I will contact the Stasi. I have read the protocol and this statement to you is true.

The document was signed by 'Bernd' and 'Rudi Ringel'.

Poor 'Rudi Ringel' (described in this interrogation report as a lathe operator). He must have been enthralled by the revelations in *Freie Welt* and come forward of his own volition, probably hoping to win kudos with the local party, possibly a glass of *schwarzbier* or a holiday in the spa town of Friedrichroda. Instead, he was whisked off to Moscow and then Kaliningrad, forced to become a party to state secrets, interrogated by Kuchumov, then Enke and now 'Bernd'. But the one thing he could never do, after writing that fateful letter to *Freie Welt*, not if he wanted to stay alive, was back down.

On 9 November 1979 'Bernd', a.k.a. Uwe Geissler, reported back to the Stasi Secretariat. He had at last found trace of 'Rudi Ringel's' father and what he revealed was not what he told us in the concrete chalet in 'Goat's Throat Village'.

'Rudi Ringel's' father was a member of the NSDAP but from 1940 was attached to a post office protection unit. 'Bernd' wrote: 'After an injury [name blacked out] suffered while serving in occupied Poland he was disabled out of the service. According to his daughter, since then he had made a living by manufacturing bags from scrap fabric.' It was highly unlikely that an invalided post office security guard would have been entrusted with the Amber Room by Erich Koch.

At the back of 'Rudi Ringel's' Stasi file is this conclusion:

The statement made by ['Rudi Ringel'] is wrong. He either deliberately or indirectly made difficulties for the Amber Room investigation and misdirected the search, causing it great harm. It is suggested that judicial responsibility should be examined according to paragraph 228, concerning false accusations, and paragraph 233, aiding and abetting.

'Rudi Ringel' also stood accused of 'providing false information to Soviet organs'. All of the Soviet excavations in Kaliningrad based on 'Rudi Ringel's' evidence had been a waste of time.

We call Geissler at his apartment in East Berlin, near Allee der Kosmonauten, and ask him what happened to Enke and his digs to find BSCH, the secret hiding place for the Amber Room? Was it these digs that led to the outing of 'Rudi Ringel' as the son of a lame post office guard?

All we can hear on the line is the wheezing of Geissler's emphysemic lungs. 'We dug,' says Geissler. 'We dug and dug. Pulled in experts from Switzerland. Heavy machinery hired from abroad. Paid for it all in hard currency. Spent 6 million or thereabouts [500,000 dollars] on excavating just one of the mines. And eventually we did get into the tunnels of Schwalbe V, near Gera. It had been a Nazi underground factory where scientists were trying to synthesize petrol from coal. Enke had told the bosses, "We are the first to get in." But when we lit up our torches...'

The line goes silent. A crackle as Geissler inhales. 'We found nothing but small, charred, rolled-up pieces of *Pravda* dating from July 1945. The Red Army had been there, decades before us, and left behind their cigarette butts. We even knew the date. Back in 1945 supplies of everything were low, including cigarette papers, and the Soviet troops used pages from *Pravda* instead. Enke had been wasting our time.'

As we ponder how everything came to a grinding halt in an empty mine already searched by the Soviets (with 'Rudi Ringel' in the dock), the functionary in pearls enters the room. 'Time, please,' she says, tapping her wristwatch.

10

In the last week of May 1980 Generalmajor Karli Coburger and Generalmajor Jochen Büchner, two of the Stasi's most senior directorate heads, met to discuss Paul Enke's career.[1]

According to Enke's personal file, KSII404/82, he had 'exposed 100 possible locations for the Amber Room' over twenty-five years of service. Using the pseudonym Dr Paul Köhler and the cover 'functionary at the State Archives Administration', Enke had 'got in touch with West German citizens and with FRG journalists' in connection with the issue of restitution of stolen Soviet art.[2] But his career was not without blemish.

The generalmajors also had before them this reference from 15 April 1952, written when Enke was a young police recruit: '<u>Character Appraisal</u>. The calm manner revealed by Enke in most of his dealings is quite obviously only an apparent show, hiding a vivacious and impulsive character.'[3]

Generalmajors Coburger and Büchner also read this from 5 October 1964, one week after Enke had been sworn in as a Stasi agent. While the new officer was prepared to 'carry out tasks that may exceed normal working hours... Enke tends to deal exclusively with the theory and distance himself from practical activities... Sometimes, he also tends to adopt a certain stubbornness of manner whereby he is often not open-minded enough to confront criticism of his person or decisions.'[4]

Given these doubts, we are suprised that Enke was entrusted for so many years with such a sensitive, secret and costly operation as the search for the Amber Room.

On 30 May 1980 Enke was called to Stasi headquarters at Normannenstrasse in Berlin-Lichtenberg. A report of that meeting noted: 'Comrade Büchner opened the discussion with the statement that it was necessary to raise the research work on the art robberies in the Soviet Union to a national level and thereby the results of the researches carried out by Comrade Enke should be consolidated in one official dossier.' It was concluded that the Amber Room inquiry should 'take on a more political operative character' and Enke was 'obliged to place all material relevant to the case for operative evaluation'.[5] Enke was told: 'All the above named material, accompanied by advice and annotations, must be delivered by 1.30 p.m. on 4 June 1980.' He had four and a half days to pack up his career.

Büchner called the meeting to a close. Taking into consideration increasing bouts of poor health, Enke was now 'granted sick-leave and will later be retired with a pension'. As he was shown the door, Büchner wished him 'much success in carrying out his new brief'.[6] The official retirement date was set for 1 January 1981 but in the meantime there was much for Enke to do.

Enke was being edged out and the Ministry of Truth files before us confirm that the order for a new 'systematic approach' to the Amber Room investigation came from the highest level – Erich Mielke. The files do not explain why the Minister for State Security ordered a completely new inquiry, but it must have been connected with the humiliating discovery that the Stasi had squandered millions without even having had a passable shot at the prize.

Enke's Amber Room investigation was to be renamed 'Operation Puschkin' and would receive higher levels of funding and staffing, in the form of a 'Special Task Force' that would report directly to Generalmajor Neiber, Mielke's first deputy. Enke's former boss Oberst Seufert was the only man from the old team who would remain, assisted by his new aide Oberstleutant Bauer and liaison officers Hauptmann Rudolph and Oberleutnant Kühn.[7]

While Enke's career was being deboned, he was sent home to his apartment in Berlin-Grünau. He was to remain on call, with a safe installed in his house, although the Secretariat envisaged an outflow of confidential material from the apartment rather than a continuation of the old days during which Paul Enke was left alone to stockpile documents for which there was only one index, in his head.

Enke was required to sign a form that stated 'today even more than hitherto our activities and results must be kept strictly secret and conspiratorial in order to avoid supplying arguments to our enemies that may lead to politically-hostile [*sic*] actions against the GDR and the Soviet Union'. We wonder if he had been indiscreet before as well as prone to bouts of fantasy.

In future, only Oberst Seufert and Oberst Stolze, head of the Nazi archives, would have access to the Amber Room files. Further, 'the previous permission of Seufert must be obtained if it becomes necessary to contact citizens of other countries'.[8]

Another significant player in the old Amber Room investigation was also terminated. A handwritten note by Hauptmann Rudolph recorded: 'Professor Dr Gerhard Strauss should be deleted from any further utilization in the procedure "Operation Puschkin".' An attached note (that also confirmed what we have suspected all along, that Strauss was a Stasi collaborator) stated: 'Professor Strauss has been removed from the whole process of the Amber Room after the intervention of the Comrade Minister.'[9] (After reunification Strauss's place of work, Humboldt University, would be exposed in the German press as a Stasi hothouse, with one in six professors and one in ten employees having had links to Mielke's ministry).

For Enke, there was to be some recompense. Seufert suggested that the Secretariat award him the Battle Decoration in gold (*Kampforden*) and a one-off bonus of 1,500 Ostmarks – one month's salary.[10] But surely nothing could console Enke, having been forced out of that which he created.

Once Enke had turned over his paperwork, he was ordered to complete his long-overdue book, an exercise that the Ministry of Truth files stated was 'critical to the success of the new "Operation Puschkin"'. The Secretariat had ditched Enke's dogmatic title in favour of something more pithy: *Bernsteinzimmer Report*. Enke was given just months in which to polish his manuscript and, to hurry him along, two Stasi-approved

Lektors (editors) were hired: Wolfgang Ney, Humboldt University professor of criminology and Dr Manfred Kirmse, director of the Documentation Centre at the State Archives Administration.[11] No mention yet of Günter Wermusch or Die Wirtschaft, the eventual publishers.

According to Ministry of Truth files, the latter chapters of *Bernsteinzimmer Report* would provide a 'description of the finding of the new tracks of the Amber Room in Thuringia', proving that 'arriving from Königsberg, the unique art collection of Erich Koch, including the Amber Room, had been stored in the State Museum of Weimar and that on 9 or 10 April [1945] these collections had been taken to a place of safety away from the approaching US Army. The man in charge of the double relocation of the collections was Albert Popp.' The book would 'succeed in proving that a man living in the GDR and serving as an informant to the Soviet government (a.k.a. 'Rudi Ringel') told how his father was supposed to have concealed the Amber Room and that as a result of the author's research... new tracks [of 'Rudi Ringel's' story] point to western Saxony, a version supported by information emanating from the Soviet Union which was passed under conditions of confidentiality to the author'.[12]

Given the internal investigation into 'Rudi Ringel's' evidence, the failed digs in Saxony and the pensioning off of Paul Enke, *Bernsteinzimmer Report*, still today the most famous book on the Amber Room mystery, was shaping up to be a classic exercise in disinformation. In a report to Generalmajor Neiber, Oberst Seufert confirmed this, writing: 'The book is to be published to lend new impulses to the search.'[13]

While Enke sweated over his manuscript, Seufert picked through his subordinate's files and began to discover significant gaps. Enke had never seen Professor Brusov's assessment of Königsberg Castle Museum director Alfred Rohde, written in 1945, or Anatoly Kuchumov's dismantling of it in 1946. Enke had never been shown any of Kuchumov's 1946 interrogations. Or a transcript of Kuchumov's interview with of Dr Gerhard Strauss in the Hotel Moscow in Kaliningrad in 1949. In fact, Enke had mislaid the Stasi's entire file on Gerhard Strauss, an incident that now led to a high-level inquiry, with one Stasi directorate head writing to another: 'This file could be of great importance to our investigations but for operative reasons it cannot be located. We have already been looking for it in the State Archives Administration and the Central State Archive in Potsdam with no result. Do you have it?'[14]

Although Enke's main investigations to date hinged on the theory that the former Gauleiter Erich Koch had ordered the evacuation of the Amber Room and that it had been shipped from East Prussia alongside Koch's private art collection, Seufert reported that Enke had never seen Strauss's cross-examination in Warsaw of Erich Koch from June 1959 (in which Koch stated that it would have been impossible to evacuate the Amber Room to Germany). Instead Enke had derived his intelligence on the former Gauleiter almost exclusively from Polish and Soviet newspapers.

The Gauleiter of Saxony, Martin Mutschmann, had signed off all art transports into his state and yet Enke had found no documents connecting Mutschmann with the Amber Room. Although it was an open secret that the Red Army had probably found Mutschmann in the Erzgebirge in May 1945 and taken him back to Moscow, Enke had made no formal request to the KGB for intelligence. There was no evidence (aside from that given by an aged Weimar art dealer) that Albert Popp, the man who had evacuated Hitler's half-sister, had also been the driver of the Red Cross van bearing Koch's art collection to the Erzgebirge. There were no witnesses or corroborative facts that supported the claim that the man in the passenger seat was 'Rudi Ringel's' father. Not only had Enke based his investigations on one source alone ('Rudi Ringel'), he had also tailored the source's statement to fit his own theory. While we had read in Kuchumov's original debriefing of 'Rudi Ringel' that BSCH (the supposed codename for the secret Amber Room storage facility) was described as in Königsberg, Paul Enke placed it in East Germany.

Oberst Stolze wrote to Generalmajor Neiber, warning him of an even more worrying factor. In reviewing Enke's interrogations of old East Prussians, Stolze had discovered that virtually every German citizen questioned by the Stasi in connection with the Amber Room story had already been quizzed by the Soviets at the end of the war. Stolze wrote: 'It has been ascertained that in the post-war years, the Soviet Union… undertook intensive measures in the territory of the GDR to find the Amber Room. Many of the persons and objects of these searches, which had been undertaken at the time, have reappeared in our inquiry.' If the Stasi and KGB had the same motives in searching for the Amber Room, why had the Soviets not shared their findings, Stolze queried, and saved the Stasi time and money?[15]

On 28 October 1980 the Stasi wrote to the KGB in Moscow to rectify the situation. 'In our efforts to obtain new hints, indications or documents which could lead to the finding of the Amber Room we are asking for any information from your archives, card indexes and other sources in the USSR in connection with the enclosed questionnaire.'[16] Attached was a thirteen-page list of what the Stasi needed: intelligence on Nazi organizations, eyewitnesses and suspects. The request was copied to the chairman of the KGB and the KGB liaison in Berlin-Karlshorst.

While it waited for a response, the Stasi recruited more staff to help comb through the old Amber Room files, dispatching a constant stream of briefing papers to deputy minister Neiber, including a twenty-three-page report dated 11 January 1982 containing new indexes for locations, transport firms, digging sites, witnesses and names of former Nazis. There were chronological lists of newspaper articles, alphabetical tables of Nazi art depots, maps – scores of them, now sorted and classified – and photographs too. All of Enke's theories on the Amber Room's disappearance were anatomized. Buried towards the end of one of these reports was a significant concession: perhaps the Amber Room had remained concealed in Kaliningrad after all.[17]

The Secretariat signed off a fifteen-page recommendation on 21 January 1982: 'Political-Operative Plan of Steps for Cooperation between Foreign Security Services for the "Operation Puschkin" investigation'. It was a plea to brother intelligence organizations to share information with the Stasi. The KGB in Moscow was petitioned again to open their files and the Polish security services were asked again for access to Erich Koch, who was still alive.[18]

By February 1982 Generalmajor Neiber was actively involved. He proposed a top-level delegation, 'a business trip of a working task force by five MfS members to the Soviet Union's KGB'. Steeped in Mielke's lexicon, Neiber wrote: 'Duration – four days. To take place in May 1982... for the further harmonization, liaison and cooperation in the realization of the planned political and operational measures, necessitated through the Security Process "Puschkin" No. XV 3241/80 as controlled by the office of the Comrade Deputy Minister'. Translation: let's work together, please. Yet even in matters of international significance there was the old Stasi banality. Neiber signed off his report with a coda: 'It has been agreed that the delegation will travel by aeroplane to and from Moscow.'[19]

An attached letter – 'Berlin 02/1982, For Information Only, to Generalmajor Karli Coburger' – set out the delicate nature of the trip.

The [Soviet] documents relating to persons and objects [that we have received] following a request to the Investigation Department of the KGB, which had been dispatched in October 1980, had been useful only in the partial clarification of some subjects in the range of investigations... The results transmitted remained within a narrow framework and did not lead to clarification of the basic matters of concern in this process.'

Translation: the Stasi request to the KGB for help, made sixteen months earlier, had achieved little.[20]

Neiber would sort out the trouble. He forwarded a list of key Soviet figures that the Stasi delegation would like to meet: 'Comrade A. M. Kutschumow, Comrade Xenia Agarfornova, Comrade Jelena Storozhenko (Geological-Archaeological Expedition, Kaliningrad), Comrade W. D. Krolewski (search commission, Kaliningrad), Comrade Julia Semjonow (long-term Soviet newspaper correspondent in the FRG and now in based Moscow)'.

In a correspondence file for the Stasi district office in Magdeburg we learn the fate of deputy minister Neiber's trumpeted mission to Moscow.[21] It was cancelled at the last minute – by the Soviets. Magdeburg reported to East Berlin that it had uncovered a potential informer, 'Comrade M... who is capable of making a statement clearing up some details about the Amber Room'. Magdeburg was delighted with its find and wanted to know if it should interrogate Comrade M locally or send him to headquarters. But East Berlin advised Magdeburg to do nothing: 'The proposal for [Neiber's] trip to Moscow... has been rejected. Deputy Comrade Minister Generalmajor Neiber has decided that overall charge of the political-operational handling of the entire above-mentioned complex must remain in the hands of the "fraternal authorities"...' Translation: the Stasi was bowing to the KGB. 'With a large degree of probability the main part of the Amber Room had still been stored in 1945 in Königsberg,' East Berlin informed Magdeburg, effectively telling the district office to stop looking for it in East Germany. All Stasi efforts to locate the Amber Room in East Germany had been a waste of time.

However, the Ministry of Truth files do record that there was another visit to Moscow in the spring of 1982 concerning the Amber Room. A handwritten note dated 22 February reported that Comrade Enke had called in with some startling news: 'A ten-person commission led by FRG citizen George Stein has arrived in the Soviet Union to talk about the BZ.'[22]

Moscow was courting a West German.

We have come across George Stein before.[23] Gerhard Strauss's son, Stephan, had told us that a 'George Stein' had been a frequent visitor to their house in Heinrich-Mann-Platz. We had also spotted the name on a grizzly dossier of deaths (said to be connected with the Amber Room) that had been shown to us by the staff of the Catherine Palace in St Petersburg (although we saw it so briefly we couldn't understand its meaning). And we have seen the name in a Ministry of Truth file, in papers that revealed the Stasi would have been familiar with George Stein too, since he had come to its attention during what Erich Mielke would have described as a 'favourable political-operative situation': the return to Moscow of missing Soviet treasure.

In 1966 George Stein, a strawberry farmer from Stelle, a village south-west of Hamburg, had begun to scour West German archives in his free weekends, looking for information about the Amber Room. It was an exciting hobby for a man who had been raised in the former East Prussia.

He began his research with the war. In state archives in Bonn he read how, despite the division of Germany into Allied zones at the Yalta Conference in February 1945, a race had ensued to reach the Nazi hoards. In April 1945 the US Army had beaten the Red Army to Thuringia (in the Soviet Zone) and removed the Reichsbank reserves, '100 tons of gold and silver

*Art works stolen by the Nazis, hidden in German mines
and found by American troops in April 1945*

bullion'.²⁴ From the Soviet Zone US troops also took priceless German art collections, as well as Soviet treasures looted by the Nazis that had been stored beside them. Stein considered the possibility that the Amber Room had been found by US troops and taken back to America.

He read how the USA had tried to placate Stalin in 1945 by assuring him that all Soviet art would be returned, and between 1946 and 1948 the USA sent to the USSR tens of thousands of crates. There was, however, no apology for taking the gold and German art collections from the Soviet Zone. By March 1949, with Berlin blockaded, the wrangle over reparations and the bitterness felt by the Soviets at losing out contributed to the freezing of relations between East and West.

Stein read in the Bonn archive how Marshal Vasily Sokolovsky, Commander-in-Chief of the Soviet Occupation Forces, accused his American counterpart, General Lucius Clay, of 'deliberate spoilage or theft'.²⁵ The US dismissed the claim as Stalinist propaganda, stating that the only Soviet items it continued to hold on to were politically sensitive documents, such as the Smolensk Communist Party Archive, which 'served their purpose as a training ground for American Sovietology'.[26] If we have hoarded Soviet art, the Americans challenged Moscow, show us the proof.

In 1972, Stein found it. In the Ministry of Truth files, we come across a report on Stein's researches, written by Paul Enke, that stated Stein had discovered in the Bonn archive (a place barred to the Soviets and East Germans) a letter dated 27 April 1955 from Dr Clemens Weiler, director of West Germany's Wiesbaden City Museum. In the letter, Weiler explained how he had been made responsible for numerous art works left behind by the Americans after they had closed their central art collection point, which was based in Wiesbaden, in 1951. Four years later Dr Weiler was offering some of these art works, specifically a collection of Russian icons, to another West German museum, the Kunsthalle in Recklinghausen.[27]

Stein probed and found more correspondence about the Russian icons, this time letters from Clemens Weiler to Ardelia Hall, head of the US Restitution Program at the Department of State in Washington. Weiler reported to Hall his intentions to pass on the icons and Hall advised him to dispose of them as he saw fit, requesting only that they be made 'as accessible to the public as possible'. There was no discussion about returning the icons to the Soviet Union.[28]

In 1972 Stein drove to Recklinghausen and discovered that the deal had gone ahead. In fact the Russian icons were still there, locked up in a third-floor store. He contacted a family friend who had been part of the wartime resistance in Königsberg, Marion Dönhoff, the famous 'Red Countess of East Prussia', who after the war had become the publisher of Die Zeit newspaper. The story Marion Dönhoff printed forced the Recklinghausen museum to defend itself. Its spokesman claimed that the wooden icons had been locked away only 'to avoid infestation with moths' – hardly a convincing argument – and failed to answer the question of what icons belonging to the Soviet Union were doing in a West German museum in the first place. The West German government too made little effort to apologize. Helmut Rumpf, a Foreign Office spokesman, issued a statement: 'You know what it is like, the personnel in charge changed, the files were taken to the archives and then all was forgotten.' Rumpf also turned on George Stein, describing him as 'a zealous whinger looking for a life's task'.[29] West German newspapers agreed, accusing Stein of being a traitor, a liar and a fantasist.

But the story would not go away. What Stein had found was one of the Soviet Union's most precious missing devotional treasures, the Byzantine icons from the Mirozhsky Monastery in Pskov. They had been stolen by the Nazis in the autumn of 1941, packed into crates along with ruby-studded crucifixes, bishops' crowns encrusted with precious stones, and gold and silver chalices, and shipped to Castle Colmberg in Bavaria in 1944. There they had been discovered by American forces, who had taken them to Wiesbaden in April 1945.

As soon as the story went public, the Soviets lodged an appeal for the return of the treasures and the West German Foreign Office was forced to back down. On 14 May 1973, amid a barrage of negative publicity in West Germany, where curators called for Moscow to hand back items allegedly looted by the Red Army in 1945 (including a Gutenberg Bible, stained glass from St Mary's in Frankfurt an der Oder, the 'Trojan Gold', drawings by Dürer and the entire collection of the Bremen Kunsthalle), the Pskov icons were repatriated to the Soviet Union. In Moscow, the West German Consul-General presented them to Patriarch Pimen, head of the Russian Orthodox Church, who then awarded George Stein the Star of the Order of St Vladimir Second Class, a cross worn around the fruit farmer's neck on which was embossed the motto 'Usefulness, Honour and Glory'.[30]

Lionized in Russia, George Stein returned to West Germany in June 1973 to be belittled as a meddling *hobby-Historiker* by bristling and chauvinistic elements in the West German press. But according to the Ministry of Truth files, what the Stasi had identified as a 'favourable political-operative situation' (the Soviets and East Germans portrayed as preyed upon by the greedy West, which was forced by one of its own citizens to return stolen art) rapidly deteriorated into a 'politically hostile situation' (the Soviets and East Germans demonized by that same citizen – George Stein).

Stein learned from irate West German museum curators that extensive files concerning secret Nazi art storage facilities and the fate of the Amber

Room had been amassed by the USSR and GDR. He began demanding access to them and in particular he repeatedly wrote and called the State Archives Administration in East Berlin (the place where the Stasi's own Amber Room expert, Oberstleutnant Paul Enke, worked undercover as researcher Dr P. Köhler).

In the Ministry of Truth we found this report, written by Paul Enke:

[day and month blacked out], 1975. In connection with problems of exchange of works of art, my department has unofficially learned that George Stein is... trying to force the USSR and the GDR to make available and accessible information that is closed about the hiding place of art treasures and especially the Amber Room of Pushkin. In 1974 and on 3 July 1975 George Stein has asked our Documentation Centre of the State Archives Administration for assistance in his search for the Amber Room. On 18 August 1975 he received a reply that in spite of detailed researches there is no information about the Amber Room in the archives of the GDR.[31]

But the Stasi had underestimated how tenacious George Stein could be. When he received the letter from the State Archives Administration on 18 August 1975, brushing him aside, he turned to press contacts he had made after recovering the Pskov icons. He called up 'Red Countess' Marion Dönhoff of *Die Zeit*, Anthony Terry at *The Sunday Times* in London and reporters on the *Washington Post*. He accused the East German and Soviet governments of withholding sensitive information about the Amber Room, hobbling those who were making genuine attempts to find it. Stein's accusations immediately picked up speed, as the *Freie Welt* and *Kaliningradskaya Pravda* stories had by now percolated into the West, creating great interest in the Amber Room.

In the Ministry of Truth files, the Stasi's alarm was palpable. Enke's boss Generaloberst Büchner and Stasi deputy minister Generaloberst Beater immediately demanded further intelligence about the activities of George Stein. Beater and Büchner were advised by Enke:

West German *hobby-Historiker* George Stein is talking to the English and American press, saying that the GDR and USSR are hindering attempts to find art works like the Amber Room, that the GDR and USSR have information about the hiding places of art treasures that they do not want to publish. We cannot allow this threatened press campaign by Stein to interfere with the cultural agreements being negotiated between the GDR and FRG.[32]

West German citizen George Stein had blundered into *Ostpolitik*. West Germany had held out its hand to Moscow, making peaceful overtures, and for its part Moscow and East Berlin were being made to look recalcitrant. George Stein would have to be headed off.

The files show that it was Professor Dr Gerhard Strauss who was brought in to handle the delicate negotiations. Strauss called George Stein to say that the GDR and USSR were keen to share information about the search for the Amber Room. He invited Stein to Heinrich-Mann-Platz for dinner (which must have been when Stephan Strauss, Gerhard's son, met him) and in the course of the evening explained that the GDR was not being obstructive but was a stickler for protocol. All future inquiries should be directed via him to a Dr Paul Köhler, senior researcher at the Documentation Centre of the State Archives Administration. Dr Köhler would provide relevant documents in exchange for sight of Stein's own research in Western archives and he would even pay for the material.

Stein must have been flattered to be courted by such a prestigious East German cultural scholar as Strauss and to be offered money for what he had so far had to fund from his own pocket. He readily agreed, but could not have known that Paul Köhler at the archives was Paul Enke of the Stasi.

The watchers in the East would now manipulate George Stein. A Stasi report noted: 'Based on Stein's inquiry at the State Archives in Potsdam we have the possibility of establishing specialized contacts via Comrade Enke which have been useful in giving Stein hints about objects and persons in [West Germany] which he could follow up much better than we could.'[33] The portal operated in both directions. Stein would be fed information that the East wanted publicized and fetch from the West that which the East couldn't reach.

Within two years, evidence of the success of this strategy would appear. On 23 April 1977 the West German newspaper *Der Tagesspiegel* carried an exclusive story: 'One of the most famous collections of amber in the world that belonged to Königsberg University, considered to be lost in the last days of war, has been found in Göttingen University.' During a spring-clean at the geological department, staff at the West German university were said to have broken open two wooden boxes to find 1,100 exceptionally fine pieces of amber. They bore handwritten labels in Gothic script: 'Institute of Palaeontology and Geology, Albertus-University, Königsberg, East Prussia'. We recall that part of this collection had been found in Königsberg by Soviet investigator Professor Alexander Brusov in 1945. At the time Brusov had advised Moscow that the best pieces of this collection had already been evacuated by Nazis from the city. Now they had turned up in West Germany, where it appeared that Göttingen University had been sitting on them for thirty-two years.[34]

George Stein confronted the university with a series of incriminating documents. One of them, dated 1 November 1944, was from a curator at Königsberg's Albertus-University, Herr Hoffman. Writing to Hauptmann Peters, Munitions Department, Volpriehausen, Lower Saxony (a pit village twelve miles north-west of Göttingen University), Hoffman said: 'The transporter of this letter has two wooden trunks with the most valuable pieces of amber from the collection of the Prussian state. Please keep them in a place which is specially guarded.' One wagon of valuables had already been sent, Hoffman added, and another 'containing irreplaceable art items of the university will come next week, addressed to the Bürgermeister'.[35]

Irreplaceable items – the same words used by Alfred Rohde when writing in December 1944 of his intention to evacuate the Amber Room. Across the bottom of the Hoffman letter was a postscript: 'It makes sense to address the boxes during transport with "ammo dept" so as not to bring them to the attention of others, since they are filled with priceless goods.' On the back of the letter were two handwritten notes, one of which was dated 7 November 1944, and recorded a call from Hauptmann Peters saying that 'everything went smoothly'. The other, dated 4 January 1945, advised: 'The placement of the Königsberg salvage items has been completed.' Stein had found proof that East Prussian treasures were moving west.[36] Could Stein possibly have found genuine tracks of the Amber Room too?

Reporters from *Der Tagesspiegel* learned from residents of Volpriehausen (the pit village named in the Hoffman letter) that heavily loaded trucks had been seen arriving at the mine in November 1944 and January 1945 – dates that corresponded with the transports from Königsberg. In September 1945 the entrance of the pit had been blasted shut by the Allies as they withdrew. The following year a Göttingen University professor had gathered a group of students to mount an amateur salvage operation and they had descended 1,625 feet down the main shaft on ropes, managing to recover 360,000 partially burnt books. Only the collapse of the roof at the end of the main tunnel had prevented them from continuing. When the *Der Tagesspiegel* reporters were shown some of the books in 1977, they noticed the stamp of Königsberg University library. Stein announced that the Amber Room was in the pit and he would lead a team of specialists into the tunnels to salvage it.

But George Stein had no money and in 1978 began to noisily lobby the West German Bundestag to fund the excavation. The Stasi carefully monitored each stage of this 'Volpriehausen episode'. In one report Enke wrote: 'Professor Dietrich of the SPD [Social Democrat Party] initiated several questions in the Bundestag on behalf of George Stein, including specific queries about fascist depots in Volpriehausen.'[37] Enke reported that in the village of Stelle, Stein and his wife, Elisabeth, were besieged by newspaper reporters and that right-wing newspapers were asking why West Germans should be concerned with restocking Russian museums when their own were still bare.[38]

The Bonn government was unimpressed with Stein's campaign. Chancellor Helmut Schmidt refused permission to excavate. There was insufficient evidence to warrant the expenditure. And what was in it for the FRG, apart from expiation of guilt?

On 1 December 1978 *Die Zeit* published more evidence from George Stein that he claimed connected the Amber Room to the Volpriehausen pit. It included a letter from 6 March 1944, written by the Nazi Kreisleitung (district administration) that identified the Volpriehausen pit as a vital storage depot with 7,000 square feet of available space. Another document, dated 29 December 1944, reported how twenty-four railway wagons filled with books and valuables had safely arrived at the pit. *Die Zeit* informed readers that the source of much of Stein's classified and pristine material was 'Dr Paul Köhler in the GDR', whom Stein described as 'my good friend'. Stein claimed that the most compelling document was a copy of a wartime telex concerning 'enterprise Amber Room' that showed how the treasure had been evacuated from Königsberg in the spring of 1945. Stein told *Die Zeit* that the telex reported how the room was eventually concealed 'in a place codenamed BSCHW, a cipher that could be unpicked to mean 'B-Tunnel [Volpriehausen]'. The head of the secret operation SS Sturmbannführer Ringel apparently signed the telex.[39]

Suddenly we realize that the Volpriehausen episode was a highly successful diversionary ploy. While the Stasi had secretly suspended all of its own operations connected to the source 'Rudi Ringel', it had recycled his dubious evidence for a new purpose – through George Stein. BSCH, the secret hiding place of the Amber Room, was becoming nomadic: first in Kaliningrad, then in East Germany and now in West Germany, alongside 'Rudi Ringel's' father, the lame post office security guard who appeared to have signed a telex in 1945 using a pseudonym given by the Stasi in 1959. It was all getting rather far-fetched.

We can see how conveniently this bad publicity played out for the Stasi. To the delight of the authorities in the East, Bonn once again appeared to be intransigent and chauvinistic, while the Soviet Union's wartime losses were highlighted through the fate of the Amber Room.

The Soviets contacted the Stasi, asking for more background information and a character assessment of George Stein. In his reply, Paul Enke made certain that he was not eclipsed by his West German mole:

I suggest you don't really expect anything sensational from this source... Stein works with somewhat dubious methods, for instance with forgeries. The motives for these practices are not quite clear to us. Maybe it is only the greed for sensationalism and the need for so-called scoops inherent in Capitalism. Just recently Stein published in the Hamburg weekly *Die Zeit* four reports about the storage of the Amber Room in the pits near Göttingen. According to a statement by Stein... he has a copy of a wartime telex that writes about the conclusion of 'enterprise Amber Room' that is supposed to be graced with the signature 'Ringel'. But as we are all aware, the name Ringel is only a pseudonym given to our 'object' in 1959, therefore it can hardly be the signature on a letter from 1945. This is only one further example of Stein's talent for invention.⁴⁰

This was a bold statement from a Stasi man who would already have known that he was about to be investigated in connection with his reliance on the dubious evidence presented by 'Rudi Ringel'. But Enke's unflattering portrait of Stein failed to put the Soviets off the scent.

Five months later, flattering articles about George Stein began to appear in the *Literaturnaya Gazeta*, a highbrow Soviet literary journal, under the byline of its Bonn correspondent, Julian Semyonov. This must be the 'Comrade Julia Semjonow' that Stasi deputy minister Neiber requested to see on his planned mission to the KGB in Moscow in 1982.

In May 1979 Semyonov wrote an article headlined 'A West German Citizen from the Village of Stelle'.⁴¹ He described the scene:

I am sitting here in the home of the married couple Stein in the village of Stelle near Hamburg. Wooden beams blackened by the wind from the sea lie across the white walls of this genuine Hanseatic house as I listen to the story. Like every enthusiastic person [George Stein's] language is unclear, rapid and jumps from one subject to another. George Stein knew that the search for the Amber Room had to continue and this is his story...

The thousands of words that follow tell how Stein had inadvertently become 'Europe's most successful Second World War treasure-hunter'. Semyonov revealed that Stein's interest in Nazi loot was sparked in 1966 when, laid up in a sanatorium at the foot of the Matterhorn, recovering from a car accident, he read a series of articles by Anthony Terry in *The Sunday Times* about Erich Koch's prison-cell confessions concerning the Amber Room.

Semyonov revealed that Stein, a native of East Prussia, vowed to find the Amber Room as a tribute to his family. His father, a Königsberg industrialist, had been part of the wartime resistance, while Dorothea-Luisa, Stein's sister, had worked at Königsberg Castle as an assistant to Alfred Rohde. Can this possibly be true? It seems a little neat. Semyonov continued: George Stein had been conscripted to defend the city, which he did until he was captured by the Red Army in May 1944, only learning after his release from camps in Uzbekistan and Leningrad that the SS had executed his entire family on discovering their links to the resistance and the 'Red Countess' Marion Dönhoff. Putting his tragic past behind him, Stein had migrated to Stelle, married Elisabeth, the daughter of a local farmer, and settled down to grow strawberries, until he crashed his car into a traffic policeman and ended up in Switzerland, bored and compulsively scanning the newspapers.

A photograph of Stein shows a large, jovial man with a harelip and thick-rimmed glasses, ostentatiously smoking a cigarette at a dinner table, a wine glass before him – a *bon viveur* dining out on a flush of stories.

George Stein

Julian Semyonov revealed that, having pressed the West German government to dig at Volpriehausen, Stein's life was now in danger. Hate mail had arrived at his home in Stelle. Semyonov wrote: 'George Stein has found out through innumerable threatening letters and public hostility how close the criminal past is connected with the present in the Federal Republic of Germany.'

Enke clipped everything Semyonov wrote about Stein and the Amber Room, pasting it into his files. Several translations have notes scribbled in the top left-hand corners, showing that the articles were referred up the hierarchy to the deputy minister and to Mielke himself. Key sentences were underlined, all of which were quotes from George Stein about 'my good friend Dr Paul Köhler in the GDR'. Paul Köhler was in danger of being unmasked as Stasi agent.

Paul Enke had to get alongside Semyonov. The flamboyant, hard-drinking Soviet journalist was well known to the Ministry for State Security. A graduate of Moscow University, Semyonov had begun publishing fiction in 1958 and by the time he was posted to Bonn in the early 1970s, he was the author of a bestselling series of spy novels starring Maxim Stirlitz, a cultured Soviet agent who could speak almost every European language 'with the exception of Irish and Albanian'. While readers in the West were thrilled by Ian Fleming's *You Only Live Twice* and *Diamonds are Forever*, bibliophiles in the East bought Semyonov's *Diamonds for the Dictatorship of the Proletariat* and *He Killed Me Near Luang Prabang*. However, unlike James Bond, the Stirlitz novels were meticulously rooted in historical fact and advanced a propagandist agenda, such as the storyline in which the spy exposed an attempt by Britain and the United States to make a peace-pact with Hitler, opening a united front against the Soviet Union (something that the KGB archives reveal that Stalin had actually believed when he forged the non-aggression pact with Germany of 1939). With access to limitless visas and a capacious expense account, Semyonov travelled the world researching his books. By the time he began to write about George Stein he had served as president of the International Association of Crime Writers. Semyonov insisted that it was his success with Stirlitz that bought him his freedom and connections, but few other writers in the Soviet Union at this time were given *carte blanche* like this.[42]

The Stasi Secretariat viewed Semyonov's interest in Stein as a possible threat. Stein was a Stasi source, a useful tool that it did not want to lose to the Russians. The German Amber Room operation was run by the Stasi from the East and not George Stein in the West. The Stasi would have to engineer a collaborative relationship with Semyonov. They would do it 'through the mediation of a female comrade by the name of [name blacked out]'.

We do not know what actually happened between Semyonov and this 'female comrade' (name blacked out), but on 31 October 1979 Enke received a series of telephone calls at his home, 'several very urgent requests' to meet Semyonov at the Soviet Embassy at 10 p.m. Enke wrote an account of what happened next for his deputy minister Generalmajor Neiber: 'At 22:00, on return from his official trip, I met [Semyonov] at the embassy and I then accompanied him to the railway station, from where he continued his journey to Moscow around midnight.' Always the minutiae before the meat. 'Semyonov informed me as follows. He had concluded his activities in Bonn, Vienna, Geneva and The Hague and intended to get on with some of his literary projects during the following period of time.'

Both men talked about the fact the other was preparing a book on the Amber Room and, according to Enke, agreed to co-author a two-volume edition. Enke wrote: 'The first volume would deal with the history of the room as well as the activities of the imperialist secret services and the counter-espionage engaged in the fight against such machinations.' It sounded like a plotline from Stirlitz. Enke, who, according to his personal file, had as a young man been desperate to become a journalist, was flattered by the attentions of his new and famous acquaintance. There was even an invitation dangled by the celebrated Soviet writer. Enke wrote: 'Julian Semyonov announced a forthcoming visit for me to Moscow for the premiere of a play he has written.'[43] It is a shame we cannot see what Semyonov reported to the KGB about Paul Enke.

Believing they had engineered a positive relationship with Julian Semyonov, the Stasi now felt confident enough to reactivate Stein and soon he was used to plant another story. A letter written by Enke on 10 September 1981 reported that Alfred Rohde's written assurances of September 1944 that the Amber Room had survived the Allied air raids 'will [soon] be utilized in the article to appear in October in *Die Zeit*. On this occasion we will remember that 14 October is the fortieth anniversary of the date on which the Amber Room was dragged out from Pushkin on eighteen trucks laden with works of art... We will continue to support [Stein] as much as we can.'[44]

But the following February, in 1982, George Stein was invited to

Moscow without the Stasi's prior knowledge at a time when the Stasi deputy minister's request for a visit to Moscow had been rejected by the KGB. A West German *hobby-Historiker* was welcomed to the Soviet Union at the head of a commission searching for the Amber Room, while the dutiful Stasi's Amber Room operation remained marooned in East Berlin.

There was now even more need for the Stasi to find the Amber Room and return it to Russia.

'All these comrades are our models and teachers for our work,' Erich Mielke once wrote of the leaders of Soviet Russia.[45] He and his ministry would, at least in public, maintain unquestioning loyalty to Moscow Central until the very end.

The KGB made certain. Moscow attached a KGB colonel to every Stasi directorate and all Stasi intelligence was fed back to Moscow and into a super-computer called SOUD (System of Unified Registration of Data on the Enemy) that could place an enemy operative into any one of fifteen categories. Regardless of how it was treated by the KGB, George Stein or no George Stein, the Stasi always gritted its teeth.[46]

In September 1982, four months after Stein's mission to Moscow, Mielke also flew to Russia for talks with his KGB counterpart, Chairman Vitaly Fedorchuk. East German workers already footed the bill for apartments, kindergartens, cars, furnishings and everything else needed by the 2,500-strong KGB team at Berlin-Karlshorst. And on 10 September 1982 Mielke signed a thirty-eight-page protocol pledging absolute loyalty and a further extension of his ministry's financial support. An indication of the enormity of the sums involved comes from a Soviet estimate equivalent to 19,000 dollars to refurbish just one KGB apartment in East Berlin, at a time when the average East German earned the equivalent of 33 dollars a month.[47]

So tight-knit were the connections between the KGB and the Stasi that in November 1989, as the Berlin Wall came down, dozens of KGB teams flew into Berlin to destroy documents stored at Stasi headquarters, preventing the exposure of live operations and the links between Moscow and the Stasi leadership.

However, the KGB sweepers were not entirely thorough. Amid the thousands of pages of Amber Room files at the Ministry of Truth we found an extremely rare letter written by Erich Mielke (famous for his reluctance to commit anything to paper). It concerned the Amber Room and was addressed to Comrade Viktor Mikhailovich Chebrikov, who became chairman of the KGB in December 1982.

The letter revealed how Mielke had used his scheduled September 1982 trip to Moscow to resuscitate 'Operation Puschkin'. Although the Stasi must still have been smarting from seeing George Stein reach Moscow before them, Mielke put the episode behind him and sought out Chebrikov, who was then KGB deputy chairman.

'Dear Comrade Tschebrikow!' Mielke wrote. 'During my visit in the autumn of 1982 I passed to you a progress report on the state of the search [for the Amber Room] in the GDR. As it made clear the search on the territory of the GDR has been and still is justified. I wish to assure you that the GDR and her MfS will not rest or relax in their search for the whereabouts of the Amber Room and other treasures of world culture.'

Viktor Chebrikov, KGB chairman, with Erich Mielke (right), East Germany's Stasi chief, at Stasi headquarters, East Berlin, 1987

The minister wrote that he was certain that documents, witnesses and maps could still be found in East Germany to help unravel the mystery. But he was also at pains to assure the KGB that he did now recognize 'the possibility' that the Amber Room could have remained in the former Königsberg 'or its nearer or further vicinity'.[48] Mielke was distancing himself from the German theory, banked on by the Stasi for so many years, most likely in recognition of the damage caused by the 'Rudi Ringel' episode.

In February 1983 the Stasi received a response to Mielke's Amber Room progress report, but it did not come from the KGB. Oberst Seufert reported that Professor Vladimir Andreievich Bojarsky, of the Soviet Academy of Sciences, had made contact and 'stated that he was running a commission for research into the natural resources of the earth and... that his academy had recently been commissioned to carry out a further search after the Amber Room'. Seufert concluded: 'Bojarsky stated his conviction that it would be helpful to arrange a working consultation to be held in Moscow with Paul Enke.'[49]

That was it. No round of toasts at the Lubyanka, KGB headquarters. No dinner at the Kremlin. There was no way to disguise the poverty of relations. But the Stasi needed to grab any line it could get into the Soviet Amber Room inquiry and ordered Enke to reply.

However, even this lowly offer of a scientific exchange failed to materialize. More than a year later, Seufert wrote that Enke was still waiting for his invitation. All that had been received from Professor Bojarsky (and therefore from the USSR) over the past twelve months was 'noncommittal cards with good wishes on the occasion of certain [public] holidays, without any obligation'.[50]

But still the Stasi would not give up. Preserved in Generalmajor Neiber's files in the Ministry of Truth is a series of letters that reveal that while the deputy minister was 'rejected' by Moscow, Paul Enke (now retired on medical grounds) kept relations between the GDR and the USSR going by establishing a back-channel with Julian Semyonov. Most of their discussions concerned the ongoing work of George Stein.

April [day blacked out] 1984. My dear Julian, There have been no sensational developments about the Amber Room but I am sure you have seen the article published by Stein in the periodical *Die Zeit*. It contained a lot of nonsense. Stein seems to be becoming dangerous, due to his unrealistic trains of thought with the resulting self-deception, to which he seems to fall prey. If he continues as he proceeds at the moment he will certainly become a case for treatment.[51]

A search through *Die Zeit*'s archive shows that in 1984 George Stein had revived his discredited Volpriehausen theory (that the Amber Room had been evacuated to a pit near the West German city of Göttingen). That year Stein also made new approaches for funding to West Germany's conservative coalition of Chancellor Helmut Kohl. It declined but, aware of how previous governments had been portrayed as unrehabilitated nationalists, the coalition issued a holding statement: 'For some time the Federal Government has made efforts to clarify the whereabouts of the lost Amber Room [and] will continue her efforts to find it.'[52]

Enke's letter to Semyonov continued:

After an interruption of several months we are working again on the opening of an old mine for which there are indications that it might have been selected in 1944–5 as a depository for works of art. At the request of my comrades we have now decided to publish the provisional results of our researches. It will turn out to become two publications around which I currently negotiate with publishers. Due to the shortage of paper the print run may be too low. I embrace you and send you the warmest fraternal regards and messages of congratulations on the anniversary of the victory over Hitler's fascism.

The Ministry of Truth files confirmed that in 1984 Seufert's 'Operation Puschkin' team was targeting a new site at Langenstein, a village in the foothills of Brocken Mountain, an area riddled with lead, copper and zinc reserves.[53] It was miles away from the Erzgebirge and Enke's previous hypothesis and the dig site was surely symbolic, located near a high-security Soviet military base and a Stasi electronic eavesdropping station that overlooked the West German border. The Stasi would be seen digging by Russians and West Germans. We are pulled up short by the language Enke uses. 'We are working'. 'Our researches'. In fact Enke was at home with his incomplete manuscript, fighting to save *Bernsteinzimmer Report* from budget cuts. It must have been now that Enke called up Günter Wermusch at *Die Wirtschaft* publishing house.

Another letter from Paul Enke.

15 May 1984. My dear Julian, I have heard that you have returned from South America to your native country. I do hope the large tour has been a success. Your readers and I myself will obviously be especially interested if you manage to trace the tracks of Martin Bormann. Following the forged *Hitler Diaries*, *Der Stern* of Hamburg has warmed up the legend that surmises that Martin Bormann could still be alive. Since Bormann was so obviously involved in the concealment of the Amber Room, the story would certainly create interest. I have just looked again at the correspondence between Martin Bormann and his wife. Extremely meaningful for the study of the psyche of this criminal. An author with whom I have become friendly claims to have located Gerda Bormann in Italy and to have spoken personally with her. He swore by all the saints in the calendar that this woman was really and truly Bormann's wife. You know my attitude to such 'sensations'. Comments are superfluous.[54]

Another month, another letter to Julian Semyonov and another conspiracy for Enke, who clearly yearned for the respect of his brother writer. His own problems, over forgeries and the 'Rudi Ringel' débâcle, seemed to have been forgotten.

Enke continued:

Last month George Stein called at the State Archives Administration in Potsdam. He also tried to make contact with P. Köhler. But Köhler had been at the time on an extended journey to Cuba. I therefore had to represent Köhler and look after Stein... discussions that lasted four days. He informed us extensively about his work and about the clues he has been following, whereby I am afraid, regarding the Amber Room, the tracks followed were more in the realm of wishful thinking than in the region of reality. In spite of all this, it is still regrettable that although in this way a so-called German–Russian dialogue and exchange of experiences on the subject of the Amber Room has materialized it is, however, only in Berlin instead of in Moscow.

In creating his persona of a senior researcher at the Ministry of the

Interior archives, Stasi officer Enke had borrowed the identity of a real employee, a man George Stein thought he had telephoned and even quoted in his articles, without realizing that he was actually dealing with a Stasi agent. Now Stein had arrived to meet Köhler in person and, with the real archivist on leave, Enke was brought out of retirement to maintain the deception. Enke obviously felt comfortable enough in his relationship with Semyonov to bemoan the state of play that had reduced the Stasi and KGB dialogue on the Amber Room to a circuitous correspondence, with Stein acting as witless intermediary.

'Translation from the Russian. Dear Paul' – an undated letter from Julian Semyonov to Paul Enke:

I was happy to receive a letter from you, many thanks. Following my Latin American impressions – I had been from January to April in Argentina, Paraguay, Peru, Costa Rica, Panama, Nicaragua – I have in spite of everything arrived at the full conviction that Bormann had been alive here. Especially since they mentioned to me the day of his death in Asunción. He died seven years ago from [line blacked out]. He was too old (he did not deserve to live that long). The matter of George Stein is more complicated: his wife had died and this had affected him very much and then somebody – this has been my feeling – had begun to work against us, to try and influence him subtly against us, because he knew too much about the Nazis – this is very rare in the West. I am not going to write anything about this in the letter, <u>better when we have a chance to meet face-to-face</u>. I embrace you [name blacked out]. Kindest regards to all the buddies, comrades and friends, until we meet again, Julian Semyonov.[55]

What had led Semyonov to write in such a conspiratorial tone? We search newspaper archives in Hamburg and discover something shocking. Two years before this letter was sent, George Stein had reported to the police that on Good Friday he had been attacked by masked men who had stormed his house in Stelle, drugged him, tortured him and interrogated him about the Amber Room. Stein woke up later covered in blood and found a sheet of paper lying beside him on the floor with a strange motto in Latin scrawled upon it: 'If your disgraced servant is White, then Christ should spray his blood. If he is Red, Christ should extinguish him. If he is Black, Christ should let him die.'[56] Another newspaper report revealed that, in the following summer, Elisabeth Stein was found hanged in the cellar of the family home. Semyonov claimed that Stein 'knew too much' and that 'somebody had begun to work against us', and yet while he suggested that Stein's injuries and his wife's death were somehow connected to the Amber Room search, he didn't want to write down who was responsible, possibly fearing that the letter would be intercepted.

We had taken lightly the *Kaliningradskaya Pravda* claim that Alfred Rohde had been murdered to stop him revealing the location of the Amber Room. In the 1960s it was revealed that his children, Lotti and Wolfgang, had in fact survived the war and were living in West Germany. Yet Semyonov was hinting at another possible murder. Was someone so desperate to keep the location of the Amber Room a secret that they were willing to kill? We read on and see that the last letter to Julian Semyonov was from an entirely different correspondent in the West. We have no idea how it ended up in the Stasi files.

8 December 1984. My dear Julian, I have not heard from you for some time. I do hope your health has improved. Good health is the most important thing in life... Amber Room: I am often corresponding and telephoning Stein. He really has no more money to carry on with his research trips and I am the only one who supports him financially. The sums I have lent him are already considerable. I do hope the two of us achieve positive results soon otherwise it would be a great pity for the pair of us to have made such a big effort. I wish you and your family a Happy New Year. Please tell your cousin Serge, I will bring his stomach pills with me when I visit in the spring (I have just received his order through TASS). Eduard.[57]

The letterhead is embossed with a crest: two horses rearing above a name and address, Baron Eduard von Falz-Fein, Villa Askania Nova, Vaduz, Liechtenstein. We have never heard of him, but for someone who clearly knew Stein intimately we are surprised that he makes no reference in this letter to Elisabeth Stein's recent death or to the attack on Stein himself. We are also surprised to see that George Stein must have been receiving two wage cheques for his Amber Room investigation from opposite ends of the political spectrum, one from the Stasi and another from a baron whose villa was named after a region in the southern Ukraine, making it possible that he was a White Russian exile. Maybe Stein was playing one off against the other and someone had had enough. Maybe this was the reason Stein was tortured and his wife found hanged.

There is one document left in our Ministry of Truth file, a KGB communiqué to the Stasi Secretariat. It abruptly states:

We... wish to let you know that according to a statement received from the authorized department at Section 5 of our Establishment, the search for the Amber Room has been discontinued on the territory of the Soviet Union... This decision was taken according to a resolution by the Council of Ministers of the RSFSR [Russian Soviet Federated Socialist Republic], adopted in October 1983. All the Organizations and Authorities which took part in the measures and searches will no longer occupy themselves with these tasks.[58]

Barely a year after George Stein was brutally assaulted and just months after Elisabeth Stein was found hanged, the Council of Ministers, the highest executive body in the Russian Federation, ordered the end of all searches for the Amber Room, bringing to a close thirty-seven years of secret investigations in a single paragraph. But for some reason they had failed to tell the Stasi for over two years, since this KGB communiqué was dated 15 April 1986.

11

The Hamburg phone book brims with 'Stein's. But there are none with the initial 'G' listed as living in the village of Stelle. Maybe the family fled the tragic house in whose cellars Elisabeth Stein was found hanged and in whose living room George Stein was drugged and tortured by men apparently seeking or protecting the Amber Room.

There is nothing to do but ring them all.

Do you know George Stein, we ask repeatedly. One male voice eventually answers 'Who's this?' At least he hasn't hung up. We are calling in connection with the Amber Room. *Das Bernsteinzimmer*. 'My father can't speak to you,' the man replies.

His father? Have we reached the right number for George Stein? 'Well, I – I suppose so. I – I – I am his son. I better see you. Not at the house, it is impossible. I – I will meet you outside Hamburg station tomorrow night. I sell strawberries in the day. My name? I am Robert, Robert Stein,' the man stammers in broken English, before replacing the handset.

George Stein's son had volunteered no description of himself and the next evening thousands of commuters mill around the Hamburg terminus. But at 8.10 p.m., as a stream of roller-bladers swoosh past, a lopsided man with wild hair and a beard, his black jeans held up by leather braces, wades through their midst, sending them flying, his eyes zeroing in on the copy of *Bernsteinzimmer Report* we hold in our hands.

'*Ja, ja*, Robert Stein. Sorry, I – I missed the train,' he mumbles. We sit at a station café and he looks over his shoulder before talking. '*Das Bernsteinzimmer* broke our family. My mother said to my father, "You're a fruit farmer." Four children and 4,000 bushes. But our father ignored us and now I work on another man's farm. People say I – I am like him, that I am crazy. No, it is not true. I am finished with *das Bernsteinzimmer* story. I – I do not want to be a lost-treasure artist. I sell strawberries. Police came to the house in Stelle and took away thousands of pages from my father's archive. They said he had stolen them. "Good, I said. Take it all away."'

Had the authorities come to the house as a result of Elisabeth Stein's death, we ask? Had the family sold the house in Stelle soon after? 'I will never go back to Stelle. There is too much there to remind me of what happened,' he says distractedly.

What happened, we ask, trying to settle him down? Robert Stein's eyes are fearful: 'People came to the house. I – I don't know names. All the time my father, he goes away. I don't see him.' He is staring mournfully at his empty beer glass. 'The Baron, he finds people who say they know where is *das Bernsteinzimmer*. He asks my father to run all over Germany. My father spends all our money. He sells our bushes, he sells our land, he sells our farm, our home.'

Is he talking about Baron Falz-Fein, the man who wrote to Soviet crime writer Julian Semyonov about George Stein and the Amber Room in December 1984, we ask? 'I cannot talk about the Baron, you must ask him yourself.' So the Baron is still alive. Robert Stein starts rambling again. 'My father was always afraid. I don't know of what, but it started in Königsberg in the Second World War.' He curls strands of hair around his fingers, singeing the ends with a roll-up cigarette. 'He broke my mother's heart. She murdered herself. Too much blood.'

Desperate for precision, we ask directly if Robert Stein's mother killed herself. Was her death connected to the Amber Room? 'Of course my mother's death was connected to *das Bernsteinzimmer*. To my father's search for it,' he says. 'Everything comes back to the *das Bernsteinzimmer*. Three days before my father was in blood, a man came to the house. I rang this man later and he denied having been there. Why? I learned from many people that my father had been in touch with Paul Enke. You may have heard of this man from the Stasi. My father went to see him in the GDR. He was on his way to see him again in 1987.'

What does Robert mean his 'father was in blood'? Is George Stein dead? Does Robert believe that the Stasi killed his father? Robert produces from his jeans pocket a used white envelope that might have once contained a bank statement. 'I have learned to say, "It's enough."' He smooths the envelope on the table.

Without saying another word Robert Stein stands up and walks off, leaving the envelope. We see he has drawn on it rows of crosses with the letters RIP written beneath each one. Across one corner he has scribbled: 'Deceit. Lies. Fear.'

Robert Stein does not want to answer any of our questions or is incapable of doing so. We have no idea why he agreed to meet us. All we can see is that he is haunted by the Amber Room and the catastrophic effect it has had on his family. Faint and distorted, flickering like a light bulb about to pop, Robert Stein is overshadowed by whatever happened to his parents.

There is a Baron Eduard von Falz-Fein listed with international directories at Villa Askania Nova, Liechtenstein. Before calling the number we check the Ministry of Truth files to see if the Stasi was interested in him too.

It was. We find a report from 1987 to Stasi deputy minister Neiber.[1] Baron Eduard von Falz-Fein was obviously a significant player. Here he was described by a Stasi watcher as 'a descendant of Tsar Nicolas II, a cousin of Vladimir Nabokov, and last in line to a *boyar* title from Askania Nova, in the southern Ukraine'. The report stated:

Baron Eduard von Falz-Fein uses his entire influence to return looted Russian works of art to the Soviet Union... It is known that he maintains contacts up to the highest Soviet leadership. For instance, he travelled with Comrade Gorbachev on his trip through the Baltic Soviet Republics in the spring of this year [1987]. [Falz-Fein] spoke on Soviet television and he took part in discussions lasting several hours with the Soviet Minister of Culture about the search for stolen works of art.

So this would explain his connection with the Amber Room. We call.
'My dears, who did you say you were?' asks a reedy voice.
Baron Eduard von Falz-Fein says he is busy packing his travelling

wardrobe. 'I'm sorry, dears, but I have a very important tea appointment with Prime Minister Yushchenko in Kiev on Thursday. Yush-chen-ko. That's it.'

Can we talk about George Stein, we ask? 'Oh.' The line goes quiet. 'George Stein.' A lengthy pause. 'That was a long time ago. If you can make it down here tomorrow, then I'll see if I can squeeze you in. But I have a young lady to escort to Switzerland at 1 p.m., so I won't be back until 1.30 p.m.' He lives in a small world, a principality of sixty-two square miles squeezed between Switzerland and Austria. 'Have your lunch before you come, dears. I'm a simple bachelor of ninety-one years old and I don't entertain. You'll find my little place up Schloss Strasse, the last house before the castle. Look for the name, Askania Nova, my beloved birthplace.'

In Vaduz, Liechtenstein's capital, where the air is filled with a rich scent of warm milk and the gentle thrum of cash machines, we find the Baron's white stucco villa wrapped in wisteria, overlooked by that of his next-door neighbour, Crown Prince Hans-Adam II, ruler of the tax haven.

Baron Eduard von Falz-Fein might be ninety-one years old but in his fawn moccasins and slacks he looks like a youthful playboy. 'You are journalists, I take it? I hope you have brought your tape recorder.'

Closer to, the Baron's full head of hair has a sandy tint and he shaves patchily. The scent of spiced fruitcake wafts around him. 'My pedigree is very important to me, my dears, and I am very proud to be still alive.' Can we come in? 'No.' He bars the entrance and points with an exquisite feminine finger to half a dozen rusting coats of arms bolted around the door. 'First you must understand I am a legend in Russia and the Ukraine. This one on the right is the oldest coat of arms in the whole of Russia, it came down to Mummy directly from Peter the Great. And here, this is the Falz-Fein coat of arms. From Daddy. Died of a broken heart after we fled the Bolsheviks.'

The Baron steers us over the doorstep. 'Now you know a little, you may enter my humble refugee's abode.' He stops again in the hall. The walls are lined with oils, many of which look familiar. 'Here is the last Tsar. Here is his wife,' the Baron gushes over a murky portrait whose original certainly hangs in the Russian Museum in St Petersburg. 'What a beautiful lady she was. What a tragedy. Murdered in that filthy cellar in Ekaterinburg.' The Baron clutches his breast. 'I gave DNA to identify the Romanov bones. I was the only "foreigner" invited to the funeral when they were laid to rest in St Petersburg in 1990. Such an honour.

'Here is my grandfather Nikolai Alexeievich Epanschin, the General of Infantry and Director of the Emperor's Page Corps.' The Baron trails a protective finger across a line of blurred portraits. We notice the clock on the wall is set four hours ahead. To Ukrainian time.

An hour into the tour we reach the Baron's own generation. We are ushered into his living room. In one corner is a vast nineteenth-century *boyar*'s desk and next to it a well-used exercise bike. 'Everyone wants to give me a special order,' says the Baron with mock fatigue, opening a glass cabinet crammed with citations and medals, a glittering mass of hammers, ribbons, sickles, red stars and even a black iron cross. 'They want me to wear them.' He doesn't say who. 'But heaven forbid! I would look like Brezhnev.'

The Baron leads us to a red leather sofa from which we can see sweeping views over the velvety Liechtenstein valley. How did you meet George Stein, we ask? 'My life has taken ninety-one years to live and you cannot understand my motivations for hunting for the Amber Room unless you understand my background. Allow me this short summary.' He checks to see that our tape machine is whirring. '*L'Equip* snapped me up in Paris and sent me to cover the 1936 Olympics. I saw how Hitler was mad when Jesse Owens won the 100 metres! The Führer was only twenty yards from our press box.' After his stint in journalism, the Baron became a cycling champion, a *luge* champion and then a racing driver.

'Eventually my friend Porfirio 'Rubi' Rubirosa said to me, "Eduard, there is a time in every man's life when it is no longer appropriate to be flirting with little girls." No more Casanova. I went to see cousin Vladimir Nabokov in New York, where I proposed to my first wife.' In 1950 the Baron married Virginia Curtis-Bennet, the daughter of Sir Noel, a president of the International Olympic Committee and mandarin at the British treasury. 'I asked the Archbishop of Canterbury's permission for an Orthodox service with a Russian choir. We married in the Savoy Chapel. It was a sensation, dears. All the royalty came.

Baron Eduard
von Falz-Fein
reporting at the
1936 Munich
Olympics

'But later, oh, we fought like cats. She tried to convince me that everything English was best, like your chocolate and cars, but it is not so. I told my darling, "Don't be silly. Only Swiss chocolate is the finest in the world. Your cars are tin cans." Eventually a very fine American author, Paul Gallico, rescued me. He took her off my hands. Afterwards they married and moved to Monte Carlo and started hanging out with Princess Grace. After Gallico died, Prince Rainier took my former darling on as *Dame d'Honour du Château*. When Princess Grace died, my former darling looked after the royal children. *Quelle tragédie*. She is still there and we are the best of friends. Whenever I come down to Monte Carlo I'm very nicely treated. The Prince invites me for lunch.'

So extraordinary is the story of this life that if it were not for the grand piano that prominently displays the photographic evidence, Baron Eduard von Falz-Fein could pass as a slick confidence trickster. But here he is as a young hack in the Berlin Olympics press box with swastikas flying around his head; dining with Princess Grace in Monte Carlo; and then walking across the *piste* in the 1960s with British royals, Prince Philip and Prince Charles; even in a clinch with Joan Crawford.

The Baron's mobile phone trills a fragment from *Swan Lake*. It is the office of Mr Yushchenko, the Ukrainian Prime Minister, and he fields the call in halting Russian before hanging up and finally turning to the subject of the stolen art. 'I began looking for art stolen from Russia in the 1950s. I found a Gobelin tapestry from the tsar's family that had been looted from the Livadia Palace. I outbid the Japanese for it, at a sale in Bonn. *Mon dieu, mon dieu*, what a welcome the Russians gave me when I returned it to the palace.' The Baron's eyes prick with tears: 'Dum, didum, didum. Thousands of people there to see me give back what had been stolen. Little me, a poor refugee living in Liechtenstein!'

And what of George Stein, we ask?

'Yes, yes, I'm coming to him. After I found the Gobelins I got a call from a Soviet writer stationed in Bonn. He was a working for *Literaturnaya Gazeta. Mon dieu*, Julian Semyonov.' The Baron strikes his forehead in horror. He is talking about the Soviet crime writer whose letters and articles about George Stein we have read in the Stasi files.

'The first time Julian Semyonov came here he stayed fifteen days. Sat there, where you are, on the red sofa, drinking half a bottle of vodka for breakfast and then falling asleep until lunch. Julian cost me a fortune, creeping around the house looking for gluggables. I never touched a drop or smoked a single cigarette in my entire life. When Julian woke up, all we talked of was the Amber Room. He said he needed my help to find it. In 1975 he introduced me to George Stein, who had returned the Pskov icons to Moscow. I thought Stein was a little crazy but we had a common interest. He had a theory about a mine in Volpriehausen, near Göttingen. Irreplaceable amber buried in that pit. So exciting. George Stein said: "I know where the Amber Room is. Give me some money and I'll go and find it for you."' So after the West German government had turned him down, George Stein had sought out a private source of finance to pursue the story planted by the Stasi.

Was it worth it, we ask?

The Baron walks over to an enormous antique carved oak chest, a family heirloom from the Ukraine that is filled with a jumble of paperwork.

'Our archive,' he declares. 'Myself, Julian and George, we decided to form a little committee. To look for the Amber Room. George had all these wartime documents that suggested that the Amber Room might have been concealed in Volpriehausen in West Germany and we were so excited, because until then all the searches had been beyond our reach – in Russia and the GDR. Now we could search for buried treasure in the West too and, my dears, we worked *so* hard.'

The Baron hands us a photograph of Semyonov, a bull-necked man with a bushy black beard. 'I like to think I played a small part in his career.'

Was Semyonov KGB, we ask?

'My dears, I wouldn't be so rude as to ask and he never volunteered. Let's just say he went on a lot of foreign holidays.

Julian Semyonov

'Amber Room fever hit the West in the 1970s and journalists, detectives and writers flocked to join our little committee: Georges Simenon, the *Belge* who lived in Paris making a fortune from his character Inspector Maigret. Simenon was a friend of Julian Semyonov's too. We also had darling "Red Countess" Marion Dönhoff, the Grand Dame of the East Prussian resistance. Somehow George Stein had convinced her that their fathers had been great friends in Königsberg.

'So, through Marion we had the influential *Die Zeit* on our side. There were others circling on the periphery. A little Englishman from

Marion Dönhoff

the intelligence services, MI6, perhaps he was called Eldridge. Or was it Aldridge? Oh, I don't know.' The Baron's eyes are gleaming like a child's on Christmas morning. 'It was all done with our own money, a lot of money, crazy money. For a time the Amber Room held such a fascination for all of us. It was like a drug. And I poured money in.'

The Baron pulls newspaper cuttings out of the old chest. By the early 1980s 'the Amber Room committee' was hogging increasing amounts of newsprint, its activities gobbled up by the West German, British and American press, willing it on to find the Russian treasure ahead of the Communists. *Komsomolskaya Pravda*, 1983: 'Face to Face – an Interview with George Stein'. *The Sunday Times*, 20 October 1985: 'The Theft of the Amber Room'. Digs in Carinthia. Hunting in the Odenwald, east of Mannheim. Secrets buried in classified US Army files in Washington. Julian Semyonov and Baron Falz-Fein debating the Amber Room mystery over cups of champagne at Maxim's in Paris. The Baron staying over at cousin Vladimir Nabokov's, researching the last months of the war. And the Baron's committee infecting others with the Amber Room bug, spawning feverish speculation about where the treasure lay buried. Magazines. Books. TV documentaries.

Did the Baron know that much of Stein's intelligence was coming from the Stasi, possibly Moscow? We show him some of the papers we have found in the Ministry of Truth.

He shrugs. 'Paul Enke. He told us he was from the Ministry of the Interior. I didn't know for sure that he was Stasi. But we had our suspicions since Enke could never come out of East Berlin. We always had to go there, as tourists through Checkpoint Charlie.'

But what of the Volpriehausen episode, where George Stein relied on a fake telex from 'Rudi Ringel's' father to prove that the Amber Room was buried in the pit? We show the Baron the report of 'Rudi Ringel's' interrogation by Uwe Geissler in 1979 that revealed how 'Ringel's' father was in reality an invalided post office guard. The Baron pushes it away. 'I'm an old man now. Talk to the ones continuing our search.' His eyes well up as he embarks on what sounds like a well-rehearsed story. 'I had to get involved. When I was a little boy, only five, my grandfather the General took me to see the Amber Room and said, "When you are a bigger boy you will remember that I showed you one of the wonders of the world." I never forgot. And when I came to a time in my life where I could help return it, I saw it as my duty. To give back the Amber Room.' He stands up. 'Now I must go to a meeting.'

We show the Baron the Stasi report that accused Stein of doctoring documents to fit his theories.

'No one paid more heavily for following the Amber Room than dear old George Stein,' he retorts.

Is the Baron referring to the death threats, the assault and Elisabeth Stein's death, we ask?

He sits back down. 'So, you know. George's problems began when his wife died in terrible circumstances in 1983 and then, the following year, his mentor in the East, Berlin art historian Gerhard Strauss, dropped dead too. Without Gerhard Strauss, Stein had to deal with Enke directly and those two never got on, dears. So protective of their respective versions of the story, they fought like tom cats. Everyone had a version in those days. Anyway, I must take your leave,' he says, standing up again.

Why did the Soviets close down the Amber Room inquiry and fail to tell anyone else, we ask? We are trying to keep the conversation alive.

The Baron's mood darkens. 'It all collapsed in the summer of 1987. Stein phoned me and said, "I don't know where to go. Can I come over to see you, as I have sold everything." He stayed one, two, three weeks, I can't remember, writing, writing, writing. Then one day I said, "Tomorrow I must go away." It was the start of the Tour de France. I had been invited, personally. Stein said he had a friend in Munich. I drove him to the station. Gave him money. I felt terrible packing him off. Miserable. I told him, "Please be careful." Imagine if it had happened here in Vaduz. What a horror.'

What happened, we ask?

The Baron forces a bundle of documents into our hands and urges us out into the hall. 'Here, this is everything you need to know. So nice to meet you,' he beams and opens the door. As it shuts behind us we notice on the papers the insignia of the Bavarian police force, Criminal Investigations, Ingolstadt. Case: George Stein: 20 August 1987.[2]

'Villa Askania Nova, Schloss Strasse, Vaduz.' A letter from the Baron to Julian Semyonov. The first document in the bundle he has given us:

8 April 1985, Dear Julian, yesterday I spoke to your daughter and found out that you are in the Argentine. Please call me in ten days on your return. The visit I desired is now coming about and I shall arrive [in Russia] on 27 May, 17.05, with the *Swissair* from Zürich. I took a *visum* for three weeks and therefore I will have time to fly with you also to Yalta. Please organize my stay as well as the planned detour to Leningrad for the rededication of the tombs of the Admiral Epanschin. I greet you in order to renew our old friendship and I am very pleased to see you again. Eduard.

The Baron and Julian Semyonov, once close friends, were planning his Grand Tour of the Soviet Union.

'Ashhausener Strasse, Stelle, Hamburg.' A letter from George Stein to Julian Semyonov:

10 November 1985, My dear Julian! I have been very surprised that you have

surfaced so suddenly but anyhow have a good time in Geneva. I am enclosing an article from *The Sunday Times* on the subject the 'Theft of the Amber Room'. The contract for the filming of "The Amber Room" I also enclose. It has been decided by the Bavarian Broadcasting Corporation that shooting should begin in early 1987. The plan is to produce an evening-long documentary and later a feature film. The basis of the film will be my archive with *circa* 2,300 documents. On the basis of my negotiations with the central archive of the GDR in Potsdam, we pursue clues that lead to the FRG... We must talk about these matters several times... the first chance for such a contact would be Friday a.m. at 7.45, with kindest regards, your friend George!!!

Having learned from the Baron that Semyonov was back in touch, Stein immediately began bombarding the Soviet crime writer who had made him famous in 1973 with wild Amber Room theories, fed by documents from the Stasi.

'Ashhausener Strasse, Stelle, Hamburg.' Another letter from George Stein, the same day:

10 November 1985, Dear Baron von Falz-Fein, please show Julian... a copy of the article written by Anthony Terry [*The Sunday Times*]... Please send back the original contract from the Aktive Film Company... I am not sure if Julian wishes to help. He was trying to make some films about the subject [of the Amber Room] himself. Could you sound him out?... We must discuss these questions in detail before you meet Julian... He is a nice enough chap but he is just not reliable. It would be favourable for an increase in my finances as well. With the kindest regards, as ever, sincerely yours, George Stein.

Always the showman, Stein's greatest fear was losing control of the Amber Room story and particularly to the already famous Soviet crime writer Semyonov. But in the end it was not Semyonov that he would fear.

There is a significant gap in the bundle of correspondence, presumably the period in which Stein's Amber Room documentary was being filmed, before this flurry of press releases in 1987:

Deutsche Press Association, ARD [Channel One television] and NDR [Norddeutscher Rundfunk]. 16 April 1987. Headline: Amber Room taken to the USA on 15 May 1945. George Stein reveals that the room was transported via Grasleben [mine in Helmstedt, eighty miles north-east of Volpriehausen] – to Wiesbaden [US central collection point] – and then Antwerp [sea port] – finally arriving in the USA [secret depository].

Bayern 3 TV: 16 April 1987. A 90-minute documentary screened tonight will show how the hunt for the Amber Room led by *hobby-Historiker* George Stein has revealed that it was taken to the United States.

Die Zeit, Hamburg: 18 April 1987. Mystery of Amber Room Now Solved?

Stein had been passed documents by the Stasi that showed how the Amber Room had been taken by US forces and smuggled to America, a revelation that, although surely a fake, created a press frenzy.

'Hamburg-Eppendorf Psychiatric Hospital.' A letter from George Stein, 13 May 1987. Less than one month after the German media aired Stein's controversial American theory, he was in a psychiatric hospital.

My dear Baron! I am lying here for the last three and a half weeks exactly. Why, you shall find out today. On 15 April [the day before Stein's TV documentary was broadcast], I received an ultimate demand from the Inland Revenue for the amount 400,000 DM. My children have been induced to clear the house in Stelle. It is now standing empty and will be auctioned in the near future by the state. The Amber Room affair is at an end and that probably was the main aim of the 'State Action'. We were nearly at the final stage. Revenge for the little matter of the monastery treasure [Pskov] is also playing a role in this affair. I myself own nothing except the clothes I am wearing.

'The Amber Room files are locked up in the empty house. Friends are trying to rescue these and take them to safety... I have no money at all. Somebody has given me the stamps for this letter. In spite of all this I retain courage and hope. Please inform all our friends, you know who I mean. Please do not forget me. I often think about all of you... My children despise me and they don't visit any more... With kind regards, George Stein.

P.S. How do I get out of here? Can our friends help?'

Stein was in a manic state, on the verge of bankruptcy, and we wonder if he was seeing clearly, fearing that the West German government was trying to silence him about the Amber Room before he made his controversial revelation. But we are beginning to understand what contributed to Robert Stein's state of mind. We read on, as fast as we can.

'Files of the Criminal Investigation Department, Ingolstadt.' Extract from a report by Professor Götze, senior physician, Hamburg-Eppendorf Psychiatric Hospital, May 1987:

The patient always reacted in an identical manner, when challenged directly about mysterious or occult facts; emphasizing the importance of his own person, hinting at his function as a confidant of secrets, as a researcher of complicated areas and a connoisseur of international political entanglements – and of the dangers arising for him out of such matters.

Professor Götze was suspicious of his conspiracy theories.

'Villa Askania Nova, Schloss Strasse, Vaduz.' A letter from the Baron:

1 June 1987, Dear Mr Stein! Enclosed please find a letter from Mr Popov, Deputy Director of the Soviet Television Corporation and a telegram from Julian Semyonov. You can see that you have not been forgotten. I have naturally replied that it is impossible that you and [Robert Stein] accept the invitation to the Soviet Union for 3 June, especially as no financial proposals for the flight have been mentioned. I am enclosing a 100-DM note for your expenses. With all my heart I wish you an early convalescence. Eduard von Falz-Fein.

George Stein and his son had obviously been planning to take the controversial American theory to Moscow, where it would be broadcast to maximum effect. The Baron seemed to be keeping his distance.

'Files of the Criminal Investigation Department, Ingolstadt.' Extract from Professor Götze's case notes, 16 June 1987:

Mr George Stein has been treated in our ward between 23 April and 16 June 1987 after being treated in the Chirurgical Dept. 5 for an abdominal cut... during the operation we carried out a partial resection of the colon, which was followed by intensive medical care. We succeeded in stabilizing the patient's post-operative condition in such a way that after a few days we were able to recommend his transfer to a ward... Mr Stein left our ward on 15 June, with the intention of travelling to Switzerland.

When Stein was hospitalized, one week after his Amber Room documentary was broadcast, he had suffered a serious abdominal injury. But there was no explanation of the circumstances in which Stein was stabbed and we cannot understand why Stein made no mention of it in the letter to the Baron. Maybe the men who drugged and tortured him in 1982 had returned to finish the job. Stein's fears might have been genuine after all.

'Files of the Criminal Investigation Department, Ingolstadt.' Extract from a report by Dr Benno Splieth, Clinical Assistant, District Hospital, Starnberg, Bavaria. Another medical report, this one originating from southern Germany, was written twelve days after Stein was discharged from a hospital in northern Germany.

29 June 1987... We report about the patient who was found yesterday in Starnberg woods with abdominal trauma and brought to our clinic by the emergency doctor. The exploratory laparotomy revealed a 5–10 cm long diagonal gaping wound in the middle of the upper abdomen with an opening into the peritoneum, which was contaminated with grass... two damaged veins in the vicinity of the transverse colonic-mesenterium were noted, from which the patient had lost an estimated two litres of blood.

Only two months after the unexplained stabbing incident in Hamburg, George Stein was seriously injured again. Stein appeared to have been pursued across Germany. We calculate that this second incident must have happened shortly after Stein visited the Baron in Vaduz. The Baron had told us that he had put Stein on a train to Munich when he turned him out of villa, Askania Nova, at the end of June 1987. But why had the Baron not mentioned to us that Stein had been stabbed, once before arriving in Liechtenstein and again, shortly after he left?

'Krieskrankenhaus Starnberg am See, Bavaria.' A letter from George Stein. '7 July 1987, Dear Baron, I have now been here one week. Berlin had to be cancelled. Dr Enke could not get a visa for me. I will be here for another six days. Where am I going to then?... Couldn't cash the cheque. Regards, G. Stein.' We cannot understand why none of Stein's correspondence mentions the fact that he was stabbed twice and nearly died. Instead, he was preoccupied with his failure to get a visa from Paul Enke, whose real identity he had learned at last.

'Krieskrankenhaus Starnberg am See, Bavaria.' Another letter from George Stein, whose hospital stay was much longer than he had predicted:

13 August 1987, Dear and honoured Baron! After six weeks here at the clinic I will move at the weekend; my surgeon has a weekend house, so for a start I can shelter there temporarily. I cannot go home because my children have sold everything... I am left without a penny to my name. The next three weeks are going to be difficult for me... I must manage to get through with only 120 DM... I suppose one can also live from dry rolls... What is going to happen later, I still don't know. But the Amber Room research goes on!!! And this is the only thing that matters!! Please send me something I can smoke. When are you going to Russia? With the kindest regards, George Stein. Forwarding Address: George Stein c/o 8079 Altdorf, Post: Titting, Bavaria. No Telephone Connection.

Although weak, Stein was still obsessed with the Amber Room. Once again he put pressure on the Baron.

'Files of the Criminal Investigation Department, Ingolstadt.' Extract from an outpatient referral from Starnberg to Hamburg. As far as hospitals staff were concerned, Stein was heading back home.

15 August 1987. Dear [Dr Arlt, Ward Registrar, Hamburg-Eppendorf Psychiatric Hospital], enclosed please find some additional information about George Stein, who will attend your clinic on 25 August 1987... Stein is an intelligent, subtly sophisticated personality in full possession of his mental faculties... Stein's strategic guideline for his life [is to] look for much honour even at the price of large numbers of unwanted enemies... Many kind regards, Dr Benno Splieth, Clinical Assistant.

George Stein's Bavarian doctor was upbeat about his patient's recovery prospects but concerned about the forces pitted against him. We still do not know if his enemies really existed or if they were in his head.

'8079 Altdorf, Post: Titting, Bavaria.' A postcard from George Stein who was recuperating from his recent traumas in the countryside.

18 August 1987, Dear Dr Splieth! I am well, I am walking a lot, write and make

new plans! Your parents have been here yesterday, we hung up the laundry, which had become quite stiff in the sun. I intend to walk now to Eichstädt to post the mail. In the enclosure you can see how the publication of one of my books is being planned. Kind regards, yours George Stein.

The enclosure is missing, so we can only presume that the book was about the Amber Room and Stein's American theory. It is remarkable that Stein had lost none of his bravura and even intended to set out on a round trek to the post office that we calculate would be forty miles.

According to a report in *Bild*, a farmer claimed to have seen George Stein emerging from a hotel, Pension Schneider, in the small Bavarian hamlet of Altdorf in the early hours of 20 August 1987, shortly after sending his postcard to Dr Splieth. The owner of Pension Schneider told the police that Stein had arrived days before in a highly agitated state and during his stay ate very little, spending most days out walking.

We drive across the belly of Germany, following the line of the Austrian Alps, then turn north, through Bavaria. We skirt Munich and head along the A9 autobahn, past the medieval city of Ingolstadt (the setting for Mary Shelley's *Frankenstein*), where George Stein's criminal file originated. A side road plunges between hop poles and low-slung whitewashed farm buildings. Twelve miles down the road lies Altdorf, a hamlet of less than half a dozen houses, fringed by Titting Wald.

We read in *Bild* how, on the afternoon of 20 August 1987, Aloise Dirch, a resident of Altdorf, found a body lying in the ruins of the fourteenth-century castle that stands on a hill above the village. Kriminalhauptkommissar Wermuth from Ingolstadt wrote in his report that the victim has been stabbed in the abdomen several times.[3] The pathologist from Ingolstadt hospital, who examined the body, wrote that most of the wounds were made 'using a dissecting scalpel'. He also found disturbing evidence of other recent 'sacrificial cuts to the [victim's] abdominal wall'.

Two police photographs exist of the body as it was discovered, lying beneath fallen beech leaves, a relatively tidy scene for such a violent death. In the first picture there are few signs of struggle, only smears of dried blood on the victim's fingers and caked beneath his nails. The face, with its slightly perplexed expression, as if he had consumed too much red wine and fallen off his chair, is instantly recognizable. The thick-rimmed glasses slightly askew, shirt buttons undone. And in the second crime shot, an unseen hand has brushed aside the leaves and raised the victim's shirt to reveal a series of deep gashes across the upper abdomen. Beside the body lie two pairs of scissors and a scalpel. Next to them is a half-empty packet of Malboros and a glass flask, its contents either drunk or spilt, as if a stake-out or perhaps a night-time rendezvous had been envisaged.

Police photograph of the body of George Stein,
20 August 1987

When we arrive in Altdorf it is drizzling. We cannot find Pension Schneider or anyone who knows Dr Benno Splieth's parents, who sup-posedly had a weekend house here. In fact, although we try many doors, everybody is determined to be out. We spot a small sign, pointing to a footpath up the hill in the direction of 'Ruine Brunneck, 1.5km', and see a castle on top of the hill. We follow the track beside a barn filled with lowing cows and pass a young woman gardening who runs off as we near. We press on into a copse of beeches. Dry leaves crunch beneath our feet. The canopy is thick. The wood gloomy. And then we hear a slow, deep drumming. Quietly at first and then more percussive, it nears. Finally, there are gusts of breath and snapping branches. We jump back as a deer skitters across the path.

Climbing a muddy bank up through the trees, we spot a castle turret and a gateway. Inside the ruin is an amphitheatre of old trees. A recent fire pit. Some charred branches. Old graffiti scored in Gothic script on to the trunks: 'SCH 1', '1964/66', 'LOEH 76/77'. The letters 'B', 'Z', and 'CH'. The word 'Goppingen'. All of it is familiar, but not quite right. In the distance we hear a chainsaw scream.

We imagine George Stein here at dawn, having climbed up from Pension Schneider in the dark, looking out across the vale of Altdorf, watching the green tractor below churning the rust-red soil. And by the time the sun had risen high in the sky, he had bled to death.

The discovery of George Stein's disembowelled corpse was front-page news across Germany and the Soviet Union. Many of the reports lingered over the ritualistic nature of his death and his proclivity for embarrassing the West German government with revelations about wartime loot. Reporters converged on the torpid hamlet of Altdorf and besieged the bankrupt fruit farm in Stelle. Rumours spread that the West German *hobby-Historiker* had been murdered to stop him revealing the hiding place of the Amber Room. *Izvestiya* reported:

Historian George Stein for twenty years searched for the Amber Room and other works of art. He achieved much and was able to help several former owners retrieve their property – including the Soviet Union... Unknown assassins have already tried to murder Stein on several occasions... The circumstances and motives of his death have not yet been satisfactorily cleared up.[4]

The official Stasi reports concerning Stein's death were also conspiratorial. One to Deputy Minister Neiber, stated:

The starting point for many of our contacts concerning the Amber Room was George Stein, who has died under mysterious circumstances... During the period of collaboration Stein passed us more than 150 files and diligently followed any clues received... George Stein cooperated regularly and was an important person for our investigations in West Germany.

But there was no time for mourning: 'Now that [Stein's] dead it is advisable to try to create active connections with... Baron Falz-Fein.'[5]

Regardless of whether Stein's death was murder or suicide, it played into the hands of someone with whom he had continually competed with for suzerainty over the Amber Room investigation. The previous summer, on 30 June 1986, a meagre paperback volume with a cheap, pliable cover had appeared in East German bookshops promising to unravel the thrilling mystery of the 'missing Eighth Wonder of the World', proving that, 'contrary to other claims and suspicions, the Amber Room was not destroyed'. *Bernsteinzimmer Report*, Paul Enke's *magnum opus*, had been published, at last, by Die Wirtshaft and edited by Günter Wermusch. Those who asked for biographical information were advised that Enke was a functionary in the GDR Ministry of the Interior. Unsurprisingly, there was no mention of the Stasi.

With George Stein dead (and a strong suspicion he had been murdered for spreading Amber Room secrets), *Bernsteinzimmer Report* became a bestseller. Vlad Lapsky, Berlin correspondent for *Izvestiya*, wrote: 'A short time ago the book's second edition appeared in a relatively high run only six months after 20,000 copies of the first edition had been sold. It practically never reached the tables of the bookshops.'[6]

Public imagination, pricked in 1958 by *Kaliningradskaya Pravda* and in 1959 by *Freie Welt*, now fed off the chilling drama surrounding Stein's death and the authoritative details contained in *Bernsteinzimmer Report*: interviews with real eyewitnesses, original Nazi documents saved from the fire, explosive allegations linking the West German, British and American governments to a vast conspiracy to steal the world's most valuable treasure.

The climax of *Bernsteinzimmer Report* was set in the spring of 1945: a Red Cross van driven by Albert Popp and probably SS Sturmbannführer 'Ringel', loaded down with the art collection of the Gauleiter of East Prussia, Erich Koch, and the Amber Room. Skirting Allied bombers, Popp and 'Ringel' raced through Nazi Weimar to a disused mine in the western Erzgebirge in Saxony. Page 227 concluded: '[Gauleiter of Saxony] Mutschmann, Albert Popp and SS Sturmbannführer 'Ringel' have taken the secret with them to the grave of where some of the most valuable goods of world culture were hidden for the filthy fascist plans of the future.'

For once the Stasi was delighted with the out-of-favour Enke and, in assessing the impact of *Bernsteinzimmer Report*, Oberst Seufert revealed that its sole aim was 'to reawaken awareness of the FRG's public' in the hope they would write in, leading 'to new hints'. Seufert reassured the Secretariat that Enke's book 'is not a diary of the search' and there were no secrets in it 'as the documents and facts used are... practically accessible to everyone'.[7]

One of the key facts, the Erich Koch connection with the Amber Room, would be revealed as a bogus story just months after the book came out. In an interview conducted with the elderly ex-Gauleiter in his Polish prison shortly before his death on 15 November 1986 (thirty-seven years after he was diagnosed as suffering from a terminal illness), Koch told journalist Mieczyslaw Pozhinsky that he had never known what had happened to the Amber Room. 'Do you think that in the spring of 1945, with the Red Army attacking in all directions, I had time to worry about those boxes?' he asked.[8]

However, the readers of *Bernsteinzimmer Report* were not listening. Thousands wrote in to GDR publishers Die Wirtschaft with new angles on old scenarios. 'After careful perusal of your book about the disappeared Amber Room, I suddenly recalled everything,' wrote Herbert from Zeulenroda, a town twenty miles north-east of the Erzgebirge.[9] In 1953 Herbert had trained as a fireman at a castle near Weimar, where he had discovered 'in the half-open drawer of a cupboard and also on the floor in a shallow dish were lying small honey-yellow stones of amber'.

Other correspondents were more imaginative. Gerhard from Uder, a village twelve miles south-east of Göttingen in West Germany, wrote: 'My life has been tragically involved with these events. I have lived to see some quite incredible things.' Most incredible was Gerhard's claim that, on 22 January 1945, he had seen a Special Gauleiter Train packed with the Amber Room panels, commanded by SS Sturmbannführer 'Ringel'. Gerhard claimed even to have heard 'Ringel' talking on the telephone to Erich Koch and then Hermann Göring.[10] Since the Stasi inquiry was still underway, Enke was called on to weed out the fantasists.

Then, on 7 December 1987, Paul Enke was found dead, at the age of sixty-three. Another death connected with the Amber Room. But this one barely raised a murmur in the press, as Paul Enke had hardly existed. Very few people were invited to attend his funeral at an East Berlin cemetery, his casket lowered into the grave in the rain, watched by a gaggle of sodden and disparate associates including his *Lektor*, Günter Wermusch. And afterwards Oberst Seufert licked and stuck shut the composite file on a life. Enke, Paul, file number KSII404/82, was deactivated, filed away with the cold cases on one of the seven reinforced floors of the Stasi's central archive.

However, the hunt for the Amber Room would carry on. Despite the orders from Moscow of 1986 to desist from searching, the death of the agent closest to the inquiry and his main source in the West, the Stasi would not give up on 'Operation Puschkin'. We are amazed to see a report fired off to Deputy Minister Neiber: 'What can be done now that Enke is dead? How can we utilize Enke's contacts and extend them for further measures in searching for the Amber Room?' The Stasi was obsessed with finding the Russian treasure, even though they had discovered nothing new and had had all their old Erzgebirge theories seriously undermined. There was no good operational reason for the Stasi to persist (alone without their Soviet comrades), so the impetus must have come from on high, possibly a 'minister's must'. Maybe Erich Mielke was unable to let go of his fantasy of winning plaudits in Moscow by presenting them with the ultimate prize, the Amber Room.

We read in the Ministry of Truth files that within days of the funeral the Stasi approached Günter Wermusch: 'After the unexpected death of Comrade Enke it became essential to find a person suitable to continue his work who would at the same time be acceptable to the public. Comrade Wermusch, who identifies himself totally with this task, has been persuaded by Seufert to accept the job.'[11] So Wermusch was more than just an editor and had gone on to run part of the Amber Room inquiry.

His first job was to process and reply to all *Bernsteinzimmer Report* correspondents, aided by 'Bernd', a.k.a. Uwe Geissler, the Stasi informer we had met in 'Goat's Throat Village'. So this was how they knew each other. We recall that Wermusch had told us that he had travelled the

GDR with Geissler after Enke's death, but he had not said it was on Stasi business (although nothing in the files indicate that Wermusch was a paid employee of the ministry).

Seven months after Enke's death, someone else we know well contacted Wermusch. We found this letter in the Ministry of Truth files. 'Villa Askania Nova, Schloss Strasse, Vaduz.' Baron von Falz-Fein.

18 July 1988, Dear Mr Wermusch! My German secretary is on holiday and I am thinking in French and Russian. I do hope that my [German] lines are comprehensible to you. George Stein: I do not know whether you are aware of my close cooperation with Stein. We were introduced ten years ago by Julian Semyonov in Bonn. As a five-year-old I saw the Amber Room and I was enthusiastic about its splendour. As a Russian I set myself an aim to help both of them wherever I could. I am sure you are aware that I spent a lot of money on Stein's trips and researches.

The same old story the Baron told us. Everyone connected to the Amber Room was regrouping and the Baron continued:

Archive Stein: I used to help Stein's children bridge the economic emergency they found themselves in and that is why I received [Stein's archive] after his death. It is now in the Sovetskaya Kulturnaya Obschestvo [Soviet Culture Fund]. The last information I have received was that the people engaged in translation have found many positive and interesting matters relevant to their researches. Paul Enke: a huge loss for us researchers. Julian Semyonov has given up on our work and taken off to Yalta.

In the absence of Enke, Semyonov or Stein, the Baron had a proposal:

International Commission. Such weekend hobby enthusiasts as we are, without experts like Stein and Enke, we cannot be totally successful. Official help is required otherwise the case is finished. My dear Mr Wermusch, as a Russian I thank you for the great help you have accorded to Mr Enke and that you as a German wish to restitute that which your countrymen destroyed and that brought shame on your culture. Your hobby collaborator, Eduard.[12]

The Stasi barely had time to consider the Baron's proposal, as two weeks later its attention was drawn elsewhere. News arrived that the

Soviets had begun digging for the Amber Room again, in Kaliningrad, even though they had told the Stasi two years before that they had given up the search. 'The Scent Leads to Ponarth,' declared *Izvestiya*.[13] Vlad Lapsky, its Berlin correspondent, wrote: 'Another version of a hiding place of the Amber Room emerges. There will be confirmation of this new scenario soon.' Then a report from TASS, dated 2 August 1988, read: 'Amber Room found in Kaliningrad?' And twelve days later Aktüllen Kamera (the GDR state TV news programme) reported: '19.30 hours. 14 August 1988. Kaliningrad. Population 400,000. City on the Soviet Baltic coast. An unusual search started this weekend here at the [Ponarth] brewery, which took us back to the last months of the war. A group of experts, students and workers, led by operation director Colonel Avenir Ovsianov, are hoping to find the world-famous Amber Room.'[14]

By the second week of August 1988 there was so much publicity surrounding this new Soviet dig that Erich Mielke, the Minster for State Security, felt compelled to write to Viktor Chebrikov, the chairman of the KGB:

Dear Comrade Tschebrikow! The TASS report about the location of the Amber Room has finally brought about my writing of this letter. The alleged facts of the case emanated from a female citizen of the GDR. You are aware that the GDR and especially the [Stasi] have been pursuing the traces of the Amber Room since 1945 in order to return this work of art to its legal owner, the Soviet Union.

These activities reveal our continued interest in the fate of this work of art. I would therefore be grateful to you if you could let me know the results of your search in Kaliningrad. In the event that you have achieved success, we would call off our searches.[15]

Translation: the trials and tribulations of the Amber Room were as much a part of the GDR as they were of the USSR. But the most feared man in the GDR, someone who had risen to power by forging the closest possible ties with Moscow, suspected that he was so far out of the Soviet loop that even if the Amber Room was found, he might learn of it only from the newspapers.

While he was on the subject, there were other matters of concern. Mielke continued:

I also believe it could serve our joint purpose if we could have sight of the archive accumulated by the FRG citizen and *hobby-Historiker* George Stein, which has been passed to the Soviet Culture Fund. The same also applies to certain fascist files that are held in Soviet archives. It could prove useful if an exchange of information between the experts in the search after missing works of art could be set up.

I wish to ensure you the GDR and her MfS will not rest or relax in their search for the whereabouts of the Amber Room and other treasures of world culture.

Erich Mielke promised to give the Soviets his all, even though he surely now realized there was only one possibility, that all the German versions of the Amber Room story were spent and the answers if there were any, lay with the Soviets, who were not going to share their findings with anyone.

There are no more files in the Ministry of Truth for us to decrypt and it is as we feared. Mielke must have felt trapped by the Amber Room saga, or at the very least misled by Moscow. Perhaps the Soviets were using their German comrades to distract attention from the one direction in which answers lay.

We too feel that the German version was a snare, serving to bog us down and distract us from the real work in Russia.

12

The cherry-lipped Pulkova Airlines stewardess has had years of experience shuttling passengers from St Petersburg to Kaliningrad, and before the Tupolev takes off she emerges from the galley with a tray laden with vodka and beer.

'A can for you, sir.' 'A shot for you.' Eight fishermen on their way back to a fleet of rusting hulks that plunder the cod banks of the Baltic rise like a swell in the rows behind us. The sour stench of Baltika beer fills the cabin.

Through the fatigued plastic portholes we watch a snowstorm whip us along the runway. It is early March 2003, ten months after our last trip to Russia, and we are heading towards the source of the mystery of the Amber Room: the former East Prussian city of Königsberg, which fell to the Red Army on 9 April 1945.

Professor Alexander Brusov went there in May 1945, only to conclude that the Amber Room had been destroyed. Anatoly Kuchumov and his friend Stanislav Tronchinsky followed in March 1946 and argued that Brusov was mistaken. Kuchumov returned in December 1949 to interrogate Dr Gerhard Strauss, who claimed to know where the Amber Room was but then forgot. A decade later it was the local newspaper, *Kaliningradskaya Pravda*, which broke the story that the Amber Room had been concealed in a secret bunker and was being hunted for, setting Europe abuzz with excitement about lost treasure. Within weeks GDR citizen 'Rudi Ringel' had emerged and was brought to Kaliningrad to be interrogated by Anatoly Kuchumov as the Soviets struggled to locate SS Sturmbannführer 'Ringel's' hiding place, codenamed BSCH.

After 1959 an untold number of secret Soviet investigations dug for the Amber Room in the province, but their findings were never published. If it is true what they say about Kaliningrad, that tens of thousands of Soviet citizens were brought here by force after the war and none of them ever left, then some of those involved in these investigations should still be around.

Once airborne, the fishermen all light up cigarettes and pound the backs of our seats as they regale one another with holiday tales of losing their hearts to girls on the Gulf of Finland. 'No-smoking flight,' the stewardess barks across the PA. Half a dozen figures stagger off to the toilet cubicle.

By the time we descend into Kaliningrad International Airport, the beer and vodka have gone and the fishermen are agitated. As the Tupolev makes its final approach, one of them picks up his kitbag and staggers down the aisle. When the plane touches down and the engines flick into reverse thrust, he collides with the galley. A loud cheer resounds as the stewardess steps over his prone body to open the cabin door.

A wrought-iron hammer and sickle spins like a weather vane on top of a hangar containing a single metal desk. Although opened up to the world in 1991, hardly anybody visits Kaliningrad. The immigration officer lazily stamps our paperwork and we emerge into the forecourt to face a wall of leather-coated taxi drivers.

We pick the man whose car seats are covered with fake Siberian tiger fur. 'It was a shock when I first arrived too,' Valery, the taxi driver, says, grinning at us in the rear-view mirror. 'Got sent here from Minsk in the 1960s. It was like a lottery. And I lost. I had to leave everything behind for our new frontier.'

News footage from after the war showed garlanded Soviet farmers and their families jiggling into the new Kaliningrad on party-issue tractors. And then the province sealed itself off from the outside world: the ancient amber pits of Palmnicken becoming the Yantarny Mining Combine No. 9, while the Teutonic town of Pillau was levelled to become Baltiysk, new home to the Baltic Fleet. Hundreds of thousands of troops converged on Kaliningrad to transform it into one of the Soviet Union's most secure military bases. Only party officials would come and go, holidaying in exclusive spas that popped up along the seashore.

'Now everyone is trying to leave,' Valery murmurs. Disconnected from Moscow by 1,000 miles, the amber capital of the world is plagued by poverty and a trigger-happy mafia, and is best known as Europe's epicentre of gun-running, drugs and AIDS.

We bump along a raised road to where the city begins and the potholes open up, patches of cobble poking through the meagre Soviet crust of asphalt. East Prussia refuses to die. Old photographs show Königsberg as a bustling medieval town hunched over canals and rivers, dominated by God and the rule of law, the forbidding cathedral and the dark turrets of the castle.

Now the signs of Kaliningrad's Teutonic antecedence are more subtle: the battered iron tramlines, the manhole cover embossed with a Prussian eagle, the avenues of linden trees, antiques shops stuffed with white crockery stamped with a crimson swastika and the logo of the Blutgericht, the Nazi's Blood Court restaurant, which once occupied the cellars of Königsberg Castle.

Pre-war Königsberg

The 'Monster'

Where Leninsky Prospekt (the road once called Steindamm Strasse) merges with Ulitsa Shevchenko, Valery the driver points to a giant concrete tower-block, the windows of which have all been blown out. It is a building so eye-blindingly hideous that it provides the dour residents of Kaliningrad with a moment of levity every time they sit here in the traffic and contemplate it. 'Monster,' Valery declares, telling us how the city council spent years building it upon the ruins of Königsberg Castle without having surveyed the flooded cellars, into which their 'Monster' immediately began to sink. It was on this junction that Kuchumov and Tronchinsky must have posed for one of their photographs taken in 1946, trouser bottoms stuffed into socks, a pork-pie hat and a black beret.

We have an appointment with the Kaliningrad Centre for Coordinating the Search for Cultural Relics, an organization whose name suggests that it can tell us something about the state investigations into missing art works. We pull up outside a pebbledash 1930s-style villa. We ring and hear a scraping as a key is inserted in a lock. We follow a silent woman upstairs.

'The Colonel isn't here,' she announces, as we enter a darkened office, lined with maps and locked cupboards. 'But he knows you have arrived.'

Who is she talking about, we ask?

'Colonel Avenir Ovsianov. He runs the centre. He'll be back tomorrow.'

The last time we had seen Colonel Ovsianov's name was in a news report from August 1988 that revealed he was heading a dig in the suburbs of Kaliningrad city for the Amber Room (the same report that drove Erich Mielke to write in haste to the chairman of the KGB).

At the Kaliningrad Hotel a receptionist offers us a view for a few dollars extra. We reach the third-floor room and pull back the curtains to see an expanse of concrete and, rising from it, the 'Monster'.

We close the curtains. We were in St Petersburg's airport just long enough to catch up with Our Friend the Professor. She thrust a large envelope into our hands as she waved us off. All the papers come from the literature archive and concern Kaliningrad, she said. Our reader's tickets have expired but she has gutted the Kuchumov files and will post on the rest of the documents when she has translated them.

We open a file. The first page is stamped 'For Official Use Only'. In the top left-hand corner is written: 'Approval of the chairman of the Committee on Searching for Museum Treasures, Deputy Minister of Culture for the Russian Federation, Comrade Vasily Mikhailovich Striganov, 1969.'[1]

As with all the papers from the Kuchumov archive, the readers' slip confirms that we are the first to study this file and we expectantly turn the page. Here is the material that the Stasi was never permitted to see, a table of Soviet officials who searched for the Amber Room in Kaliningrad from December 1949 to January 1984. It is also material that previous Amber Room researchers have been prevented from reading, since the original copies of all documentation connected with Kaliningrad search committees remain classified in the State Archive of the Russian Federation in Moscow.[2]

Vasily Striganov's report fills twenty pages. It lists search sites covering the entire province, teams sponsored by almost every organ of the Soviet state, a secret exercise in discovery that was extensive and frenetic (churches surveyed, thirty-five; former Nazi offices visited, forty-seven; major excavations conducted, sixteen).

Striganov's report confirms what the Stasi long suspected: that the Anatoly Kuchumov–Gerhard Strauss mission of December 1949 was the beginning of intensive Soviet investigations in Kaliningrad, not the end.

Even while Kuchumov was interrogating Gerhard Strauss in the freezing Hotel Moscow about the location of the Amber Room, a powerful provincial search committee was already being formed. It was led by Comrade Veniamin Krolevsky, the Secretary of Kaliningrad ObKom (the *oblast* or provincial committee of the Communist Party of the Soviet Union) and slotted between the technical experts were agents of the security apparatus including the provincial KGB chairman and the director of Kaliningrad UVD, its Department of Internal Affairs or security police.

While it was standard practice for intelligence agents to be attached to every civil organization, office, factory and college, the fact that such high-ranking officials sat on Krolevsky's committee suggested that its work was being closely observed.

We see that against Comrade Krolevsky's name Kuchumov has written in pencil 'a.k.a. Vladimir Dmetriev'. This is a vitally important piece of information.[3] We immediately recall the July 1958 *Kaliningradskaya Pravda* articles written by Vladimir Dmetriev of July 1958, in which he claimed: 'I was really involved and excited. I had never done anything so interesting before. We reported every day to ObKom our measurements of the castle and during the evening analysed results, as if it was a difficult crossword... This was vital work...'

We could find no record of a journalist called Vladimir Dmetriev and had assumed (incorrectly) it was a pseudonym for Anatoly Kuchumov. But here we see that Vladimir Dmetriev was a *nom de plume* for the Secretary of the Kaliningrad Communist Party, one of the most powerful men in the province, Veniamin Krolevsky. This means that the articles *Kaliningradskaya Pravda* published and *Freie Welt* regurgitated had emanated from the Communist Party of the Soviet Union. This puts the claims made in them in a different light.

It was the party, then, that had revealed that the Amber Room had survived and was being secretly hunted for. It was the party that publicly humiliated and defamed Professor Alexander Brusov, who, the Party claimed, had incorrectly concluded that the Amber Room had been destroyed. And it was the party that decided to keep Kuchumov's name out of print, shielding his role in the Amber Room investigation for some reason.

It is beginning to look as if Brusov was sacrificed for some greater purpose. So eager was the party to keep the Amber Room alive, while punishing the man who had killed it off, that it begins to feel as if the Soviet authorities were covering something up.

Striganov's report continued. It revealed that on 9 September 1959 Party Secretary Krolevsky's committee was subsumed by another, more powerful one led by his superior, Comrade G. I. Harkov, the vice-director of ObalIsPolKom (the Kaliningrad Executive Committee of the People's Deputies).

Harkov enlisted a twelve-man team, pooled from practically every Soviet security, party and defence organization: the vice-director of the Cultural Department, two vice-directors of the Kaliningrad Department of Internal Affairs [UVD], a vice-commander of the Baltic Fleet DKBF (building committee) and the provincial KGB deputy. A column marked 'Findings' stated: 'No archive documents available.' Perhaps they had found nothing and wanted no one to know, or perhaps they had found something that they wished to keep a secret.

On 11 March 1967 Comrade Harkov's search was also taken over. An executive directive issued by the Council of Ministers of the Russian Federation, the highest executive body of state, ordered a new search team be formed.[4] We have before us the minutes of its first meeting, on 25 March 1967:

Comrade Yermoliev [director of the Central Museum Committee of the Russian Federation] opened the meeting of the newly named Working Group on the Search for the Amber Room.

COMRADE YERMOLIEV: 'Let me start [by saying] there have been many attempts to search for the Amber Room and the Kaliningrad authorities have played an important part. However, not enough has been done and the work has not been systematic, the analysis unscientific.

A stinging attack on the Kaliningrad authorities and evidence that Moscow was intent on taking over the search.

COMRADE JAKOBOVICH [chief of Kaliningrad air-raid defences]: How much time do we have for finding the Amber Room? Do we have to do it by the fiftieth jubilee of the Soviet Union [the founding of the Bolshevik state was only seven months away]?

COMRADE YERMOLIEV: Well, that would be very good, to make a gift to the Motherland for the jubilee. However, it would be very difficult to set a time limit.

COMRADE GLUSHKOV [director of the Kaliningrad Cultural Department]: One of the most important questions we should put to Soviet ministries of the Russian Federation is about financing.

MAJOR V. V. BOGDANCHIKOV [vice-chairman of the Kaliningrad Communist Party]: Our group should have its own car and we are bound to have a lot of material. So we need someone who can type up everything.

COMRADE VASHNA [a senior official from Moscow]: I want to ask a question of Comrade Maximov. What hindered the previous searches and have there been any significant findings to date that need our attention? And if things have been found, where are they now?

COMRADE MAXIMOV [civil engineer and a member of the old Krolevsky team]: There were no valuable findings.

COMRADE JAKOBOVICH: Well, all valuable findings were sent to the KGB.

Maximov and Jakobovich were tripping over each other. Here the minutes abruptly move on to a discussion about the previous search commissions' lack of equipment. We wonder what was found and spirited away by the KGB.

COMRADE MAXIMOV: For example, we went into dark basements and we had no torches so we could see nothing.

It seems almost unbelievable that the Kaliningrad KGB and MVD, which backed the searches, were not able to provide their teams with even the most basic equipment like torches. Unless, of course, there was nothing worth illuminating.

Before the issue could be discussed further there was a suggestion from the floor. Why not round up everyone living in the *oblast* who had been a resident since 1945 and interrogate them about the Amber Room?

According to Comrade Yermoliev: 'It is not a good idea. The bigger the circle of people knowing the problem the greater the problem. We need secrecy. Well comrades, today's meeting was a very useful one because we have all expressed our concerns and suggestions.' Secrecy was a strange notion to introduce after millions of newspaper readers of *Pravda* and *Freie Welt* had been alerted nine years earlier to the existence of a secret search for the Amber Room in Kaliningrad.

Then, in March 1969, seventeen months after the fiftieth jubilee of the Soviet Union, with the search for the Amber Room still ongoing, Moscow took over completely. A telegram dated 15 April 1969 arrived for the investigation's new chairman, Comrade Jakobovich.[5] In it the Deputy Minister of Culture of the Russian Federation, Comrade Vasily Striganov, instructed him on the theory he was to follow:

Since the end of the war our stolen art collections that were stored in East Prussia haven't turned up. You might think that somebody is still hiding them. That seems unlikely, as not one jot of information over fifteen years has emerged... If the Germans had taken out the treasures, they were bound to turn up in Germany and yet nothing has. So what can we see from this?

One can come to a conclusion that the Amber Room is still in Kaliningrad. I think that the Germans never thought East Prussia would remain within the USSR. They thought they would return to the province and we would leave.[6]

This summary dismissal of the Stasi's theory, which held that the Amber Room had been taken to Germany, was written as Paul Enke was beginning his monumental trawl of archives in Potsdam. It seems bizarre that the KGB would let the Stasi run with this theory for so many years when even at this early stage no one in the Soviet Union believed it. Unless, of course, the entire Stasi investigation into the Amber Room was a lure of some sort, to distract public attention away from Kaliningrad. Or perhaps it was simply an elaborate ruse to weed out old Nazis.

For Striganov, secrecy was a critical issue:

Four days ago in Western Germany people were interested once again with a question of the Amber Room, trying to find out through our embassy whether there is progress, what is new. We should not give them a straight answer. [As Germany was the country that stole it,] they have too big an interest in this matter... The question is: how will our work continue to be secretive? What is going to be done to make sure of this?

He offered some patrician advice: 'One has to think of a cover story, for example the examination of the soil, and this cover story we give to the press so all our real conclusions from the expedition can remain top secret.'

Comrade Jakobovich, the mission chairman, worked on Striganov's idea. Why not say the investigation team was digging for oil and call it the Kaliningrad Geological Archaeological Expedition of the State Historical Museum for the Ministry of Culture of the Russian Federation (KGA), Comrade Jakobovich suggested?

Striganov liked the title but in his subsequent reply pointed out an obvious flaw: 'There is no oil in Kaliningrad.'

Within three months Jakobovich was replaced by his deputy and the KGA began its secret work. There are no reports here about what the KGA found in its early years, but there is something else, something unexpected, written many years later, that brings Anatoly Kuchumov, the Leningrad curator, back into the frame.

It is a twenty-page statement dated 19 July 1986, by Comrade Jelena Storozhenko, a linguistics scholar and someone whose name we have read before. We go through an index of our characters and see that Storozhenko was one of those who regularly sent greetings cards to Kuchumov. Here we read that Storozhenko took over the chair of the KGA in 1974 and led it until it folded ten years later. Attached to Storozhenko's statement is a covering letter addressed to Anatoly Kuchumov, a person she evidently knew well and trusted. She wrote:

Dear Anatoly Mikhailovich, I am giving you these notes in the hope that they would be printed for the world to see in memory of everyone who to the last of their days devoted their lives to searching for the Amber Room.[7]

This is surprising. Storozhenko was attempting to publicize the sensitive findings of her mission, whatever they were. When the Russian authorities closed the KGA in 1984, no public statements were made. We already know that even the Stasi was kept in the dark for another two years about the closure of the mission. The KGA's findings were boxed up by the KGB and classified, locked away in the State Archive of the Russian Federation in Moscow, where they remain to this day. And yet this bureaucrat wanted everything she knew out in the public domain.[8]

Storozhenko explained her motivation to Kuchumov: 'On 1 January 1984 [the KGA] was wound up and we were asked to hand over all documents.' Her next statement comes as a great disappointment to us. 'We did not find the Amber Room.'

Having concluded that the German episode was a red herring, we have come back to Russia only to discover that here too investigators failed to make any progress on the Amber Room. But Storozhenko was not happy. She wrote in her covering letter to Kuchumov:

No one could doubt that the search should continue and we could offer proposals on how to conduct that search. However, for successful searches it is necessary to have the highest levels of control and organization, otherwise further searches are not worth conducting. It is in the stated interests of the Soviet people that the Amber Room should be found and given back. My heartfelt regards to your wife, be healthy, good luck and success, and I dream of seeing you again. My son, who is standing beside me, says, 'Send my best regards.' We embrace you, always yours, Jelena and Zhenik.

The letter was very carefully worded but the message was clear. Storozhenko's search had failed because she had not been given 'the highest levels of control and organization' and she could see no reason for winding up the KGA. We wonder who was holding her back and turn to the twenty-page statement itself in which Storozhenko gave Kuchumov a frank and detailed explanation of her failed ten-year inquiry.

She confirmed that her team was financed by Moscow and that she was required to make quarterly reports back to Deputy Culture Minister Striganov. However, it was the Culture Ministry's KGB chief, G. S. Fors, who supervised the day-to-day running of the KGA operation.

Storozhenko wrote that her remit was to 're-examine all material connected directly or indirectly with the mystery of the Amber Room ...' as she had discovered that all previous searches 'have been unscientific and uncoordinated and that no digs were conducted at a depth greater than eight feet'. Storozhenko's statement reveals something significant. For fifteen years, Soviet Amber Room searchers had been sifting around only in the topsoil. If Storozhenko's predecessors had been genuinely looking for hidden cellars and bunkers, they would have had to dig far deeper. But the KGA chairman did not say whether she believed the decision not to was premeditated or simply incompetent.

Storozhenko explained that 'it was important to have a scientific foundation to our work'. Her team was ordered to 'check and analyse all previous statements of citizens of the USSR, East and West Germany and Poland. These statements were filtered and those meriting further investigation set aside... and copied to Moscow.' Everything was submitted to the KGB and vetted by Fors.

Witness accounts were checked against old maps and wartime literature, tested against other eyewitnesses and archive material. While we read in the Ministry of Truth in Berlin that the Stasi was repeatedly denied access to archive material in the Soviet Union, Storozhenko listed here more than twenty archives used by her team in Moscow, Leningrad, Kiev and provincial cities from the Ukraine to Estonia.

But it is the section entitled 'Findings' that tells the real story of the KGA. Storozhenko revealed to Kuchumov that her ten-year expedition had discovered:

Forty pieces of artillery, cannonballs, bullets and aerial bombs in the former Teutonic castle of Lochstädt, a private collection of amber (weighing nine pounds) in a blocked-up cellar. And under the floor of a private house in the centre of the city we found dead bodies, a coffin and a red flag on which was the hammer and sickle. Perhaps this flag dates from the Revolution period of 1918, when Soviet workers rose up for the first time against East Prussia. Maybe then this workers' flag flew over Königsberg.

Cannonballs and skeletons were not much to show for a scientific expedition and Storozhenko drew Kuchumov's attention to some critical factors:

The expedition had some difficulties. We worked at a time when the city was being rebuilt very quickly and it was impossible to get admission to sites having no documents. We also had no opportunity to organize invitations for those people who had made previous statements to come over here. We also suffered from a lack of technical devices.

Kuchumov had been permitted to fly witnesses to Kaliningrad and was empowered to search wherever he wanted. He even had a mechanical digger. Storozhenko advised him that a Kaliningrad Party directive supposedly backed the KGA. Issued in 1969, it ordered every administrative, military and utility office in the province to support the activities of the search.[9] But the directive had not been adhered to. Something had gone wrong. Storozhenko thought she had been prevented from looking too hard for the Amber Room. The authorities must have feared what she would find.

'I am giving you these notes in the hope that they would be printed for the world to see,' Storozhenko had written to her friend Anatoly Kuchumov. She was relying on the famous curator to publicize her predicament, perhaps in the hope that a new and unfettered investigation into the Amber Room would find it. We wonder if Kuchumov, aged seventy-four when he received this statement, still had the energy to help.

'238340 Svetly, Kaliningrad Region, Ulitsa Sovetskaya, House 11, Apartment Six, tel: 2-22-80': we copied Jelena Storozhenko's details from her letter but her telephone has been disconnected.

Valery the taxi driver volunteers to take us to Svetly via a circuitous route. 'I want you to see our amber coast and then you can attend to your business,' he says.

The city ends abruptly and Kaliningrad province sprawls across end-

The amber coastline of the Samland Peninsula

less marshy, wind-whipped fields, left lifeless and infertile by spray from the Baltic. Past the military listening station and abandoned fighter-jet hangars is Yantarny, the amber capital of the world. Boys sledge on gunnysacks down the blue-clay hillsides. Listless men in army coats and tracksuit bottoms drink silently on collapsing Prussian-built verandas. Enormous overground pipes carrying seawater, which is used to blast the mud and amber apart at the impoverished Yantarny Mining Combine No. 9, strangle the village.

'Beautiful, isn't it?' Valery says.

We follow the coastline of the Samland Peninsula south, towards the closed military city of Baltiysk (where security permits are still required), before turning sharply into Svetly. House 11, Apartment Six is boarded up, but from a neighbouring building that also looks abandoned emerges a *babushka*.

'Storozhenko?' we ask. 'Jelena.'

'Dead,' she snaps. 'Gone in 1994. Strange. There was a stepson. Zhenik. He's disappeared.' She scuttles back into the ruin.

Valery is anxious to get home before dark and we clatter through yet more mournful villages that are slowly slipping into the Baltic.

The next morning Colonel Avenir Ovsianov, director of the Kaliningrad Centre for Coordinating the Search for Cultural Relics, is waiting for us at the care-worn 1930s-style villa. '*Dobry*,' he says, offering us a large, hard hand that feels as if it has spent a lifetime wielding the pick we can see propped behind his desk. 'Kaliningrad welcomes you.' He solemnly pours into our cupped hands lemony grains of amber fished from the beaches of Yantarny and we notice a picture on the wall of him as a younger man, with Red Army comrades in military uniform and armed with metal detectors.

Today, the colonel looks every inch the grand old Soviet commissar: thick waves of silvery hair, gold teeth, unsmiling wintry face, piercing eyes peeping over Politburo glasses.

Why was the Storozhenko inquiry shut down in 1984, we ask?

The colonel draws breath. 'Everything here was secret. This was a

Avenir Ovsianov (centre), digging for the Amber Room
in Kaliningrad Province, 1970s

secret place. You are only here on the invitation of our government. I report to the FSB [the successor to the KGB].' Surely the colonel isn't threatening us?

'We are here on state salaries. Will you be paying?' the colonel asks, walking over to a cabinet and flashing us a view of hundreds of files, neatly stacked in rows. 'I managed to get these. From my military sources.'

What are they, we ask?

'I have some of Jelena Storozhenko's papers in here.'

We thought everything was locked up in Moscow.

'There are always ways of getting information,' the colonel says. He is as hard to hook as a wily old pike, but when we hand over dollars he begins to open up.

The colonel tells us that, as a military engineer in the Red Army, he had specialist knowledge of the subterranean infrastructure of Kaliningrad and in 1971 was called to assist the search for the Amber Room. 'That was the first time I met Jelena. And at that meeting I contracted an illness, searching for treasure. Jelena told me to keep absolutely silent about my involvement in the KGA and anything I learned. She told me her organization was secret. I said, "I am a soldier and not a journalist."'

We try to speed things along. We need to know why Jelena Storozhenko's investigation was closed down. We show the colonel her report to Kuchumov of 1986. Perhaps it might jog his memory. Was Jelena Storozhenko correct in believing that her investigation had been hijacked, we ask?

The colonel slips on his heavy glasses. He thumbs through our twenty-page statement. He makes appreciative grunts. 'It's interesting,' he says. 'But you do not have the full story.'

Hel unlocks a cupboard and takes from it a small black-and-white photograph that shows ten people huddled in a group, standing inside an anonymous hall. Six men in black lace-up shoes. Four women in high-heeled leather boots. Smart *shapkas* on everyone's head and fur-trimmed coats wrapped tight against the Kaliningrad chill. The woman at the centre clutches a plastic bag that is stuffed with paperwork and a bunch of flowers.

'Chairman Storozhenko,' the colonel says.

*Kaliningrad Geological Archaelogical Expedition team
photograph with chairman Jelena Storozhenko at centre*

We look closer. Jelena Storozhenko is almost smiling, her lips parted as if she is joking with the photographer. How innocuous her KGA looks, like middle-aged teachers preparing for a union conference, not a top-secret investigation ordered by the Kremlin.

The colonel leans over the desk. 'They operated out of the Church of the Holy Family, near the railway station. Called themselves "the Choral Society" to prevent any unwelcome inquiries.

'After the KGA was closed down in 1984, the state too wanted to inhibit unwelcome inquiries and for several years denied it had any papers belonging to the KGA. But I knew Jelena had amassed a vast archive and I told the authorities I had seen it in her office. Eventually I got hold of some of her things, including this, her personal ready-reckoner, which she carried with her every day of her investigation. Would you like to see it?'

We try not to grab at the small exercise book with a hard cover that the colonel has taken from his grey briefcase. A label on it states: 'Not to be removed from the State Archive of the Russian Federation, Moscow.'

We scan the contents page. A list of possible locations and witnesses.

Transcripts of statements by Ernst Schaumann (friend of Alfred Rohde), Paul Feyerabend (director of the Blood Court restaurant at Königsberg Castle) and Otto Smakka (another contemporary of Rohde's). Nothing new here. We have seen all of this before in Kuchumov's private papers.

There follows a short history of previous Amber Room searches and an essay, 'On Hunting for Cultural Treasures', by Comrade Jakobovich, the first head of the KGA. There is a translation of Alfred Rohde's *Pantheon* article, the piece in which he announced the public display of the treasure in Königsberg Castle in 1942, then a review of Soviet searches 1945–67 and a plan of work for the future.

We see that Storozhenko has a copy of Kuchumov's conclusion of 1946, in which the curator stated that the room survived the war and remained concealed in the city. It was obviously a critical document for her too. Finally there are three statements from Professor Alexander Brusov: his original findings of 12 June 1945, a statement made in December 1949 and another on 29 July 1954. This is interesting. We have only ever seen the statements made by Brusov in 1945 after his trip to Königsberg and in 1946, when Kuchumov and Tronchinsky quizzed him in Moscow. We turn to look at the 1949 and 1954 statements, but see that both have been cut out of the binding.

'State censors. They went through everything before I saw it,' the colonel says, watching us.

A long pause. He fiddles with some Nazi dog-tags that he found in a local ruin, then says: 'There was very strong centralization in Jelena's day and without permission from Moscow nothing could happen. It would take months for a request from the KGA to be answered. Can we dig? Can we have some shovels? But the problem she faced went beyond bureaucracy and inefficiency. I think that Storozhenko's expedition was deliberately hampered. The Ministry of Defence intervened.'

He looks down the pages of our Storozhenko statement and taps on the line where she complained that she was hindered by the rebuilding of the city. 'She was being euphemistic. It was worse than that. In 1947 the Council of Ministers of the Russian Federation passed an order handing over all areas of the *oblast* that were in any way connected to the amber industry to the Ministry of Defence.[10] Amber was a lucrative asset, after all. Beaches, villages, forests, marshes and factories all went under the control of the military. Anywhere Jelena wished to dig, she had to seek permission from them. And they seldom gave her that permission. Why would they do that when they were also supposed to have been part of the effort to find the Amber Room?'

We have no idea. Maybe the Ministry of Defence was simply trying to protect its assets, we suggest. The Baltic coast was a strategic area.

The colonel sips from a glass of water. 'You misunderstand the Soviet Union. Obstacles were placed in Jelena's way. Let me give you another example. In your document Jelena writes of the twenty archives she visited, but she does not mention the others that were out-of-bounds. Brezhnev once declared: "We should make access to special military archives more restrictive to make sure that filthy people will not use them for their own dirty purposes." And they did.'[11] He drains his glass.

But for what reason, we ask? What was there to hide?

'Jelena was pursuing her own theory. Something that Professor Brusov had subtly alluded to in 1945. Our Red Army was heroic and long-suffering. But this was not the only truth. There was also theft and terrible destruction of treasures by our side.'

Is the colonel suggesting that the Red Army stole or destroyed the Amber Room, we ask, our hearts in our mouths?

He ignores the question and carries on: 'Jelena had stumbled over a few Ministry of Defence papers that had been misfiled. One from 15 June 1945 referred to a [Soviet] trophy brigade opening and emptying a safe in the Königsberg Volksbank. I have the document.' He reads aloud from it: '"What we recovered: eighty kilos of cultural treasures, including a huge amount of platinum, gold and silver, among them one kilo of gold chains, rings, medallions and watches, silver coins, medals and 353 silver soup spoons, 244 forks, 107 knives. Report of Major Germani of the 5th Trophy Department [sic], assisted by Major Makarov, head of the travelling department of the State Bank 168, and Lt Suzlova, representative of Königsberg Military HQ."'[12]

The colonel looks up: 'Later this Volksbank haul disappeared. And this was just one example. When Jelena attempted to trace what had happened to these treasures and the people who found them, Moscow informed her that there was no surviving archive material. Why would they do that? Why cover up the disappearances and the work of these so-called trophy brigades? Unless they wanted to preserve intact the image of the heroic Red Army fighting the Great Patriotic War.'

The colonel launches into a crisp lesson in Soviet military history.

In 1942 reports about the Nazi pillaging of the Leningrad palaces in 1941 and 1942 prompted officials in Moscow to propose that the Soviet Union was entitled to compensation, he says. An Extraordinary Soviet State Commission to investigate German war crimes was established in November that year and sanctioned the idea of taking 'Replacement Treasures', art works gathered from German territory to replace those that had been lost in the USSR.

On 25 February 1945, two weeks after Stalin returned from the Yalta conference (where compensation for Soviet losses had been set by the Allies at 10 billion dollars), a new body was established in Moscow to realize the sum. The Special Committee on Germany was staffed by Nikolai Bulganin, the deputy head of defence, Georgy Malenkov, a member of Stalin's war cabinet, and Nikolai Voznesensky, the powerful head of Gosplan, the organization responsible for implementing the planned economy. The colonel says that the Special Committee sanctioned the gathering of 1,745 specific works of art chosen from German museum catalogues.[13]

Soldiers could not do such a specialized job and so conscription orders were sent to industrialists, artists, curators, writers and scientists. They were invested with military ranks and uniforms so that the Red Army would respect them. Armed with lists, targets and *Baedeker* guides to Germany, they would be known as the 'trophy brigades' and dispatched to the front.

The colonel looks at us over his glasses. 'I began to investigate the behaviour of these brigades and our regular troops in East Prussia. Among the Soviet forces storming Königsberg in April 1945 were the 11th Guards Army, the 50th Army and the 43rd Army. Each of these armies had trophy brigades attached to them and these experts hit the ground running as soon as the city fell on 9 April. When the 50th and 43rd armies were dispatched to the Far East, the 11th Army under General Galitsky was left behind and its trophy brigades carried on with their work.'

We know that Professor Alexander Brusov, who led the first official search for the Amber Room, only reached Königsberg sixty-one days after the city fell. According to Colonel Ovsianov's research, this meant that there were sixty-one days during which the city was crawling with regular troops and trophy brigades whose actions were not always co-ordinated or accountable.

'Even after Brusov arrived, his was not the only team in town,' the colonel says. 'Several units of the trophy brigades were still operating. Colonel D. D. Ivanyenko, the man who found the Castle Gift Book, recording the arrival of the Amber Room in December 1941, was not a real army officer. He was conscripted from Moscow State University to a trophy brigade and remained in the city until August, accompanied by political commissar Major Krolic and translator Lieutenant Malakov.

'In June 1945, the Brigade of the Committee of Arts Affairs, led by N. U. Sergeiyevskaya, Secretary of Moscow's Purchasing Committee of the Commission of Cultural Affairs, arrived with First Lieutenant I. I. Tsirlin from the Pushkin Museum. The same month, another brigade, headed by Comrade S. D. Skazkin and Comrade Turok of the Academy of Science in Moscow, arrived. And then a fourth search team came from the Voronezh Museum, under the chairmanship of Professor I. A. Petrusov. All of these teams had overlapping responsibilities for recovering loot and all of their findings came under the Ministry of Defence.

'No one was to supposed to know of the existence of these brigades. Certainly not the Allies. Secrecy was understandable at that time. And during the Cold War, when you and I were enemies. But now we are at peace, I cannot understand the behaviour of our officials, who still block access to the trophy brigade archives.'

Is the colonel saying that the Gauleiter of East Prussia, Erich Koch, was right, we ask? He had told Gerhard Strauss at the special interrogation in the GDR's embassy in Warsaw in 1959 that he believed the Red Army had stolen the Amber Room.

'I am not saying that,' the colonel replies. 'I am saying that by keeping the trophy brigade files closed, the Ministry of Defence is obstructing investigators and creating suspicion. It cannot sanction a probe into the Amber Room and then remove from it one of the most vital sources of reference material.'

He bangs his fist on the desk. 'For thirty years I served in the military and even I cannot get certain files out of the Central Archive of the Ministry of Defence that relate to the trophy brigades. I have come up against very thick walls of Soviet bureaucracy.'

In June 1996 Colonel Ovsianov learned from a colleague in Moscow that files concerning the activities of the trophy brigades attached to the 11th, 50th and 43rd armies of the Third Belorussian front (those active in East Prussia) did exist and were kept in a closed section of the Central Archive of the Ministry of Defence (TsAMO). He applied for a permit to the repository, which is tucked away in Podolsk, a hard-nosed industrial city south-west of Moscow.

'On 17 July 1996 I received a reply from Colonel Vimuchkin. "In your letter you petitioned to get various documents. After our analysis we have ascertained that the material that is interesting to you is not to be found anywhere in our archive. There is no reason for you to research this any further." I wrote back, this time with names and titles of documents, to the chief of the unit.' [14] The colonel pulls another letter from his grey case. 'Then I received this. "At the moment in the Central Archive of the Ministry of Defence we have special works which are connected to a new law about restoration of art treasures and due to this reason the access to these documents is restricted."'

In May 1997 the law was passed and on 16 October the colonel reapplied to Podolsk for the papers. 'This time an answer came from a Colonel Dorothiayev.' Another letter emerges from the grey case. '"We have received your petition... and we are trying to extract the following documents and will let you know in due course."

'I am still waiting to hear from the archive,' the colonel says. 'Is the truth still so powerful and strange that no one can be allowed to see it?'

13

Colonel Ovsianov is a watchful man. He believes that there was some kind of Soviet cover-up concerning the Amber Room. But he won't be drawn until he gets into the military archive in Podolsk.

He might be waiting a long time. However, there are strong indications about what this cover-up involves: the Red Army doing the unthinkable, destroying the Soviet treasure or stealing it in the last days of the battle for East Prussia. This is the last thing we expected to discover when we began our search. But now Ovsianov has raised it, the story begins to make sense for the first time.

Professor Alexander Brusov voiced similar concerns in 1945, killing off all hope about the Amber Room just weeks after he had been sent to Königsberg to find it, concluding that it was burned in the Knights' Hall by troops as the city fell.

The point at which the Amber Room story changed forever was when the Soviets ordered a reinvestigation in 1946. Then Anatoly Kuchumov returned to the scene of the crime and forensically analysed the castle ruins, finding new evidence that led him to conclude that Brusov was wrong, febrile and misinformed. And since then there have been many searches for the Amber Room – in the GDR and Soviet Union – based on Kuchumov's hypothesis. Ridiculous amounts of money have been thrown at recovering the missing treasure from its Nazi hiding place. Politicians and security officials from both countries have urged on the investigations. Yet nothing has been found and the possibility that the culprits might have been Soviet was never even considered.

*

At the Kaliningrad Hotel reception, squeezed between counters selling garish amber jewellery and German posters advertising nostalgia tours for old East Prussians, a package is waiting. A parting gift from the literature archive in St Petersburg, a miscellany of biographical and research information connected to Anatoly Kuchumov. This will be our last foray into the curator's private papers.

Anatoly Mikhailovich Kuchumov, the man who had panicked and left the Amber Room in the Catherine Palace in 1941, had leapt at the chance of reinvestigating its fate in Königsberg in 1946. Having knocked out Brusov's evidence, he had pursued his own theory to Berlin in 1947 and the new Kaliningrad in 1949 and again to that city in 1959. The story keeps coming back to the man who resurrected the Amber Room.

We take the file up to the third floor and close the curtains in our room. We cannot bear looking at the 'Monster'. In the packet is a small hard-backed volume with a grey and beige cover, *The Amber Room* by Anatoly Kuchumov and M. G. Voronov.

The book was published in 1989, as the Soviet Union staggered to its end, forty-eight years after Kuchumov had begun to research in frozen Novosibirsk. *The Amber Room* came out when Kuchumov was seventy-seven years old, twelve years after he officially retired from the Leningrad palaces with a serious heart complaint.[1]

It began with Kuchumov in a reflective mood: the court of the tsars; Peter the Great's dreams of owning the Amber Room; Peter's frustration at his experts' inability to reconstruct it in his Summer Palace; the triumph of empresses Elizabeth and Catherine in resurrecting the treasure in the Catherine Palace; its emergence as the 'Eighth Wonder of the World'.

But when Kuchumov addressed the fate of the Amber Room in the final pages, his tone changed:

The failure of the searches for the Amber Room should not be an embarrassment for the Soviet people, particularly museum workers. The Amber Room did not die. This masterpiece could not have been deliberately destroyed. There are many secret places that we still have not discovered left by the Nazis in the territories of Germany, Austria and other countries. It is only a question of time before it is found, by chance or the continuation of searching. Lovers of beauty, you must not reject the continuation of the search.

We are struck by Kuchumov's choice of words. 'embarrassment', 'the Amber Room did not die', 'deliberately destroyed'. It is as if he was defending himself, and yet as far as we know, he faced no accusers in 1989.

What is also striking is that Kuchumov's book failed to reveal any of the sentiments expressed by Jelena Storozhenko in her twenty-page statement to Kuchumov in 1986. *The Amber Room* made no mention of Storozhenko's paltry finds or her fears of official obfuscation. For some reason, Kuchumov decided that, even though the Soviet Union had embraced glasnost and perestroika, Storozhenko's allegations were not 'for the world to see'.

We close his book and turn to a file of papers from the literature archive with a growing feeling that Kuchumov was struggling at the end of his life to deal with the consequences of his actions in 1941. Perhaps he was trying to keep something alive that he knew had in reality died.

The documents are in reverse order, the most contemporaneous, a newspaper cutting from 1986, at the top. *Leningradskaya Pravda* reported on 22 April 1986: 'Mikhail Gorbachev, Secretary of the Central Committee of the Communist Party of the Soviet Union, and Nikolai Richkov, Chairman of the Council of Ministers of the USSR, announce... recipients of the Lenin Prize.'[2]

Among the handful of those chosen to receive the Soviet Union's highest civilian honour in 1986 we spot the name 'A. M. Kuchumov (art historian)', awarded in recognition of 'outstanding achievements' and 'the solution of tasks vital to the state'.

A telegram sent to Kuchumov from Minister of Culture Comrade Dermichev read: 'Honoured Anatoly Mikhailovich! Heartfelt congratulations... your many years and creative labours have returned to life that destroyed by the Hitlerite occupants...'

We recall the man in the photographs: Kuchumov portly in his tatty suit, a provincial curator who rolled up his shirtsleeves to help track down and recover art stolen by the Nazis. Self-taught, as blind as a mole, Kuchumov appeared to live a commonplace existence with his wife, Anna

Anatoly Kuchumov reading in the mauve boudoir of Empress Alexandra, Alexander Palace, Pushkin, 1940

Mikhailovna, in their threadbare Pavlovsk apartment. But here, we see that the party's Central Committee and the chairman of the Council of Ministers of the USSR had plucked Kuchumov out as an exemplary comrade. Many curators we met at the St Petersburg House of Scientists had also struggled with virtually no resources to rebuild Russia's cultural heritage, yet who among them had been recognized? Kuchumov must have done something special, and yet in his book, the epitaph on his career, he was regretful.

Dozens of telegrams arrived after news of the 1986 award was published. From First Secretary Comrade Solavyiov of the Leningrad Communist Party. From the Supreme Architect of Leningrad, Comrade Bulkdakov ('we are proud'). From Dushanbe in Tajikistan ('your old friend Vsevolod... I heard it on the radio!').

And lastly, from unprepossessing Svetly in Kaliningrad Province: 'Dear Anatoly Mikhailovich, heartfelt congratulations. So glad to hear your success. Kiss you always. Jelena Storozhenko.'

So glad. However, according to the correspondence that comes next, the man Storozhenko perceived as a friend and a servant of the state was already its agent.

The file goes back to the 1970s. A bundle of letters, all of them penned by a comrade, G. S. Fors, and sent to Kuchumov's home address. We recognize the name: G. S. Fors. He was the KGB chief at the Ministry of Culture in Moscow to whom Jelena Storozhenko was required to report her findings about the Amber Room.

The earliest letter is dated 5 July 1970, one year after the Kaliningrad Geological-Archaeological Expedition (KGA) was established:

Dorogoy Anatoly Mikhailovich. In Kaliningrad our affairs are multiplying and becoming more interesting. The investigation has developed its own technique and we are digging without any help. I write to you with the intention of knowing confidentially when you are coming to Kaliningrad. The affair demands your presence and it would be good if you could come for ten days in August. G. S. Fors.[3]

The KGB was reporting to Kuchumov about the new Amber Room investigation, although it is not clear who was in charge.

The next letter Kuchumov kept was sent eighteen months later, on 27 December 1971:

Dorogoy Anatoly Mikhailovich! Heartfelt congratulations to you and your respected wife on the occasion of New Year's Eve. Long years of heart-beating to come, as there are many affairs to be done. I ask you to come to Kaliningrad at the start of 1972 for eight to ten days. We must discuss the state of affairs and manage the researches. We would like to scale down the digging... With a bow, I leave you, G. S. Fors.

They had only been excavating for two years and already the KGB was keen to curtail the work. Perhaps Moscow was concerned that too much money was being spent in Kaliningrad. Maybe the KGA was getting dangerously close to that which the Ministry of Defence wanted to keep secret. Since there are no replies here, we do not know whether Kuchumov agreed.

There is gap of three and a half years before the next letter:

2 May 1975, *Dorogoy* Anatoly Mikhailovich! I am passing you letters (attached) that have been registered with my department. They might help your work [on the Amber Room]. But I must ask you, remember these are confidential documents. Keep them safe! Anything you glean from them must be held as a separate affair. And all of these letters must be returned to me before 1 July personally or via a trusted person. G. S. Fors.

The documents Fors sent are no longer attached but what this letter tells us is that the KGB man trusted Kuchumov sufficiently to quietly share intelligence with him. We wonder if the letters concerned the activities of the Soviet trophy brigades or witness statements that Kuchumov was being asked to vet.

The final letter Kuchumov kept was sent on 29 August 1978:

Dorogoy Anatoly Mikhailovich! The Lord is my witness. I have received your letter and I am immediately answering. Our affair continues... in meetings with eyewitnesses from different periods of time... I feel uncomfortable because we are wasting state funds... I am on holiday until 4 October and after that we must think of a very good reason for calling you to Moscow. Think of a reason. I embrace you heartily. G. S. Fors.

Whatever they were doing in the province, the KGB was conscious that it was not cost-efficient. One thing we can think of that would not be cost-efficient would be digging pointlessly for something that the KGB knew did not exist. But the letters do not confirm this.

We have only a fragment of the correspondence, but from the tone and language of these letters Fors and Kuchumov enjoyed a close relationship at a time when most citizens lived in fear of the security services. '*Dorogoy* Anatoly Mikhailovich!' each letter began – my dear Anatoly Mikhailovich. Kuchumov was always addressed with a warm-hearted greeting by the KGB official. Our Friend the Professor notes in the margin that she is surprised to see anything from the KGB in which the phraseology used was familiar rather than formal, the Russian equivalent to the French *tu* rather than *vous*.

We have never even considered that Kuchumov might have had KGB connections until now, other than having to deal with the local KGB officials at the Pavlovsk and Catherine palaces, as every other curator did as a matter of course. There must have been a significant political dimension to the Amber Room search for the KGB to have become so closely involved, and whatever it was, Kuchumov was evidently up to his neck in it.

Beneath the KGB letters are *komandirovat* passes, similar to the ones we have seen before that authorized a worker to be transferred to another town or city.[4] They show that, while corresponding with the KGB, Kuchumov bobbed back and forth, at its behest, between Leningrad, Moscow and Kaliningrad throughout the 1970s, always telling his colleagues that he was on holiday – keeping in touch with KGB chief Fors about the failings of the Kaliningrad search team, sharing intelligence about the Amber Room that appears not to have been shown to chairman Jelena Storozhenko. It is beginning to look as if Kuchumov's loyalties lay more with the KGB than his fellow academics on the dig team in Kaliningrad. If there was a cover-up of any kind involving the Amber Room, Kuchumov must have been in on it, maybe while those physically searching were kept in the dark.

The file goes back to the 1960s, a page ripped from a school exercise book, a diary jotted down by Kuchumov over three days in 1969:

26 May: I came by plane to Kaliningrad at 9.40 a.m, settled in my hotel, got very comfortable and quiet suite No. 182. Meeting with G. S. Fors (KGB chief) and people from State Historical Museum, Moscow... Preparing documents and papers for the meeting of the State Commission that will take place tomorrow.

27 May: 10 a.m. meeting with Major Bogdanchikov. Also here are... military regiments and some from geophysics, some from local museums, some from Moscow. Evening: my birthday.

28 May: went with specialists to see bunker. Looking at area near Steindamm Strasse. Trip to garden of Alfred Rohde's house on Bickstrasse and former estate of Erich Koch at Gross Friedrichsberg...[5]

We recall a previous document stating that in May 1969 Deputy Culture Minister Vasily Striganov had ordered a major revamp of the Amber Room investigation, Moscow seizing control of the provincial search. And here was Kuchumov in Kaliningrad at that time advising, leading, coaching and preparing, guiding a string of dignitaries and security officials through the stage set of the last days of the Amber Room (and into a bunker).

But frustratingly the information here provides only snapshots in time. The file flips back to 1967. A succession of orders and telegrams show how Kuchumov had come to Striganov's attention two years earlier.[6] On 11 March 1967 Striganov called Kuchumov to address a committee in Moscow, comprising a phalanx of security and military officials: Comrade Z. V. Nordman, vice-director of the KGB; Comrade T. M. Shukayev, vice-directors of the MVD; M. G. Kokornikov, the chief of engineering regiments of the Red Army; Major Bogdanchikov of the Kaliningrad Communist Party. The committee asked Kuchumov to prepare a briefing for the Executive Committee of the Council of Ministers, the highest administrative organ of the Russian Federation.[7]

Kuchumov presented his briefing on 21 March 1967 at 4 p.m. He was asked back two weeks later, on 5 April. The minutes of these meetings are not here. But the title of the topic of discussion is: 'A plan of practical affairs to organize the search [for the Amber Room]'. So the Soviet authorities were absolutely serious about the Amber Room and Kuchumov, the son of a carpenter, had become a driving force behind national policy on the matter.

We rifle through the file. We find a letter that explains how Kuchumov's Amber Room plan came to the attention of the authorities in Moscow. In October 1963 he wrote to Mrs L. S. Karpekina, vice-director of the Committee of Culture of the Executive Committee of LenGorSoviet: 'I treat it as my debt to say to you the following. 1. The searching for the Amber Room in which I took part in 1946 and 1949 had mostly the character of observation or scouting, a preparation exercise for a wider-scale search with modern techniques.' Kuchumov confessed there were no special funds and that the investigations he conducted with Tronchinsky in 1946 and then Gerhard Strauss in 1949 were superficial.

This is bizarre. Superficial? A scouting exercise? The 1946 mission was a watershed, the investigation that overturned Brusov's findings. We can only presume that Kuchumov was downplaying his success in 1946 and 1949 to appeal for more resources.

Kuchumov continued: '2. Having analysed the documents and witness statements, one can suppose that the Amber Room was not transferred from Kaliningrad and was hidden in a special bunker.'[8]

Kuchumov appeared to have compelling new evidence. He claimed to have identified a specific bunker in which the Amber Room might have been concealed, a reason to resume the search.

The file goes back to the winter 1949, revealing where the bunker story came from. We already know that in 1949 Kuchumov had quizzed GDR art historian Gerhard Strauss in the Hotel Moscow in Kaliningrad about the location of a bunker. But we did not realize how critical this bunker would be. In the report before us, Kuchumov revealed that when he failed to get results from Strauss, he summoned Professor Brusov from Moscow – someone we had assumed had dropped out of the picture in 1946.

According to the file, Professor Brusov was sixty-four years old in 1949 and had been retired from his job at the State Historical Museum. He gave a new witness statement to Kuchumov, the one that had been cut out of Jelena Storozhenko's ready-reckoner. But it is here in the file from St Petersburg and it makes for startling reading. In it Brusov completely contradicted his conclusions of 1945. Originally Brusov had written that the Amber Room had been destroyed. In 1949 he claimed: 'I think that the Amber Room exists because in the Knights' Hall, the place where Alfred Rohde said he had stored it, we found only the remains of burned doors. We did not find pieces of bronze or any other anti-inflammables [glass, mirrors, stone mosaics].'[9]

It was an incredible about-face, and Kuchumov must have presented Brusov with incontrovertible new evidence to jog his memory but it has not been detailed here. What has been noted in this file was that once the professor had reviewed his main conclusion, he revisited all of his 1945 findings. On 29 December 1949 Brusov stated:

When I was [in Kaliningrad] in 1945, Rohde suggested to me that I search a cellar on Steindamm Strasse. Rohde, who had a key to this cellar, went three floors underground and I found several museum items there. I was not looking for the Amber Room since I thought it had been burned. I only searched the rooms that Rohde showed me and did not pay attention to several others in this large bunker.

Here was the root of Kuchumov's bunker theory. There were rooms in a bunker that had never been searched. It was the same bunker that Brusov had talked to Kuchumov about in 1946. It was not a new story. But in 1949, when Kuchumov asked to be taken to the bunker, Brusov was unable to find it again. 'My memory is not good,' he conceded. 'I could remember the street, Steindamm Strasse, but I could not exactly point out the building [beneath which the bunker lay].'

Our file from St Petersburg shows that after Brusov was sent back to Moscow in 1949, Kuchumov sat as a special adviser to a Kaliningrad-based team that searched for this bunker from that year until 1960 and it was shortly after this date, having failed to find it, that Kuchumov contacted Mrs L. S. Karpekina in Leningrad, appealing for more backing.

As we scan the members of the 1949–60 search team that hunted for the bunker, a piece of the puzzle slips into place. We see that the chairman was Comrade Veniamin Krolevsky, secretary of the Kaliningrad Communist Party, the man who wrote (under an alias) the *Kaliningradskaya Pravda* articles of 1958.[10] This was the series which first revealed to the Soviet public that Professor Brusov's original findings were wrong, his powers of deduction at fault, and that the Amber Room had in fact survived the war and was being concealed in a secret bunker.

So the Leningrad curator Kuchumov, Krolevsky's special adviser, had not stopped at disproving Brusov's 1945 findings. He had brought Brusov back to Kaliningrad in 1949 and made him recant. And then in 1958 a close colleague of Kuchumov's had launched a broadside against Professor Brusov in *Kaliningradskaya Pravda*, ridiculing his findings and his powers of recall. We can only conclude that Kuchumov had a hand in these articles. With the professor out of the way, Kuchumov was free to promote his bunker theory to Leningrad, pushing it ever higher until he and his plan reached the Executive Committee of the Council of Ministers of the Russian Federation. But what was it that made everyone so sure that Brusov had got it wrong in 1945?

The file from the literature archive goes back to the 1940s. One year before Kuchumov's second visit to Kaliningrad, he joined the Communist Party of the Soviet Union, his card number 08740331.[11] Kuchumov was now among the 7 per cent of Soviet citizens who chose to embrace the system.[12] He began to write propaganda. Among the papers we have here is a draft of an article by him, entitled 'The Wonderful Palaces of Pushkin and Pavlovsk Rise out of the Ash and Rubble'.[13] In it he praised the actions of the Red Army in Königsberg during the summer of 1945:

The Soviet army preserved cultural treasures, even those that belonged to the enemy. The soldiers of the Königsberg regiments, when they learned that under the rubble was hidden the famous Amber Room, took part in the searching, within the ruins, cellars and bunkers... with an enthusiasm that never waned.

Some were so industrious that Kuchumov gave them a special mention:

A feat was achieved by Guard Major Rakitsin, who found gilded furniture stolen from the Catherine Palace in the rubble of Königsberg. With the help of his men, he carried forty pieces through the city to an empty apartment where he was staying. They were damaged. The silk was ripped. The legs were broken and during the evenings, after serving his duty, the major glued back together every broken part.

Kuchumov described:

a Red Army recruit from Potava, Misha Kulot, who wrote to me in February 1947. '... I worked in the rubble and I found 100g piece of beautiful amber. If you need it I can send it to you. This piece was with me everywhere. Even in Sakhalin Island. Now I have brought it home.' Kulot was an ordinary Russian soldier who carefully took with him an amber detail, believing it was part of the Amber Room that he wanted to give back to us. What a contrast to the behaviour of the Nazis in our Motherland.

He concluded:

At the end of the war it was impossible to say 'my story', only 'our story', about the preserving and returning of treasures from the palace museums. I have enough examples to prove to you [the reader]... the high-spirit and culture of all Soviet soldiers and officers who carefully guarded the peaceful works of our nation built on Communism.

Colonel Avenir Ovsianov, director of the Kaliningrad Centre for Coordinating the Search for Cultural Relics, had told us a strikingly different version of events, one that raised questions about the discipline and motives of the Red Army in Königsberg. If Ovsianov was right, then Kuchumov was blinkered by his patriotism. We will have to read everything else Kuchumov wrote with this in mind.

The last report in the file was compiled by Kuchumov and takes us back to the critical year of 1946. 'Destiny of the Amber Room' is its title.[14] There are no official stamps. It is full of crossings-out. As we begin to read, we see that in it Kuchumov rehearsed his argument for Moscow, preparing the conclusions that would eventually topple Professor Brusov and reinstate the search for the Amber Room. The document is vital. It should explain what evidence Kuchumov amassed, illuminating the critical new facts that the Leningrad curator had discovered, evidence that eventually persuaded Professor Brusov himself to reconsider his conclusions.

Kuchumov began this draft (as he began his final report to Moscow) with his most important discovery of 1946: the remains of three stone mosaics in the Knights' Hall of Königsberg Castle. '22 March 1946. Near the entrance to the Knights' Hall, beneath a staircase we found three totally burned and discoloured mosaic pictures from the Amber Room... only when touching them did they disintegrate into tiny pieces.' These stone mosaics had once hung from hooks on the large amber panels of the Amber Room and had been commissioned by Catherine the Great in the eighteenth century.

In his final report to Moscow, Kuchumov would argue: 'This [discovery of the stone mosaics] cannot serve as evidence that the Amber Room was lost in a fire.' He pointed out that only three out of four stone mosaics were to be found in the Knights' Hall. This suggested that the Amber

Room had been broken up and, wherever the fourth mosaic had been hidden, the amber panels would be there too.

Kuchumov told Moscow that he was convinced of this theory because he had found no other charred pieces of the Amber Room in the Knights' Hall (amber and wooden backing boards). He advised Moscow that the space where the stone mosaics had been discovered, under the stairs beside the door, was far too small to have also accommodated the constituent parts of the Amber Room – a dozen large panels twelve feet high made of amber, ten amber panels just over three feet high and twenty-four sections of amber skirting board. 'This forces us to reject the loss of the amber panels in this room,' he concluded to Moscow.

We had found this argument slightly difficult to follow the first time we had read it in papers from the literature archive. We could not understand why Kuchumov's discovery in the Knights' Hall of the charred stone mosaics in 1946 did not simply reinforce the evidence found by Professor Brusov in the Knights' Hall in 1945. The logical conclusion should have been that, as everyone was finding burned pieces of the Amber Room in the Knights' Hall, it had been incinerated there. But Kuchumov concluded the opposite and Moscow accepted his findings. Until now we had given Kuchumov the benefit of the doubt, presuming that he must have gathered additional evidence, complex technical details that he had decided not to burden the senior bureaucrats with. But where were they? Not in this report.

This report is bereft of any new evidence. It reveals how Kuchumov failed to explore the most obvious possibilities. Although he was at pains to describe the cavity where he found the stone mosaics as too small to house the amber panels, he did not even consider that the crates containing other sections of the Amber Room could have been stored elsewhere in the Knights' Hall (which was vast and still half empty by April 1945).

Kuchumov made much of the fact that he could not find a single charred remnant of amber in the Knights' Hall, but in his analysis he ignored a fact he must, as an amber expert, have known: the melting point for amber (between 200°C and 380°C) was far lower than that needed to incinerate the kind of stone used by Florentine carvers like Dzokki. If three stone and glass mosaics were reduced to a fine powder, including pieces of malachite that burns at 1,084°C and pieces of glass that burns at 1,400°C, then there would have been nothing left of the amber panels themselves.

Kuchumov highlighted his failure to find in the Knights' Hall other elements of the Amber Room (bronze candelabras, glass mirrors, glass and crystal pilasters). But he failed to consider that Soviet troops and trophy brigades had occupied the castle site for sixty-one days prior to Brusov's arrival in May 1945. The crime scene had never been secured. Almost a year passed before Kuchumov came to the Knights' Hall (in March 1946), plenty of time for the hall to have been swept clean of souvenirs of value by Soviet troops.

Kuchumov would write in his 1948 propaganda articles that some soldiers had come forward with amber trophies, such as Misha Kulot, who admitted to carrying a nugget that he believed had come from the Amber Room all the way to Sakhalin Island and back again. And yet Kuchumov never mentioned the possibility that Soviet soldiers had looted as he drafted this report, one that is for us beginning to resemble a 'cheat sheet' in which the curator assembled the argument that the Amber Room had survived.

Kuchumov assured Moscow that he had conducted a 'very scrupulous search'. But we now know that there was no more evidence. No great discoveries. Nothing. There were no additional technical data. The truth was that Kuchumov's investigation had been superficial and prejudiced.

We can see nothing in this report that would have convinced Professor Brusov he was wrong. He must have been coerced into abandoning his findings by other means.

We turn to the next page and find a collection of interrogation reports. Across the top Kuchumov wrote: 'Statements of citizens of Kaliningrad, collected by myself. 1946. Original papers in German'.

The first interrogation was of Paul Feyerabend, the director of the Blutgericht restaurant, which occupied the cellars beneath the Knights' Hall. We already know that Kuchumov questioned Feyerabend on 2 April 1946, but here is a statement made by Feyerabend that we have never read before. The restaurant director told Kuchumov:

At the beginning of April 1945 the packed Amber Room stood in the Knights' Hall. Several days later the city's resistance began. I was located in the cloakroom and the Knights' Hall and during the [Soviet] attack [of 7 April onwards] Alfred Rohde was nowhere to be seen. On the afternoon of 9 April... I was in the wine cellar with several servants. Later, with their agreement, I hung from the north wing of the castle a white flag as a sign of surrender.

At 11.30 p.m. that night [9 April] a Russian colonel came. When I told him everything and gave statements, he ordered the evacuation of the castle. At 12.30 a.m. [10 April], when I left, my restaurant was occupied by artillery regiments of the Red Army. The cellar and Knights' Hall were not damaged at all. After I came back from Elbing, where I had been hospitalized, I heard from Alfred Rohde that the Knights' Hall and the restaurant [beneath it] had been burned down.

This is extraordinary. According to Paul Feyerabend, the fire that incinerated the Knights' Hall had begun after the Red Army occupied Königsberg Castle. The Amber Room was, according to Feyerabend, packed into crates in the hall when he surrendered to a Russian colonel. This can only mean one of two things: the Amber Room was removed by Soviet troops from the Knights' Hall after the German surrender or it was destroyed in a fire started by the Red Army.

Kuchumov dismissed Paul Feyerabend as an unreliable witness who 'mixed up facts and dates'. He chose not to attach any importance to the restaurant director's statement. In fact he ignored it all together, making no mention of it in the reports to Moscow we have seen. The great curator was intent on providing only one view of history. Our view of him is changing.

If Feyerabend was telling the truth, then Kuchumov knew as early as 1946 that the Amber Room had been stolen or burned by the Red Army. Yet he chose to promulgate a line that would lead to a search across the Soviet Union and Germany in pursuit of Nazi thieves and their hiding place.

If Feyerabend had recalled correctly, then George Stein, the West German *hobby-Historiker*, had been remarkably close to the truth when he threatened to go public in 1975, accusing the Soviet and GDR government archives of sitting on data that would solve the mystery of the Amber Room.

If Feyerabend was right, then so was Colonel Avenir Ovsianov, and it is more than likely that the Ministry of Defence archives in Podolsk contain documents that would corroborate the story that units of the Red Army or trophy brigades inadvertantly destroyed the Amber Room and stole any pieces that survived the fire.

Tucked at the back of Kuchumov's report, 'Destiny of the Amber Room', are a few loose documents written on graph paper that take the story back to the beginning. The summer of 1945.

We have before us 'Extracts from report notes of Professor A. Brusov to Special Committee of Cultural and Educational Institutions. Note: It concerns the fate of the Amber Room, which was gifted to Peter I and located in the Tsarskoye Selo and moved by the Germans from there.'[15]

We have previously seen only an extract from Professor Alexander Brusov's diary of his mission in 1945, sent to us from the Leninka, the Lenin Library in Moscow.

This document might hold the key. In this report, Brusov wrote:

I was lucky to learn the following. Packed into cases, the Amber Room was placed in the Knights' Hall of Königsberg Castle beside another collection, the furniture of the Countess Keyserlingk. In the spring of 1945 it was decided to evacuate the Amber Room to Saxony (document attached) and for this reason Rohde visited Saxony...

Brusov described how, after returning from Saxony, Alfred Rohde prepared the room for evacuation but then fell ill: 'For some weeks he did not appear in the museum, according to witness Paul Feyerabend, who ran the Blutgericht...' By the time Rohde had recovered, there were no train carriages available to take the room to Saxony, a story that Brusov verified with local people, who told him that the last chance to evacuate anything to central Germany by train had been at the end of January.

Brusov reported: 'The same Paul Feyerabend was in the castle up until the capture and says the Amber Room was in cases at the moment of surrender and burned there later during a fire that destroyed the north wing of the edifice.' When Brusov inspected this area he found 'traces of fire, ash heaps and ash covering the entire floor' and also 'small pieces of burned wooden strips and parts of cases and some parts of mouldings and copper hinges from the doors, which were taken by Germans from the Tsarskoye Selo and moved to Königsberg along with the Amber Room'. He drew a clear conclusion: 'Summarizing all the facts, we can say that the Amber Room was destroyed between 9 and 11 April 1945 since some officers of the Red Army who inspected the castle on 11 April could find no cases in the Knights' Hall.'

Kuchumov had kept this crucial report that repeated Feyerabend's evidence and yet when Feyerabend told Kuchumov exactly the same story one year later, the curator chose to dismiss it.

Kuchumov also transcribed, on this graph-paper addendum, extracts from Brusov's diary that extend beyond the entries we have read in the photocopies from the Lenin Library.

On 25 June 1945 Brusov wrote: 'I can't get anything out of Alfred Rohde. He barely talks. I would like [the NKVD] to interrogate Rohde. I would like them to talk to him seriously rather than treating him with kid gloves. I believe that Rohde will not say anything when you are nice to him as he is a committed fascist.'[16] So when Kuchumov told Moscow in 1946 that 'the mistake of Professor Brusov was that he believed easily the words of Rohde... forgetting that he was dealing with a Nazi fanatic', he had already read this entry in Brusov's diary and knew his accusation to be false.

In another extract, dated 2 July 1945, Brusov wrote:

We asked General Pronin, commander of Königsberg, for a car to collect the archive of Castle Wildenhoff. He refused, saying there was not enough petrol. But around us everyone is using cars. For want of twenty-five litres of petrol the archive is going to die. 1st Moscow Division is using [Wildenhoff] Castle as barracks. Storerooms are never locked. What can I do? I must try and persuade the military to go to the archive, but I am not confident.

Even in 1945 Professor Brusov was worried about the behaviour of the Red Army, believing that treasures were at risk.

According to these extracts from Brusov's diary, he was not the only one concerned at the mêlée. On 8 July 1945 Brusov wrote: 'General Galitsky of the 11th Guards Army arrived and gathered a meeting of trophy brigades, treasure hunters and *komandirovochnya* [people on *komandirovat* trips] and in very rough speech called everyone "free-marketeers". Galitsky said: "I will not allow anything else to be taken from the city. I will cancel the guards in all the store places."'

Trophy brigades and *komandirovochnya*, treasure hunters part-time and professional, exactly the scene in Königsberg described by Colonel Avenir Ovsianov. Even General Galitsky had become concerned at the level of looting, threatening to throw all the thieves out of Königsberg. The Soviets would have to stamp on the story.

Brusov continued in his diary:

We are still working in the castle. We have found very interesting Chinese, Meissen and Berlin porcelain and two marble busts given by Mussolini. What is going to happen to all these things? My mood is spoilt. Why should we continue working? Should I go back to Moscow?'

This was a very different Königsberg from that conjured by Kuchumov in his propaganda articles of 1948. Brusov's city was occupied by thieves and nothing in it was safe, as all of them were wearing the uniform of the Red Army. Kuchumov's Königsberg was a crime-free zone where the Soviet troops struggled to piece together the shattered legacy of the tsars.

Brusov's last diary entry was dated 13 July 1945. He wrote:

I found four boxes with very good porcelain that fell down from the [castle's] third floor to the second. Lots of things were broken but forty pieces survived. I have packed them into five boxes for Moscow. I have stopped searching. Everything is packed into sixty boxes. I will give things to the archive where they have special security.

We know from reading previous extracts from Brusov's diary that among the items in these crates were thousands of pieces from the Königsberg Albertus-University amber collection. Brusov told Kuchumov that he had handed these sixty crates to a Red Army guard, and they had subsequently vanished. It was another incident that Comrade Krolevsky (a.k.a.

Dmetriev) would distort in *Kaliningradskaya Pravda* in 1958, accusing 'Barsov' of the theft.

Kuchumov kept something else we had never seen before, a 'fourteen-page defence', written by Brusov after *Kaliningradskaya Pravda* published its assault on him. Professor Brusov was incandescent: 'This story is portrayed in the most fantastic way. So many facts are distorted and of course as I appear in the story, thinly disguised as "Barsov", I am strongly against this rubbish.'[17] Brusov repeated his concerns about indiscriminate Red Army looting and added that, far from not thoroughly investigating the bunker on Steindamm Strasse (which Kuchumov would develop into his major theory of the 1960s and 1970s), he had visited it in 1945 and discovered that 'Some people had got there before me and taken all the important things.'

The 'people' were undoubtedly Soviet troops or trophy brigades and their reports are probably in the closed section of the Podolsk archive.

Kuchumov wrapped distorted evidence around his theory of 1946 to make it fly. He joined the Communist Party in 1948 and wrote stories about the Red Army that he knew not to be true. He rail-roaded Brusov in 1949, forcing him to recant, and was closely connected with the *Kaliningradskaya Pravda* articles of 1958 that destroyed Brusov's character and conclusions. Kuchumov steered all subsequent Amber Room searches to follow his reasoning. In the early 1970s, he forged a conspiratorial relationship with the KGB, reporting to it far more intimately than he did to his colleagues in Kaliningrad. While Brusov sank, it was Kuchumov who would be embraced by the Motherland, fêted by Gorbachev with the Lenin Prize. And then of course there were the regrets of an old man, the embarrassment and shame hinted at in his book, *The Amber Room*.

Anatoly Kuchumov had lied. His die was cast on 30 June 1941 when seventeen train carriages pulled out of Leningrad bound for a secret location in Siberia without the panels from the Amber Room. At this moment the life of the inexperienced curator, who had concealed the Soviet's unique treasure rather than evacuate it, changed for ever. We know from his book that Anatoly Mikhailovich Kuchumov was haunted by his decision, realizing that, had the panels from the Amber Room been evacuated to Siberia, they would have been returned to Leningrad in 1944, with all the other saved treasures, and reinstalled in the Catherine Palace when it was restored.

By the time Kuchumov was sent to reinvestigate the fate of the Amber Room in March 1946, he had good reason to be worried about his error of judgement. The literature archive files show that Kuchumov was monitoring the fate of a colleague, Ivan Mikryukov, the former director of Pavlovsk Palace, who had been exiled to Kazakhstan, accused of having packed his palace treasures too early and being 'defeatist'. It would soon be well publicized in the Soviet Union that a team of Nazis had taken only thirty-six hours to dismantle and carry off the Amber Room. Working in a climate of spiteful recriminations, Kuchumov must have felt extremely vulnerable.

He had no choice other than to dedicate the rest of his career to bringing back to life that which he had lost, spending thirty-nine years looking for it and forty-eight years writing about it in a book that concluded with the words 'the Amber Room did not die'. It could not have been 'deliberately destroyed'.

But the reason why the Soviet authorities were so ready to dismiss Brusov's conclusions of 1945 in favour of Kuchumov's ramshackle theory of 1946 is less obvious and has to be prised from the history of the Cold War.

We know that in April 1945 the US Army broke its agreement with the Soviet Union, stalking into the Soviet Zone of Germany to take the Reichsbank gold and priceless caches of German art. But we also read in the files of the National Archives and Records Administration (NARA) in Washington and in war-time papers kept at the Public Records Office in London that when Berlin fell in May 1945, Allied intelligence immediately began picking up reports that the Soviets were plundering the British, French and US sectors in retribution.

By 18 October 1945, when the International Military Tribunal opened at Nuremberg, emotions were running high. A favourite story doing the rounds among British and American prosecutors was that the Soviet Union only erected fences around its military camps to give the animals in the woods some peace. The Soviets countered with a saying of their own (reminding all that it was the USA that had first broken international compensation agreements by seizing the Nazi gold): 'While we were taking the Reichstag,' the Soviet slogan went, 'who was taking the Reichsbank?'[18]

However, soon there were so many priceless things missing from German collections in regions swarmed over by the Red Army that allegations of wanton behaviour by Soviet trophy brigades and regular troops would not go away. Where was the 'Pergamum Altar', American journalists asked, referring to the ancient Hellenistic altar of Zeus that had been on display in Berlin until it was evacuated to an anti-aircraft tower in the capital? Where was the 'Trojan Gold', excavated by Heinrich Schliemann and bequeathed in 1881 to the Pre and Early History Museum in Berlin as 'a gift to the German people for ever to be shown in the German capital'.[19] It was last seen on 1 May 1945 in three crates that were also stored in a Berlin anti-aircraft tower. Where was the Bremen Kunsthalle collection? The 1,715 drawings, 3,000 prints and fifty paintings by Dürer, Goya, Titian, Rembrandt and Cézanne had been evacuated to Karnzow Castle, a country estate north of Berlin. And the list went on and on: a Gutenberg Bible (one of only forty still in existence); the stained glass from St Mary's Church in Frankfurt an der Oder; the entire Dresden State Art Collections (including works by Rembrandt, Vermeer, Velázquez, as well as Raphael's *Sistine Madonna*). The Red Army was implicated in all of these disappearances.

In 1946 Dr Hermann Voss, director of the Dresden State Art Collections, had told American interrogators, preparing evidence for Nuremberg: 'Immediately the Russians occupied Dresden, a commission called the Trophy Organization [*sic*] appeared to make a choice of the best works of art belonging to the Saxon state... Almost all... were selected by the Russians and disappeared.'

The Soviets denied any responsibility but, to assure the Allies, Stalin ordered an investigation into the behaviour of his trophy brigades, appointing Alexander Porivayev, a member of the Central Committee of the Communist Party of the Soviet Union, as inquiry chairman.[20]

In February 1946 the USSR opened its case at Nuremberg, calling to the stand Joseph Orbeli, then director of the State Hermitage museum in

Leningrad, who drew the world's attention to German looting and the destruction of Leningrad's cultural trophies as acts that encompassed all Soviet suffering. Orbeli talked of 'intentional wrecking', the burning down of great halls, the stealing of parquet floors, priceless treasures ripped from the walls. These palaces were not military installations, Orbeli said. They were ambassadors of Russian culture that spoke on behalf of the Motherland. They should have been accorded the privileges due to them under international law.

One month after Orbeli spoke Anatoly Kuchumov was put on a train to Königsberg, with orders to staunch another allegation about wilful destruction by the Red Army. Only this one was far more dangerous, as it involved one of the Soviet Union's own treasures. Professor Brusov had already given an interview to TASS revealing that the Amber Room had been destroyed or looted, implicating Soviet troops in its demise. Moscow had to prevent this potentially explosive news from spreading before it could be manipulated by the Allies. Kuchumov would quickly turn the Amber Room story on its head, delivering a different (and more useful) conclusion that enabled the authorities in Moscow to point to a 'still-missing' Amber Room as evidence of how the Motherland had suffered at the hands of the Nazis.

Stalin's inquiry into the actions of the trophy brigades dragged on in secret but claimed some high-profile scalps. Marshal Zhukov, who had led the fight-back against the Nazi invasion and the battle for Berlin, was exiled to Odessa, accused of filling his Moscow dacha with German art works. General Ivan Serov, head of the NKVD in Germany, was accused of looting by MGB director Viktor Abakumov. In the furore, Serov turned the tables on his rival, and in 1951 it was the MGB chief who was arrested, and three years later tried for treason and executed. Stories of Abakumov's fate spread panic throughout the Red Army and security services. Any Soviet citizen who had stolen art works would never talk about them again. The chances of finding the Amber Room, if pieces from it had been looted or rescued from the fire in the Knights' Hall, were remote.[21]

Then history was edited again.

*

335

On 31 March 1955 the Council of Ministers of the USSR announced that 'in the course of the Great Patriotic War, during battles on German territory, the Soviet Army saved and removed to the Soviet Union masterpieces of classical painting from the collection of the Dresden Gallery'.[22] This was a revelation. The treasures from Dresden had not been seen since April 1945, when the Nazis concealed them in a salt mine, twelve miles east of the city. As well as confirming that the art works had been 'rescued' from this mine by the Red Army, the Council of Ministers also announced in *Pravda* that they were to be returned to the GDR 'for the purpose of further strengthening and developing friendly relations between Soviet and German people'. The news provided a fraternal backdrop to critical negotiations in the Eastern bloc, the revelation coming just six weeks before Moscow signed the Warsaw Pact.

In the Soviet capital a million citizens queued outside the Pushkin Museum for a glimpse of the 'rescued' German collection that went on display before it was given back. Exhibition catalogues and posters of Raphael's *Sistine Madonna* sold out. Soviet magazines published interviews with members of the trophy brigades, who were presented as Red Army heroes who had rescued German art from the firing line.

Then in January 1957 another exchange was proposed. Soviet tanks had rolled into Budapest the previous November to crush a nationalist uprising. Poland too was in a state of unrest. On 8 January, *Pravda* reported that the USSR's First Secretary Nikita Khrushchev and Otto Grotewohl, the GDR premier, had signed a protocol reaffirming fraternal ties. At the bottom of the statement was a pledge: 'Both sides affirmed their readiness to discuss questions connected with the return on a mutual basis of cultural valuables'.[23]

Two lists would be drawn up, one of art works 'that are in the Soviet Union for temporary storage' and another of Soviet art that was in East Germany. When the Soviet list was approved on 30 July 1958, it consisted of an incredible 1,990,000 art works that had been 'rescued' from Germany. Here was the altar of Zeus from Pergamum and many other items that had vanished at the end of the war and been secreted in Soviet stores. The Soviet trophy brigades had been far more industrious than even the Allies had suspected.

The East German list was delayed until 19 October 1958 and when it arrived the Soviet authorities realized why. 'No cultural valuables from the USSR [had been found] in the GDR.' Nothing. Not a stick of furniture could be returned to Moscow, as the Americans had already given back to the Soviet Union half a million valuables at the end of the war.

Moscow had a serious problem. The forthcoming exchanges had been publicized around the world. But now the Soviets would have to hand back nearly 2 million German art works and get nothing back. They would appear to be voracious thieves while the Germans, convicted at Nuremberg for the decimation of Soviet culture, would be portrayed as victims.

The Soviets launched a damage limitation exercise. In July 1958 the Pushkin Museum in Moscow and the State Hermitage in Leningrad announced that they were to stage joint gala exhibitions of 'saved treasures'.[24]

Newspaper editors were called in and briefed on what stories to run. It was now that *Kaliningradskaya Pravda* (and then practically every other paper in the Motherland) published their dubious stories about the Amber Room. The articles revealed how 'the most valuable international art trophy in the world' had not been destroyed by fire in April 1945 but concealed by Nazis in a secret location known only to a handful of Germans. The story of the Amber Room helped to divert attention away from the embarrassing questions being asked in the Western media about why Moscow had lied for so long about looting German treasures? What else was concealed in its archives and stores?

Anatoly Kuchumov had revived the Amber Room story to save his career. Moscow had snapped his report up to ward off American allegations of Soviet impropriety. Now in 1958 revelations about the secret search for the world's most valuable missing art treasure would grab the headlines once again and save Soviet face.

Six months later East Germans joined the clamour for news about the Amber Room, having read the sensational articles in *Freie Welt*. It was fate that the *Freie Welt* articles appeared as would-be Stasi agent Paul Enke graduated from the Walter Ulbricht Academy in Potsdam-Babelsberg. This was his cue to begin searching for the Amber Room in the GDR, forming the embryonic Amber Room study group that would play into Soviet hands by generating yet more rumours about the 'still-missing' Amber Room (while ascertaining what the Germans really knew about the truth).

And once Moscow had launched the story, they had to keep looking for it in the Soviet Union too. As the mystery of its hiding place gathered momentum, ever-higher figures in the Soviet establishment became attached to what was now a patriotic mission. Perhaps, as time went by, the Soviets forgot the real story, believing instead the dogma, until 1984, when Moscow tired of paying out in pursuit of nothing and secretly called it a day, shutting down all Amber Room inquiries after thirty-eight exhausting years.

But Colonel Avenir Ovsianov, the director of the Kaliningrad Centre for Coordinating the Search for Cultural Relics, told us that this was not the end of the Amber Room story. When Communism began to teeter in the late 1980s, several high-profile art collections looted during the Second World War emerged in the Soviet Union. All of these long-concealed treasures materialized through the mediation of a quietly spoken academic from Bremen University, a man able to play all sides: trusted by Soviet apparatchiks; tolerated by former Nazi looters; courted by politicians in the Bundestag.

And after these missing art works floated to the surface in Moscow, pieces of the Amber Room emerged in Germany.

14

'So you want me to tell you about the recovered pieces of the Amber Room?' Professor Wolfgang Eichwede says, raising his eyebrows, when we meet in his study at Bremen University in April 2003. He pushes a box of Russian chocolates across the table and we see that the Catherine Palace in St Petersburg is pictured on the lid. 'Take one,' he says, popping a soft centre into his mouth. 'They're really very good.'

He settles back in his chair. 'A few months before the Berlin Wall came down in November 1989,' he recalls. 'I received a phone call from a man in Moscow. His name was Viktor Baldin and he was the director of the Shchusev Museum of Architecture. He told me he had a secret.'

Baldin confessed to Eichwede, director of Bremen University's Research Centre for Eastern Europe, that his institution had, locked away in its stores, 364 pictures and drawings that belonged to the Bremen Kunsthalle.

Not parts of the Amber Room, we ask?

'No, they appeared much later. Viktor Baldin told me that he had known about these pictures since in July 1945, while serving as a captain with the Soviet's 38th Field Engineers Brigade, he and other soldiers had found them in the cellars of Karnzow Castle, forty miles north of Berlin. They all bore markings of the Bremen Kunsthalle. Several comrades, including Baldin, brought art works back to Moscow.'

Viktor Baldin said that after the war, when Stalin ordered an investigation into looting, he panicked and gave his cache of 364 pictures to the Shchusev Museum of Architecture, where he worked. In 1989, with the Cold War coming to an end, Baldin, who had risen to become the museum's director, wanted to return the Bremen drawings as a sign of friendship. However, the authorities in Moscow had found out and were trying to block him.

Eichwede says: 'His phone call began a chain reaction. Just days after he rang me, Russian Culture Minister Nikolai Gubenko and the KGB raided the Shchusev Museum in Moscow, confiscating the 364 Bremen Kunsthalle works, sending them to the closed stores of the State Hermitage in Leningrad.' He glances up at an exhibition poster on the wall from the State Hermitage. 'I began ringing Gubenko's deputy. I made no demands. Said I simply wanted to see the Bremen items.'

A graduate of the radical student movements of 1968, Eichwede was familiar with the Soviet mindset and already had connections in Moscow. In the early 1970s he had helped initiate the first post-war public discussions about Soviet–West German relations. In 1992 the professor finally won an invitation to see the Bremen drawings.

'When I arrived at the State Hermitage, director Mikhail Piotrovsky had laid them out on the table in his office beside the Neva. We looked at them together as the snow fell outside. I was the first German to see the Bremen drawings in forty-seven years. I would not leave with them on that day but strong friendships were struck.'

On 1 March 1993, after negotiations stage-managed by Eichwede, Russia agreed to give back the Bremen works in exchange for a collection of German-owned drawings and funding from the German Bundestag to restore churches in Novgorod that had been damaged by the Nazis.

Eichwede says: 'Having agreed to the deal, my government got cold feet and blew the arrangement out of the water, saying that Germany could not be seen to reward looting. A ridiculous point of view given that we had betrayed and ransacked the Soviet Union. But our politicians said: "What else do the Russians have? We want everything back and not just the Bremen pictures." I had to go to Moscow and tell them the deal was off.'

Weeks later, more of the missing Bremen Kunsthalle collection surfaced in Moscow, when another Red Army veteran came forward after reading about Viktor Baldin in the Russian papers. The veteran had 101 drawings that he said a friend had found in Karnzow Castle in 1945. He took them in a suitcase to the German Embassy. When the Soviets found out they issued an immediate export ban. Now two parts of the missing Bremen Kunsthalle collection were stranded: one in St Petersburg, the other in Moscow.[1]

What was the connection between the Bremen drawings and the Amber Room, we ask?

'Be patient,' Eichwede says, 'The negotiations were labyrinthine. Then another missing German treasure emerged in Russia. Gregory Koslov, a curator from the Pushkin Museum in Moscow, a man who had helped to negotiate the handing over of the 101 Bremen drawings to the German Embassy, found a pile of documents in his museum that were about to be shredded. In these documents were references to German art works taken to Russia at the end of the war. There were pages of lists naming priceless exhibits we Germans all thought had been destroyed, including the so-called "Trojan Gold". What a discovery!'

The 'Trojan Gold', a hoard of ancient diadems, necklaces and earrings, a highlight of Berlin's pre-war art collections, had been among the things the Allies had accused the Soviets of stealing in 1945. The Soviets had categorically denied any responsibility, but the documents that Koslov found proved that the gold had arrived in Moscow, had been secretly taken to the Pushkin Museum and was inventoried there on 28 June 1945.

Koslov went public with the story. The German government was furious. So was Irina Antonova, Koslov's boss and the director of the Pushkin Museum. She had begun her career by helping to compile the inventory for the gold, a secret she had kept for almost fifty years.

Antonova called Koslov to her office. He later recalled: 'I told her I wanted to tell the truth. She retorted, "There are different truths... there are foolish truths and wise truth and your truth is foolish. There is also justice... You are young and inexperienced. You didn't see Peterhof burn down, but I did..."'[2] The Soviet deception over the 'Trojan Gold' was entirely excusable, nothing compared to the scale of the Nazi destruction in Leningrad, she argued.

Eichwede rolls his eyes. 'In October 1994 a German delegation arrived in Moscow to see the "Trojan Gold".[3] When they left, Irina Antonova said that although the Russians would not give it back they would display it soon. But one year later, she wrote an article in *Nezavisimaya Gazeta*, headlined: "We Don't Owe Anybody Anything."[4] Now there were three German treasures revealed as stranded in Russia: 364 Bremen drawings in St Petersburg; 101 more in the German Embassy in Moscow; and the 'Trojan Gold' locked in the Pushkin Museum stores.

Eichwede says: 'I had to break the impasse. To bring the sides together. I organized a conference in 1994, "*The Spoils of War*", to get the Germans and the Soviets to talk. I suggested they make a unique kind of exchange that didn't involve giving anything back.'

We look perplexed. He signals us to be patient and says: 'Why not help re-create the Amber Room, I asked the Germans? Prussian King Frederick William I gave the original Amber Room to the Russian Tsar Peter the Great as a diplomatic gift. Why couldn't the Chancellor of the new Germany build for the President of the new Russia another Amber Room and soothe old wounds?'[5]

Initially no one took up Eichwede's idea and criticism of Russia intensified when, in January 1996, it was admitted to the Council of Europe.[6] The action should have resolved arguments over looted art works as Russia was now bound by international restitution law that forced it to cooperate with Germany over returns. All looted archives and art works belonging to member states were to be given back.

But Culture Minister Nikolai Gubenko, who had thwarted Baldin's attempts at returning the 364 drawings to Bremen in 1989, was still determined that nothing from Russia would go to a nation that had wrought destruction on the Soviet Union. He convinced the Duma to set in passage a bill to nationalize all cultural properties seized by the Red Army during the war so that German treasures would be redefined as 'reparations for damages incurred'.

Eichwede pops a Russian chocolate into his mouth. 'What a nightmare. Then, in the summer of 1997, I got another phone call. In the middle of the night. Half an hour later I was sitting in a dubious restaurant in a Bremen backstreet with a man who, quite frankly, was mentally destroyed. Now I come to your topic. This man told me that his father, a Wehrmacht veteran, had fought outside Leningrad in 1941 and had stolen part of the Amber Room and that he still had it.'

We look aghast.

Eichwede stifles our attempt to ask another question. 'It sounds ridiculous but it was true. This man, Hans Achterman, had a Florentine stone mosaic depicting the senses "Touch and Smell" in his bedroom.'

A stone mosaic from the Amber Room. Anatoly Kuchumov had found only three of the Amber Room's four Florentine stone mosaics in Königsberg in 1946. One had been missing and Kuchumov had reasoned, wherever that was, so were the panels of the Amber Room.

Eichwede continues: 'Achterman told me that while watching a television documentary about the Amber Room in 1978 featuring *hobby-Historiker* George Stein, he recognized a picture of the missing mosaic when it flashed up on the screen. It was identical to the one that lay in his parents' attic. At the time he did nothing. He was frightened. However, eight years later, with his father dead and local newspapers carrying stories about priceless German artefacts stuck in Russia, Achterman thought he could make some money. By 4 a.m. we were talking cash for the mosaic.

'Achterman dithered. Eventually as the sun rose, the restaurant manager came over and said, "Hans, you're discussing with a professor who understands these issues. This is your one chance. For God's sake, tell him how much you want for the stone mosaic." We started at 400,000 DMs and got down to 250,000. I wrote the agreement on the back of a beer mat and then, with the pen in his hand, Hans Achterman changed his mind and left me there. With the cigarette butts.'

Although Achterman went to ground, news of the reappearance of the missing stone mosaic from the Amber Room travelled fast when the German police announced they would arrest him for theft. The *Daily Telegraph* reported: 'One of the greatest art mysteries of the century, the whereabouts of the sumptuous Amber Room, took a new twist yesterday after the discovery in Germany of a mosaic, believed to have been part of the priceless palace treasure.'[7]

US News reported: 'Missing: Priceless Room Last Seen in World War. Bits of Tsarist Treasure Mysteriously Resurface.'

Having endured eight years of vilification over the Bremen pictures and the 'Trojan Gold', Russia leapt on the PR opportunity. Russian Prime

Minister Viktor Chernomyrdin called for the mosaic's return. It was evidence that the Germans were still clinging on to his country's most precious treasure. There was hysterical speculation in the Russian press that the Amber Room was about to be found – in Germany. All of the hoary old stories about its disappearance – an élite unit of Nazis evacuating the room from Königsberg to a secret location codenamed BSCH – were regurgitated. But of course the Amber Room failed to materialize.

Eichwede says: 'It was the break that Russia needed. All eyes were on the Amber Room and memories were jogged about Soviet loss. Germany was now on the defensive.'

The German Foreign Office appealed for calm, while further inquiries into the provenance of the stone mosaic were carried out. And then a wealthy housewife from West Berlin came forward, saying that she owned a chest of drawers that had come from the Amber Room, too.

The housewife had seen an article about Hans Achterman's stone mosaic that was illustrated with a picture of the original Amber Room. Among the furnishings she had spotted a delicate, intricately inlaid eighteenth-century chest that was now in her living room, filled with tablecloths and napkins.

Then newspapers picked up on a sale at Christie's in London. Two years earlier the auction house had sold for 15,000 dollars a palm-sized centurion's head carved from amber. Eichwede says: 'It was an old piece. Mature. Honeyed. Christie's speculated that it was connected to the Amber Room.'

However, what the Russians made no mention of in the ensuing publicity was that the stone mosaic, the centurion's head and the chest of drawers proved nothing about the fate of the Amber Room itself, since all of these pieces had become separated before the Amber Room reached Königsberg in December 1941, and therefore could not have been transported to the supposed secret Nazi hiding place in which the Amber Room was allegedly stashed.

We traced the centurion's head to Munich, where an art dealer acting for the collector who bought it (a German with a passion for old amber) revealed that there was an auction label stuck to the back of the head that dated from the 1920s. It probably left Russia after the Revolution.

The chest of drawers. There was no mention of it in the Königsberg Castle Gift Book, which carefully listed each item that Alfred Rohde received in December 1941. The chest must have been stolen from the Catherine Palace before the Amber Room was transferred to Königsberg.

And finally the stone mosaic. Hans Achterman maintained up until his death that his father had taken the mosaic as a souvenir when he and five other soldiers had dismantled the Amber Room in the Catherine Palace in 1941. If what he claimed was true then he was a member of the squad that packed up in just thirty-six hours that which Anotoly Kuchumov failed to save. The fact that the fourth stone mosaic also never reached Königsberg is confirmed by studying the photographs taken to illustrate the *Pantheon* article written by Alfred Rohde in 1942. In one photograph of the room reassembled in Königsberg Castle, the reflection in a mirror revealed an empty space in the opposite wall where the fourth mosaic would have hung.

Rather than proving that German thieves were still concealing the Amber Room, the discovery of the fourth mosaic undermined the central plank of the Soviet case that the Amber Room had survived the fall of Königsberg. In Anatoly Kuchumov's private papers he argued that the absence of the fourth mosaic from the pile of ash he found in the Knights' Hall was proof that the fourth mosaic was concealed elsewhere, together with the amber panels. But of course the mosaic did not reappear until after Kuchumov's death and so he would not live to see his theory undermined.

These details did not matter in Russia, where former Culture Minister Nikolai Gubenko, now a deputy in the Duma, claimed that his nation's greatest missing treasure was buried in Germany. The Amber Room was being hawked bit by bit by German thieves, Gubenko and Russian newspapers speculated. The fate of the Amber Room was once again manipulated, this time to justify Russia's decision never to return to Berlin anything taken by the Red Army during the war. In April 1998 the Russian constitutional court ordered an unwilling President Yeltsin to authorize the law nationalizing wartime loot.

In Germany some would benefit from the renewed interest in the Amber Room too. Ruhrgas AG, a German energy provider with considerable

*Dr Ivan Sautov (left), director of the Catherine Palace, signing
the deal with German energy provider Ruhrgas AG executives
to sponsor the reconstruction of the Amber Room*

assets in Russia, agreed to sponsor the building of a new Amber Room in
St Petersburg, taking up Eichwede's idea.

The Russians had already begun this huge project but had run out of
money. On 6 September 1999, Ruhrgas AG representatives met Dr Ivan
Sautov, director of the Catherine Palace, and the Russian Minister of
Culture to sign with amber fountain pens a sponsorship deal worth 3.5
million dollars. The German government was peeved, sending its ambassador from Moscow to witness the occasion rather than its Minister of
Culture from Berlin.

Eichwede smiles. 'Ruhrgas wanted a high-profile cultural project
to buy into. Their first and only interest was a commercial one. The
Amber Room was worth a fortune for Russian politicians and German
businessmen.'

He stifles a yawn. 'It was exhausting. And then things got really complicated. Achterman and his stone mosaic reappeared. He wanted to
reconsider the deal we had worked out on the back of the beer mat and

eventually agreed to sell me the stone mosaic at 210,000 DMs. It was all incredibly secret. No one could know until the mosaic was back in Russia. The money was to come from Bremen businessmen. The German government could not be seen to pay.'

Eichwede called the Russian Deputy Minister of Culture in Moscow. '"I've got your missing mosaic," I told P. V. Khoroshilov. He was shocked and said, "Maybe we can come to terms."' Khoroshilov secretly flew into Bremen and struck a deal: Hans Achterman's stone mosaic would be returned to St Petersburg and the 101 Bremen pictures stranded in the German Embassy in Moscow would be released to travel to Berlin. 'We said, "We get the drawings first and then you get the stone mosaic." Khoroshilov signed the deal.'

All Eichwede needed was Berlin's approval. He flings his arms into the air. 'They said no.' Having promised to return the stone mosaic to Russia, the German government now advised that it too had changed laws governing art and reparations. The Amber Room's stone mosaic had been put on a list of items banned from export. Eichwede says: 'I was on the verge of giving up when the Mayor of Bremen rang me and said, "Look, this is ridiculous. I'm flying tomorrow to Moscow anyway, with the mosaic."' Fearing a scandal, the German government capitulated, and on 30 April 2000 the Mayor of Bremen, the president of the city's Chamber of Commerce and the German Minister of Culture presented the mosaic to President Putin and brought home 101 Bremen drawings. (However, Viktor Baldin's collection of 364 Bremen drawings would remain in the St Petersburg Hermitage and the 'Trojan Gold' would stay locked in the Moscow's Pushkin Museum stores.)

Once the story of the Amber Room had popped out of its box again, it was impossible to force it back in. Treasure hunters returned to the Erzgebirge nature park in western Saxony with metal detectors and picks. *Der Spiegel* magazine announced it was funding digs in Kaliningrad, beneath the 'Monster' and on the junction of Steindamm Strasse and Lange Reihe. Baron von Falz-Fein began writing to all his old friends, asking them to renew their efforts to find the room. A Second World War veteran in Weimar claimed to have found evidence that the Amber

Room was concealed in the tunnels that ran beneath the city. And a book dealer in Göttingen announced that he had discovered files that proved the Amber Room was buried in the Volpriehausen mine (where *hobby-Historiker* George Stein had tried to make the German story work, armed with documents suppied by the Stasi).

In St Petersburg, Dr Ivan Sautov announced that the new Amber Room would be opened on 31 May 2003 to mark the three-hundredth anniversary of the founding of that city.

Wolfgang Eichwede's telephone rings. He talks rapidly into the handset for ten minutes and then, after finishing the call, turns to us: 'The dealing is still going on. That was our Minister of Culture. He's been in St Petersburg recently to receive back the missing stained-glass windows from St Mary's in Frankfurt an der Oder. The windows vanished in the war, but now that Germany has offered to restore the organ of the Leningrad Philharmonic and the churches of Novgorod, the windows have reappeared. He took them to St Petersburg airport in the back of a taxi.' Eichwede beams.

What of the endlessly recycled Amber Room story? Does Eichwede believe that it will ever be buried?

The professor sighs, slinging his green-and-black tartan jacket over his shoulder like a hunting cape and looks us directly in the eyes. 'What can I say? Some people have princesses and fairies. Others have the Amber Room.'

In January 2003 the presses in St Petersburg were working double time. Before the new Amber Room could be unveiled to an international audience of VIPs, hundreds of copies of a special catalogue had to be printed.

Each guest arriving in St Petersburg on 31 May 2003 for the three-hundredth anniversary celebrations of the city would be able to read the *Summary Catalogue of the Cultural Valuables Stolen and Lost During the Second World War. Volume 1. The Tsarkoye Selo State Museum Zone. The Catherine Palace. Book 1.*[8] Out of a possible 100,000 lost items, the Russian government chose to illustrate the catalogue cover with a large hand-tinted photograph of the Amber Room.

In a foreword, the Deputy Minister of Culture P. V. Khoroshilov declared:

The West and especially Germany prefers to keep silent about Russia's cultural losses. Nevertheless everybody is interested in finding out how many German paintings, drawings, engravings, sculptures and objects of decorative art, archaeological finds and collections of books, still remain in Russia and what museums house them.

The Amber Room was once again listed as officially missing, the lead item in a 300-page inventory of works stolen by the Nazis from the Catherine Palace.

The Deputy Minister of Culture concluded with praise for only one West German: 'Of great help was the archive of the German scholar George Stein, who dedicated many years of his life to the search for the Amber Room... Unfortunately the work was interrupted by this scholar's tragic death.' We are sure that Stein would have been delighted to know he had made the final edit of the Soviet's Amber Room story.

Dr Sautov, director of the Catherine Palace, wrote an introduction. The Amber Room was a 'symbol of Russian cultural and art losses' and he and his staff 'are convinced that it has not perished and will be found as a result of properly organized searches'.

Director Sautov continued: 'The aim of this [catalogue] is... a concrete wish of real men to [publicize] which unique pieces of art were lost during the occupation, the Amber Room among them.' No mention here of the fire set by the Red Army that destroyed everything in the Knights' Hall of Königsberg Castle.

There followed a ten-page summary of the Amber Room story written by Larissa Bardovskaya, the head curator of the Catherine Palace, who freely lifted material from Paul Enke's book and from the untrustworthy George Stein. She concluded poignantly: 'The artistic valuables of the Catherine Palace museum are still waiting for the return to their home. The problem concerning the cultural trophies of the Great Patriotic War demands the most thorough attention from the representatives of the international community.' And these representatives were set to arrive in St Petersburg on 31 May 2003, to celebrate the city's tercentenary.

But in February 2003 another row had threatened to overshadow the unveiling ceremony. Culture Minister Mikhail Shvydkoi announced that Russia was at last to return to the Bremen Kunsthalle the 364 works taken by Red Army veteran Viktor Baldin. However, Nikolai Gubenko, now head of the Duma's Culture and Tourism Committee, appealed directly to President Putin to prevent the collection from leaving. First Deputy Prosecutor General Yury Biryukov summoned Shvydkoi to his office and warned that if he went ahead with the return he would face criminal charges.[9]

On 17 March Valentina Matviyenko, Putin's plenipotentiary in St Petersburg, waded into the row by rounding on German newspapers that had described the theft of the Bremen collection by the Red Army in 1945 as immoral. 'Destroying Peterhof was immoral,' Matviyenko said. 'It was immoral to steal the Amber Room, besiege Leningrad, destroy thousands of Soviet cities and kill millions of Russians... We have every right to make terms on the returns for it is us who paid the highest price for the Great Patriotic War.' Matviyenko concluded by accusing German private collectors of continuing to secrete Russian masterpieces in attics and cellars.[10]

On 8 April 2003, the eve of a Russian presidential visit to Germany, Putin raised the issue too. When asked about the repayment of Russian debts, run up during GDR times, a subject that was to be discussed in Berlin, Putin replied: 'The debt problem is very painful for Russia and Germany as well, not only because it is often said that Russian culture and arts were seriously damaged during the Second World War. It is also because a part of the art works removed from Russia during the war are now in private collections.'[11]

On 8 May more than 400 decorated heroes of the Great Patriotic War were invited to examine the reconstructed Amber Room as part of the commemorations for Victory Day, which is still regarded by the majority of Russians as the most important event in the political calendar. We will not forget or forgive, the veterans told Russian reporters, recalling how the original room had been 'ripped from the Motherland' as the 'Hitlerite evil-doers' pulled the siege noose tight around Leningrad in the winter of 1941.[12]

And then 31 May finally arrived. Although the VIPs had officially come to St Petersburg to attend a Russian–EU summit (whose symbolic backdrop was the three hundredth anniversary of the founding of the host city), the first major event on the itinerary was the unveiling of the new Amber Room.

Pravda online monitored the day's events.

15.30 hours. Russian President Vladimir Putin and German Chancellor Gerhard Schröder ascended the Monighetti staircase, an elaborate Italian marble flight draped with heavy crimson curtains. Above their heads was the recently restored *plafond* (Tercentenary Media Pack, Russian Federation Summary Catalogue: 'the staircase was ruined during the war and most of its [ceiling] decorations were lost').

Damaged Monighetti staircase, Catherine Palace, 1945

Following them were first ladies Doris Schröder and Lyudmila Putina, and then Tony Blair, Silvio Berlusconi, Jacques Chirac, Kofi Annan, Romano Prodi, Atal Bihari Vajapyee, Hu Jintao and thirty more heads of state and government from across the continents, the former Soviet Union and its allies.

Pravda reported: 'Russia's pride: leaders of foreign countries visit an exquisite monument of the Catherine Palace.'

Beside Brodzsky's marble *Sleeping Cupid*, the procession filed into the Formal White Dining Room and on through the gilded double-doors into the Crimson and Green Pilaster Dining Rooms (Tercentenary Media Pack, Russian Federation Summary Catalogue: 'having been completely damaged during the war the rooms acquired a new life in 1980').

Shepherded past cabinets displaying broken cherubs, crystal teardrops and fragments of Sèvres, past black-and-white photographs of Soviet craftsmen in overalls piecing back together the Leningrad palaces, the entourage entered the Portrait Hall (Tercentenary Media Pack, Russian Federation Summary Catalogue: 'the furniture set was re-created in 1970 using samples that were saved by evacuation during the war').

Having walked down corridors lined with evidence of Nazi barbarism, the world leaders and first ladies were finally led across a floor inlaid with rare hard woods, rose and amarantus, into a curtained chamber of light for the climax of the tour.

15.35 hours. *Pravda* reported: 'Russia's fabled [Amber] Room dazzles again. Twenty years of work by Russian craftsmen has returned what was called the Eighth Wonder of the World to its place in the Catherine Palace. The fate of the original is not known to this day and the long search for it proved futile.'

On an easel was displayed a delicate eighteenth-century stone mosaic ('Touch and Smell', the one that Wolfgang Eichwede had bought from Hans Achterman in a deal struck on a beer mat). Against a wall stood a chest of drawers that had once belonged to a housewife from West Berlin.

15.40 hours: Pooled footage from the VGTRK Rossiya (All-Russia State Television and Radio Company) showed a large man in a glossy Italian suit with a plump salt-and-pepper moustache glad-handing the guests. Tatiana Kosobokova, reporting for *Pravda*, wrote: 'Ivan Sautov, the head of the museum, assumed responsibilities as private tour guide to Vladimir Putin.'

A day that had begun with performances by Luciano Pavarotti, Demis Roussos and 'the famous German hard-rock group Scorpions' (who sang 'Anthem to a Great City') ended with an evening of candlelight, fountains and music. All of St Petersburg, from the acquisitive former palace deputy director Valeria Bilanina in Pushkin to the thrifty journalist Vladimir Telemakov in Ozerki, and from furniture expert *Malinki* Albina in Pavlovsk to Our Friend the Professor in the northern suburbs, sat back with thimbles of Pertsovka vodka and slivers of herring to watch great volleys of fireworks cascade over Putin's 'Window on the West' (restored at a cost of 1.5 billion dollars).

Nothing had been allowed to get in the way of this Great Day. The smarting Culture Minister Mikhail Shvydkoi, the vengeful Duma deputy Nikolai Gubenko and the patriotic plenipotentiary Valentina Matviyenko were all present and smiling (as was Professor Wolfgang Eichwede of Bremen University). And the sun too had been made to shine. Russian air force jets, armed with freezing agents, had been mobilized on missions to 'influence the rain clouds', banishing them from the skies above St Petersburg (at a cost of twenty-nine million roubles).[13]

As for the story of the Amber Room, it had been sealed forever, like an insect trapped in resin, a facsimile of the original room now served as a constant reminder of Russia's greatest loss to anyone who walked through it.

Epilogue

In the summer of 2003, we were sent more extracts of a report from the Hamburg-Eppendorf Psychiatric Hospital to the Ingolstadt coroner. Dated 25 August 1987, it stated that there was 'mutual hatred within George Stein's family'. It revealed that Elisabeth, Stein's wife, was not murdered in 1983 but committed suicide, in fear of her husband.

The report noted: 'Exactly fifteen years ago on Good Friday [1972], [George Stein] had encouraged his wife to make sacrificial cuts in his abdominal wall, using a dissecting scalpel. On Good Friday in 1982 he asked her to do it again.' On both occasions George Stein had called the police, claiming to have been attacked by knife-wielding masked raiders who warned him off the Amber Room mystery. But he had invented the stories, after forcing his wife to perform sadomasochistic acts.

When Stein was admitted to hospital for the first time in 1987, having been found in a wood outside Hamburg with stab wounds, it was on Good Friday. When he was discovered three months later, bleeding in woods outside Starnberg, his injuries were similar. And when his corpse was recovered on 20 August 1987 from a clearing in Titting Wald, the wounds from which George Stein bled to death were in the same position on his abdomen. They were all masochistic mutilations.

Stein was compulsive, convincing and manipulative. Brilliant at first, he located the missing Pskov icons. Then he became careless and clumsy. Even Stasi agent Paul Enke warned of Stein's unreliability, his propensity to tamper with Nazi documents. One of the many doctors who treated Stein realized these qualities too late, writing to a colleague, just five days before Stein died: 'I have involved myself in this case perhaps excessively and certainly in a somewhat amateurish manner.'[1]

George Stein took his own life in such a dramatic fashion, bleeding to death in an amphitheatre of beech trees, that he ensured his name would forever be associated with the Amber Room riddle he had failed to solve. In choosing ritual suicide by disembowelment (a formal act known to Japanese warriors as *seppuku*), Stein had also found a respectable alternative to dishonour and defeat.

But these truths, like so many surrounding the Amber Room, have been suppressed and deceit has been allowed to fill the resulting vacuum. The Russian government and museum authorities continue to promote the 'German scholar' George Stein whose laudable attempts to find the Amber Room were 'interrupted' by his 'tragic death'. Russian and German newspapers still suggest that Stein was murdered and speculate about fascist assassins or Cold War hit-men. All of this keeps alive the unsupportable and yet widely held view that the Amber Room was stolen and conceded as part of a Nazi conspiracy that has destroyed so many of those who have attempted to uncover it.

Some of the same newspapers that publish these claims continue to fund costly searches for the Amber Room. In summer 2003, teams from Hamburg excavated the tail end of the 'Rudi Ringel' story in Kaliningrad, looking for the secret hiding place known as BSCH. Others were scouring the old fortifications of Königsberg and the castle cellars beneath the 'Monster'. In Saxony, as we write, two competing expeditions are approaching one tunnel in the Nicolai Stollen silver mine from opposite directions. Heinz-Peter Haustein, Mayor of Deutschneudorf, burrows on the German side. Helmut Gänsel, a mining entrepreneur from Miami, digs from the Czech village of Štěchovice. And in the virtual tunnels and castles of Internet chatrooms, website editors continue to spin the Amber Room story. An e-mail sent to us in December 2003, from a website we had contacted that sponsors digs for the Amber Room in the German state of Thuringia, concluded: 'Please send some donations now. Give us what you can. We have made some major, ground-breaking discoveries and within a month, or two, will reveal the burial location of the Amber Room.'

However, the evidence, when we examined it, is clear. Soviet news footage shot inside Königsberg Castle shortly after the city fell on 9 April 1945 shows that some rooms in the castle remained intact. German eyewitnesses hiding inside the castle told Soviet interrogators that it was not burned to the ground when they surrendered on the evening of 9 April, or in the early hours of 10 April. Yet when the first official Soviet investigators arrived in Königsberg, on 31 May 1945, they reported that the castle was a charred ruin and the city's storage facilities in disarray. Professor Alexander Brusov wrote in his diary in June 1945 that many of the hiding places carefully selected by Alfred Rohde, the director of the Königsberg Castle Museum, were flooded, on fire and empty, having been opened, torched or vandalized after the German surrender by the Red Army.

We know the Soviet authorities were presented with these facts and advised by Brusov that, alongside many other treasures, the Amber Room had been destroyed between 9 and 11 April 1945. His findings were classified and buried for more than five decades, and in their place Leningrad curator Anatoly Kuchumov, who directed the campaign to discredit Brusov, fostered a fragile theory that depended for its success on no one examining it too closely.

The great curator feared that his failure to dismantle the room in the summer of 1941 would be judged as negligent. His guilty response fitted the needs of the Motherland: its Red Army stood accused by the Allies of wanton destruction and its museum storerooms were revealed to be brimming with looted German treasures. A great untruth was born and it enabled the Soviet people and their sympathizers in Europe and America to continue to believe that the East was the victim of the worst excesses of the West. The real story portrayed the Soviets as rapacious liars, something the leadership feared, given the instability across the bloc in the tumultuous decades after the war when Poland, Hungary and Czechoslovakia all threatened to break loose.

The story that the Nazis had concealed the Amber Room was given the backing of the Executive Committee of the Council of Ministers, the highest administrative organ of the Soviet Union. Who would be foolish enough to contradict it? The agony of the Soviet people was now enshrined in the missing Amber Room and it was enduring.

The world should remember Stalingrad, the 900 Days, the obliteration of so many Soviet cities, towns and villages, and the sacrifices made by the Red Army during the Second World War. But history is untidy, and as well as being the victim of unbridled German aggression, the Soviet state was a manipulative victor. Having seen their country burned, raped and robbed, Soviet soldiers became vengeful and careless.

There are only a handful of tangible truths in the saga of the Amber Room and they are enshrined in twenty-eight small pieces that fell off the walls, long before the Second World War. Today these broken amber nuggets are locked away in the Catherine Palace stores, having been glued on to a cardboard mount. They are all that is left of a Russian dream.

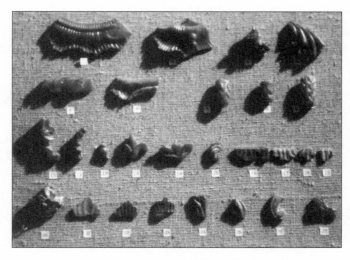

Last surviving pieces of the Amber Room

Notes

EPIGRAPH

1. Konstantin Akinsha and Gregory Koslov, *Stolen Treasure*, Weidenfeld & Nicolson, London, 1995, p. 233.

INTRODUCTION

1. Susanne Massie has researched an account of the evacuations of the Leningrad palaces. See Susanne Massie, *Pavlovsk*, Hodder and Stoughton, London, 1990.
2. See Théophile Gautier, *Voyage en Russie*, Paris, 1866.
3. The Catherine Palace had some of its rooms transformed into a museum as early as 1918.
4. Hans Hundsdörfer, who served with the 6th Panzer Division, quoted in Paul Enke, *Bernsteinzimmer Report*, Die Wirtschaft, East Berlin, 1986, pp. 15–16.
5. See footnotes in Chapter 2 for a list of files to access in the National Archives, Kew, Surrey.

CHAPTER I

1. Vera Lemus, *Pushkin Palaces and Parks*, Aurora Art Publishers, Leningrad, 1984.
2. Ibid.
3. Alexei Tolstoy began his *The Road to Calvary* trilogy in 1922 and an English translation appeared in 1946, published by Alfred Knopf, New York.
4. We later found a report critical of the 1936 evacuation plan written by Communist Party Secretary Stanislav Tronchinsky: see Kuchumov archive, Central State Archive of Literature and Art – Tsentralny Gosudarstvenny Arkhiv Literatury i Iskusstva (TGALI) 468, Opus 1, File 108.
5. Anna Podorozhnik Akhmatova, *Plantain*, Petropolis, Petrograd, 1921. Nikolai Gumilev, Akhmatova's husband, was arrested and shot that year.

6. Geraldine Norman, *The Hermitage*, Jonathan Cape, London, 1997.

7. Ibid. for the best version of the culling of museum staff.

8. We found an original version of this document in the Kuchumov archive, TGALI 468, Opus 1, File 108.

9. We later found a version of this report written by Communist Party Secretary Stanislav Tronchinsky: see Kuchumov archive, TGALI 468, Opus 1, File 108.

10. Not much is known about Schlüter's family or his early years, but the best account is carried in Heinz Ladendorf, *Der Bildhauer und Baumeister Andreas Schlüter*, Deutscher Verein für Kunstwissenschaft, Berlin, 1935.

11. Ibid.

12. Winfried and Ilse Baer, *Charlottenburg Palace, Berlin*, Fondation Paribas, Paris, 1995. Letter written on 12 November 1701.

13. J. M. de Navarro, 'Prehistoric Routes Between Northern Europe and Italy Defined by the Amber Trade', *Geographical Journal*, Vol. LXVI, No. 6, London, December 1925.

14. A. M. Kuchumov and M. G. Voronov, *The Amber Room*, Khudozhnik RSFSR, Leningrad, 1989.

15. Arnolds Spekke, *The Ancient Amber Routes and the Geographical Discovery of the Baltic*, M. Goppers, Stockholm, 1957.

16. Helen Fraquet, *Amber*, Butterworth, London, 1987.

17. Baer, *Charlottenburg Palace*.

18. Fraquet, *Amber*. Also see George and Roberta Poinar, *The Quest for Life in the Amber*, Addison & Wesley Publishing, New York, 1994.

19. Kuchumov and Voronov, *The Amber Room*.

20. Benson Mates, *The Philosophy of Leibniz*, OUP, New York, 1986, pp. 26–7.

21. Heinz Ladendorf, *Der Bildhauer und Baumeister Andreas Schlüter*.

22. Kuchumov and Voronov, *The Amber Room*.

23. Ibid.

24. *Diary of Peter the Great*, second part, Hermitage Library, St Petersburg, 1772.

25. Kuchumov and Voronov, *The Amber Room*. One taler was equivalent to just under an ounce (23.4 g) of silver.

26. Ibid.

27. 'The Amber Room of the Tsarskoye Selo Palace', *Ruskii Vestnik*, November 1877, Vol. 132, p. 391.

28. *The Letters of the Russian Tsars*, Hermitage Library, Moscow, 1861, p. 5.

29. M. P. Putzillo, 'The Beginning of Friendship between Russia and Prussia: Russian Giants in Prussian Service, 1711-1746', *Ruskii Vestnik*, March 1878, Vol. 134, pp. 376–92.

30. Ibid., p. 391.

31. Ibid.

Peace

O Come, O Come, Emmanuel

Lord Jesus Christ,
Prince of Peace and Light of the World,
may you find a generous welcome
in our hearts and homes this Christmas
as we wait in joyful and hopeful expectation
for your coming.

With profound reverence we celebrate this
wonderful Gift of your presence among us.

Draw us ever more deeply into the
Mystery and Radiance of the Incarnation
trusting that you, Emmanuel,
- are with us always.   Amen.

32. Russian State Archive for Ancient Documents – Rossiiskii Gosudarstvennyi Arkhiv Drevnikh Aktov (RGADA): Collection 11, Inventory 53, File 1, p. 9.

33. RGADA: Collection 9, Inventory 33, File 103.

34. RGADA: Collection 2, Inventory 34, File 417, p. 404.

35. O. N. Kuznetsova, *The Summer Garden and Summer Palace of Peter I*, Lenizdat, Leningrad, 1988, pp. 22–4.

36. *Pravda* means 'truth' and *Izvestiya* means 'news', literally the 'News of the Councils of Working People's Deputies of the USSR'.

CHAPTER 2

1. Author interviews with professor from Leningrad University.

2. Personalities of St Petersburg, www.ceo.spb.ru.

3. V. Telemakov, 'Secrets of Saving Museum Treasures', unpublished manuscript, 1986.

4. National Archives (NA): HW/5/29, Commander Saunders, 9 September, 1941.

5. PRO: CX/MSS/237, Commander Saunders, 13 September 1941.

6. Kuchumov Archive, TGALI 468, Opus 1, File 108, contains a similar account by Curator Popova.

7. Antony Beevor, *Berlin: The Downfall 1945*, Viking, London, 2002.

8. W. Bruce Lincoln, *Sunlight at Midnight*, Basic Books, New York, 2000.

9. Anna Podorozhnik Akhmatova, *Plantain, Petropolis*, Petrograd, 1921.

10. Telemakov, *Secrets of Saving Museum Treasures*.

11. Helen Dunmore, *The Siege*, Penguin, London, 2001.

12. Lincoln, *Sunlight at Midnight*.

13. RGADA: Collection 467, Inventory 2 (73/87), File 87b, pp. 523–4.

14. Ibid.

15. Approximately 100 lb of silver.

16. RGADA: Collection 470, Inventory 6, File 30, pp. 18,19 and 32.

17. RGADA: Collection 470, Inventory 1 (82/516), File 9, p. 1 (1746).

18. Henri Troyat, *Catherine the Great*, Phoenix Press, London, 2000.

19. Ibid. and Laurence Kelly, *St Petersburg: a Travellers' Companion*, Constable, London, 1998.

20. A. M. Kuchumov, and M.G. Voronov, *The Amber Room*, Khudozhnik RFSSR, Leningrad, 1989.

21. Théophile Gautier, *Voyage en Russie*, Paris, 1866.

22. Dr Norman Paul Förster's testimony, given at Nuremberg, 14 February 1946.

23. Author archive.

24. Unpublished letters from Anatoly Kuchumov, author archive. For more letters, see Susanne Massie, *Pavlovsk*, Hodder and Stoughton, London, 1990.

CHAPTER 3

1. Kuchumov archive: TGALI 468, Opus 1, File 123.

2. A selection of Gorky's letters, including this one and several others to Stalin, is in the Library of Congress's Soviet Archive. A facsimile of this one can also be found on www.ibiblio.org/pjones/russian/outline.html.

3. W. Derham, *The Philosphical Experiments and Observations of the Late Eminent Dr Robert Hooke*, London, 1726, p. 315.

4. Adam of Bremen, quoted in A. Spekke, *The Ancient Amber Routes and the Geographical Discovery of the Baltic*, Stockholm, 1957.

5. J. M. de Navarro, 'Prehistoric Routes Between Northern Europe and Italy Defined by the Amber Trade', *Geographical Journal*, Vol. LXVI, No. 6, London, December 1925.

6. Olaus Magnus, *Carta Marina*, Venice, 1539. See also Olaus Magnus, *De Gentibus Septentrionalibus*, Rome, 1555

7. P. J. Hartmann, *Succini Prussici, physica et civilis historia*, Frankfurt, 1677, appendix 1, translation into German of Simonis Grunovii's 1521 account, entitled *Amber and Its Sources*.

8. Gotthard Treitschke, *Origins of Prussianism: The Teutonic Knights*, G. Allen and Unwin, London, 1942.

9. Central State Archive of Moscow: Collection 8, Opus 659, File 2.

10. Antony Beevor, *Berlin, The Downfall 1945*, Viking, London, 2002.

11. Ibid.

12. Ibid.

13. Ibid.

14. Paul Enke, *Bernsteinzimmer Report*, Die Wirtschaft, East Berlin, 1986.

15. Files of the National Archive in Washington: OSS Art, US Assets. XX 8775–6.

CHAPTER 4

1. Henri Troyat, *Catherine the Great*, Phoenix Press, London, 2000.

2. Kuchumov archive, TGALI 468, Opus 1, File 119.

3. Ibid.

4. Ibid.

5. Russian translations of all letters by Alfred Rohde contained in Kuchumov archive, TGALI, Collection 468, Opus 1, File 119, pp. 39–47.

6. The letter carried a reference: '323 I–5'.

7. V. Telemakov, 'Secrets of Saving Museum Treasures', unpublished manuscript, 1986.

8. Kuchumov archive, TGALI 468, Opus 1, File 122.

9. Telemakov, 'Secrets of Saving Museum Treasures'.

10. Kuchumov archive, TGALI 468, Opus 1, File 48.

11. Ibid.

12. Telemakov, 'Secrets of Saving Museum Treasures'.

13. Kuchumov archive, TGALI 468, Opus 1, File 48.

14. Heinrich Himmler planned to raise an army of Werwolfs that was to fight a guerrilla war from secret bases in the Bavarian and Austrian Alps.

15. Kuchumov archive, TGALI 468, Opus 1, File 48.

16. Alfred Rohde, *Bernstein ein Deutscher Werkstoff*, Denkmäler Deutscher Kunst, Berlin, 1937.

17. Alfred Rohde, 'Monatsschrift für Freunde und Sammler der Kunst', *Pantheon*, Vol. XXIX, F. Bruckmann, Munich, July–December 1942.

18. Telemakov, 'Secrets of Saving Museum Treasures'.

19. Kuchumov archive, TGALI 468, Opus 1, File 48.

CHAPTER 5

1. Kuchumov archive, TGALI 468, Opus 1, File 253.

2. Edvard Radzinsky, *Stalin*, Anchor Books, New York, 1996.

3. Ibid.

4. Kuchumov archive, TGALI 468, Opus 1, File 108.

5. Kuchumov archive, TGALI 468, Opus 1, File 119.

6. Ibid.

7. V. Telemakov, 'Secrets of Saving Museum Treasures', unpublished manuscript, 1986.

8. Konstantin Akinsha, and Gregory Koslov, *Stolen Treasure*, Weidenfeld & Nicolson, London, 1995.

9. Ibid.

10. Telemakov, 'Secrets of Saving Museum Treasures'.

11. Ibid.

12. Radzinsky, *Stalin*.

13. Story told to authors by professor at St Petersburg University.

14. Kuchumov archive, TGALI 468, Opus 1, File 121.

15. Author archive.

CHAPTER 6

1. Quoted by J. O. Koehler, *Stasi*, Westview Press, Boulder, Colorado, 1999.

2. Kuchumov archive, TGALI 468, Opus 1, File 119, pp. 15–23.

3. Edvard Radzinsky, *Stalin*, Anchor Books, New York, 1996.

4. See also Helmut Müller-Enbergs, *Wer war Wer in der DDR?*, Christopher Links Verlag, Berlin, 2000.
5. Kuchumov archive, TGALI 468, Opus 1, File 119, pp. 15–23.
6. Ibid.
7. Kuchumov archive, TGALI 468, Opus 1, File 48.
8. Kuchumov archive, TGALI 468, Opus 1, File 48, p. 1.
9. Kuchumov archive, TGALI 468, Opus 1, File 120, pp. 22–3.

CHAPTER 7

1. Alexandra Hildebrandt, *The Wall*, Verlag Haus am Checkpoint Charlie, Berlin, 2002.
2. Data supplied by Forschungs und Gedenkstätte Normannenstrasse, Berlin.
3. For the history and administration of the Stasi, see J. O. Koehler, *Stasi*, Westview Press, Boulder, Colorado, 1999, and Timothy Garton Ash, *The File*, Flamingo, London, 1997.
4. BBC News reports, March 2002.
5. The Federal Authority for the Records of the State Security Sevice of the former GDR – Die Bundesbeauftragte für die Unterlagen des Staatssicherheitsdienstes der ehemaligen Deutschen Demokratischen Republik (BStU) AV14/79.
6. Helmut Müller-Enbergs, *Wer war Wer in der DDR?* Christopher Links Verlag, Berlin, 2000.
7. Ibid. See also Paul Enke, *Bernsteinzimmer Report*, Die Wirtschaft, East Berlin, 1986, for an account of Strauss's archival and Saxony investigations.
8. Gräfe interview, 'Spasennie shedevri' (Saved Masterpieces), *Sovetski Khudozhnik*, Moscow, 1977.
9. Also quoted in Enke, *Bernsteinzimmer Report*.
10. Ibid.
11. Kuchumov archive, TGALI 468, Opus 1, File 45.
12. Kuchumov archive, TGALI 468, Opus 1, File 123.
13. Sefton Delmar, *Trial Sinister* and *Black Boomerang*, Viking, New York, 1961 and 1962.

CHAPTER 8

1. BStU, KSII404/82, pp. 1–17, dated 1 October 1964.
2. Schmalfuss was the director of Stasi Department 2.
3. BStU, KSII404/82, pp. 1–17.
4. BStU, KSII404/82, p. 23, report from 23 October 1950.
5. BStU, KSII404/82, pp. 26–7, report by Oberrat Gustin.
6. Ibid.

7. BStU, AV14/79, and quoted in Paul Enke, *Bernsteinzimmer Report*, Die Wirtschaft, East Berlin, 1986.

8. BStU, 915 MfS Sekretariat d. Ministers.

9. Dated 24 June 1941.

10. Enke, *Bernsteinzimmer Report*, p. 52.

11. See BStU, AV14/79; Enke, *Bernsteinzimmer Report*; and J. Petropoulos, *Art as Politics in the Third Reich*, University of North Carolina Press, 1996.

12. Enke, *Bernsteinzimmer Report*, pp. 55-7.

13. Ibid.

14. BStU, 915 MfS Sekretariat d. Ministers.

15. For background on Rosenberg and art, see J. Petropoulos, *Art as Politics in the Third Reich*, and NA files, 'Dossier of Alfred Rosenberg', WO 208/44 94, 16 October 1946.

16. Ibid.

17. BStU, 915 MfS Sekretariat d. Ministers, and Enke, *Bernsteinzimmer Report* p. 139.

18. Ibid., p. 82.

19. The letter was dated 22 September 1962.

20. BStU, KSII404/82, pp. 146-9. Schliep served within HA VII.

21. BStU, KSII404/82, pp. 35-6.

22. See Forschungs und Gedenkstätte Normannenstrasse, Berlin, for detailed wording.

23. Enke then served within Department HA VII.

24. BStU, KSII404/82, p. 285.

25. Ibid., pp. 66-70.

26. Alfred Rohde, 'Monatsschrift für Freunde und Sammler der Kunst,' *Pantheon*, Vol. XXIX, F. Bruckmann, Munich, July–December 1942.

27. Enke, *Bernsteinzimmer Report*, pp. 114-16.

28. For details about Königsberg evacuations, see *Bernsteinzimmer Report* and Antony Beevor, *Berlin: The Downfall 1945*, Viking, London, 2002.

29. For a summary of Enke's research into troop and civilian movements and the removal of the von Hindenburg corpses see his *Bernsteinzimmer Report*, pp. 109-115.

30. BStU, AV14/79.

31. J. O. Koehler, *Stasi*, Westview Press, Boulder, Colorado, 1999.

32. D. Lewis, *The Lexicon of the Stasi: Language in the Service of the State*, University of Exeter, *Europa Magazine*, Vol. III, No. 1, 1999.

33. BStU, Neiber file 381, pp. 1-18.

CHAPTER 9

1. J. O. Koehler, *Stasi*, Westview Press, Boulder, Colorado, 1999.

2. Seufert told this to Günter Wermusch when they worked together.

3. The appeal was sent to Sir Brian Robertson, High Commissioner of the British Sector in Berlin. This, together with other information on the Koch arrest operation and prosecution, comes from NA, FO 371.

4. The Soviets submitted their brief letter on 11 June 1949.

5. Bobidanosov was chairman of the Leningrad Committee for State Inspection of Landmark Preservation. Kuchumov archive, TGALI 468, Opus 1, and see also Avenir Ovsianov archive, Kaliningrad.

6. BStU, AV14/79, Vol. 28.

7. Kuchumov archive, TGALI 468, Opus 1, File 119.

8. Ibid., pp. 4–9.

9. Kuchumov archive, TGALI 468, Opus 1, File 123, interview conducted by Vladimir Orlovsky for *Zszysze Warschawy*.

10. Kuchumov archive, TGALI 468, Opus 1, File 123, cutting dated 20 October 1961.

11. Koch's prison was near the village of Barcikowo, outside the northern Polish city of Olsztyn.

12. Kuchumov archive, TGALI 468, Opus 1, File 123.

13. Ibid.

14. BStU, AV14/79, Vol. 1, pp. 365–70.

15. For a summary of the findings of this trip, see Paul Enke, *Bernsteinzimmer Report*, Die Wirtschaft, East Berlin, 1986, pp. 179–92.

16. Ibid.

17. Ibid. See also BStU AV14/79, Vol. 1.

18. BStU, AV 14/79, Vol. 1, pp. 362–3.

19. Enke, *Bernsteinzimmer Report*.

20. Kuchumov archive, TGALI 468, Opus 1, File 121, pp. 6–7.

21. BStU, AV14/79, Vol. 29, pp. 322–89.

22. Enke, *Bernsteinzimmer Report*, and BStU, AV14/79, Vol. 1, pp. 365–70.

23. Ibid., pp. 360–4.

24. Ibid., p.356.

25. Ibid., pp. 357–8.

26. Ibid., pp. 360–4.

27. Ibid., pp. 322–89.

CHAPTER 10

1. Coburger was director of HA VIII (observation and investigation) and Büchner was director of HA VII (defence in the Ministry of the Interior, Volkspolizei).

2. Documents concerning this review of Enke's career are all from BStU, KSII404/82, and AV14/79, Vol. 1, pp. 7–11.

3. Written by Volkspolizei Oberrat Gustin: see BStU, KSII404/82, pp. 26–7.

4. Written by Major Schmalfuss: see BStU, KSII404/82, pp. 1–17.

5. BStU, AV14/79 Vol. 1, pp. 7–8.

6. Ibid., p. 7.

7. All the above are taken from ibid., pp. 5–12.

8. Ibid.

9. BStU, AV14/79, Vol. 28, p. 92.

10. BStU, KSII404/82 p. 285 and Neiber file 386, p. 180.

11. BStU, Neiber file 386, pp. 40–7.

12. BStU, AV14/79, Vol. 1, pp. 360–4.

13. BStU, Neiber file 386, pp. 40–7.

14. Generalmajor Fister, director of HA IX (investigative body), was writing to the director of HA XX (counter-dissidence, culture, church, underground): see BStU, AV14/79, Vol. 1, pp. 335–6.

15. Ibid., pp. 132–4.

16. The deputy director of Main Department Investigations wrote to Comrade Volkov, Director of the KGB Investigations Department, Moscow: see BStU, AV14/79, Vol. 1, pp. 90–113.

17. Ibid.

18. Ibid., pp. 114–29.

19. Ibid., pp. 132–4.

20. Ibid., pp. 130–31.

21. Oberstleutnant Bauer wrote to Magdeburg in 1983, see: ibid., pp. 185–6.

22. BStU, AV14/79, Vol. 28, p. 34, written by Hauptmann Rudolph.

23. The information about Stein derives from author interview with Robert Stein, Paul Enke's *Bernsteinzimmer Report*, Die Wirtshaft, East Berlin, 1986, and BStU, AV14/79.

24. J. A. Bustered, 'The Treasure in the Salt Mine', *Army Magazine*, USA, March 1997.

25. Letter dated 5 March 1949, quoted by Patricia Grimsted, 'Spoils of War Returned' *Prologue*, Vol. 34, No. 3, Washington DC, Fall 2002.

26. Ibid.

27. Ibid. The recipient of the letter was the director, Thomas Grochowniak. See also Günter Wermusch archive, Berlin.

28. Ibid., letter dated 2 May 1955.

29. See Enke, *Bernsteinzimmer Report*.
30. Ibid.
31. BStU, AV 14/79, Vol. 28, p. 37.
32. Ibid.
33. Ibid.
34. See Enke, *Bernsteinzimmer Report*.
35. Tete Böttger archive, Göttingen.
36. Ibid.
37. BStU, Neiber file 386, pp. 40–7.
38. See Enke, *Bernsteinzimmer Report*.
39. Ibid.
40. BStU, Neiber file 409, pp. 56–9.
41. BStU, AV 14/79, Vol. 3, pp. 281–9.
42. For a short biography of Semyonov, see www.sovlit.com.
43. BStU, Neiber file 409, pp. 10–12.
44. Ibid., pp. 100–104.
45. Mielke wrote this on his German Communist Party questionnaire in July 1945. See J. O. Koehler, *Stasi*, Westview Press, Boulder, Colorado, 1999.
46. Ibid.
47. Ibid., p. 75.
48. The letter was written in 1988: BStU, Neiber file 381, pp. 49–51.
49. Ibid., pp. 45–8.
50. Ibid.
51. BStU, Neiber file 409, pp. 129–30.
52. See Enke, *Bernsteinzimmer Report*.
53. BStU, AV 14/79, Vol. 30.
54. BStU, Neiber file 409, pp. 120–1.
55. BStU, Neiber file 381, p. 61.
56. E. Wiedemann, 'New Traces in the Search for the Amber Room', *Der Spiegel*, 2001.
57. BStU, Neiber file 409.
58. The Soviet communiqué was entitled 'To the measures adopted for the search after the Amber Room': see BStU, Neiber file 381, p. 72.

CHAPTER 11

1. BStU, Neiber file 386, pp. 40–7.
2. All the following documents were taken from the archive of Baron Eduard von Falz-Fein or from the private archive of Günter Wermusch.
3. See Kriminalhauptkommissar Wermuth's report in Ingolstadt No. K1-1380-1230-7/8.

4. BStU, Neiber file 381, pp. 65–9.
5. BStU, Neiber file 386, pp. 142–52.
6. *Izvestiya*, 15 May 1988. See also BStU, Neiber file 381, pp. 65–9.
7. BStU, Neiber file 386, pp. 40–7.
8. See the ground-breaking documentary *Bernsteinzimmer*, MPR Film and Fernseh Produktion, produced and directed by Maurice Philip Remy, Munich, 1987.
9. Letter from Herbert Müller to Enke, via *Wochenpost*, which ran the article, 2 January 1988: Wermusch private archive.
10. Gerhard Schröter, letter to Wolfgang Mertin and Günter Wermusch, 1 November 1988. See Wermusch private archive.
11. BStU, Neiber file 381, pp. 45–8.
12. BStU, Neiber file 381. See also Günter Wermusch's private archive for copies of the correspondence.
13. 28 May 1988. See BStU, Neiber file 381, p. 74.
14. BStU, Neiber file 381, p. 73.
15. BStU, Neiber file 381, pp. 49–51.

CHAPTER 12

1. Kuchumov archive, TGALI 468, Opus 1, File 121.
2. Gosudarstvennyi Arkhiv Rossiiskoi Federatsii (GARF).
3. Kuchumov archive, TGALI 468, Opus 1, File 123.
4. The directive was 526-R. See Kuchumov archive, TGALI 468, Opus 1; Avenir Ovsianov, private archive, Kaliningrad; and Avenir Ovsianov, *Mine Anna*, Yantarny Skaz, Kaliningrad, 2001.
5. Ibid.
6. Ibid.
7. Kuchumov archive, TGALI 468, Opus 1, File 123.
8. GARF.
9. The directive was 181-R and was passed on 13 May 1969.
10. Order No.2599.
11. D. A. Volkaganov, *Seven Leaders*, Vol. II, M. Novosky, Moscow, 1997.
12. Avenir Ovsianov private archive, Kaliningrad.
13. The best description of the action of the trophy brigades, their formation and activity, is in Konstantin Akinsha and Gregory Koslov, *Stolen Treasure*, Weidenfeld & Nicolson, London, 1995.
14. Act 241, Op. 2618, d 67, L93 n 107–111; Op. 2621, d 16, L60; Op. 2656, d 207, L22. See also Ovsianov, *Mine Anna*.

CHAPTER 13

1. A. M. Kuchumov and M. G. Voronov, *The Amber Room*, Khudozhnik RSFSR, Leningrad, 1989.

2. This and telegrams concerning Kuchumov's Lenin Prize can be found in Kuchumov archive, TGALI 468, Opus 1, File 257.

3. All of the Fors letters can be found in the Kuchumov archive, TGALI 468, Opus 1, File 121, pp. 13, 24, 29 and 34.

4. All of these passes can be found in the Kuchumov archive, TGALI 468, Opus 1, File 120, pp. 3, 6, 9, 10, 13 and 14.

5. Ibid., p. 11.

6. A *komandirovat* for 9 March, signed by Striganov, orders Kuchumov down to Moscow and on to Kaliningrad for ten days: 'ref. order number 145-k. Participation in the function of forming a State Committee on the question of the Amber Room of the Catherine Palace' following order 526-R of the Russian Federation and 161 of the Ministry of Culture.

7. Kuchumov archive, TGALI 468, File 120, pp. 14–19.

8. Ibid., p. 20.

9. Kuchumov archive, TGALI 468, File 119, p. 37.

10. Kuchumov archive, TGALI 468, File 121, pp. 7–11.

11. Kuchumov archive, TGALI 468, File 248.

12. The Library of Congress Country Studies carries a profile of the Soviet Union and its administrative and political structure. This estimates party membership and USSR census information. See http://lcweb2.loc.gov/frd/cs/sutoc.html.

13. Kuchumov archive, TGALI 468, File 61.

14. Kuchumov archive, TGALI 468, File 48, pp. 1–38.

15. Kuchumov archive, TGALI 468, File 119, p. 35.

16. Kuchumov archive, TGALI 468, File 119. See also Avenir Ovsianov, *Mine Anna*, Yantarny Skaz, Kaliningrad, 2001.

17. Ibid. See also Ovsianov, *Mine Anna*.

18. Patricia Grimsted, 'Spoils of War Returned', *Prologue*, Vol. 34, No.3, Washington, DC, Fall 2002.

19. Klaus Goldmann, 'The Treasure of the Berlin State Museums and its Allied Capture', *International Journal of Cultural Property*, Vol. VII, No. 2, 1988.

20. Konstantin Akinsha and Gregory Koslov, *Stolen Treasure*, Weidenfeld & Nicolson, London, 1995.

21. Ibid., pp. 172–80.

22. *Leningradskaya Pravda*, 31 March 1955.

23. Akinsha and Koslov, *Stolen Treasure*, pp. 189–215.

24. The exhibitions officially opened on 7 August 1958.

CHAPTER 14

1. See account of Baldin story in Konstantin Akinsha and Gregory Koslov, *Stolen Treasure*, Weidenfeld & Nicolson, London, 1995.
2. Ibid., pp. 233–5.
3. See Klaus Goldmann, 'The Trojan Treasures in Berlin', in Elizabeth Simpson (ed.), *The Spoils of War*, Harry N. Abrams, New York, 1997.
4. The article was published on 5 March 1995.
5. For a full version see Wolfgang Eichwede, 'Models of Restitution', in Simpson (ed.), *The Spoils of War*.
6. For full account of negotiations see Patricia Grimsted, 'Spoils of War Returned', *Prologue*, Vol. 34, No.3, Washington, DC, Fall 2002.
7. Article published on 16 May 1997.
8. *Russian Federation Summary Catalogue of the Cultural Valuables Stolen and Lost During the Second World War, the Tsarskoye Selo State Museum Zone, the Catherine Palace*, Book I, Ministry of Culture of the Russian Federation, Department of Cultural Heritage, ICAR inc., St Petersburg, Russia, 1999.
9. See the report 'Russian minister wants booty art back in Bremen', carried by www.Gazetta.ru, 14 March 2003 and also article by Andrei Zolotov Jr., *St Petersburg Times*, 14 March 2003.
10. See 'Vladimir Putin's representative is against returning Baldin collection to Germany', *Pravda*, 17 March 2003.
11. See 'Never read a book written about me', *Pravda*, 8 April 2003.
12. See 'Amber Room reconstruction in Catherine Palace of Tsarskoye Selo is completed', *Pravda*, 13 May 2003.
13. See *Pravda*, 31 May 2003.

EPILOGUE

1. The letter is dated 15 August 1987 and was sent to a Hamburg ward registrar who was to have supervised Stein when he was discharged and returned home.

Bibliography

BOOKS AND JOURNALS

Adamovich, Alex, and Granin, Daniil, *A Book of the Blockade*, Raduga, Moscow, 1983

Akhmatova, Anna, *Anno Domini MCMXXI*, Prideaux Press, Letchworth, 1978

— *Evening Poems*, Lincoln Davies, Liverpool, 1980

Akinsha, Konstantin, and Koslov, Gregory, *Stolen Treasure*, Weidenfeld & Nicolson, London, 1995

Alford, Kenneth, *The Spoils of World War Two: The American Military Role in Stealing Europe's Treasures*, Birch Lane Press, New York, 1994

Andree, Karl, *Der Bernstein, und seine Bedeutung... Nebst einem kurzen* Führer *durch die Bernsteinsammlung der Albertus-Universität. Mit 51 Abbildungen*, Albertus-Universität, Königsberg, 1937

— *Der Bernstein*, Kosmos Verlag, Stuttgart, 1951

Andrew, Christopher, and Gordievsky, Oleg, *KGB: The Inside Story of Its Foreign Operations from Lenin to Gorbachev*, Hodder and Stoughton, London 1990

— *Comrade Kryuchkov's Instructions: Top Secret Files on KGB Foreign Operations, 1975–1985*, Stanford University Press, Stanford, 1994

Andrew, Christopher, and Mitrokhin, Vasily, *The Sword and the Shield: The Mitrokhin Archive and the Secret History of the KGB*, Penguin, London, 1999

Baer, Winfried and Ilse, *Charlottenburg Palace, Berlin*, Fondation Paribas, Paris, 1995

Beevor, Antony, *Stalingrad*, Penguin, London, 1998

— *Berlin: The Downfall 1945*, Viking, London, 2002

Benois, Alexander, *Tsarskoye Selo in the Reign of Empress Elisabeth*, St Petersburg, 1910.

— *Memoirs*, trans. Moura Budberg, Chatto and Windus, London, 1960

Beria, Sergo, *Beria My Father*, Duckworth, London, 1999

Birukov, Valery, *Yantarnaya Komnnata: Mifi i realnost*, Planeta, Moscow, 1962

Buffum, W. Arnold, *The Tears of Heliades; or Amber as a Gem*, Sampson Low, London, 1896

Carcopino, Jerome, *Daily Life in Ancient Rome*, Routledge, London, 1941

Conquest, Robert, *The Great Terror*, Macmillan, London, 1968

Cook, John, *The Natural History of Lac, Amber, and Myrrh, with a plain account of the many excellent virtues these three medicinal substances are naturally possessed of*, Woodfall, London, 1770

Cunliffe, Barry, *Pytheas the Greek*, Allen Lane, London, 2001

Dunmore, Helen, *The Siege*, Penguin, London, 2001

Ehrhardt, T. *Die Geschichte der Festung Königsberg 1257–1945*, Würzburg, 1960

Enke, Paul, *Bernsteinzimmer Report*, Die Wirtschaft, East Berlin, 1986

Figes, Orlando, *A People's Tragedy: the Russian Revolution, 1891–1924*, Jonathan Cape, London, 1996

— *Natasha's Dance: A Cultural History of Russia*, Penguin, London, 2002

Fraquet, Helen, *Amber*, Butterworth, London, 1987

Garton Ash, Timothy, *The File*, Flamingo, London, 1997

Gautier, Théophile, *Voyage en Russie*, Paris, 1866

Grass, Günter, *Crabwalk*, Faber and Faber, London, 2002

Grimaldi, David, *Amber Window to the Past*, Harry N. Abrams, New York, 1996

Haddow, J. G., *Amber. All About It*, Cope's Smoke Room Booklets Number 7, London, 1889

Harding, A., and Hughes-Brock, H., 'Amber in the Mycenaean World', *British Society of Archaeology*, Vol. 69, 1974, pp. 145–72

Hartmann, P. J., *Succini prussici physica et civilis historia*, Frankfurt, 1677

Hildebrandt, Alexandra, *The Wall*, Verlag Haus am Checkpoint Charlie, Berlin, 2002

Hooke, Dr Robert, *The Philosophical Experiments and Observations of the Late Eminent Dr Robert Hooke*, Derham, London, 1726

Hosking, Geoffrey, *Russia: People and Empire 1552–1917*, HarperCollins, London, 1997

de Jaeger, Charles, *The Linz File: Hitler's Plunder of Europe's Art*, Webb and Bower, Exeter, 1981

Kelly, Laurence, *St Petersburg: A Traveller's Companion*, Constable, London, 1998

Klobius, Justus Fidus, *Ambrae historiam*, Wittenberg, 1666

Koehler, John O., *Stasi*, Westview Press, Boulder, Colorado, 1999

Kostenevich, Albert, *Hidden Treasures Revealed*, Ministry of Culture of the Russian Federation and State Hermitage Museum, St Petersburg with Harry N. Abrams, Inc. New York, 1995

Krollmann, Christian, *East Prussian Book of Legends*, Insel-Bücherei, Leipzig, 1931

— *The Teutonic Order*, Preussenverlag, Elbing, 1938

373

Kuchumov, A. M. and Voronov, M. G., *The Amber Room* [*Yantarny Komnata*], Khudozhnik RSFSR, Leningrad, 1989

Kuznetzova, *The Summer Garden and Palace of Peter I*, Leningrad, 1973

Ladendorf, Heinz, *Der Bildhauer und Baumeister Andreas Schlüter*, Berlin, 1935

Laue, George, and Lachenmann, Julia, *The Amber Cabinet*, Kunstkammer George Laue, Munich, 2000

Lemus, Vera, *Pushkin Palaces and Parks*, Aurora Art Publishers, Leningrad, 1984

Lewis, D., 'The Lexicon of the Stasi: Language in the Service of the State', *Europa*, Vol. 3, No. 1, 1999

Linck, Hugo, *Königsberg 1945–8*, Oldenburg, 1950

Lincoln, W. Bruce, *Sunlight at Midnight*, Basic Books, New York, 2000

Magnus, Olaus, *Carta marina*, Venice, 1539

— *De gentibus septentrionalibus...*, Rome, 1555

Massie, Susanne, *Pavlovsk*, Hodder and Stoughton, London, 1990

Ministry of Culture of the Russian Federation, *Russian Federation Summary Catalogue of the Cultural Valuables Stolen and Lost During the Second World War, The Tsarskoye Selo State Museum Zone, The Catherine Palace*, Book I, Department of Cultural Heritage, ICAR Inc., St Petersburg, Russia, 1999

Mirabeau, Count of, *Memoirs of the Courts of Berlin and St Petersburg*, P. F. Collier, New York, 1910

Mitrokhin, Vasily, *KGB Lexicon: The Soviet Intelligence Officers' Handbook*, Frank Cass, London, 2002

Müller-Enbergs, Helmut, Wielgohs, Jan, and Hoffmann, Dieter, *Wer war Wer in der DDR?* Christopher Links Verlag, Berlin, 2000

de Navarro, J. M., 'Prehistoric Routes Between Northern Europe and Italy Defined by the Amber Trade', *Geographical Journal*, Vol. LXVI, No. 6, December 1925

Norman, Geraldine, *The Hermitage*, Jonathan Cape, London, 1997

Oliphant, Ernest, *Germany and Good Faith. A Study of the History of the Prussian Royal Family*, Critchley Parker, Melbourne, 1914

Ovsianov, Avenir, *V Ruinakh Starogo Zamka: Dokumental'nye Ocherki o Poiskakh Utrachennykh Kul'turnykh Tsennostei*, Yantarny Skaz, Kaliningrad, 1998

— *Mine Anna*, Yantarny Skaz, Kaliningrad, 2001

— *Yantarny Komnata: Vozrozhdenie Shedevra*, Yantarny Skaz, Kaliningrad, 2002

Pelka, Otto, *Die Meister der Bernsteinkunst*, Leipzig, 1918

Petropoulos, Jonathan, *Art as Politics in the Third Reich*, The University of North Carolina Press, Chapel Hill, NC, 1996

Petrova, Ada, and Watson, Peter, *The Death of Hitler*, Richard Cohen, London, 1995

Prussian Year Book and Almanac, MD, Berlin, 2000

Radzinsky, Edvard, *Stalin*, Anchor Books, New York, 1996

Reed, John, *Ten Days That Shook the World*, Penguin, London, 1966

Reineking von Bock, Gisela, *Das Gold der Ostsee*, Callwey Verlag, Munich, 1981
Rohde, Alfred, *Bernstein*, Berlin, 1939
Rosenberg, Alfred, *Protestantische Rompilger: der Verrat an Luther und der 'Mythus des 20. Jahrhunderts'*, Hoheneichen Verlag, Munich, 1937
Rürup, Reinhard, *Topography of Terror*, Verlag Willmuth Arenhövel, Berlin, 1989
Schön, Heinz, *Das Geheimnis des Bernsteinzimmers*, Pietsch Verlag, Berlin, 2002
Screbrodolsky, B., *Amber*, Science Publishing House, Moscow, 1984
Seiffert, Rachel, *The Dark Room*, Viking, London, 2002
Serov, V., *75 Years of V. M. Striganov*, National Library of Russia, St Petersburg, 1995
Service, Robert, *Lenin: A Political Life*, Vol. I, Macmillan, London, 1991
— *Lenin: a Political Life*, Vol. II, Macmillan, London, 1995
Simpson, Elizabeth (ed.), *The Spoils of War*, Harry N. Abrams, New York, 1997
Sovetski Khudozhnik, *Spasennie Shedevri*, Moscow, 1977
Speer, Albert, *Inside the Third Reich*, Weidenfeld & Nicholson, London, 1970
Spekke, Arnolds, *The Ancient Amber Routes*, M. Goppers, Stockholm, 1957
Tikomirova, Marina, *Lithuanian Gold*, Vilnius, 1973
Tolstoy, Alexei, *The Road to Calvary*, Alfred Knopf, New York, 1946
Troyat, Henri, *Catherine the Great*, Phoenix Press, London, 2000
Tsarskoyselskaya Yantarnaya Masterskaya, *Catalogue of Items*, St Petersburg, 1999
Volinsky, Leonid, *Sem Dnei*, Detgiz, Moscow, 1958
Volkaganov, D. A., *Seven Leaders*, Vol. 2, M Novosky, Moscow, 1997
Volkov, Solomon, *St Petersburg: A Cultural History*, Sinclair-Stevenson, London, 1996
Wermusch, Günter, *Das Bernsteinzimmer Saga*, Christopher Links Verlag, Berlin, 1991
Whiting, Charles, *Werewolf*, Corgi Books, London, 1972
Williams, Robert, *Russian Art and American Money 1900–1940*, Harvard University Press, Cambridge, Mass., 1980
Williamson, George, *The Book of Amber*, Ernest Benn, London, 1932
Zarhovich, Y., *Yantar*, Kaliningrad Book Publishing House, Kaliningrad, 1971
Zheleznova, Irina, *Northern Lights: Fairy Tales of the Peoples of the North*, Progress, Moscow, 1976

ARCHIVES

Die Bundesbeauftragte für die Unterlagen des Staatssicherheitsdienstes der ehemaligen Deutschen Demokratischen Republik, Berlin (BStU) [The Federal Authority for the Records of the State Security Service of the former GDR]
Gosudarstvennyi Arkhiv Rossiikoi Federatsii (GARF) [State Archive of the Russian Federation, Moscow]

Kaliningrad Centre for Coordinating the Search for Cultural Relics, Kaliningrad

Königsberg Documentation Centre at the Museum Stadt Königsberg, Duisburg

National Archives, London: HW 1 series, GC and CS Churchill files; HW 3 series, GC and CS official histories and personal memoirs; HW 14 series GC and CS correspondence files; WO 208 series, War Office intelligence files, and 44/94 for Alfred Rosenberg dossier; HW 5 series; FO 1019/16 Alfred Rosenberg's Nuremburg defence; FO 1019/40 final application for witnesses and documents, Alfred Rosenberg; T 209 series for War Office field reports on looting and preservation of monuments; FO 139, 371, 937, 1023, 1038, 1060 and also WO 354-24 series for capture and extradition of Erich Koch

National Archives and Records Administration, Washington, DC, for Holocaust assets files and for documentation on restitution issues during and after the Second World War compiled for and by Office of Strategic Services (OSS) and Monuments, Fine Arts and Archives Section (MFAA) (see also: http://www.archives.gov/research_room/holocaust_era_assets/ art_provenance_and_claims/ descriptive_list_of_key_records.html)

Rossiiskii Gosudarstvennyi Arkhiv Drevnikh Aktov (RGADA) [Russian State Archive for Ancient Documents, Moscow]

George Stein Private Archive, Kaliningrad

Tsentralny Gosudarstvenny Arkhiv Literatury i Iskusstva (TGALI) [Central State Archive for Literature and Arts, St Petersburg]

Tsentralny Gosudarstvenny Arkhiv Kinofotofonodokumentov Sankt-Peterburga (TsGAKFFD SPb) [Central State Archive of Documentary Films, Photographs and Sound Recordings of St Petersburg]

MANUSCRIPTS AND PRIVATE PAPERS

Telemakov, Vladimir, 'The Secrets of Saving Museum Treasures', unpublished manuscript, St Petersburg, 1986

Valeria Bilanina private papers, Tsarskoye Selo

Tete Böttger private papers, Göttingen

Baron Eduard von Falz-Fein private papers, Liechtenstein

Vica Plauda private papers, St Petersburg

Maurice Philip Remy private papers, MPR Films, Munich

Günter Wermusch private papers, Berlin

Index

Abakumov, Viktor, 131, 140, 163, 335
Achterman, Hans, 343–7, 352
Adam of Bremen, 71
Adriatic Sea, 71
Agarfornova, Xenia, 128, 148, 228, 232, 245
Age of Reason, 4
Akhmatova, Anna, 20, 132
Alatau Mountains, 98
Albina, Bolshoi, 90, 121–5, 133
Albina, Malinki, 93–4, 353
Albrecht, Grand Master, 74
Albrechtsburg Castle, 171
Alexander I, Tsar, 106
Alexander II, Tsar, 89
Alexander Palace, 12, 17, 19, 49, 51, 106, 121
Alspector, V. A., 22
Altdorf, 283–5
amber, 24–5, 28, 41, 55, 70–3, 79, 173, 303–6; fishing, 24, 72, 73; origins, 70; trade, 73; Königsberg University collection, 83–4, 116, 251–2, 331; mythical source, 194; industry controlled by Ministry of Defence, 309–10
Amber Room: difficulty

of evacuation, 22; construction, 25–6; concealment, 31–2, 64; gift to Peter the Great, 28–30; replica, 40, 43–4, 342, 346, 348, 350–3; renovated under Empress Elizabeth, 53–5; renovation under Catherine the Great, 55–6; stone mosaics, 56, 108–10, 114, 325–6, 343–7, 352; nineteenth-century reputation, 56; Nazis enter, 57; surviving photograph, 60–1; apparent destruction in Catherine Palace, 64, 66; in Königsberg, 67–8, 74–5, 86–7, 107, 110–17, 151–2, 155, 175, 198–9, 327, 329; destruction in Königsberg Castle, 82–3, 87–8, 92, 100, 108–9, 115–16, 153, 314, 329–30; skirting board, 100, 110, 114; evacuation from Königsberg, 101, 103, 110, 113–14, 116, 129, 131, 152, 156, 170, 172, 174–5, 180, 183, 199–202, 214–17, 222–4, 329, 344; displayed in

Königsberg, 113–14, 151, 198, 309, 345; articles published, 175–80, 203, 206, 250; premeditated theft by Nazis, 193–5; candelabras, 231–2, 327; not found by KGA, 302; Kuchumov's conclusions, 315–16; Kuchumov's bunker theory, 322–3; pieces emerge in Germany, 338; final conclusions, 356–7
Amber Routes, 71
Anatolia, 127
Andrea del Verrocchio, 85
Andree, Karl, 83
Anna Ivanovna, Empress, 134
Antipin, Georgy, 126, 129
Antonova, Irina, 341
Askania Nova, 269, 270
Assyria, 127
Augustusburg Castle, 171

Bad Sulza, 226
Bähr, Oberrat, 189
Baldin, Viktor, 339, 340, 342, 347, 350
Baltic Brotherhood, 194
Baltic Sea, 24, 25, 28, 39, 71, 75, 188, 195, 305–6
Baltiysk, 293, 305

Bandemir, Captain, 29
Bardovskaya, Larissa, 40–3, 349
Bauer, Oberstleutnant, 240
Beater, General Bruno, 183–4, 208, 234–5, 250
Beliaeva, Elena Nikolaievna, 49
Beliaeva, Tatyana, 69, 75–6, 79, 85, 88, 116, 178
Belokhov, Nikolai, 67
Berchtesgarden, 170, 230
Beria, Lavrenty, 79, 131, 139, 140
Berlin, 23, 25–7, 42, 54, 57, 74, 159–60; surrender, 78, 333–4; Kuchumov's trip, 117, 122, 126–31, 132, 148, 174, 228, 315; blockade, 247; 1936 Olympics, 271, 272; Humboldt University, 175, 220, 241, 242; Kaiser Friedrich Museum, 100; Museum Insel, 127; Pankow, 138–9, 141; Pergamon Museum, 127; State Museums, 192
Berlin Wall, 196, 259, 339
Bielefeld, 217
Bilanina, Valeria, 121, 133–5, 142, 149, 353
Bilebin, Ivan, 134
Binanen Castle, 103
Biryukov, General Yury, 350
Bismarck, Otto von, 171
Black Crows, 19–20
Bobidanosov, A. V., 219–20
Bogdanchikov, Major, 320, 321
Bojarsky, Professor Vladimir Andreievich, 261
Bonn, 246, 247, 248, 273
Bormann, Gerda, 263
Bormann, Martin, 171, 194, 217, 224, 263, 264

Bremen, 342, 347; Kunsthalle collection, 249, 334, 339–42, 343, 347, 350; University, 338, 339
Breslau, 150
Brezhnev, Leonid, 12, 310
Brocken Mountain, 262
Brueghel, Pieter, the Younger, 85
Brusov, Professor Alexander Ivanovich, 68–9, 91, 242, 252; mission to Königsberg, 75–6, 78–88, 292; concludes Amber Room destroyed, 92, 292, 322, 329–30, 333, 335, 356; interviewed by Kuchumov, 99, 309; investigations reviewed, 100–4, 106–8, 110, 113, 115–17, 125, 150, 153, 155–6, 171, 175, 315, 321, 323; attempt to discredit, 177, 178–80, 298, 323, 331–2, 356; statements suppressed, 309; beaten to Königsberg by trophy brigades, 310–11, 327; compelled to recant earlier conclusions, 322, 325, 327; Kuchumov's treatment of his evidence, 325–7, 329–32; concern about Red Army looting, 330–2; defence of his actions, 331–2
BSCH, 215–16, 233, 238, 243, 254, 292, 344, 355
Büchner, Generalmajor Jochen, 239–40, 250
Buckingham, Lord, 55
Budapest, 336
Bulganin, Nikolai, 311
Bush, John, 55

Cameron, Charles, 11, 16
Castro, Fidel, 139
Catherine II (the Great), Empress, 11, 55, 93, 134, 315, 325
Catherine Palace, 1–4, 10–11, 40, 54, 108, 114, 134, 194, 219, 246, 315, 345; evacuation, 17, 19, 51; amber workshop, 43–4; archive, 45, 58, 59; war damage, 63–5, 66; curators' salaries, 90; fate of Lyons Hall, 130; fragments of items found in Königsberg, 106, 324; German occupation, 107, 192; statues of Hercules and Flora, 131; restoration, 333, 351–2; inventory of stolen works, 349; unveiling of new Amber room, 351–3; see also Amber Room
Caucasus, 195
Charlottenburg, 23–4
Chebrikov, Viktor Mikhailovich, 260, 290
Cheka, 14, 19
Chekhov, Anton, 46
Chernihiv, 195
Chernishov, Captain, 29
Chernishov, Captain E. A., 78, 84, 85
Chernomyrdin, Viktor, 12, 44, 344
Christie's, 344
Christine, Queen, 139
Churchill, Winston, 100
Clay, General Lucius, 247
Clinton, President, 40
Coburg, 228
Coburger, Generalmajor Karli, 239, 245
Cold War, 175, 312, 333, 339

Colditz, 171
Colmberg Castle, 249
Committee for Cultural
  Institutions, 126
Copenhagen, 25, 27
Council of Europe, 342
Courland, 188
Crawford, Joan, 273
Crimea, 195
Crimmitschau, 233
Curtis-Bennet, Virginia, 271
Cyril I, Emperor, 90
Czechoslovakia, 356

Daily Telegraph, 217, 343
Danube, River, 71, 193
Danzig, 23, 24, 154; Guild,
  26, 74
Delmar, Sefton, 182
Die Zeit, 250, 253–4, 258,
  262, 274
Dietrich, Professor, 253
Dirch, Aloise, 283
Dmetriev, Vladimir, 176–80,
  297; *see also* Krolevsky,
  Veniamin
Dnipropetrovsk, 195
Dohna-Schlobitten, Prince
  Alex, 85, 101–2, 140,
  157, 211
Dönhoff, Marion, 248, 250,
  256, 274, 275
Dönitz, Admiral, 200
Dorothiayev, Colonel, 313
Dresden, 131, 170, 171,
  172, 229, 230, 334;
  Gallery, 136, 155, 171,
  192, 336
Dürer, Albrecht, 249, 334
Dzerzhinsky, Feliks, 163
Dzokki, Giuseppe, 55, 326

Eichmann, Adolf, 217
Eichwede, Wolfgang, 339–
  44, 346–8, 352, 353
Einsatzstab Reichleiter

Rosenberg (ERR), 86,
  129, 192, 195
Eisenhower, Dwight D., 83
Eisenstein, Sergei, 131
Ekaterinburg, 12, 90, 271
Elbe, River, 126
Elberfeld, 226
Elbing, 73, 85, 174, 201,
  226, 328
Elizabeth, Empress, 10,
  53–4, 56, 315
Elsterberg, 233
Emden (ship), 200
Enger, Master, 54
Enigma files, 6, 50
Enke, Gerda, 196, 226
Enke, Paul, 184–5,
  186–209, 210, 300,
  337; *Bernsteinzimmer
  Report*, 184–7, 197,
  204–5, 208, 234, 241–2,
  263, 267, 286–7, 349;
  joins Stasi, 196–8, 239;
  discovers Amber Room
  evacuation, 199–202,
  214, 216; 'Ringel'
  investigation, 216, 225–6,
  232–3, 235–7; search in
  Saxony and Thuringia,
  225–30, 232–4, 238,
  242; correspondence
  with Kuchumov, 230–2;
  taken off Amber Room
  investigation, 234–5;
  Stasi career ended,
  239–41; completion of
  book and Amber Room
  theories, 241–4, 286–7;
  mislays Strauss file,
  242; involvement with
  Stein, 248, 250, 251,
  253–7, 263–4, 268, 276,
  281, 354; contact with
  Semyonov, 257, 261–4;
  back in favour with Stasi,
  287–8; death, 288–9

Enke, Sonia, 196
Eosander, Johan Friedrich d',
  23, 26, 74
Erzgebirge, 229, 232–4, 243,
  262, 286, 287, 288, 347
Estonia, 191, 194, 195, 303

Falz-Fein, Baron Eduard
  von, 265, 268, 269–77,
  347; correspondence
  with Stein, 278–82; Stasi
  connection, 286, 289,
  290
Fechter, Peter, 196
Fedor III, Tsar, 24
Fedorchuk, Vitaly, 259
Fennoscandia, 24
Fermor, V., 54
Feyerabend, Paul, 111–
  14, 116, 152, 309;
  interrogation evidence,
  327–30
Fichtner, Professor, 229
First World War, 150
Fischhausen, 73
Focke, Dr, 57
Fors, G. S., 303, 318–20
Förster, Norman, 56–7
France, 54
Frankfurt, 70, 194
Frederick I, King (formerly
  Elector Frederick III), 23,
  25, 26, 75, 199
Frederick II (the Great),
  King, 54, 170
Frederick IV, King of
  Denmark, 25
Frederick William, Great
  Elector, 23, 24
Frederick William I, King,
  26, 27–9, 342
Freiberg, 229
Freiburg im Breisgau, 201
Freie Welt, 175, 180–3, 203,
  206, 212–16, 220–1, 224,
  236–7, 250, 286, 297,

300, 337
Friedlander Tor, 156
Friesen, Helmut, 170–1,
    177, 211
Frisches Haff, 71
FSB, 95, 307
Fulda, River, 199
Fulton, Missouri, 100
Fussy, Gottfried, 174

Galitsky, General, 312, 331
Gall, Dr Ernest, 100, 177,
    211
Gallico, Paul, 272
Gänsel, Helmut, 355
Gatchina, 17, 63, 193
Gautier, Théophile, 56
Gdingen, 188
Geissler, Uwe, 208, 210–17,
    221–2, 224–6, 231, 232,
    288; interrogates 'Ringel',
    235–8, 276
Gera, 228, 238
German Democratic
    Republic (GDR), 135–7,
    149, 162, 164, 168,
    173, 188, 203, 290–1;
    foundation, 139; Amber
    Room articles published,
    175, 179–80, 182–3, 213;
    possible locations for
    BSCH and Amber Room,
    216, 225; return of art
    treasures, 336
Gert, Dr, 115
Goebbels, Joseph, 192, 194;
    diaries, 235
Goering, Marshal Hermann,
    194, 288
Goethe, Johann Wolfgang
    von, 185
Golovkin, Count Alexander,
    28, 29
Gorbachev, Mikhail, 12,
    139, 269, 316, 332
Gorky, 50, 51, 52

Gorky, Maxim, 53, 68, 90
Görlitz, 149, 155, 169
Göttingen, 254, 262, 273,
    287, 348; University,
    252–3
Götze, Professor, 280
Grabar, Igor, 67
Gräfe, Arthur, 170–2, 174
Grasleben, 279
Greiz, 233
Grimm, Brothers, 199
Gross Dirschkeim, 73
Grossgrabe Manor, 171
Grotewohl, Otto, 336
Grunovii, Simonis, 70–4
Gubenko, Nikolai, 340, 342,
    345, 350, 353
Guber, Andrei, 192
Gulf of Finland, 10, 39, 50,
    293
Gulf of Venice, 71

Habelberg, 27, 28
Hall, Ardelia, 248
Hamburg, 27, 150, 264,
    267, 281, 282
Hanover, 26
Harkov, G. I., 298
Hartmann, Philipp Jacob,
    28, 70, 75
Haustein, Heinz-Peter, 355
Hels, Helmut, 157
Henkensiefken, Friedrich,
    115, 158–61, 164, 177–8,
    211
Hess, Rudolf, 182
Himmler, Heinrich, 194,
    217, 222
Hindenburg, General von,
    200
Hitler, Adolf, 50, 77, 78,
    191–5, 198, 271
Hoffman, Herr, 252
Hohenzollerns, 23, 24
Holst, Dr Nils von, 191–2
Hooke, Robert, 70

Hopp, Hans, 151
Hungary, 356
Hut, Oberstleutnenant, 196

Igdalov, Boris, 43–4
Internet, 6, 58, 355
Irving, David, 235
Istomina, Alexandra
    Vasilevna, 96, 118–19,
    133
Ivanyenko, Colonel D. D.,
    67, 74, 78, 82, 312

Jakobovich, Comrade, 299,
    300, 301, 309
John, Elton, 42

Kalinin, Mikhail, 121
Kaliningrad, 8, 44, 69, 121,
    126, 160, 292–5; secret
    visit, 132–3, 136–7, 140,
    143, 147, 149, 156–8,
    167–8, 170, 173, 177,
    180, 242; Germans
    expelled, 212; supposed
    location of BSCH and
    Amber Room, 215–16,
    224, 238, 244, 254;
    'Ringel' visits, 222, 236–
    7; renewed investigations,
    290, 293–304, 307, 320,
    347; see also Königsberg
Kaliningradskaya Pravda,
    176–80, 212, 224, 250,
    265, 286, 292, 297, 300,
    323, 331–2, 337
Kant, Immanuel, 105
Karlshorst, 144
Karnzow Castle, 334, 339,
    340
Karpekina, Mrs L. S., 321,
    323
Kassel, 199
Kaunas, 16, 195
Kazakhov, Simeon
    Pavlovich, 132–3, 137,

140, 147, 156, 158, 159
Kazakhstan, 125, 132, 333
Kedrinsky, Alexander
  Alexandrevich, 12–19,
  20–2, 26, 30–4, 38, 43,
  58, 59, 97, 98
Kerensky, Alexander, 12
Keyserlingk, Countess
  Sabina, 85, 87, 102, 108,
  211, 329
KGA, 301–4, 307–9, 318
KGB, 47, 68, 94–5, 140,
  143, 175, 203, 211;
  Amber Room search,
  215–16, 224–5, 299–300,
  320; relations with Stasi,
  244–6, 259–61, 264,
  266, 300–3; Kuchumov
  connection, 318–20, 332
Kharkiv, 86, 88, 195
Kherson, 195
Khoroshilov, P. V., 347, 349
Khrushchev, Nikita, 336
Kiel, 188
Kiev, 16, 67, 85, 86, 88,
  129, 131, 151, 154, 270,
  303
Kinburn, battle of, 33
Kirch, 129
Kirmse, Dr Manfred, 242
Kirov, Sergei, 19
Koblenz, 191
Koch, Gauleiter Erich,
  87, 103, 113, 115,
  148, 150–1, 154, 170,
  198, 244; supposed
  role in Amber Room
  evacuation, 199–200,
  214, 217, 230–3, 242–3,
  286–8; arrest and trial,
  217–19; interrogation and
  revelations, 220–1, 223–
  6, 235, 243, 255, 312;
  birthplace, 226–7; reveals
  ignorance of Amber
  room, 287; death, 287;

estate in Kaliningrad, 320
Kochina, Elena, 52
Kohl, Helmut, 166, 191, 262
Kokornikov, M. G., 321
Könisgsberg, 24, 28, 54,
  66–7, 69, 70, 102–3,
  124, 130, 144, 148–9;
  Guild, 55–6; Brusov's
  visit, 75–88, 92, 178;
  Kuchumov's mission, 92,
  99, 100, 104–16, 125,
  128, 315, 335; Rohde's
  activities, 150–8, 169,
  198–9; art evacuation,
  170–5, 227–8, 242–3,
  254; 'Ringel' map, 222–3;
  possible location of
  BSCH and Amber Room,
  233, 243, 246, 261;
  wartime resistance, 248,
  255–6; medieval town,
  294; trophy brigades
  enter, 311–12, 331;
  Albertus-University, 83,
  116, 140, 199, 252, 253,
  331; Hofbunker, 85–6,
  99–100, 155–7; Library,
  156–7; Steindamm
  church, 223, 224,
  236; synagogue, 235;
  Volksbank, 310; see also
  Kaliningrad
Königsberg Castle, 25,
  67, 73–4, 75, 79–88,
  100, 103–17, 147, 152,
  154–5, 167, 171; Soviet
  specialists killed, 106;
  Amber Room displayed,
  113–14, 151, 198, 309,
  345; 'Monster' Soviet
  tower block built on
  ruins, 295, 347, 355;
  unveiling ceremony
  for Amber Room, 198;
  occupied by Red Army,
  328

Blutgericht, 80, 111–12,
  199, 294; Knights' Hall,
  79, 82–3, 85, 87–8, 92,
  105, 107–11, 114–16,
  153, 154, 159, 170, 179,
  314, 322, 325–30, 345,
  349; Museum, 81, 117,
  150, 156, 178; Nazi Gift
  Book, 67, 74, 78, 82, 87,
  110, 152, 312, 345
Koslov, Gregory, 341
Krasnoye Selo, 50, 192
Kriebstein Castle, 103, 171,
  172–4
Krolevsky, Veniamin, 215,
  297, 298, 299, 323,
  331–2; see also Dmetriev,
  Vladimir
Krolic, Major, 78, 312
Krupskaya, Nadezda, 96
Küchler, General George
  von, 107, 114, 150, 151
Kuchumov, Anatoly
  Mikhailovich, 12, 13;
  background, 14–15, 122,
  321; diary, 15–18, 21,
  31–2, 48, 52, 70, 98;
  evacuation of Leningrad
  palaces, 17–19, 20–2,
  26–7, 31, 98, 199, 332–3,
  356; marriage, 18;
  attempts to understand
  construction of Amber
  Room, 26–30; leaves
  Leningrad with treasures,
  32–3, 48–50, 51–3; death,
  34, 59, 345; biography,
  47–8; writes history of
  Amber Room, 53–4,
  56, 92, 315; returns to
  Leningrad, 62–3;
  promotion, 62; returns
  to Catherine Palace,
  63–5, 66; thwarted trip to
  Königsberg, 67–8; private
  persona, 91, 122–3;

mission to Königsberg, 92, 98, 99, 100, 104–17, 125, 128, 292, 295, 297, 314, 335; interviews Brusov, 99, 309; reads Rohde correspondence, 100–4; Rohde interview, 104, 110; greetings cards, 119–21, 133, 301; colleagues' admiration, 122; Berlin mission, 126–31, 132, 148, 174, 228, 315; Red Army contacts, 132; obituary, 135; secret trip to Kaliningrad, 136–7, 140, 147, 177, 180, 242, 315; interviews Strauss, 149–58, 167–8, 173, 175, 177, 198, 242, 297, 322; cartoon, 158–60, 178; interrogates 'Ringel', 222–3, 226, 237, 243, 292; correspondence with Enke, 230–2; receives Storozhenko report, 301–4, 307, 316; *The Amber Room*, 315–16, 332; conclusion about Amber Room, 315–16, 333; awarded Lenin Prize, 316–17, 332; KGB connection, 318–20, 332; leads Amber Room policy, 321; bunker theory, 322–3, 332–3, 345, 356; compels Brusov to recant, 322, 332; joins Communist Party, 323, 332; propaganda writings, 324–5, 327, 331; 'Destiny of the Amber Room' report, 325–9
Kuchumova, Anna Mikhailovna, 18, 32–3, 68, 105, 316–7

Kühn, Oberleutnant, 240
Kulot, Misha, 324, 327
Kümmel, Otto, 192–4
Kunyn, Major, 141, 147–9, 154, 169
Kunz, Walfried, 174
Kurisches Haff, 71
Kursant, 189

Ladukhin, Vladimir Ivanovich, 17, 18, 21, 32
Lake Krossinsee, 210, 212
Lake Ladoga, 36, 45
Lammers, Reichsleiter, 194
Langenstein, 262
Langheim Palace, 157
Lapsky, Vlad, 286, 290
Lasch, General Otto, 77–8, 153
Latvia, 154, 191, 195
Lau, Herr, 102
Lebedev, L., 215
Leeb, General Wilhelm von, 32, 51, 107
Lengefeld, 229
Lenin, Vladimir Ilyich, 12, 134, 182
Leningrad, 159–60, 194, 256, 303; evacuation of treasures, 17–19, 20–2, 26–7, 50–1, 332; defence, 30–1, 33, 49–50; assault, 50–3; liberated, 61–2; rebuilding, 124; war damage, 199; destruction of treasures, 334, 341 Armoury, 22; Art Institute, 18; Institute of Engineering, 38; State Hermitage, 17, 27, 28, 121, 128, 148, 228, 232, 334, 337, 340; *see also* St Petersburg
Leninsk-Kuznetsky, 98
Leo X, Pope, 70, 74
Liburnika (yacht), 27

Lithuania, 191, 195
Lochstädt Castle, 156
Luga, 195
Luther, Martin, 74

Magdeburg, 188, 189, 245, 246
Malakov, Lieutenant, 312
Malenkov, Georgy, 131, 311
Marburg University, 150
Marchukov, David, 126
Maria Fyodorovna, Empress, 122
Maria Pavlovna, Grand Duchess, 89
Marienburg Castle, 226
Martelli, Alexander, 53–4, 55
Matviyenko, Valentina, 350, 353
Maximov, Comrade, 299
Memel, 24, 27, 28
Mengele, Dr, 217
Menshikov, Governor General Alexander, 29, 51
Merkers, 228
Mertz, Amtmann, 199–200
Mga, 4
MGB, 140, 141, 147, 149, 157, 158, 159, 163, 335
Mielke, Erich, 163, 183, 204, 234, 244, 246; involvement in Amber Room investigations, 240, 257, 260–1, 288; Moscow visit, 259–60; letter to Chebrikov, 290–1, 296
Mikryukov, Ivan, 125, 333
Ministry of Defence, Central Archive, 313, 329
Minsk, 85, 86, 88, 129, 131, 154, 195
Mohrungen, 140, 144
Molotov, Polina, 132
Molotov, Vyacheslav, 16,

33, 191
Montgomery, General
  Bernard, 83
Moscow, 18, 84, 126,
  236–7, 303
  Lenin Library (Leninka),
  70, 75, 88, 329–30;
  Pushkin Museum,
  336, 337, 341–2, 347;
  Shchusev Museum of
  Architecture, 339–40;
  State Archive, 296, 302,
  308; State Historical
  Museum, 69, 98–9, 126,
  322; State Tretiakov
  Gallery, 99; State
  University, 312; Theatre
  Library, 75–6
Mosdok, 57
Munich, 194, 277, 281, 344
Mussolini, Benito, 331
Mutschmann, Gauleiter
  Martin, 170, 171, 200,
  229–30, 243, 286

Nabokov, Vladimir, 269,
  271, 275
Napoleon Bonaparte, 18
Naumann, Konrad, 207
Neiber, Generalmajor, 208,
  240, 242, 243–5, 255,
  258, 261, 269, 285, 288
Nering, Arnold, 23
Nerling, Dr, 195
Neva, River, 10, 53, 89, 94
Nevsky, Alexander, 33
New York, 60
Ney, Wolfgang, 242
Nicholas I, Tsar, 63
Nicholas II, Tsar, 12, 51,
  269
NKVD, 19–20, 22, 50, 57,
  79, 85, 88, 110, 124, 140,
  149, 330, 335
Nordman, Z. V., 321
Novgorod, 129, 340

Novosibirsk, 52–3, 56, 61,
  63, 98, 125, 315
Nuovo Suzi, 63
Nuremberg, 194; trials,
  56, 124, 155, 217, 218,
  333–4, 337

Oder, River, 71
Odessa, 335
Olaus Magnus, 71, 72
Operation Barbarossa, 114,
  192
Oranienbaum, 17, 192
Orbeli, Joseph, 334–5
Orlov, Gregory, 55
Orlovsky, Vladimir, 223
Orwell, George, 96
Ostpolitik, 251
Ovsianov, Colonel Avenir,
  290, 296, 306–13, 314,
  325, 331, 338; close to
  truth, 329

Palmnicken, 201, 293
Paris, 60, 150
Paul I, Emperor, 93, 122
Pavlov, Dmitry, 51, 52–3
Pavlovsk, 17, 19, 31, 62, 91,
  129, 133–4, 231, 333,
  353; library, 59, 92–3;
  Kuchumov's apartment,
  66, 176, 317; curators'
  salaries, 90; palace
  evacuation, 125
Pergamum Altar, 127, 334,
  336
Perleberg, 235
Persia, 127
Peter I (the Great), Tsar, 10,
  24, 27–30, 53, 70, 270,
  315, 329, 342
Peter III, Tsar, 55, 170
Peterhof, 17, 192, 194, 341,
  350
Peters, Hauptman, 252
Petrusov, Professor I. A., 312

Pieck, Wilhelm, 168
Pillau, 73, 156, 200, 201,
  293
Pimen, Patriarch, 249
Piotrovsky, Mikhail, 340
Piotrovsky, Professor Boris,
  20, 48
Plauda, Vica, 59–60, 63, 92
Podolsk, 313, 314, 329, 332
Poland, 24, 28, 123, 149,
  156, 235, 237, 336, 356
Poltavsev, Major, 148
Ponarth, 236, 290
Popova, Sophia, 51
Popp, Albert, 230–3, 242,
  243, 286
Porivayev, Alexander, 334
Porschin, Christian, 25
Pönsgen, Captain Dr, 193
Posse, Dr Hans, 192
Potsdam, 28, 169, 190–1,
  194, 198, 226, 243, 251,
  263, 278, 300
Pozharsky, Ivan, 75
Pozhinsky, Mieczyslaw, 287
Pregel, River, 73, 79
Pretoria (ship), 200
Primorskaya, 39
Prokofiev, Sergei, 132
Pronin, General, 330
Prussia, 23, 25, 28, 55,
  66–7, 70, 114
Pskov, 129, 195; icons, 249,
  250, 273, 279, 354
Pushkin, 5, 47, 49–53, 57–8,
  61–4, 160, 193–4, 221,
  231, 353; items from,
  67, 129–30; workers'
  apartments, 134; *see also*
  Tsarskoye Selo
Pushkin, Alexander, 11
Putin, Vladimir, 12, 40, 347,
  350, 351, 353

Rachmaninov, Sergei, 89
Rakitsin, Guard Major, 324

Rastrelli, Bartolomeo, 10, 16, 55
Rautenburg, 82, 85, 102
Recklinghausen, 248
Rekhlovo, 63
Ribbentrop, Joachim 16, 57, 191, 194
Richkov, Nikolai, 316
Riga, 154, 195
'Ringel, Rudi', 215–16, 224, 232–3, 242, 286–7, 355; interrogations, 222–3, 226, 235–8, 243, 276, 292; dubious evidence, 243, 254–5, 261, 263, 276
Rochlitz, 172
Roggenbuch, Friedrich, 55
Rohde, Alfred, 109–17, 140, 144, 223, 255, 258, 323, 328; interrogated by Brusov, 81–2, 84–7, 330; correspondence, 99, 100–4, 107, 110, 125, 153, 155–6, 158, 173, 211; planned evacuation of Amber Room, 101, 103, 113–14, 131, 224, 252, 329; interviewed by Kuchumov, 104, 110; death, 110–11, 114, 146, 147, 178–9, 265; *Bernstein*, 113, 114; Strauss's account, 148, 150–8, 169, 171–4, 198–9; *Pantheon* magazine article, 198, 309, 345; house in Kaliningrad, 320
Rohde, Ilse, 111, 178
Rohde, Lotti, 111, 179, 265
Rohde, Wolfgang, 111, 265
Rome, 71, 74–5
Rosegarten Tor, 156
Rosenberg, Alfred, 86, 129, 192, 194, 195, 198, 217
Rostock, 154

Rovno, 218
Royal Society, 70
Rubirosa, Porfirio, 271
Rudolph, Hauptmann, 240, 241
Ruhrgas AG, 44, 345–6
Rumiantseva, V. F., 99
Rumpf, Helmut, 248
Runstedt, Field Marshal von, 57
Russia, 7, 37, 59, 68, 195; history, 89–90
Russian Academy of Arts, 12
Russian Revolution, 12, 303, 344
Russo–Japanese war, 94
Rust, Bernard, 199

Sachsenburg Castle, 171
St Petersburg, 10, 26, 35–6, 154, 192; Red Terror, 14; treasures removed before Napoleon, 18; Stalinist purge, 19–20; Romanov funeral, 271 Bolshoi Dom, 94; Hermitage, 48, 53, 347; Imperial Lyceum, 11; Literature Archive, 94–7; Nevsky Prospekt, 35, 104; Russian Museum, 270; Summer Palace, 29, 30, 53, 315; Vasilevsky Island, 14; Winter Palace, 53–5; *see also* Leningrad
Sakhalin Island, 46, 324, 327
Sakharov, Andrei, 68
Samland Peninsula, 41, 55, 70–1, 73, 157, 159, 201, 305; map, 72
Sardovsky, Lieutenant, 78
Sautov, Dr Ivan Petrovich, 38, 40–3, 45, 58–9, 346, 348, 349, 353
Saxony, 7, 103, 110, 113,

131, 149, 153, 170–1, 173, 200, 286, 329, 347; Enke's search, 225–6, 228–9, 232–3, 242; continuing searches, 355
Schacht, Ernst, 26
Schaumann, Ernst, 113–14, 116, 153, 309
Scheidig, Dr Walter, 226–8
Schlema, 233
Schliemann, Heinrich, 334
Schliep, Hauptmann, 197
Schlobitten Castle, 101–2, 140, 156, 157
Schlüter, Andreas, 22–6, 40, 75
Schmalfuss, Major, 188, 189
Schmidt, Helmut, 253
Schröder, Gerhard, 351
Schwerin, Countess von, 84, 85, 101–2, 211
Semyonov, Julian, 246, 255–8, 261–5; connection with Baron Falz-Fein, 268, 273–5, 277, 278, 280, 289
Sergeiyevskaya, N. U., 312
Serov, General Ivan, 335
Seufert, Oberst Hans, 183–4, 186–7, 206–8, 213–14, 216, 225–6, 230, 232–3; retained on Amber Room investigation, 240–1, 242, 243, 261–2, 287
Sevastopol, 16
Seydervitz, Mr, 136
Shaliapin, Fedor, 89
Shostakovich, Dmitri, 132
Shukayev, T. M., 321
Shukin, Captain, 150, 154, 155
Shvydkoi, Mikhail, 350, 353
Siberia, 52, 53, 56, 67, 332
Simenon, Georges, 274
Siverskaya, 195
Skazkin, S. D., 312

Slavyanka, River, 92
Smakka, Otto, 114, 151–2, 309
SMERSH, 79, 110
Smolensk, 48, 123–4, 192, 195
Sokolovsky, Marshal Vasily, 247
Solms Laubach, Dr Ernst-Otto Count zu, 193–5, 199
Sonderkommando Ribbentrop, 57
Sophie Charlotte, Queen, 23–4, 25, 26
Soviet Academy of Sciences, 261
Soviet Union, 89, 124, 131, 136, 151, 257, 310; German invasion, 1, 16; Amber Room articles published, 176–7, 179–80, 183, 184; return of art treasures, 247–9, 269, 311, 313, 336; glasnost and perestroika, 316; looted art collections emerge, 338
Speer, Albert, 193
Spielberg, Steven, 42
Splieth, Dr Benno, 281–4
Sprecht, Jürgen, 113, 115
Spree, River, 127, 129
Stalin, Joesph, 16–17, 33, 68, 79, 83, 100, 159, 217, 257, 311; purges, 19, 52; his times, 89, 96; demolition of Leningrad cathedral, 94; Ivan the Terrible role model, 132; 'Lord God on earth', 133; pact with Ulbricht, 139; return of Soviet art treasures, 247; orders investigation into looting,

334–5, 339
Stalingrad, 101, 124, 357
Stasi, 139, 140, 162–7, 175, 180–5, 187–8, 202–3, 207, 210; archives, 137, 138, 161; Amber Room study group, 183–4, 186, 198, 207, 211, 213–14, 217, 337–8; Enke joins, 196–8, 239; Amber room search, 216, 221, 223, 224–8, 230–2, 234–7, 240, 246, 261; Enke's career ended, 239–41; relations with Soviets, 243–6, 259–61, 264, 266, 296–7, 300–3; Operation Puschkin, 240–1, 244–5, 260, 262, 288; and Stein's activities, 250, 253–4, 257–9, 266, 273, 276, 278–9, 285–6; connection with Baron Falz-Fein, 286, 290; Enke back in favour, 287–8
Steffani, Agostino, 23
Stein, Elisabeth, 253, 256; death, 265–6, 267–8, 276, 354
Stein, George, 144, 246, 248–57, 262–4, 267–8, 348; visit to Moscow, 258–60; attacked and tortured, 264–5, 266, 267, 276; connection with Baron Falz-Fein, 271, 273–7, 278–82, 289; death, 276–7, 283–6, 349, 354–5; Amber Room documentary, 278–9, 281, 343; hospitalized, 279–81; archive, 279, 291, 349; stabbed, 281–2, 283, 354; close to truth, 328; sadomasochism, 354
Stelle, 246, 253, 255–6, 264,

268, 279, 285
Stettin, 55, 56, 200
Stolze, Oberst, 241, 243
Storozhenko, Jelena, 121, 245, 305, 308–10, 318, 320, 322; report to Kuchumov, 301–4, 307, 316; investigation closed down, 304, 306–7, 309–10; congratulates Kuchumov, 317
Strauss, Dr Gerhard, 137, 138–49, 214, 225, 228, 292, 321; interviewed by Kuchumov, 149–58, 167–8, 173, 175, 177, 198, 297, 322; cartoon references, 159–60; activities revealed in Stasi records, 163, 164, 167–75, 200; *Freie Welt* articles, 175, 177, 181, 183–4, 203, 206, 215, 220; interrogates Koch, 220–1, 223, 243, 312; taken off Amber Room investigation, 241; file mislaid, 242–3; meets Stein, 251
Striganov, Vasily Mikhailovich, 296, 298, 300–1, 303, 320–1
Suvorov, General, 33
Svetlogorsk, 41
Svetly, 304, 305, 317
Sweden, 10

Tallinn, 29, 38, 194, 195
Tannenberg, 200
Tatars, 52
Tartu, 195
Telemakov, Vladimir, 45–9, 51, 53, 56–7, 66–8, 92, 94, 98, 176, 353
Tellerhäuser, 229
Terry, Anthony, 250, 255,

278
Teutonic Knights, 72–3, 82, 140
Thule Society, 194
Thuringia, 7, 246; Enke's search, 225–6, 228, 231, 234, 242; continuing searches, 355
Tilsit, 102, 157
Tolstoy, Alexei, 14, 36
Tomsk, 52
Treskin, Anatoly, 59
Trieste, 71
'Trojan Gold', 127, 334, 341–2, 343, 347
Tronchinsky, Stansilav Valerianovich, 98, 99, 100, 102–11, 113–14, 116, 135, 292, 295, 309, 321
Tronchinskaya, Katya, 105, 106, 108, 110, 111
trophy brigades, 310–13, 319, 327, 331–7
Trotsky, Leon, 30
Tsarskoye Selo, 11, 17, 18, 31, 47, 133, 329–30; see also Pushkin
Tsirlin, First Lieutenant Ilya, 86, 312
Tsiten, 157
Turau, Gottfried, 26
Turkey, 127
Turok, Comrade, 312

Ukraine, 57, 195, 217, 226, 266, 269, 270, 303
Ulbricht, Walter, 139, 168

Urals, 15
USA, 247, 279, 333
Uzbekistan, 256

Vasilev, General, 104, 110
Velichko, Mikhail, 63
Versailles, 30
Vimuchkin, Colonel, 313
Vladimir, Grand Duke, 89
Vo Slavu Rodini, 115, 129
Volkmann, Mr, 147
Volpriehausen, 253–4, 256, 262, 273–4, 276, 348
Voringer, Professor, 157
Voronezh, 195, 312
Voronov, M. G., 315
Voronova, Nadezda, 92, 98
Voroschilovgrad, 195
Voss, Hermann, 155
Voznesensky, Nikolai, 311

Wagner, Richard, 105, 131
Waldheim 174
Wandel, Paul, 167–8, 169, 170, 172, 173, 174, 200
Warsaw, 23, 218, 219, 243, 312
Warsaw Pact, 336
Wechselburg Castle, 103, 153, 171–4
Wedelstädt, Captain Helmut von, 198
Weiler, Dr Clemens, 248
Weimar, 7, 226–8, 230, 232, 233, 242, 286, 347
Wermusch, Günter, 185–7, 204–8, 210–14, 242, 263, 286; works for Stasi,

288–9
Wiesbaden, 248, 249, 279
Wildenhoff Castle, 84, 86, 101, 102, 330
Wilhelm Gustloff (ship), 7
Will, Dr Helmut, 112, 115, 169, 177, 211, 223–4
Wolf, Markus, 162, 208
Wolfram, Gottfried, 25, 26, 27
Worringer, R., 151
Wrangel Tor, 156
Writers' Union, 132

Yalta Conference, 246, 311
Yantarny, 293, 305, 306
Yeltsin, Boris, 12, 38, 345
Yermoliev, Comrade, 298–300
Yezhov, Nikolai (Karlik), 19–20, 79
Yezhovshchina, 19

Zhdanov, Andrei, 124, 126, 128, 131
Zhitomir, 16
Zhukov, Marshal, 78, 335
Ziegenhals, 210
Zimmerman, Dr Gerhard, 100, 177, 211
Zorin, General Leonid Ivanovich, 128–31, 132, 140, 158
Zoshchenko, Mikhail, 132
Zschopau, River, 172
Zubov, Count Platon, 11
Zuyeva, T. M., 126
Zwickauer Mulde, 171